CAPE COD

ITS PEOPLE AND THEIR HISTORY

JAMES OTIS

CAPE COD

ITS PEOPLE AND THEIR HISTORY

BY

HENRY C. KITTREDGE

Second Edition
with a Post-Epilogue, 1930 – 1968
by John Hay

WITH ILLUSTRATIONS

PARNASSUS IMPRINTS, INC.

Orleans, Massachusetts

PUBLISHED BY ARRANGEMENT WITH HOUGHTON MIFFLIN COMPANY
ALL RIGHTS RESERVED
PARNASSUS IMPRINTS EDITION PUBLISHED JUNE, 1987
ISBN 0-940160-35-8
PRINTED IN THE UNITED STATES OF AMERICA

TO
G. L. K.

ACKNOWLEDGMENTS

I AM indebted to Alfred Crocker, Esq., of Centerville, for detailed information about salt-making in the salt works of his father, Loring Crocker, of Barnstable. Mr. Alfred Crocker spent several years in this business and is one of the few persons alive who is qualified to give first-hand information on it. Thanks are due to Mr. Thomas F. Hall, of Omaha, Nebraska, for facts about the Shiverick clipper, Belle of the West, in which he sailed for over four years, part of the time as mate. I wish to thank Mr. Gilbert Coleman, one of the leading oyster dealers of Cotuit, for information about the shellfisheries in that village for the last seventy years; and Mr. Elmer Rich, chairman of the Board of Selectmen of Wellfleet, and Mr. Frank A. Williams, town clerk, for information about the oyster and quahaug industries in their town. Both these men have long been engaged in the business there. Particular thanks are due to Mr. Elmer Mayo, of Chatham, for permission to copy a letter to him from L. M. Shaw, Secretary of the United States Treasury, recounting the facts of Mr. Mayo's rescue of surfman Ellis off Monomoy. This letter accompanied the medal which the Department presented to Mr. Mayo on that occasion. I am also indebted to Ezra H. Baker, Esq., of Boston, for information about anchor-dragging off the south side of the Cape in the eighties, when he used to watch the boats thus employed. I have especially to thank Mr. John H. Edmonds, State Archivist, for the map showing locations of wrecks and for his perfectly authenticated narrative of the Whidaw episode.

Mr. and Mrs. Lewis Crowell, of East Dennis, have shown me every courtesy and assistance in obtaining the photograph of the Wild Hunter, which is taken from the original painting in the possession of Mr. Crowell's mother, Mrs. Louisa M. Crowell. I wish also to thank Miss Edith M. White, of Yarmouthport, for her great kindness in lending me pictures of Captains Asa, John, and Oliver Eldridge, reproductions of which appear in this volume. The portrait of James Otis is copyright by A. W. Elson, of Belmont, to whom thanks are due for permission to use it. The same acknowledgment is due Mr. Fred Small, of Buzzards Bay, for his photographs of marsh and beach. The picture of the Dillingham house in Brewster is reproduced with the kind permission of Mr. Isaac Dillingham, of Newton Center, and that of the old Sears house in Dennis with the permission of Mrs. Margaret Richardson, its present owner, to whom I am also indebted for the date of its construction. The present volume would never have been undertaken without the advice and assistance of my father, George L. Kittredge, whose collection of documents pertaining to the Cape has always been at my disposal, whose knowledge of the bibliography of Cape history has saved me months of searching, and whose suggestions for the arrangement of material have been as happy as they were welcome.

PREFACE

Some years ago, being idly present at a tiny harbor — a mere nook in the coast of the Cape (for *the* Cape it is to all good Americans) — I scraped acquaintance with an ancient and solitary fisherman who had just landed and was lunching in the shade. He was so quietly at home in the landscape that I felt a scrupulous and uneasy impulse to authenticate myself as the real thing and not a naturalized colonist or a floating element in the population. I told him, accordingly, that I claimed all the rights and privileges of a native (which, be it remembered, are many and important), because, though I was born in Boston, my mother came from Barnstable and was a direct descendant of the first settlers of 1639. 'And so,' I concluded with modest triumph, 'I may claim to go back pretty far as a Cape man.' 'Yes,' he replied, with a slow smile, 'you have a good claim; and as for me, I go back pretty far too.' 'How far?' I asked. 'Oh, my great-grandmother was descended from the Hockanom Indians of Yarmouth.' As Artemus Ward puts it, 'He *had* me there!'

The author of this book, it may be inferred from this anecdote, has grown up in propitious nurture and admonition. He, too, in his daily walk, claims with pride the privileges of a native, and he writes with that intimacy and understanding which befit the chronicler of so distinguished a region as Cape Cod. It is 'a piece of prudence, as well as good manners,' Swift tells us, 'to put men upon talking on subjects they are best versed in.' And so I leave him with confidence to the friendly reader.

GEORGE LYMAN KITTREDGE

CONTENTS

ILLUSTRATIONS

CAPE COD

ITS PEOPLE AND THEIR HISTORY

CHAPTER I

GEOLOGY AND EARLY APPEARANCE

A GENERATION or two ago the notion existed in the minds of those who were at all interested that Cape Cod had risen from the sea — a Cytherea of sand and scrub pine — washed into being by the whim of tides and currents. There was good reason for this belief. Every year new sand bars appeared in the harbors, and old bars changed their shape. Year by year the inhabitants watched their long peninsulas of outer beach stretch farther and farther into the sea, the wind piling them into sand dunes as they went. Sometimes, too, they saw whole sections of beach washed away, leaving new channels between sea and harbor, until the tides of another year closed them with solid barriers of sand.

In the face of such performances it is no wonder that our fathers believed they were watching miniature manifestations of the same forces that little by little had swept the Cape itself out of the sea. Not until geologists advanced the glacial theory, and laymen accepted it, did it occur to any one that Cape Cod as it appears to-day is the result of the passing of glaciers, and that the activity of winds and tides in shifting the restless sands of its coast line was merely the trimming off and polishing of what the glaciers had left in the rough. But such was the case.

The speed with which Science marches from discovery to discovery, leaving behind her a trail of shattered theories, compels the most dogmatic of us to be cautious. Nowadays, if we are wise, we qualify our boldest assertions with some verbal loophole or other through which we may escape when our thesis is shattered by the findings of a new decade. The geology of Cape Cod is a case in point. But the most widely accepted theory at the moment — one that has held for more than

thirty years and is probably correct — is that the foundation of
the Cape, the solid bed of clay that lies under the loose gravel
and sand on the surface, antedates all glaciers, and is one of the
'ancient drainage divides of the country.' This very old foundation exists under almost the whole length of the Cape, cropping
out at the surface here and there, as in the clay deposits that
supply the West Barnstable Brick Yard, and the spectacular
cliffs, called the Clay Pounds, at North Truro. For the rest, it
is the despair of well-drivers, who have the greatest difficulty in
working through it. What the glaciers did, then, was merely to
cap this antique foundation with a blanket of light, loose soil.
This fact should be borne in mind in connection with all that
follows.

It took two glaciers, it seems, to apply this top layer of earth.
One, called the Buzzards Bay Glacier, stopped its journey
southward with its southern edge resting along the curving line
of the Elizabeth Islands, and its eastern side lying along the
eastern shore of Buzzards Bay. From here it stretched north
along the coast line of Massachusetts. Close beside it on the
east was the Cape Cod Glacier, the southern edge of which
exactly fitted the curve of Cape Cod Bay. The movement of the
ice in glaciers is in three directions. It crawls southward, of
course, but at the same time spreads sideways in both directions; thus the upper part of the Cape (from Bourne south to
Falmouth and thence northeast through Mashpee to the Bay
at Sandwich) consists of the rubbish of earth, gravel, and
boulders that was pushed east by the eastern edge of the Buzzards Bay Glacier, and west by the western edge of the Cape
Cod Glacier. In the same way the north shore of the Cape
was formed by deposits of earth that were scooped up in front
of the southern edge of the Cape Cod Glacier, while the eastward motion of its ice pushed into place the section of the
Cape from Orleans north to Truro.

But the process was only begun. No sooner had these glaciers
come to rest than they began to melt, and a thousand streams
appeared flowing out from under them, carrying more soil with
them. These rivers forced their way through the earthy deposits already piled up in front of the glaciers, and carrying the
lighter material along, spread it out in the broad gentle slope

that forms the southern shore of the Cape, all the territory, in fact, from the high ridge that runs east and west along its axis, south to the beaches that border it from Cotuit to Chatham. Similar rivers flowed out from under the eastern edge of the glacier and gave breadth to the plains of Nauset.

In connection with this part of the Cape — to be more explicit, the Ocean side from Chatham to Highland Light — another geological conjecture must be mentioned. The existence of Nantucket Shoals and Georges Bank is best explained by the theory that they are respectively the southern and southeastern moraines deposited by a third glacier called the South Channel Glacier. If such an ice field existed, the westward spreading of its pack certainly contributed to the creation of the region between Chatham and Highland Light, dividing the honors for this achievement with the Cape Cod Glacier on the west. This hypothesis is supported by the presence, in Eastham, Wellfleet, and Truro, of a series of parallel valleys, the floors of which slope from east to west. Such valleys may have been formed by glacial rivers flowing out from the west edge of the South Channel Glacier. In fact, it is hard to account for them in any other way.

In brief, then, the Cape is composed of earth piled up by glaciers on top of a preglacial foundation of clay, and then spread out and added to by rivers of melting ice flowing out from under them. This process was doubtless repeated. The quality of the ice varied greatly; it was harder in some spots than in others, and melted more slowly. So it happened that the rivers sometimes encountered in their course isolated blocks of very hard ice from which the glacier itself had melted away. These abandoned glacial fragments were often several acres in extent. In time they were buried under the earth that was washed over them by the rivers, and presented what was to all appearances solid land. But when its ice foundation finally melted, this land sank, forming pockets into which the ground water promptly seeped. These water pockets are to-day the ponds that are found scattered thickly over the whole length and breadth of the Cape.

Of course the retreating glaciers did not leave anything like the smooth and regular shore line that the maps show to-day from Provincetown to Monomoy Point. The coast was ragged and notched with a hundred shapeless coves and spits, most of them composed of loose gravel, just the sort of shore that the sea likes to fall upon and trim smooth. Two of these irregularities, unlike the rest, were of sufficient size to be classed as headlands and had enough rock in their composition to present an obstinate front to the waves. Naturally, therefore, they lasted long after the rest of the coast had been swept smooth. The existence of the first of these, known as Webb's Island Point, is conjectural, but there is a stubborn local tradition, supported by a certain amount of evidence, that such a body of land once stretched southeast from Chatham several miles into the sea. If it ever did exist, it had certainly been washed away before the first European arrived on the coast.[1] Of the existence of the other headland, called 'Île Nauset,' there is no doubt. It projected seaward from Eastham, and remained undemolished long enough to play an important part in New England history, for it was the surf breaking on this promontory that caused the Mayflower to turn back to Provincetown, instead of continuing her voyage to the Hudson. With the exception of these two tongues of land, however, the sea made short work of the irregularities along the outer beach and used the material it dislodged to lengthen the Cape by making the land that is now Provincetown and the miles of barren sand hills that lie behind it.

The process was simple. Every northeaster sent a tremendous surf breaking against the new and loosely packed outer shore of the Cape all the way from Chatham to its original limit at North Truro. The power of these waves bit great pieces out of the invitingly irregular bluffs and sent whole sections of them sliding down to be swept away by the next roller.

'Till the slow sea rise and the sheer cliff crumble,
Till terrace and meadow the deep gulfs drink,
Till the strength of the waves of the high tides humble
The fields that lessen, the rocks that shrink —'

Once dislodged, this loose sand and gravel was swept in both directions, north and south, and as winter followed winter and

[1] See notes to Chapter I.

century followed century, that which was carried north formed shoals beyond High Head in North Truro. By degrees these shoals were piled higher, attached themselves to the mainland, and finally became dry land. In this way the whole end of the Cape beyond North Truro was built by the sea out of material that it had sliced away from the shores of Truro, Wellfleet, and Eastham. The process still goes on. Every winter sees more gravel and sand torn away from the sea front of these towns, and carried north until it comes to anchor on Peaked Hill Bars. These bars will eventually rise from the sea as a low island; the wind will blow its sand into dunes; a beach will form along its outer edge; and our great-grandchildren will see a neck of sand hills and beach-grass projecting northeast from the present shore line. Such, at any rate, was the process that built Race Point, and left Race Run as a salt creek splitting it from the mainland. Little by little this creek is being filled with sand blown into it by the northeasters that howl over Race Point. By and by the Run will be entirely obliterated, and Race Point will have become throughout its whole length an integral part of the mainland. And the same end, we may safely assume, awaits Peaked Hill Bars, that embryonic strip of dune and beach that lies still unborn beneath the sea.

Monomoy Point and the whole stretch of Nauset Beach were formed in the same way by loose material washed from the coast of Chatham and Orleans and swept south. Prophets delight in foretelling how long it will take at this rate for the Cape to be demolished. One guess is as good or as bad as another. A recent authority predicts that five thousand years will suffice for the waves to eat through from the Clay Pounds at Highland Light to the Bay. He may be right. But the accuracy of such forecasts is interfered with by the whimsical way in which the elements, though they rob Paul one winter, turn the plunder over to Peter the next. Mr. Isaac Morton Small, who has watched the sea's activity at North Truro for seventy years, makes a statement that should shake the assurance of the most robust seer: 'Three years ago,' he writes, 'the ocean waves were pounding into the base of the cliffs one half mile south of Highland Light, and tearing away great patches of earth. To-day the beach is one hundred yards wide at that point, and the highest tides do not reach to the foot of the bank.' The British vessel Somerset, which came ashore not far from this spot during the Revolution, has been buried, unburied, and buried again in the century and a half since she was wrecked.

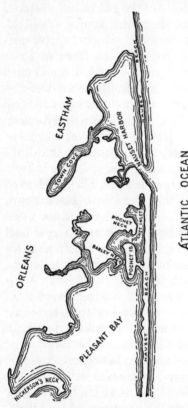

EASTHAM, ORLEANS, AND NAUSET BEACH

Sketch showing how Nauset Beach protects the old irregular glacial shore front of Eastham and Orleans. Nauset Harbor, so called, is filled with marshes; so is Pochet Inlet; but they are not shown in the sketch, because they did not appear until after the beaches had formed.

Another geological phenomenon should give the prophets pause. The old glacial shore line of Eastham, which lies well inland from the present beach, has been perfectly protected, and the town has been given a harbor of sorts, by the gradual formation of Nauset Beach, a low-lying barrier of sand dunes built up from material washed away from the bluffs to the north and swept south in perfect conformity with the whole outer shore. Monomoy Point is in fact a prolongation of this beach. The harbor with which Eastham was thus unexpectedly furnished has had many entrances; the sea will break through the beach during a storm, and sweep a channel into existence that in time is washed wide and deep enough to serve small craft. The next storm will completely block this entrance and open a new one somewhere else. In this way the entrance to Nauset Harbor has been shifting from point to point, usually in a southerly direction, until to-day it is not in Eastham at all, but lies well south of it in Orleans. But through all the rains and ruins of a thousand winters, the old original seacoast has lain far inland, in unbattered serenity. In the same way the east shore of Orleans has been protected by a continuation of Nauset Beach that stretches south from the entrance of Nauset Harbor and continues all alongshore.

The Bay shore has seen changes, too, though of a less spectacular nature than those on the exposed Ocean side of the Cape. The most important of these is Long Point, the long and incredibly narrow sand spit that protects Provincetown Harbor on the west and south. The material for this frail barrier was washed into place by waves and currents set in motion by the northerly and northwesterly winds. The powerful allies could not have done a better piece of work if their sole object had been the creation of a perfect harbor. The same southerly wash of sand and gravel appears at other points along the Bay shore. To-day three large islands (Bound Brook, Griffith's, and Great Islands) stretch out in a northeast and southwest line to form the western boundary of Wellfleet Bay. Originally these were true islands, completely surrounded by the waters of Cape Cod Bay; but now, though still called islands, they are joined with each other and with the mainland by narrow strips of beach that have been washed up in the same way as Long Point. Lest the process become too uniform, however, and tempt us into laying down laws for wind and wave, the northwesters have cut off Billingsgate from this chain of islands, leaving a wide stretch of shoal water between it and Great Island, with which it was formerly connected. By the same token, the waves first chopped off and then obliterated a small island that was once a part of Billingsgate.

Proceeding farther south, we come to Sandy Neck — a seven-mile strip of high and very old dunes that stretch east from the mainland at West Barnstable and make Barnstable Harbor. Sandy Neck is a prolongation of Spring Hill Beach, just as Monomoy is a prolongation of Nauset Beach, and it protects the old glacial shore line of Barnstable in the same way that Nauset Beach protects the high shore of Eastham. Though much older than Monomoy and generously sprinkled with patches of trees, it was formed in the same way from débris washed south and east from the bluffs of Manomet. Like Monomoy it is

growing longer year by year, reaching out easterly across the
entrance to the harbor toward the Dennis shore; whether or not
it will ever reach this goal no one can say. It is true, however,
that while the Neck is stretching farther and farther east, the
bar across the mouth of Barnstable Harbor is at the same time
growing wider and higher, and the channel through it is fast
silting up. There is nothing to counteract this combination of
forces except the tide, which, as the channel narrows, sweeps in
and out of the harbor with terrific and annually increasing force.
Perhaps this tremendous scour will be sufficient to keep a
channel of some sort open forever; perhaps not. Another thousand years will write the answer.

The marshes which invariably lie between these barrier
beaches and the mainland are comparatively recent additions to
the Cape scenery. As soon as a beach has grown long enough to
provide calm water inside, marshes begin to make their appearance and spread fast or slowly, depending on the proportions of mud and sand that are washed into the embryonic
harbor: the more mud, the faster the growth. So it happens
that there are as many salt marshes on the Cape as there are
sandy necks.

Inland, changes equally extensive but less varied have taken
place. One great transformation, indeed, covers them all: to-
day no timber of any account grows on the Cape. Formerly it
was heavily wooded from end to end with a wide variety of
trees. The old records are unanimous on this point. Provincetown itself — the most barren region of all — was once covered
with a thick mantle of woods. Mourt's 'Relation' describes the
shore front as it looked to the Pilgrims when they saw it for the
first time from the deck of the Mayflower: 'It is comaspsed
about, to the very sea with oaks, pines, juniper, sassafras and
other sweet woods.' Bradford says 'the whole countrie full of
woods and thickets, represented a wild and savage heiw.' Even
the sand hills of Provincetown shore were covered with a layer
of good soil that supported considerable vegetation: 'They
found . . . the ground or earth sand hills much like the Downes
in Holland, but much better all wooded with oaks, pines,
sassafras, juniper, birch, holly, some ash, walnut, the wood for

the most part open and without underwood, fit to go or ride in.'

Not content with these bits of indisputable testimony, tradition — persistent as tradition will always be while men remain greedy for marvels — tradition perseveres in the assertion that large trees once stood well out in what is now Provincetown Harbor, and vanished when the shore line of those days was washed back to its present position. Stranger things have happened in the history of Cape Cod; but the evidence for this theory, consisting of the stumps of a few trees that formerly appeared on the flats in front of Provincetown at low tide, is hardly convincing, particularly when we reflect that the tide — the only agent that could have performed this feat — has acted in quite a different way only a mile or so up the shore, and, instead of washing anything away, has built up a solid bar in front of the entrance to East Harbor. However, tides have ways past finding out, and anything is possible on a sea coast. Furthermore, the local historians of Eastham and Dennis, not to be outdone, have reported similar stumps on the flats off the Bay side of their towns.

There were trees enough on the Cape, anyhow, without going to sea for them. Kendall in his travels took a trip down the Cape in 1807–08, and, on reaching Truro, was sufficiently impressed with its forests to call them 'lofty.' It was in Truro, too, that the Pilgrims became lost in one stretch of woods and were torn to pieces by briars in another. Clearly, then, its trees in those times bore small resemblance to the scrub pine and oak that to-day comprise Truro's 'lofty' forests.

The same story is repeated a little farther up the Cape at Wellfleet, where, until the middle of the nineteenth century, the local shipbuilder found plenty of oak and pine growing ready to hand. Many of the fishing vessels and whalers that hailed from this town were made of timber that once covered its present scrubby barrens. Bound Brook Island, which now boasts hardly a tree, was well wooded a hundred years ago. Eastham had all the woods its inhabitants could use for both building and fuel until the end of the seventeenth century, when the town fathers began to show signs of uneasiness at the dwindling supply. It is in Eastham too that the crumbling outer shore has laid bare the edge of a peat bog which for years supplemented its inhabitants' supply of fuel. There must have been woods enough there once, then.

Champlain reports that Chatham, except for the clearings where the Indians had their villages, was overgrown with walnut, oak, and cedar. Some fifty years later, when William Nickerson arrived there as its first white settler, he found its hills still covered with forests of oak, and the swamps filled with gigantic cedars. Dennis and Yarmouth, like Wellfleet, built their own fishing vessels and packets, as well as some crafts for neighboring towns, from lumber produced on the premises. When the first settlers arrived in Barnstable in 1639, they found, in the words of Amos Otis, 'almost an unbroken wilderness'; and more than a century later, in 1762, Deacon John Hinckley cut timber for the East Parish Meeting-House at Barnstable in the woods behind the village. Until 1711 there were enough pines on the common lands to allow them to be boxed and milked. The surplus wood from the Shootflying Hill region was exported to Boston by water. The Reverend Timothy Dwight, traveling down the Cape about 1820, makes the startling assertion that thirty vessels in Sandwich were likewise engaged in this traffic. These items, covering most of the early settlements from Provincetown to Sandwich, are enough to show that in its day the Cape boasted a fair share of forests. But with a wanton extravagance that ill accords with their frugality in other respects, the first settlers demolished the timber wholesale. This ruthless conduct, strangely enough, turned out to be a blessing in disguise, for by ruining the soil, it drove the Cape Cod farmer to sea for a livelihood; and there he won fame such as no farmer can ever hope for. But this is trespassing on topics that belong to other chapters.

CHAPTER II

THE EXPLORERS

LIKE every other part of the Atlantic Coast from Newfoundland to the Delaware Capes, Cape Cod is said to have been one of the ports of call of the Norsemen in their coastwise tour about the year 1000. Of evidence there is none. To identify the places described in their sagas is like trying to identify the particular vintage that Homer had in mind when he sang of the wine-dark sea. Human nature is too frail for such a task, and too readily bends the large phrases of the sagas to fit the contours of any desired landscape. We read, for example, that Thorwald, an Icelandic Viking, younger brother of Leif the Lucky, was shipwrecked at Provincetown, landed and built a house, and later was buried there. An ancient stone cellar is the foundation of this theory. Another authority asserts that his grave was in Plymouth. Somewhat later, we are told, the Icelandic navigator Thorfinn Karlsefne was so struck with the dazzling whiteness of the Monomoy Sands that he called them the 'Marvellous Strands,' and then sailed up Buzzards Bay and spent the winter near Woods Hole. But the wisest men and the best authorities unite in their skepticism regarding all such alleged Norse itineraries, and are content to leave the Cape shores unmolested by white men for another six centuries, when Bartholomew Gosnold dropped anchor off Provincetown.

Visitors there were, no doubt, before him — men who either sailed past the Cape or landed on its shores, sometimes inadvertently, like many a good mariner since. Doubtless John and Sebastian Cabot took a look at Cape Cod on their way from Labrador to Virginia in 1498, but their glances have not altered its history. Sailing in the opposite direction, the Italian Giovanni da Verrazano rounded it on his way north to the coast of Maine in 1524, but there is no evidence that either of these navigators ever landed on the Cape. In 1609, Henry Hudson, on the way to the discovery of the great river that bears his name, may have allowed some of his men to land not far from

Provincetown and pick grapes, before sailing on past the Chatham shore to New York. In 1611, Edward Harlow, an Englishman, raided the Cape shores at various points and after several skirmishes carried off two Indians. George Weymouth, another Englishman, after a narrow escape from the Monomoy shoals in 1605, prudently decided to explore some other region. His countryman, Thomas Dermer, who had formerly been a captain on the New England coast under John Smith, came again in 1619, and, even more restless than most explorers, paid flying visits to the Cape with bewildering frequency, darting back and forth between its shores and Monhegan Island, rescuing two Frenchmen who had been shipwrecked three years before, getting himself captured by the Indians, and finally sailing away for good to Virginia, where he died of wounds received from the natives of Cape Cod. Other random visitors there were, whom in the words of Captain John Smith 'I must entreat to pardon me for omitting,' for their visits were of no consequence.

With Gosnold, however, the case was different, for he was the first European whose voyage gives us any real information about the appearance of the Cape at this early date. He sailed from Falmouth early in the spring of 1602 in the ship Concord, with the object of founding a colony in some agreeable spot, preferably one where gold was abundant. After a voyage of a little over six weeks, his men 'smelled the land' (they were real sailors), and the next day, May 14, they sighted a spot on the Massachusetts coast somewhere near Bass Rock. This place Gosnold named Savage Rock because some Indians sailed out in a Biscay shallop to meet him there and paid a short visit on board the Concord. He then sheared off Southwest and, sailing across the mouth of Cape Cod Bay, sighted the end of the Cape. He called the Bay Shoal Hope, and supposed, not unnaturally, that it cut off the end of the Cape from the mainland. He did not investigate, however, but anchored off the outer Beach behind Provincetown and, excited by the numbers of codfish that surrounded his vessel, caught as many as he wanted and named the land Cape Cod. This happy accident has been worthily celebrated in a poem by Benjamin Drew, whose lively fancy justifies him in taking certain liberties with the facts.

Gosnold went ashore, cut some firewood, made sure that the

pebbles on the beach were not nuggets of gold, had a friendly
though unilluminating encounter with a genial young Indian,
and rowed back to the Concord. So far things had gone well;
but his troubles were about to begin. He weighed anchor and
headed south along the outside of the Cape. After sailing about
thirty-five miles, he was alarmed by surf breaking on a point of
land that projected across his course. In trying to double this
point, he narrowly escaped running aground on shoals that
stretched out from it, but finally, by a smart bit of seamanship,
he got safely into deep water and rounded the point. He called
the surf Tucker's Terror and the point Point Care. Tucker's
Terror is best identified as Île Nauset, a point of considerable
size which once stretched seaward from Eastham. Point Care
was Gosnold's name for the northeast extremity of this point.
Once around it, he breathed more freely and, coming up under
the mainland, anchored for the night. The next day, May 17, a
fresh breeze kicked up enough sea to show him that he was not
yet out of trouble, for it broke white on shoals that lay off a
sandy point to the south'ard.

The next morning the weather moderated, and Gosnold sent
a boat to test the depth of water off this point, which he called
Point Gilbert, now Monomoy Point.[1] Next day he brought his
vessel safely round Monomoy and anchored well inside it. The
following morning he weighed anchor and coasted along westerly, passing an opening which he judged to be the other end
of Shoal Hope. This may have been Lewis Bay in Hyannis,
or possibly Cotuit Harbor. Because of shallow water, Gosnold
sailed by without investigating it and arrived the same day at
one of the Elizabeth Islands which he called Martha's Vineyard — not to be confused with the present large island of the
same name. Here he spent a day fishing and exploring. He
sailed on past another of the Elizabeth Islands, naming it
Dover Cliff (perhaps a part of the present island of Naushon)
to the 'stateliest Sound I ever was in' — Buzzards Bay itself,
which he named Gosnold's Hope. He decided to settle on an
island that lay about ten miles off shore, which he named
Elizabeth's Isle. But the crew were better sailors than they were
pioneers; and all wanted to go home. After a short sojourn,

[1] See notes to Chapter II.

therefore, during which they built a house and a fort and cut a cargo of cedar and sassafras, the Concord set sail June 17 and reached Exmouth in the remarkably good time of thirty-six days.

The next explorer to visit the Cape was Champlain, an extremely intelligent young Frenchman, a good cartographer, and a man whose lively interest in anything new made him a keen observer. He made, in fact, two expeditions to the Cape. The first one sailed early in the summer of 1605, from the French colony on the St. Croix River, in search of a warmer climate. He coasted along for a month, was hooked in by the end of the Cape, took a look at Wellfleet with its harbor, though he did not land, named it St. Suzanne de Cap Blanc, as being a sort of adjunct to Provincetown (which he called Cap Blanc), rounded the Cape, and, late in July, sailed into Nauset Harbor. He had to hurry back for lack of provisions and so spent only three or four days in Eastham. But he had seen enough to tempt him to come again the following year.

Accordingly in the fall of 1606 Champlain again left the St. Croix River, this time with Poutrincourt in command of the expedition, to reëxplore the regions around Eastham and Chatham, still with a view, albeit a somewhat vague one, of establishing a colony there. They were a little out of their reckoning, and, instead of raising Provincetown, as they intended, they dropped anchor an hour before daylight somewhere inside Cape Cod Bay, two or three miles from land. As soon as it was light, they went a shore in their tender and explored a harbor which they called Port aux Huitres because of the abundance of oysters. It has been thought that this was Wellfleet, but, as Champlain had visited Wellfleet the year before and named it, he could hardly have failed — accurate observer that he was — to recognize it now. Barnstable Harbor is a better guess, for although there are no oysters there to-day, huge oyster shells of great age are sometimes picked up on the flats, and they may have been abundant in 1606. But before they could land, a favorable slant of wind sprang up and proved a stronger temptation than the lure of an unknown shore. They therefore sailed fifteen miles northeast, rounded Provincetown, and arrived off Eastham, which they had named Malle Barre the year before.

Here a southerly blow compelled them to anchor and Poutrincourt went ashore, where he was greeted by a hundred and fifty
inquisitive Indians. When the weather moderated, they skirted
the coast southerly, got in trouble among the Monomoy shoals
(which Champlain called Cape Batturier), smashed their rudder, and, despairing of ever extricating themselves without aid,
anchored and went ashore in the shallop. They found an Indian
who consented to act as pilot, and brought him off to the vessel,
which he took safely round Monomoy Point into Stage Harbor,
Chatham. Some of the ship's company stayed there to mend the
rudder, while others in the shallop coasted along southerly with
an Indian as guide. The strain of being alone among white men
proved too great for the Indian, and he took to the woods somewhere in the neighborhood of Point Gammon. The Frenchmen
were afraid to proceed without him, and made their way back
to Chatham.

The anchorage was so good that Poutrincourt was reluctant
to leave, and the explorers made themselves very much at home,
taking frequent excursions inland, inspecting the Indian villages, and doubtless bringing back with them whatever of interest or value the country yielded. They also built baking
ovens on the shore, where they made their bread. After this had
gone on for a fortnight, the Indians began to wonder what the
end would be. A friendly visit was one thing; a permanent
settlement quite another; so they decided to speed their guests
into departure. Accordingly one afternoon they began to take
down their lodges and send the women and children off into the
woods. The French rightly interpreted these demonstrations
as the preliminaries of an attack, and toward evening Poutrincourt sent the shallop ashore to bring off the men, for some of
them always slept on the beach near the ovens. But they found
the shore more comfortable than the ship, and refused to leave.
The shallop returned without them. Early in the morning, the
Indians crept up on the shore party, found all but one of them
asleep, and let fly four hundred arrows, such a volley that 'to
rise up was death.' The Frenchmen fled in bewildered disorder
and with some losses, the Indians meanwhile making a 'desperate noise with roaring which it was terrible to hear.' To add to
the confusion, the shallop, which started from the vessel to help

the fleeing Frenchmen, stuck on a sand bar, and the rescuers had
to jump overboard and plough their way ashore through the
water. On their arrival, the Indians fled, and the explorers,
prudently concluding not to follow them, buried their dead,
erected a cross over the grave, and returned to the bark.

No sooner were they aboard than the Indians emerged from
the woods, dug up the corpses and threw down the cross. The
French went ashore again, reburied the dead, replaced the cross,
returned to their vessel, and the next morning sailed away south,
naming the place Port Fortuné because of their disastrous experience there. They sighted what may have been Martha's
Vineyard and perhaps saw Buzzards Bay, but head winds made
progress too slow with winter at hand. Discouraged and in an
ill frame of mind, they returned to vent their spleen on the
Chatham Indians. Their object was to carry off some of them as
slaves, and to accomplish their design they hatched a plot that
would have done credit to Machiavelli. This was the scheme:
they would land and approach the natives with a string of beads
in one hand and a fathom of rope in the other, and thus try to
lure them into the shallop. If they refused to be lured, the plan
was to put the string of beads around the Indian's neck and at
the same time lasso him with the rope; then he could be dragged
to the shallop. If, even though snared, the Indians proved 'too
boisterous,' they were to be held by the rope and stabbed to
death. If, by any chance, the stabbing failed, there were to be
men standing by with swords. Meanwhile cannon on the bark
should be ready to fire on any Indian reënforcements, and under
this barrage the shallop was to row out with its captives. This
plot helps to explain, perhaps, why the French were indifferent
colonizers. It failed to bag any slaves, but a few Indians were
murdered according to schedule.

It is interesting, and not without significance, to contrast
the attitude of these Frenchmen toward Indian thieving with
Gosnold's. One day after the latter had landed on the Elizabeth
Islands, he was visited by a party of inquisitive Indians. After
they had been parleying in friendly fashion for some time, the
English saw an Indian take a shield from the shallop and put it
into a canoe. Gosnold called the attention of the chief to the
procedure, being curious to see what authority he had over his

CHAMPLAIN'S DRAWING OF THE FIGHT WITH THE INDIANS AT CHATHAM

subjects. Instantly the chief gave orders; the shield was returned, and the day ended as genially as it had begun. Truly with nations, as with individuals, there are diversities of talents.

The next explorer of importance is the celebrated Captain John Smith, who came in 1614. He is in one respect unique among the early navigators of the New England coast; he thoroughly enjoyed the business, and his accounts of his discoveries and of the beauties and excellences of the country for any purpose, from mining gold to raising corn, are full of the ardor of the enthusiast. His catalogue of the abundance and variety of fish and game reads like 'Swiss Family Robinson,' but it was substantially true. He had no doubt that gold and copper were to be found with a little patience. Corn, he declared, sprang into ripeness with unexampled speed. The climate was that of Devonshire. But Smith did more than rhapsodize over New England; he made an amazingly accurate map of its coast as far south as Cape Cod, and he was honest enough to stop drawing where his own knowledge ended. Thus we have a first-rate outline of the Bay side of the Cape, the best sketch of Provincetown Harbor that had been done up to that date, and the beginning of the back side about as far along as Truro. Farther than that the Captain does not commit himself, but says that the Indians tell him there are shoals beyond. Because of his candor here, it is safe to conclude that what else he tells us of his coasting is also true; that he skirted alongshore in a small boat, past Plymouth, Sandwich, Barnstable, and so on out of the Bay and past Provincetown. He stopped short of Île Nauset and it does not appear that he landed at any of these places for more than an hour or so, here and there. Fish and furs comprise the burden of his song, and, loading his vessel with these and a little whale oil, he returned to England, leaving Captain Thomas Hunt in command of the second ship to load with fish for Malaga. The only foolish thing that Smith did was to try to alter Gosnold's name, Cape Cod, to Cape James. Happily this change never spread beyond his own writings. Smith started another voyage to New England in 1615, but fell in with pirates, and eventually returned home without reaching our coast.

Hunt, realizing that he might never again have such a chance,

seized twenty-four Indians, some of them Nausets, and carried
them to Spain along with a cargo of fish. There he 'sold those
silly savages for rials of eight,' and thereby burned his bridges
so far as New England was concerned. Much pious indignation
has been hurled at Hunt for this transaction, and certainly Hunt
was a villain. But his performance differed from that of many
generations of the descendants of his critics merely in geography
and in degree. He stole two dozen natives from New England;
they stole thousands from Africa. Yet they were men who
read their Bibles and were doubtless familiar with the parable
of the mote and the beam.

So far, all the men who visited the Cape were frankly explorers; love of adventure and desire for gold tempted them
to come, and when they had had enough excitement and had
looked in vain for the gold, they sailed back again. Quite different from these irresponsible gentlemen were the next arrivals
on Cape soil — the Pilgrims in the Mayflower.

After a series of disappointments and deceptions that would
have utterly discouraged any mere explorers and would have
killed any motive but a stubborn desire to worship God as they
chose — deceptions, too, which so delayed their departure that
they landed at the beginning of a New England winter instead
of in May or June — the Pilgrims, battered and exhausted,
sighted the end of Cape Cod and identified it with rejoicing.
They shaped their course so as to bring them outside it, and began the last leg of their voyage, which was to land them somewhere near the mouth of the Hudson River; but after half a
day, they encountered, as Gosnold had encountered before
them, the white breakers on Île Nauset, and despairing of finding a passage through them, returned to the shelter of Provincetown Harbor, where they dropped anchor on November 11,
1620. Provincetown was not the destination they had had in
mind, but after more than two months in the cramped quarters
of the Mayflower, any port and any land looked like the Garden
of Eden to these sea-weary voyagers. Not knowing how soon
now they might find themselves established on shore, and having, along with their idealism, a good share of sturdy common
sense, they decided to draw up a constitution for their new government before they landed. This measure was the more neces-

sary as some adventurers, who, in spite of precautions, had
secured passage on the Mayflower, had been overheard during
the voyage in seditious boasts as to what they would do when
they got ashore; furthermore, the Pilgrims' patent, being for
Virginia, was worthless in New England. They therefore assembled in the cabin and composed the famous Mayflower
Compact, the text of which follows:

In the name of God, Amen. We, whose names are underwritten, the
loyal subjects of our dread sovereign Lord King James, by the grace of
God, of Great Britain, France, Ireland, King, defender of the faith, etc.

Having undertaken for the glory of God, and advancement of the
Christian Faith, and honor of our King and country, a voyage to plant
the first colony in the northern parts of Virginia, do by these presents,
solemnly and mutally, in the presence of God and one another, covenant and combine ourselves together into a civil body politic, for our
better ordering and preservation, and furthermore of the ends aforesaid;
and by virtue hereof to enact, constitute, and frame such just and
equal laws, ordinances, acts, constitutions, offices from time to time,
as shall be thought most meet and convenient for the general good of
the Colony: unto which we promise all due submission and obedience.
In witness whereof we have hereunto subscribed our names. Cape
Cod, eleventh of November, in the year of the reign of our sovereign
Lord King James of England, France and Ireland 18, and of Scotland
54. Anno Domini, 1620.

This document has been called the germ of our Declaration of
Independence; but such an interpretation is too sentimental.
What the Pilgrims did in this Compact was to assert the right
to modify the existing laws of England to suit new and unprecedented conditions which they were sure to encounter in
New England. Such right of interpretation was often ex-
pressly granted in the patents given to colonists, and was in
accord with the general policy of the Virginia Company, under
whose ægis the Pilgrims had set sail. In drawing up this Compact, therefore, they were merely assuming, here in New England, rights which would have been theirs if they had landed, as
they expected, on territory that was under the Virginia Company's jurisdiction. There was nothing revolutionary or unprecedented about it.

After the first flush of gratitude at being safe in harbor had
worn off, sober second thoughts assailed the little band. They
had reached their goal and were face to face with the reality that

heretofore they had idealized. Bradford saw the solemnity of
their situation clearly and has expressed it with eloquence:

they had now no freinds to wellcome them, nor inns to entertiane or
refresh their weatherbeaten bodys, no houses or much less townes to
repaire too to seek for succoure.... And for the season it was winter,
and they that know the winters of that cuntrie know them to be sharp
and violent, and subjecte to cruell and feirce stormes, deangerous to
travill to known places, much more to search an unknown coast.
Besides, what could they see but a hidious and desolate wildnes, full
of wild beasts and wild men? and what multitudes ther might be of
them they knew not.... If they looked behind them, ther was the
mighty ocean which they had passed, and was now as a maine barr
and goulfe to seperate them from all civill parts of the world....

From every point of view action was imperative. The shallop
had been damaged during the voyage, and several days would
be needed to repair it; so a number of them took the longboat
and rowed ashore at Long Point. They spent the day tramping
about, keeping always a weather eye open for Indians; but they
saw none, and having walked perhaps as far as what is to-day
the west edge of the town, they returned at dusk to the Mayflower, much refreshed by the excursion.

The next day was Sunday, and, though the shore must have
looked to the cramped voyagers as alluring as the Swiss landscape looked to the Prisoner of Chillon, they stayed piously on
board, thinking about heaven and to-morrow. This Sunday,
beyond a doubt, was the longest day in the lives of any of them;
but it passed, and on Monday morning, November 13, all hands
— Pilgrims, sailors and servants — hurried ashore, landing in
the very middle of the present shore front of Provincetown.
While the women were busy washing the clothes, the men
dragged the damaged shallop up above high-water mark for
repairs. Two days later, under the command of Captain Miles
Standish, a party of sixteen, wearing corselets and armed with
swords and muskets, set out to explore the region. The party
proceeded alongshore for a little way, heading east, in single file
and at equal intervals: the Captain was a believer in military
discipline. But before long they forgot their marching order in
the excitement of following a couple of Indians that they saw
running inland. The Pilgrims, hoping to find the Indians' village, and guided by the footprints of the natives in the sand,

persevered in the unequal race, until nightfall found them close to the Back Beach and near Stout's Creek (a branch of East Harbor). Here they camped for the night, and the next morning, still following the Indians' footprints, they made their way round the head of East Harbor Creek, and lost the trail in some pines. They had to plough through briars that 'tore their very armour in pieces,' until finally, suffering severely from thirst and fatigue, they came upon a spring near the edge of the marsh behind High Head, in Truro. Here they drank their first draughts of New England water and stopped for a rest. Disappointed in their hope of finding any Indian settlements, they decided to make for the mouth of Pamet River, of which they had caught glimpses from the deck of the Mayflower, on the chance that this region might turn out to be a good place to settle.

With this goal in mind they headed for the shore of the Bay, and skirted the water's edge southeasterly, through the present villages of North Truro and Truro, where they came upon Indian stubble fields and graves. They poked round a bit in the graves, but took nothing, thinking, as they piously expressed it, 'that it would be odious unto them to ransack their sepulchres.' They had no scruples, however, about helping themselves to some corn that they found a bit farther on, buried in grass baskets in the sand. They took away as much of this as they could carry, and also a ship's kettle which they found with it.

On their way back, the Pilgrims, after spending the night on the shore of the pond that gives Pond Village its name, lost themselves in the woods while trying to make their way round the head of East Harbor Creek, and finally came out on the Back Beach not far from Highland Light. Here they got their bearings once more and returned to the Mayflower, where they found their friends enjoying themselves ashore while the carpenters hammered away on the shallop. This expedition is known as the First Discovery.

For the next ten days all hands busied themselves pleasantly, cutting wood, fashioning axe-helves and getting into condition again after the enforced idleness of the long voyage. At the end of that time the shallop was ready, and on November 27 a party of thirty-four, including Captain Jones, set out for Pamet River,

Truro. The weather was bitterly cold, and their boat was driven for shelter into East Harbor; in getting ashore every one was forced to wade knee deep, and this, with the subsequent night of exposure, gave them colds from which some of the party never recovered. Rather than spend the night shivering, half the group set out alongshore on foot toward Pamet River, and were picked up next morning by the shallop. They landed on Indian Neck between the two branches of the river. The ground was frozen and covered with snow; so after an abortive excursion inland, they returned to the spot where they had previously found the corn, and helped themselves to some ten bushels more, naming the place Cornhill. Jones then returned to the Mayflower, taking with him the corn and a number of sick men.

The next day those who remained continued their explorations and came upon some more Indian graves, and one in which the bodies of a child and a sailor had been buried together. Truly more things than are known occurred around Province-town before 1620. They found also a couple of Indian houses, which had apparently been abandoned in hot haste, for utensils of all sorts were lying about. 'Some of the best things we took away with us,' says Mourt's 'Relation,' 'and left the houses standing still as they were.' The theft of the corn can be excused, for hunger is a stern dictator; but how is such filching as this to be justified? Toward evening they returned to the shallop, which had arrived to pick them up, and reached the Mayflower the same night. There they learned of the birth, during their absence, of Peregrine White, the first English child to be born in New England. This excursion is known as the Second Discovery.

The third and last Discovery was undertaken only after considerable discussion. Truro looked so good to some of the Pilgrims that they were in favor of settling there, believing that they might go farther and fare worse. But another and more adventurous group was for making wider explorations before they came to a decision. This party prevailed, and, on December 6, ten Pilgrims and eight sailors, under command of Miles Standish, set out in the shallop in freezing weather to examine the whole Bay shore. Their pilot, one Robert Coppin, told them of a place where he had once been, 'on the other headland of this Bay almost right over against Cape Cod, being a right line not much above eight leagues distant.' This, Coppin said, he and his fellow explorers had named Thievish Harbor because an Indian had stolen a harpoon from them there. It was of course none other than Plymouth. This place, it was decided, should be the limit of their explorations, and if they found a good spot nearer at hand, so much the better.

They had no more than started when the whole party were drenched with spray which froze as fast as it struck them, but they persevered and coasted along as far as Billingsgate Point. In sailing across the mouth of the harbor, they grounded on the Eastham flats and waded ashore through icy water, a process they were beginning to regard as inevitable. They spent the night round a fire on the beach, and in the morning part of them explored Wellfleet Harbor, named it Grampus Bay from the numbers of stranded blackfish they found, and returned to their first landing-place at Eastham. Here they were joined by the rest of the party, who had struck inland and who returned at night with the report that they had found more elaborate and extensive Indian burying grounds than any they had yet seen, and had also come upon the dismantled frames of a few Indian houses. They all camped again on the beach, barricaded against a possible attack.

In the gray of the dawn, while they were preparing to embark, the attack came; some shots were exchanged amid great excitement and confusion on the part of the Pilgrims; but nobody was hurt, and the Indians soon withdrew. The affair seems to have been a mere flash of hostility rather than an organized onslaught, but it so impressed the settlers that they named the spot the First Encounter.

After this lively interruption, they continued coasting along and soon ran into bad weather with a high wind and such a thick snowstorm that they sailed past the entrance to Barnstable Harbor without seeing it. The wind increased until by the middle of the afternoon it was blowing a gale. Their rudder broke, and their mast snapped in three pieces. They were in grave danger of swamping at any moment. However, they found to their joy that they were off Clark's Island at the mouth of Plymouth Harbor, and managed to make a landing there.

They shivered through the night in the rain, and spent the next two days thawing out and resting. On Monday morning, December 11, they made their way into Plymouth Harbor, where they found cleared land all ready to be occupied and plenty of fresh water. This they decided was the very place they had been looking for; they had had enough exploring to last them for a long time. They, therefore, sailed back straight across the mouth of Cape Cod Bay, carrying the good news to those who had stayed on the Mayflower. On the morning of December 15, the Mayflower set sail from the anchorage where she had lain for more than a month, and the next day dropped anchor in Plymouth Harbor. This was on a Saturday. The piety of the Pilgrims would allow them to do nothing until Monday; so they waited within a stone's throw of the goal they had been seeking through so many weary months, and did not go ashore until the Sabbath lay behind them.

CHAPTER III

THE INDIANS

WHEN the Mayflower dropped anchor in Provincetown Harbor, and her weary passengers at last had a chance to stand on a steady deck and look about them, they saw a shore wooded to the water's edge as far as the eye could reach. So, as a matter of fact, was all the rest of the Cape: a virgin wilderness, with mile on mile of continuous forest. But there was more than vegetation to be found by one who was explorer enough to pierce the veil; for the Pilgrims, instead of carving a republic from a western wilderness, stumbled into an organized community. Behind the screen of pine and oak were clearings dotted with Indian dwellings and connected by well-worn paths with other groups of dwellings. These were villages in the strictest sense: no chance camping grounds of nomadic savages, but fixed abodes, inhabited by generation after generation of natives. It was no joke to make a clearing big enough for a village in such woods as used to cover the Cape; and natural clearings were few and far between. Once they had hewn out such an area with their stone axes, the Indians kept it, for they were not adventurous, and preferred other forms of exercise to wood-chopping.

The trails that connected these villages were established routes fixed after long and painful experience. That they were indeed paths of least resistance is shown by the fact that many of the Cape roads to-day follow these Indian trails. One of them led up the Cape from Eastham to Yarmouth and was so much used by the settlers that it was beaten into a dusty bridle-path and then into a wagon-road. To-day it is substantially the route of the macadamized highway between these two towns. At Yarmouth this trail was cut diagonally by a famous thoroughfare that ran across the Cape from Hyannis. Another main artery of Indian travel was the famous trail from Sandwich off the Cape to Plymouth. No doubt, too, a path through the woods connected Yarmouth and Sandwich. At all events, there was a much-used trail across the Cape at Barnstable that has never ceased its usefulness; it is now known as Mary Dunn's Road. In short, the Pilgrims landed, not in a wilderness, but in a region that had been settled for nobody knows how many hundred years; a region that had its villages and its roads, its organization and its traditions. So much is certain, although little enough is known about its inhabitants.

All Cape Indians belonged nominally to the Wampanoags, but thanks to the geographical isolation of the Cape, each little tribe — and there were half a dozen or more of them — was free to go its own gait under its own sachem. Massasoit had no control over them. King Philip tried in vain to enlist them as allies. They were independent, peace-loving, and non-progressive. At Falmouth were the Succonessitts. The tribe that lived in and near Sandwich called themselves Manomets; those at Barnstable and Yarmouth were Mattakees and Cummaquids; the Monomoyicks occupied what is now Chatham; the Nausets controlled Eastham, and the northernmost group, who lived in the neighborhood of Truro, were called Pamets.

The notion that Indians lived only in wigwams receives a blow when one begins to read what the early explorers have to say on the subject. Wigwams existed, it is true, on the Cape as elsewhere, but the early accounts say little about them and a good deal about a different sort of structure, with a skeleton of sapling-poles bent into the shape of horseshoes about seven feet high, with both ends stuck into the ground. For greater stability a ridgepole was sometimes fastened along the top. Over these ribs the builder stretched heavy mats, woven from the long thatch that bordered every creek in the marshes. The door was another mat hung over an opening so small that it was necessary to crawl to get through it. These dwellings usually had an inner lining of mats of finer texture, embroidered with colored grass and porcupine quills. The floor consisted of mats spread on the ground.

All the houses were small, only big enough for a single family. In the middle of the floor a circle of stones served as a fireplace, and directly above, a hole in the roof let out the smoke. Beds were the most conspicuous items of furniture, and consisted of three or four thicknesses of mats. Sometimes these were raised a little off the ground on stakes.

Such houses were almost never found isolated, for Indians were more gregarious than whites. The remote New England farmhouse, standing a mile or two from its nearest neighbor and ten miles from a town, had no prototype among the Cape Cod Indians. Sometimes, to be sure, the number of dwellings was small. Bradford and his band, for example, came upon a group of only two, but probably these were what was left of a larger number that had been moved away on the arrival of the Mayflower. Champlain reports 'large numbers of little houses' seen on an expedition inland from Chatham, and describes Nauset Harbor as 'very spacious, being perhaps three or four leagues in circuit, entirely surrounded by little houses, around each one of which there was as much land as the occupant needed for his support.'

The sites of these settlements could be pretty well determined to-day by the shell deposits that accumulated beside them, even if we had no contemporary historians to tell us where they were. Such shell heaps are found in every town on the Cape from Truro to Buzzards Bay and on both the north and south shores. For the most part they are close to salt water, for the Indians, like their white successors, regarded the inland of the Cape (except for hunting purposes) as merely a distance to be covered in getting from one shore to the other. The few settlements that they did make inland lay along the banks of great salt creeks like Bass River, or beside ponds like the mill ponds behind North Brewster. But the great permanent villages were alongshore.

Of the tools and weapons found on the sites of these villages little need be said, for they hardly differ from those used by Indians throughout the country. The isolation of the Cape, though it increased the natives' happiness, retarded their progress. Their implements, therefore, were less elaborate than those made by Western Indians; but the same sort of objects are found: stone arrow- and spear-heads; knives; scrapers; the usual types of stone axes and grooved hammers; occasionally a finely polished pendant, and more rarely still a sacramental banner-stone showing fine workmanship. Once in a great while a stone pipe turns up, but none so elaborate as the Western specimens. Cape Indians had no need to make pipes out of stone: they used wooden pipes and lobster claws, and no doubt corncobs. Stone pestles are common enough, but mortars are very rare and of enormous size, obviously village property placed at some central point to be used by any member of the group, like our town pumps. They made pottery out of a mixture of clay and broken shell, surprisingly thin and light, and frequently decorated with criss-cross patterns and scalloped rims. Many implements of all kinds were made of shell — needles, hoes, arrow-heads, pendants, and the like, but these have nearly all vanished.

A significant fact about all these objects is that they are made almost without exception from local material. As far as the raw stuff for manufacture went, the Cape Indians were as self-sufficient as they were in the matter of food and clothing. One may pick up, for example, a thousand arrow-heads made from local stone, for one of copper. Gosnold, to be sure, mentions seeing an Indian off Chatham adorned with a copper pendant a foot long, but the copper for this, and for the arrow-heads as well, is more likely to have come from a wrecked French fishing vessel than from the utterly unknown and remote Michigan Indians.

One exception to this rule must be noted. Fragments of soapstone pottery are frequently found on the Cape and one soapstone pipe was picked up in Harwich Port. As no native soapstone exists anywhere on Cape Cod, this must have been imported from Johnston, Rhode Island, where quarries exist that are known to have been worked by the Narragansetts. One clay pipe of an elaboration beyond the powers of the local Indians has been found near Bourne. But with these two exceptions, the Cape tribes made their implements from local materials.

Before the arrival of the whites, wampum seems to have been used merely for ornament, never for money. For this reason there was not much of it in evidence. The Plymouth men had no idea of its value until Rasière, on a visit to them from New Amsterdam, explained that the Dutch were using it in trading with the New York Indians; he sold the Plymouth settlers a lot of it, but it took Bradford two years to get rid of it to the Indians. After that, however, it went better. Two kinds of wampum existed on the Cape — white and black. The white was made from the stems of periwinkle shell; the black from the purplish part of the inside of quahaug shells. This was worth twice as much as the white, or about twopence a bead.

The natives of the Cape were in no proper sense of the word nomadic. They found living easy where they were, and saw no reason to change. They were led away by no wandering herds of buffalo — like the Western tribes — and had no fixed seasons for hunting. Every creek was full of eels; every flat thick-sown with clams; most harbors had oysters. The marshes teemed with ducks and geese, snipe and plover. Deer were abundant in the woods, and to make hunting easier they burned out the underbrush whenever it grew too thick — a maneuver called 'firing the woods.' They spread nets for fish, and set snares for wolves and deer, so shrewdly concealed that young William Bradford was caught in one at Provincetown on his first excursion ashore from the Mayflower. Beans were sometimes planted in the same hill with corn — a sort of embryonic succotash. If the ground was poor, they spread herring over it for fertilizer and spaded it with sea-clam shells. They stored up their surplus corn by the simple method of burying it in grass baskets three or four feet deep in the sand, where it kept perfectly. By way of luxuries they may have raised tobacco, but this is quite as likely to have been a weed called poke. At all events they smoked poke, but perhaps they had a little real tobacco too. What wonder that they were content with their lot, and wisely concluded that their lines were fallen unto them in pleasant places?

Champlain speaks of the neat appearance of the Nauset girls. It would be pleasant to lend unqualified endorsement to this view, but sailors are not always discriminating in matters of feminine beauty. It was a long time since Champlain had seen any women, and he doubtless looked on the Nauset maidens with a tolerant eye. The Indians wore no clothes to speak of until cold weather forced them into a single lower garment of deerskin that served for both trousers and stockings, with another deerskin worn loosely over the upper part of the body.

Champlain mentions a short grass garment, open in front, that some of the Nausets wore when they visited his ship. One woman, he says, had a red deerskin tunic, the borders of which were ornamented with little shells. Both sexes frequently painted their faces red, black, and yellow, in whatever designs they fancied, and indulged at times in elaborate hairdressing that involved feathers, foxtails, and similar adornments. But these, like their clothes, appeared only on state occasions.

But we have already spent more time on his costume than ever an Indian did! Let us turn to the baffling question of his character. Certain of the traditional Indian traits are too well known to need more than the briefest mention. Such qualities as stoicism in pain and remembrance of injuries may be taken for granted. But quiet endurance of torture seems to be about the only sort of restraint the Indians practiced; in most respects they were like children, and restraint is not in the nature of children or of primitive man. It is no surprise, therefore, to learn that even the best of them were gluttons in the presence of food. They ate as much as they could whenever they had it. No less a dignitary than Massasoit himself — though just recovering from an almost fatal attack of indigestion — was powerless before the savor of a fat wild duck, and nearly killed himself by devouring it against the excellent Puritanical advice of Winslow. An incident that further illustrates their childishness occurred when some of Iyanough's men had stolen certain trinkets from Miles Standish on one of his excursions from Plymouth to Yarmouth for food. The Captain, with characteristic brusqueness, demanded their instant return. The Indians gathered round with wide-eyed protestations of innocence, while the culprit slipped down to the boat and placed the stolen articles on board. He then returned with the glad tidings that they hadn't been stolen after all, but had been overlooked by the impetuous Standish.

A good deal of discussion has been indulged in, first and last, on this question of Indian honesty, and wise men have raised their voices on both sides. It would be foolish to try to show that the Cape Cod Indians — or any other Indians — were not ready thieves. But if they stole oftener than civilized men, so did they more often return the stolen goods; and it is doubtful whether at any period of Cape Cod history the permanent losses suffered by the whites at the hands of the Indians have been more numerous than those suffered by the Indians at the hands of the whites.

The Indians were frequently dishonorable. It may be, indeed, that they cared nothing for honor. Thomas Dermer would have said so, for one. It was his misfortune in 1619 to be captured by the Monomoyicks near Chatham. They demanded a ransom from his crew. It was paid. 'But,' says Dermer bitterly, 'I was [then] as far from liberty as before.' Such perfidy would be shocking enough but for the cheering reflection that Lord Bacon himself, at about this time, was profiting by the same sort of ethics in the High Courts of Justice in England. It would be prudent to preface all criticisms of aboriginal honor with Addison's dictum, 'None but men of fine parts deserve to be hanged.'

Of their utter savagery at times there can be no doubt. Not even the graves of dead enemies were sacred. Champlain was horrified when the natives dug up the bodies which he had buried and threw down the cross he had erected over their graves. He had not the gift of prophecy and could not foresee that when another century and a half had wheeled round, purging the gentle weal as it revolved, a London sexton would exhume from the graveyard the body of a child and leave it on the parents' doorstep because they were slow with the burial fee. Indian atrocities were in fact no more than manifestations of the same cruelty that has existed in all human beings, in all countries, in all ages.

A pleasanter characteristic of the Cape Cod Indians was their amazing friendliness to the white men — at first to those fleeting voyagers to the Cape shores, and afterwards to the permanent settlers there. This friendliness is strongly marked among the Cape Indians. It singles them out from among all the other tribes of the New World. It made enemies for them among their own kind. Why they were friendly is a mystery. Many considerations help to explain it; none of them — nor all of them together — quite succeeds. But a few instances when their friendliness appeared may furnish a hint of the answer.

In the spring of 1602, Bartholomew Gosnold anchored off the

south shore of the Cape somewhere between Eastham and Monomoy. The apprehension which he felt when he saw his vessel surrounded by a fleet of canoes full of Indians quickly vanished before their friendly gestures, and he bore no malice for the loss of a few articles to which they inconspicuously helped themselves. When he landed on one of the Elizabeth Islands, he was cheered to find that there too the Indians were on the whole friendly and helpful. His decision to abandon his purpose of settlement was in no way attributable to their attitude.

The Indian who did more than any one else to keep his fellow tribesmen amicable to the whites was Squanto (sometimes called Tisquantum). He appeared at Plymouth very soon after the Mayflower, with the great Massasoit, and acted as interpreter in drawing up a treaty of peace which that chief made with the colonists. When Massasoit left Plymouth, Squanto stayed behind, perhaps because Plymouth was his native place; perhaps because he fared better with the whites than with his own people; perhaps, as Bradford devoutly declared, 'because he was a special instrument sent of God for their good beyond their expectation'; perhaps, as Winslow asserts, because he 'wished to make himself great in the eyes of his countrymen... not caring who fell, so he stood.' At all events, he stayed with them, showed them how to plant corn and catch fish, and took them 'to unknown places for their profit.'

One of his first helpful exploits was in connection with a worthless youngster named John Billington, who was always in trouble and who this time got lost in the woods. Less rigorous consciences than the Plymouth men's would have ascribed this happy accident to God's will and would have persuaded them that they were well rid of the young pest. But the stern daughter of the voice of God sent them off in search of him, and ten men, with Squanto as their guide, set out by water for the Bay side of Eastham. They spent the night in their boat, which had grounded at low tide on the Yarmouth flats, and in the morning were cordially greeted by some Indians who were lobstering alongshore, and who told them that the boy was safe at Nauset. They accepted an invitation to land and take breakfast with the savages, and were warmly received by the young chief Iyanough, whose 'cheare was plentiful and various.'

The white men were chagrined to find here an old woman who wept and wailed at the sight of them — the first Englishmen she had ever seen — because her three sons had been sold into slavery by the unscrupulous Captain Hunt. Notwithstanding this untoward incident, the visit passed off in friendly style, and Iyanough himself escorted them in their shallop to Nauset, and on arriving, went off inland with Squanto to tell Aspinet, the sachem, what they had come for. Here again the sins of the settlers rose up to confound them, for they met the owner of some corn they had helped themselves to when first they had landed at Provincetown. They satisfied him, however, with promises of payment, and this incident, too, was amicably closed.

Soon a great number of Indians arrived with Aspinet, bringing the lost boy. They waded out to the shallop, carrying him in their arms lest he wet his feet, and returned him bedecked with beads. The settlers bestowed two knives on the Indians and sailed away. They stopped again at Yarmouth on the way back, where Iyanough supplied them with fresh water and a necklace, and then they squared away for Plymouth.

The friendliness of the Indians throughout this expedition is of capital significance. If they had wished to wipe out the Plymouth Colony, this was their chance, for by killing the ten men who comprised the crew of the shallop, they would have reduced the number of able-bodied settlers by more than half, thereby delivering what would probably have been a fatal blow. But the Englishmen, instead of getting arrows between their ribs or knives in the back, received food, water, information, guidance, and presents. The next year the Monomoyicks of Chatham supplied Bradford with eight hogsheads of corn and beans, thereby pulling the Colony through a severe shortage of food.

In the winter of 1626, the Nausets had another chance to help the settlers. An English vessel, probably the Sparrowhawk, bound for Virginia with prospective colonists, came ashore near Eastham. She was not much damaged, and could

be made seaworthy again if materials could be had. The shipwrecked men had hardly got ashore when they were approached
by a group of Indians who asked if they were Governor Bradford's men and offered to carry the news of the disaster to
Plymouth. This offer, as a matter of fact, was made out of
friendship to Bradford rather than from any special desire to
help the new arrivals, for the Indians on the Cape had agreed to
notify the Governor of any 'roving ships upon the coast.' However, the offer was eagerly accepted, Indian runners were dispatched over the forest trails to Plymouth, and in due time
Bradford himself arrived, bringing spikes and oakum. The
vessel was repaired, but was again smashed by a storm before
she could set sail, this time beyond hope of repair. So with
Indians as guides, the newcomers betook themselves bag and
baggage overland to Plymouth, having received Bradford's
permission to sojourn there temporarily.

Five years later, in the winter of 1631, occurred an instance
of Indian humanity worthy of the good Samaritan himself.
Richard Garrett, a Boston cobbler, set sail in January for
Plymouth with his daughter and a crew of four men. They
were blown by a northerly gale across Cape Cod Bay and came
ashore somewhere near Barnstable. Two of the men started
out on foot for Plymouth and on the way met two Indians, one
of whom went along with them, while the other went back to
help those who had stayed with the boat. He found them almost frozen, built a shelter over them and started a fire to thaw
them out. Garrett died very soon, whereupon the Indian with
his tomahawk chopped a grave in the frozen ground and laid
him in it, covering the spot with a pile of brush to protect it
from wolves. Garrett's daughter and one of the men survived.
The two who had started for Plymouth died — one at the
Manomet trading post, and the other on arriving at Plymouth.

It is true that two or three instances of hostility occurred
between the Cape tribes and various explorers who visited its
shores from time to time. At first glance, these skirmishes seem
to contradict the thesis of Indian friendliness, but a little consideration will show that they were the result of panic, or else
were acts of justified retaliation for wanton aggressions of the
whites.

The first of them was Champlain's unpleasant experience with the Nausets in 1605. The trouble started with a tactless performance on the part of one of Champlain's men. Some of his sailors had gone ashore for water near Eastham, and a group of Indians had returned the compliment by going aboard the vessel for a friendly visit. As one of the shore party was filling a copper kettle from a brook, an Indian snatched it from his hand and made off into the woods. The French, with all their virtues, are an impulsive folk. One of them instantly pursued the fugitive, while the rest shouted to the men on the vessel to shoot. The Frenchmen fired muskets, and the Indians who were aboard, seeing that something was amiss, dived over the side and headed for shore — all but one, whom the sailors seized and bound. Panic is contagious. The Indians who were ashore, hearing the shouts and seeing their comrades take to the water, killed the Frenchman who had had the kettle. Some more shots were fired from the ship, and a landing party went ashore to bury the dead man. The whole affair was unfortunate and quite unnecessary. If, instead of flying off the handle and beginning to shout and shoot the minute the kettle was stolen, the French had kept calm and demanded its return from the chief, the chances are they would have got it with apologies. At worst they would have lost only a kettle instead of a kettle and a man. A few hours later, a delegation of Indians came to apologize. Champlain bore no malice and released the prisoner that had been held on board.

His encounter with the Chatham Indians the next year was more serious, and no amount of sentimentality can interpret it as friendly. One thing, however, is clear. A fortnight's association with the Frenchmen turned the Indians from friends into enemies. If they had wished to destroy the newcomers at the outset, they need only have stood on the shore and watched the vessel pound her bottom out on the worst shoals on the Atlantic Coast. Instead, they piloted her into the harbor. They could even have piloted her wrong and led the explorers into certain destruction. There was something, clearly, in the attitude of the Frenchmen — in particular in the aspect of their excursions inland — that offended or alarmed the Indians so seriously that they tried to kill the same men whom two weeks before they had saved from the Monomoy breakers. It is unfortunate that our only account of the affair is from the French angle.

The Indians were slow to forget injuries. Fourteen years later, the Nausets, remembering the experience that their neighbors, the Monomoyicks, had had with Champlain, attacked the Pilgrims who landed at Eastham in the course of the Third Discovery. Obviously the Indians supposed that these white men were the same sort of people as the French. But as soon as they learned their mistake, they changed their attitude, and on more than one occasion saved these very men from starvation.

The rumor of one more war must be silenced before the road is clear for pleasanter topics. In March, 1623 — in the midst of genial passages between the Cape Indians and their white neighbors at Plymouth — Winslow refers to a proposed insurrection of the Massachusetts Indians against Weston's colony of demoralized Londoners at Wessagussett. It is no wonder that they wanted to destroy these persons, whose actions filled the Plymouth men with pious horror and the Indians with scorn. The plot would not have come within the scope of this volume had not these Massachusetts Indians induced their brothers on the Cape to plan an attack on Plymouth at the same time. Such, at any rate, was the story that Massasoit told to Hobbamock — a staunch friend of the Plymouth settlers — with instructions that he should report it to Winslow. Massasoit's motive was gratitude to Winslow for having cured him of indigestion. According to him, all the Cape tribes except the Monomoyicks were involved in the conspiracy.

Here, then, is a fine state of affairs, coming as it does in the midst of our protestations of Indian friendliness. But there is no reason for becoming any more exercised about it than the settlers did. They ordered Miles Standish to take as many men as he needed and march off north to annihilate the Indians of the Massachusetts Bay Colony. By this procedure they deliberately deprived their town of its chief military officer and an important fraction of its fighting men. To be sure, Standish, always fond of the spectacular, took only eight men with him, but eight men were a good many in the condition of the

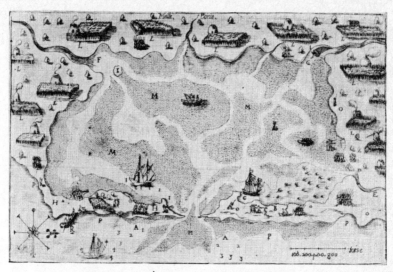

CHAMPLAIN'S MAP OF NAUSET HARBOR

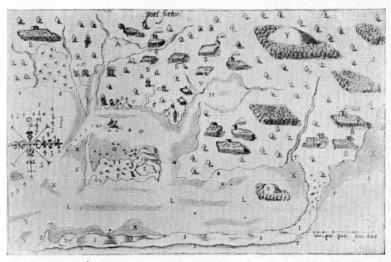

CHAMPLAIN'S MAP OF CHATHAM, SHOWING INDIAN HOUSES AND
MONOMOY

Colony. Remember that two years before, ten men had comprised more than half of its fighting force. Furthermore, the Governor and Council were themselves surprised that the Captain took so few; they had been ready to part with more.

This action when rightly interpreted, is significant. If the Plymouth Colony had felt that there was real danger of an attack from the Cape Indians from the south, they would hardly have sent off Standish and his men to the north; for though blood is indeed thicker than water, and the Pilgrims were ready to help Weston's colony if they could, yet the blood in our own veins is thicker than that in our neighbors', and not even the New England consciences of the Plymouth settlers would have jeopardized their own hard-won existence for the sake of saving profligate countrymen from a fate that they richly deserved. If, then, the men most immediately threatened by this alleged conspiracy of the Cape took such a cavalier attitude toward it, there is no reason to regard it as more than a rumor. Furthermore, the event justified their nonchalance. No attack materialized; the strength of their newly completed fort was never put to the test; and though they were stern believers in punishment where punishment was deserved, they never made the slightest move to punish the Indians of Cape Cod. It looks very much as if Winslow, through the alchemy of a close perspective, raised a dense cloud of smoke from a very small spark.

So much for the question of Indian friendliness. For the next fifty years all was quiet among them. Then came the formidable war declared by King Philip — and what the Cape Indians did at that critical period will appear in due time. These fifty years, however, formed an important epoch in their history; for it brought them their first lessons in the rudiments of civilized life. By 1644 the first four permanent settlements on the Cape had been made — at Sandwich, Yarmouth, Barnstable, and Eastham; and as time went on, the pious citizens of these towns felt moved to spread the gospel among their heathen neighbors and so were brought for the first time in contact with the primitive but in some ways beautiful religion of the Cape Indians.

This is a tantalizing subject because our information is so

meager. Our ancestors felt small interest in what they regarded as the bizarre paganism of the aborigines and were at small pains to leave exact information about it. The following facts are taken from Winslow's somewhat sketchy observations among the Indians just off the Cape in the neighborhood of Buzzards Bay.

Two major gods, it seems, presided over the Indian destinies. The greater of these they called Kiehtan. He was their creator and the creator of all else besides, earth and sea, sky and stars. The naturalness of the Adam and Eve story as an explanation for man's existence on the earth is strikingly illustrated by the Indian idea that Kiehtan had first created one man and one woman from whom they all were descended. Kiehtan lived in heaven, and to him went the spirits of all the dead; to be admitted if they had been good; otherwise to be sentenced to a wretched and restless existence of aimless wandering in a sort of Cimmerian fog. They prayed to Kiehtan for good crops and good weather and offered him sacrifices if their prayers were answered. Apparently they ran no risk of wasting a sacrifice before the event. Kiehtan seems to have been a somewhat remote deity. That he was at least partly analogous to the Christian God appears from a conversation which Winslow had with an Indian named Combatant, who, observing that he asked a blessing before meat and returned thanks after it, asked what the significance of the ceremony was. Winslow explained as simply as he could, and Combatant, nodding his comprehension, remarked that the Indians held much the same belief, but called the god Kiehtan. It is prudent to suggest, however, that this remark was probably born of the childish desire of all primitive peoples not to be outdone.

The other great divinity of the Indians was Habbamock. He was less powerful than Kiehtan, but more active, and held particular sway over the realm of disease. He disclaimed all connection with fatal diseases, however, ascribing them to Kiehtan and asserting that he himself dealt only in curable ailments, and was always ready to cure them if properly approached. This approach could be made by only two classes of Indians, the *powahs*, or medicine-men, and the *pnieses*. Obviously Habbamock's reluctance to associate himself with fatal illness was a canny invention of these medicine-men to cover their retreat when their cures failed. He appeared to them, so they declared, sometimes as a man, but more often in the form of a bird or other animal — usually a snake.

The powahs, in effecting their cures, worked themselves into a state of frenzy with loud cries and wails and other antics of so strenuous a nature that the sweat stood out on their bodies and foam on their lips. Clearly an Indian sick-bed was not a couch of roses. Winslow remarks that when he visited Massasoit in his illness, these medicine-men were 'in the midst of their charms, making such a hellish noise as it distempered us that were well, and therefore unlike to ease him that was sick.' It need hardly be observed that the office of Powah furnished a fine chance for hypocrisy and false practice.

The pnieses were quite different from the powahs, and were the finest specimens, both mentally and physically, in the tribe — a combination of priest and warrior and statesman. To become a pniese a man had to undergo a rigorous and savage training that would have discouraged or killed any but the sturdiest. They had little to do with religion, but were constantly summoned to councils of state. They were the chosen advisers of the sachem and the most powerful fighters in war. A sort of divinity hedged them in battle, the prestige of which enabled them, we are told, to put a hundred of the enemy to flight single-handed. There is a Homeric quality about these pnieses that suggests the prowess of Achilles and the wisdom of Nestor. But since their religious activities received only a small part of their attention, no more need be said about them here.

Religion among the Cape Indians was falling upon evil days as early as 1623. They told the settlers — perhaps with more evasiveness than truth — that the forms of their worship varied widely between village and village, and they added gloomily that in the olden days their ancestors had been more religious than they. Kiehtan, they asserted, was no longer worshiped as he had been. Such doleful sentiments have a familiar ring. Even the Indian, it would seem, sighed for the good old days!

Their legends were to Indian religion what the story of Adam and Eve or of Samson and Delilah is to our own. They would surely have found a place in an Indian Old Testament. Most of them were invented to account for the existence of natural objects, and show a pretty highly developed imagination. Like all legends, they might serve as fanciful answers to children's questions.

A good example is the Yarmouth Indians' explanation of fog. Long years before, they said, a huge bird used to visit the shores of Yarmouth and carry off the children in its talons, flying with them to the south out over Vineyard Sound. Maushop, a benevolent giant of Yarmouth, at last grew tired of this procedure and decided to pursue the bird and kill it. So, on its next appearance, he followed it out across the Sound, wading along as fast as he could, until finally, pretty well exhausted, he reached an unknown island on the other side, where he found a huge tree piled about with the bones of children. 'It is time for a smoke,' said Maushop to himself, and reached for his tobacco. But he had forgotten to bring any with him and was obliged to use poke instead — a plant which he found growing plentifully on the island. This poke he puffed with such effect that the whole Sound and the shores on both sides of it were enveloped with the smoke; and forever after when a fog settled down over the south shore of the Cape, the Indians would nod wisely and say, 'There's old Maushop smoking his pipe.'

The Indians on Nantucket made up a fine story to explain the existence of their island. Like the Yarmouth legend, it involves a giant — a monster who used the Cape for his bed, covering the whole length of it with his huge body, and fitting himself comfortably into its curves. One morning he awoke after a restless night, in the course of which his thrashings and rollings had ploughed the sand into hollows and dunes that have remained ever since, and struggled to his feet. To his annoyance he found that his moccasins were full of sand; so he took them off and threw the contents far into the sea, where they formed Nantucket and Martha's Vineyard.

The Cotuit Indians had a local legend to account for Santuit River and a knoll near by. A great trout, that lived in the South Sea, wanted to get into Santuit Pond to rest. So he ploughed his way overland, leaving behind him a deep, crooked furrow that was promptly filled with salt water. Finally he arrived at the pond, but was so exhausted that he had not the strength for the return trip, and died there. His path became Santuit River. The Indians covered his remains with a mound of earth that still exists and is called Trout Grave by the inhabitants.

Each of these legends, it will be observed, has something to say about fatigue, rest, or sleep. This may be chance, or it may be significant; but it is idle to try to guess what the significance may be — if there is any. It was with men who were thinking such thoughts and repeating such tales as these that the early Cape preachers had to deal when they turned missionaries in their spare time. Two or three of them, indeed, finding the virgin soil of the savage mind more fruitful than the stubborn clay of the enlightened Christian, gave their best efforts to the Indians.

The pioneer among these was Richard Bourne, who was in fact not a minister at all, but a layman of substance who moved to Sandwich early and was established there by 1641. He soon became interested in the Indians and determined to improve their condition. They could have had no better advocate. Bourne was experienced in legislative matters, having been representative to the General Court, and was a man of sound judgment and common sense. His voice carried weight in high places, and the energy of his nature made his theories work. He wisely concluded that the first step in converting the Indians was to awaken their self-respect by establishing them in a community on land of their own, and then teaching them the rudiments of self-government. It took him twenty years to accomplish this, but in 1665 the act was recorded authorizing the Indians to hold their own courts, try criminals, and pass judgments. Five years earlier they had received title to fifty square miles of ideal territory at Mashpee — shore, woods, rivers, and ponds — everything best suited to an Indian's existence.

Naturally enough, their first experiments at governing themselves often failed. The jump from a primitive tribal organization to the complex machinery of civilized government was too great. Frequently the General Court was obliged to step in and extricate them from legal tangles in which they had become enmeshed. Yet Bourne's scheme, with all its failures, was a great help in increasing the natives' self-respect; and this was the cornerstone of Bourne's structure.

Meanwhile, he kept preaching Christianity to them with considerable success, for it would be a churlish Indian, indeed, that allowed himself to be cured by Bourne's medicine, accept Bourne's land, preside over a court which Bourne had given him, and then rejected the religion that came hand in hand with these blessings. Bourne had four Indian preachers as his assistants, and reports that the whole population of Mashpee — numbering between four and five hundred — were converted. Although this district was nearest his heart, Bourne assumed responsibility for the spiritual welfare of all the Indians on the Cape, and did what he could to convert the tribes as far away as Truro. In 1670 he was regularly ordained as minister of the Mashpee church — a mere official recognition of the work he had been doing there for years. Here he continued to preach until his death in 1685.

During the last dozen years of his life, Bourne's territory was reduced to something like manageable dimensions, for in 1672 Samuel Treat, an energetic young minister who graduated from Harvard in 1669, was called to the parish of Eastham. He immediately relieved Bourne of all the territory below Yarmouth, and divided his efforts about evenly between the Indians and the whites. Treat had a genial and sociable nature with a marked vein of humor not always found in our early preachers; but there was nothing genial or humorous about his doctrine. It was the most virulent form of undiluted Calvinism, and the detailed description of the torments of hell-fire that he roared at the natives in a voice which, in the language of Dr. Freeman, drowned out 'even the winds that howled over the plains of Nauset,' were well calculated to rouse the savage instinct of even the most phlegmatic Indian.

Treat, like Bourne, was a firm believer in self-government for the natives, and was able, thanks to his proximity, to put into execution schemes that Bourne had been trying to work out at arm's length. The result was very much what it had been at Mashpee. In 1693, Treat was able to report that there were five hundred praying Indians in his district, which included

Eastham, Harwich, Chatham, Wellfleet, and Truro. Twenty years earlier there had been only three hundred in all the territory below Sandwich. This improvement shows what could be done by an enthusiast like young Treat. Four native preachers operated under his supervision, and four native schoolmasters taught the Indians to read and write their own language. The difficulties of this tongue had no terrors for Treat. He mastered it in a short time, translated the Confession of Faith, and frequently wrote sermons in Indian for his assistants to deliver.

The finest specimen of a praying Indian, however, lived neither in Eastham nor in Mashpee, but in Yarmouth. His name was Elisha Nauhaught, but he is better known as Nauhaught the Deacon, the man who stood his ground when attacked by a large number of black snakes and let them surround him. One climbed up his body and tried to put its head into Nauhaught's mouth. The Deacon opened his jaws and brought them together on the snake's neck with such vigor that the reptile was decapitated. Alarmed by the blood that flowed down in streams, the rest of the snakes fled, and Nauhaught strolled home. On another occasion he showed an interesting combination of superstition and honesty. He had found a purse full of money, but refused to open it except in the presence of witnesses, 'for if I did,' said he, 'all the trees in the woods would see me and witness against me.' This remarkable Indian died peacefully at the age of eighty-nine, and viewed the approach of death without a tremor — calm in the assurance of salvation, or, as he himself expressed it to the Reverend Mr. Alden, who was at the bedside, 'I have always had a pretty good notion about death.'

Unfortunately not all the praying Indians were of Nauhaught's caliber, nor was Nauhaught himself exempt from an occasional fall. Sometimes they found unorthodox uses for their newly acquired religion. There is, for example, the yarn of Deacon Ryder and the stolen turkeys. The language of the Reverend Timothy Alden, who tells the tale in his 'Collection of American Epitaphs,' cannot be improved upon:

The village [i.e., the Indian village near the mouth of Bass River] contained many praying Indians as well as some of a different character. Deacon Ryder, an old gentleman, had lost some turkeys on a certain time, and not being well acquainted with the character of his aboriginal neighbors, fixed his suspicions upon them. He rode into the [Indian] village very early in the morning, fastened his horse in the woods, and walked in silence to the door of one of the wigwams, where he stopped for a moment and found that the Indian was at prayer. He then, without disturbing the pious occupant in his devotions, passed on to another wigwam. The head of the family was solemnly engaged in the same manner. He felt ashamed of himself but thought he would go to one wigwam more. He did so, and it happened to be Nauhaught's. To his astonishment he found him also offering his morning sacrifice in the midst of his little family. What a delightful scene! While the groves resounded with the melodious notes of the feathered choir, the whole village seemed to echo with the prayers and praises which rose from every quarter. Deacon Ryder was extremely mortified that he should have suspected the poor Indians of theft, when he found them before sunrise pouring forth their petitions to Almighty God in such a commendable manner, while many of his whiter brethren were sleeping like the sluggard and never called upon that sacred name unless to profane and blaspheme it!

On the whole, however, Bourne and Treat ought to have been satisfied with their results even in the ticklish realm of religious conversions; and their temporal accomplishments may have saved Massachusetts, for in 1675, fifteen years after Bourne secured Mashpee for the Sandwich Indians, and three years after Treat had begun his work among the Nausets, King Philip declared war on all the white settlers in Massachusetts and Rhode Island. The condition of the Cape during this war, though actually a very happy one, was potentially critical. As long as the Cape Indians refused to join Philip or listen to his anti-white propaganda, the settlers there were in a far better position than the other colonists. King Philip was not in their vicinity, and it was unlikely that any fighting would take place on Cape soil. Nevertheless, the Cape men had a very real cause for anxiety. They had to furnish their quota for the colonial army, and every man who departed weakened the town. In the midst of them lived some five hundred braves who might at any moment leap up with a whoop and attack them in their own houses.

The alarm was universal and led to the absurd measure of seizing some of the squaws as hostages. But the settlers soon realized the folly of this and then became doubly excited for

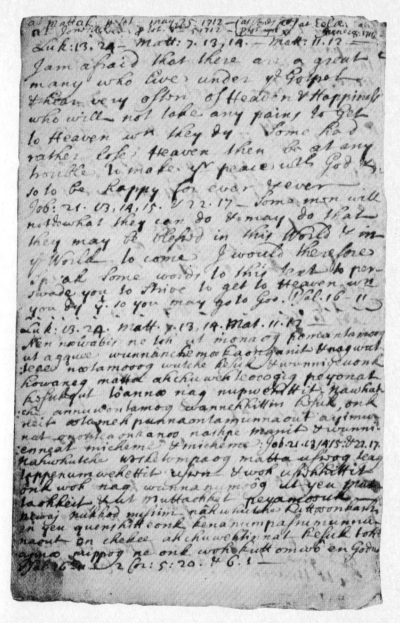

PAGE OF SERMON THAT JOHN COTTON PREACHED TO THE YARMOUTH
INDIANS IN 1712
English above; Indian below

fear the Indians would attack them in retribution. The Reverend Mr. Walley, of Barnstable, writes: 'I am greatly afflicted in my spirit to see the danger we are in and the confusion and sad disorder we are fallen into. . . . Some fear we have paid dearly for former acts of severity; and how dear we may yet pay, God knoweth.' It seems that his apprehension had so far gained ascendancy that he was living not in the present, but in a future of his own imagining; for the Cape Indians stood firm. Some of them even enlisted with the settlers and fought against their own people, thereby helping the white cause by their activity as well as by their inaction. The commanders of the colonial units soon discovered the wisdom of following the advice of their dusky allies. 'Set an Indian to catch an Indian' became the watchword of the wisest of them. Before long, the Cape was inviting the citizens of less fortunate communities, like Rehoboth, Bridgewater, and Taunton, to seek safety for their families on its peaceful shores; and though the invitations were not accepted, the incident shows strikingly what confidence Cape men put in their Indian neighbors before the end of the war.

The reasons for the fidelity of the Cape tribes during these months were many. In the first place, they were isolated from their warring brethren and so did not catch the contagion of war. Furthermore, they were of a peaceful — even a submissive — nature. But beyond a doubt a large factor in their friendliness was gratitude for the work that Bourne and Treat had done for them. Without these two men, a fire might have broken out in the rear and consumed the Cape settlements. Religious teaching alone would not have sufficed, for Christianity so far has failed to prevent wars. It would be hard to point to a finer instance of virtue receiving its reward than the staunchness which the Cape Cod Indians maintained, in considerable measure out of gratitude to Bourne and Treat.

But there was another reason why the tribes on the Cape held aloof from Philip's War. They no longer had the energy or the desire to fight with any one. Their race was run; their pride and dignity were little more than memories. Degeneration had begun as far back as 1616, when a plague swept over the Massachusetts coast from Penobscot to Provincetown and

wiped out whole villages. This disease was apparently a kind
of malignant typhus caused by filthy living conditions. The
Cape suffered less than the rest of the State, perhaps because
its sandy soil provided perfect natural drainage. But a good
many Indians died even there, as is shown by the number of
graves that Bradford found at Truro and Eastham.

Treading the shadow of this disaster came the white men,
whose arrival was the beginning of a long uneasiness among the
natives. In the modern jargon, they began to suffer from an
inferiority complex. What was the meaning of this new race
whose weapons belched fire and roared like the thunder?
Vague dread lay beneath the Indians' acts of friendliness, and
dread is a poor companion for those who are trying to swing
back into stride after a pestilence. This surely is an important
reason why the Indians of Cape Cod were so friendly to the
Englishmen. Their attitude sprang from no unnatural desire
to help foreign intruders, but rather from an underlying apprehension that tinged their generosity with fear; and the white
man, though he, too, was afraid, was shrewd enough, as he
accepted their hogsheads of corn, to smile loftily at his bene-
factors —

> '... as one great lord of fate
> Might smile upon another half as great.'

It is not hard to deceive children, and the Indians supposed that
these white strangers felt as fearless as they looked.

When, in 1639, the settlers came and built towns close beside
them, choosing the best places from Sandwich to Eastham, this
vague uneasiness began to crystallize into despair. The Indians
saw that the whites grew and prospered, while their own
strength ebbed from year to year. Their new neighbors assumed
charge of all things in a masterful way. 'This land,' they said,
'we will buy from you for five axes; that land you may keep.'
'We will tell you what God to worship, and will show you how
to govern yourselves.' But the new God seemed remoter even
than Kiehtan, and the government that the white men gave
them was an unwieldy tool in their hands. They grew more
discouraged than ever. Rum found its way among them. What
was the use of struggling? The whites were invincible and knew

everything. Blasted by such apprehensions, their native virtues withered and died. This was the effect, on these reduced and plague-ridden tribes, of the arrival of a superior race. It is not a new story. It has been the result wherever civilization has camped beside primitive man; only in the present case the end was hastened by the epidemic.

The speed with which the Indians vanished was frightful. Before the plague, there had been upwards of two thousand adult Indians on the Cape.[1] Eighty years or so later (in 1690) there were probably not more than a thousand. A little before the outbreak of the Revolution there were five hundred and fifteen. Town after town saw its Indian population dwindle to a half-dozen wretched families in an isolated cluster of huts. In 1764, only four Indians remained in Eastham and eleven in Wellfleet. Five or six families of Monomoyicks were left at Chatham. Harwich was better off with a total of ninety-one. Nauhaught reported six wigwams in Yarmouth, near the mouth of Bass River, as late as 1767, but ten years later smallpox carried away most of their occupants, and their lands were sold soon after the war. A few years later, all that remained of this village was a single wigwam occupied by a Negro and a squaw.

Mashpee, meanwhile, was in a serious condition. Numerically, to be sure, the district seemed to be holding its own much better than any other Indian community. In 1802, for example, there were three hundred and eighty inhabitants, including children, and in 1820 the number was three hundred and twenty, a very slight shrinkage compared to the death-rate elsewhere. But these figures are misleading; they do not indicate either health or prosperity in the district, for the original Mashpees were dying off as fast as any Indians on the Cape. What kept the numbers up was not a healthy birth-rate, but the fact that Mashpee was a Utopia where no inhabitant was taxed. This halcyon state of affairs brought the scum of the Indian and Negro population from all over the State drifting to Mashpee like weeds to the Sargasso Sea. These worthless immigrants — many of whom had little or no Indian blood in their veins — intermarried with the remains of the Mashpees, until, as early as 1792, at least two thirds of the inhabitants

[1] See notes to Chapter III.

were of mixed blood. The fact that the population was kept up by these unwelcome additions deceived some into believing that the district was a model Indian community, happy and prosperous, under the wise, paternal eye of intelligent overseers. A few industrious and self-respecting families there were, no doubt, like the Pocknets and the Attaquins, but on the whole the inhabitants were a lazy, improvident lot. Well into the nineteenth century many of them still lived in sedge wigwams that crawled with vermin; and the few houses that they did build were 'dirty, unfinished huts.'

The State tried various schemes for improving their condition. Before 1763, the Governor had appointed two overseers and two guardians for Mashpee, who should watch over the Indians' affairs, and in particular should see to it that the entailment on their real estate, a protection which Richard Bourne's son Shearsjushub had obtained for them, was respected, and that no white man should be allowed to buy away their land. Good men had been provided to preach the Gospel to them: after Shearsjushub's death, his son Joseph had been their minister; and after him came the Reverend Gideon Hawley and John Freeman, the half-breed. But the Mashpees remained degenerate and degraded. In 1763, the authorities, thinking that perhaps a little more self-government might increase their self-respect, answered the Indians' constant petitions for more liberty by making Mashpee a district, and allowing the inhabitants to elect for themselves five overseers and various minor officials. But all was in vain; no form of government, no amount of preaching, could make the Indians religious, virtuous, or happy; so after twenty-five years of prolonged discontent, the old order was reëstablished, and in 1788, the Governor once more appointed Mashpee's overseers and guardians. As the various committees that labored for the Indians' welfare 'could not give them temperance and industry, they still remained poor, abject and discontented.' The committees were discouraged; in the words of James Freeman, 'the melancholy reflection that they have labored in vain obtrudes itself upon the mind.' Again he writes, 'Last year (1801) their meeting house resembled a cage of unclean birds. The situation of it proved that they could take no delight in the worship of God, as the house which is dedicated to him was more offensive to the senses than even their filthy huts.... The term "Praying Indian" cannot with propriety be applied to the inhabitants of Mashpee.'

Twenty years later, the situation had not changed. Their missionary, Mr. Fish, writing in 1820, says: 'Their descent cannot be traced at this day and they have altogether adopted the habits of civilized life. They have forgotten their ancient names and languages, except a very few who retain a slight knowledge of the old tongue and can converse in it a little. The number of pure-blooded Indians is very small, perhaps fifty or sixty, and is decreasing. There is more negro blood than white in the mixture. About fifty profess religion, a few of whom are eminently pious, considerable numbers decent in their lives, and not a few shockingly profligate.'

Fifty years later, in 1869, we learn from the lips of a Mashpee Indian, Mr. Pocknet, that the foreign strain in the Mashpee blood was still more marked. Addressing the legislative committee on Indians that visited the Mashpees in their meeting-house to discuss once more the question of removing the entailment on their real estate, he made this striking statement: 'There are some Indians here two-thirds blooded, and some nigher.' The next year, 1870, the district was incorporated as the Town of Mashpee.

About this time a new ingredient was added to the already miscellaneous nationality of the Mashpees. Every returning New Bedford whaler brought home a few *bravas*, or black Portuguese, among its crew. These Cape Verde savages — a cross between exiled Portuguese criminals and the aborigines of the Islands — began to drift into Mashpee and marry into the hybrid of Indian and African Negro that they found there. This vicious mixture caused what Mr. Pocknet called 'a drift of disgust against Mashpee,' and has resulted in such a mixture of blood that the Indian strain is to-day almost lost. Only now and then, as one makes one's way through the village, is the eye caught by some leather-skinned veteran whose high cheekbones, thin lips, and straight hair suggest that his ancestors once chipped arrow-heads from the pebbles on the shores of the Cape and shot deer with them in the woods.

CHAPTER IV

THE FIRST SETTLERS

AFTER they were settled at Plymouth, the Pilgrims found the Cape both a blessing and a nuisance. It was a blessing as a granary, from which friendly Indians supplied them with corn; but geographically it was a nuisance because it lay across the water route to New York and trade with the Dutch. The voyage around the Cape was too dangerous; was there no easy way across it?

On one of his voyages to the Cape for corn, Bradford had landed at Bourne and had seen how nearly the Cape was cut in two at that point by Scusset Creek on the north and Manomet River, emptying into Buzzards Bay, on the south. The idea of avoiding the passage round the Cape by using these streams, with the short carry overland from the one to the other, now occurred to him, and by 1627 the settlers were employing this channel as an established trade route and had erected a house and a palisade near the headwaters of the Manomet River. Here they kept two men, and built a shallop large enough to navigate the waters of Nantucket Sound. This new passage was so successful that in a few years Plymouth was trading with the Connecticut River and New York.

The colonists now ceased to think of the Cape as a hindrance to their voyages, and by degrees began to realize that it was a good place to live in. The Plymouth men were not the only ones, however, who had this idea. Enthusiasts in Scituate and Lynn and Ipswich were also turning their backs on their hardly completed cabins and heading for newer pastures on the Cape. Furthermore, in 1630, Bradford at last received his patent from the Earl of Warwick, President of the Council for New England. In this document the whole Cape was annexed to the territory of the Plymouth Colony, and settlements could now be made on it with perfect legality.

Naturally Sandwich was the first site that was selected. For one thing, it was far up the Cape and close to the Manomet trading post; but more important was the extent of salt marsh that bordered it on the north. The problem of fodder for their cattle was always an urgent one with the settlers. They had no time for turning forests into meadows green with English hay. They had enough to do in building their houses and clearing land for their corn. The acres of Sandwich marshes, therefore, which yielded more salt hay than they could possibly use, to be had for the cutting, were in themselves reason enough for choosing this spot. Here, too, was a stream with herring and water-power enough for a mill. Wood in prodigious quantities was at hand whichever way they turned. There was no harbor, to be sure, but a creek navigable for small vessels served well enough instead. So Sandwich it was.

Edmund Freeman, of Lynn, was the father of the new town. He had the pioneer's restlessness to an exaggerated degree. He arrived from England in 1635, lived a year at Lynn, made his way to Plymouth in 1637, and, staying there only long enough to obtain the Governor's consent to start a new settlement at Sandwich, set out with ten others, most of them like himself from Lynn, and, making his way over the old Indian trail through the woods, arrived at his goal with his axes and his cattle and began to clear land and build houses. The Governor had authorized him and his companions to take enough land for sixty families, and almost immediately recruits began to arrive, swelling the number of the 'ten men of Saugus.' Twenty or thirty families from Lynn, Duxbury, and Plymouth came straggling in during the year that followed Freeman's arrival. Their purpose was 'to worship God and to make money.'

As the numbers in the new town grew, the question of dividing the land became acute. Not everybody, by any means, was entitled to hold land. The old order had not changed, and as yet freedom and equality were not even theories of government. But even among the potential landholders, disputes — or at least problems that bade fair to become disputes — frequently arose. They therefore wisely shifted the responsibility to the Plymouth Court, and the Court with equal wisdom ordered Captain Miles Standish to go to Sandwich and arrange the matter in an equitable fashion. John Alden went with the Captain, and between them they did the job to the satisfaction of all hands — doubtless by the usual method of drawing lots. Sandwich grew and prospered, and in 1639, two years after Edward Freeman and his little band of followers arrived, the settlement was regularly incorporated, and named Sandwich after the old town in Kent.

The story of Yarmouth, which was the next town to be established on the Cape, begins with an heroic failure. The Reverend Stephen Bachiler had for several years prior to 1638 been leading a stormy life in Lynn. He was one of those fiery malcontents whose utter unwillingness to compromise with authority defeats the very progress it strives for. He had been dissatisfied with the Church in England; he was still dissatisfied with the Church in Lynn, and tried, with the support of a handful of followers, to start a new one. He was warned to confine his preaching to the satellites he already had and to accept no new converts. He refused, and decided to move away to some spot where he would be left alone with his doctrine. Such was the man who at the age of seventy-five set out on foot for Yarmouth at the beginning of the winter of 1637–38. With him went a few of his unregenerate flock.

Such an enterprise was foredoomed to failure. Yarmouth was a wilderness, relieved only by a few Indian clearings. The flats and forests were the only possible sources of food. A wise man would have waited for spring, but wise men are never guilty of dramatic rebellion. Bachiler and his friends would certainly have starved or frozen that winter but for the Indians. As it was, their sufferings were such that they departed in the spring — just when they might have begun to be comfortable; and this admirable madman spent the last years of his life in continual religious hot water in various parts of New England. His frantic effort to settle at Yarmouth has no bearing on the town's history, but as an heroic gesture it deserves mention.

Bachiler had hardly departed when the first real settlers made their appearance. These were Anthony Thacher, John Crow, and Thomas Howes, who arrived in the late winter of 1639. Stephen Hopkins, one of the Mayflower band, also built a house that same year, but soon sold it and returned to Plymouth. Within a year other recruits arrived from various parts of the Bay Colony and built houses on the shores of the millpond. The town was incorporated almost as soon as the first settlers arrived in 1639, the same year as the incorporation of Sandwich and Barnstable, and the Indian name of Mattacheese was officially changed to Yarmouth. The new name was given, like the names of so many other Cape towns, as a reminder of the port from which a number of its citizens had doubtless embarked when leaving the old country.

Except for a few clearings that the Indians had made, and the marshes alongshore, the Yarmouth pioneers were confronted by an unbroken expanse of woods; their first labor, therefore, was with the axe. As soon as their houses were built, there arose, as there had arisen at Sandwich, the troublesome question of dividing the land. Thacher, Crow, and Howes had received somewhat embarrassing instructions in this regard from the Plymouth Court; they had been told to divide the land on the 'to-him-that-hath' principle, which was easy enough, but they were also to take into consideration each man's 'quality.' Here was a problem to daunt the most dogmatic. A committee was formed, however, and the land was divided; but nobody was satisfied. Captain Miles Standish was added to the committee, and another division was made; the citizens were no better content than before. In desperation the Court ordered the fiery Captain to act alone and gave him autocratic power. Thus armed, he proceeded to cut the Gordian knot. Half of the landholders were ejected, the claims of the others went unheeded, and Standish began again, making a complete redistribution of all the real estate. Still nobody was happy, naturally enough, but their grumbling could not pierce the armor of the Captain's plenipotentiary powers, and the landholders settled down resentfully on their new estates, while Standish made his way back to Plymouth.

It was natural enough that the troubles over land should have been greater in Yarmouth than they had been at Sandwich, for the men who settled Yarmouth were not in any department of life a unit. They had come from various parts of the Bay Colony, and for various reasons. Thacher was the only one who, after the departure of Hopkins, could be called a Pilgrim. The rest were of miscellaneous doctrines and belonged to different walks of life. A few were restless spirits from Sandwich. The one bond that could hold them together was their common interest in their new town, a bond which, as has been seen, had to be forged on the anvil of fiery misunderstanding; and Miles Standish was no gentle blacksmith.

In spite of an early restriction forbidding any man to own two house lots unless they were both occupied; in spite, too, of the alliterative dictum that the first settlements were compact in order to bring the inhabitants near the 'mill, the market, and the meeting,' it is certain that the town straggled over a large area. Richard Sears, and some friends who came about 1640, lived several miles from the rest of the settlers, and some, adventurous spirits built their houses on the shore of Bass Pond, some distance off in the woods. This wide geographical distribution reflects in a striking, though perhaps accidental, fashion the divergence of interests and opinions that long kept the Yarmouth men disunited.

Their lack of unanimity was made the more conspicuous by the harmony that reigned throughout the first years of the history of Barnstable. This town, like Yarmouth, had a forerunner who arrived before the main body of settlers and played an almost lone hand against the wilderness. The Barnstable pioneer was the Reverend Joseph Hull, with whom was associated Thomas Dimock. Hull came from England in 1635 and took up his ministry in Weymouth, where he eked out his salary by trading in cattle. Whether it was his activity in this field of endeavor or his doctrine that offended the Weymouth church does not appear; very likely both. At all events, they decided that he was 'contentious' and dismissed him. Nowhere in Massachusetts are there more extensive salt marshes than at Barnstable; these 'hay grounds,' as they were called, acted as a magnet to the cattle-raising pastor, and to Barnstable Hull came with a small number of followers. The precise date of his arrival is not known, but he was well established there in the fall of 1639. The lease which the Plymouth Colony gave him and Dimock was dated June 4, 1639 (old style), and in the following December his settlement was incorporated as a town. But he probably did not wait to receive this grant before occupying; he occupied first and got permission afterwards.

Hull was happy in his new location, and divided his time between his cattle and the souls of his diminutive congregation, some of whom were Indians. Then there arrived, on October 11, 1639, the Reverend John Lothrop and a large part of his church from Scituate. Mr. Hull welcomed them with enthusiasm and invited the whole band to dinner — some at Mr. Mayo's, some at Mr. Lombard's, and some at his own house. The newcomers far outnumbered Hull's little band, and were united in their affection and loyalty to Lothrop. Inevitably they took charge, and little by little Hull found himself a nonentity. It was nobody's fault. There was no room for two preachers — even if the Court had allowed it — and Hull's congregation — ever eager, like the Athenians, for some new thing — began to listen to Lothrop's sermons. Hull stood this neglect for a year or so and then moved to Yarmouth, where he began preaching to a few loyal friends from Barnstable and a group of malcontents from the Yarmouth church. For this act the Barnstable church excommunicated him, and the civil authorities supported the church by issuing a warrant for his arrest. He moved to Dover and later to the Isles of Shoals, where he died.

Meanwhile, Barnstable was flourishing under the wise and competent leadership of Mr. Lothrop. The remarkable thing about Lothrop — and the highest tribute to his character as a pastor — is the way in which his church followed him from point to point throughout his wanderings. Many of his original London congregation had sat under him in Scituate, and with him left Scituate for Barnstable. History can show few more perfect examples of the Shepherd and his flock. It is not without reason that the present Congregational Church in West Barnstable, which is the same organization that Lothrop brought down with him three hundred years ago, assert that their church has the longest uninterrupted history of any church of that denomination in the world. This statement would be true were it not that Henry Jacob's church in London, the first Congregational church ever founded, continued for a few years after Lothrop's departure from it.

The propriety of naming the new town after the English Barnstaple is obvious to any one who has seen the shore fronts of the two places at low tide — miles of sand flats in a long narrow harbor, crooked channels twisting their way seaward, and low, easy shore lines on both sides. Such is the aspect of both harbors, and so forcibly did their new surroundings remind the settlers of the old English town that they named it Barnstable forthwith.

Eastham, the last of the original four Cape towns to be founded, has one point in its early history in common with Barnstable; it was settled by a solidly united group of church members. They came from Plymouth, and thus was Eastham endowed at birth with a richer strain of Pilgrim blood than Sandwich, Yarmouth, or Barnstable. By 1640, Plymouth had begun to suffer from the loss of a handful of her citizens here and a handful there, as they had emigrated to one or another of the many new settlements that were everywhere springing up with bewildering speed. Business in the old town was not what it had been; men began to grumble, and for want of a better grievance, declared that the trouble was the poor soil; besides, they said, they were cramped for acreage. The truth was that they, like the rest of the early New-Englanders, were still goaded by the gadfly that later sent the prairie schooners heading westward toward the Rockies. But the soil was a good enough pretext, and satisfied everybody. It had been used to justify almost every emigration in Massachusetts so far. The Plymouth men, however, were more radical and more ambitious than their predecessors. They decided to move in a body — to transplant the entire population — and leave Plymouth, as the Indians had left it before them, a prey to the winds and the wolves. The question was, Where should they go?

It so happened that Bradford, in making over to the Colony the patent he had received in 1630 from the Earl of Warwick, had reserved for the use of the Purchasers and the Old Comers three tracts of land, one of which was Nauset. This region had for twenty years been to the Pilgrims what the Promised Land was to Moses — a land flowing with milk and honey. The Nauset soil purported to be the best in the Colony. These two considerations, therefore — the fact that it was peculiarly their own land, and that it was very fertile — induced the authorities to send a small party down the Cape to look the property over and report.

They returned with the discouraging verdict that there was room at Nauset for only about one half the population of Plymouth. The Governor and town fathers heard this statement and hoped that the matter was closed; they could not contemplate without a shudder the prospect of losing half the already depleted population of their town. A good many of the older citizens agreed with them; but there was no stopping the younger element. As Bradford ruefully put it, 'neither could the rest hinder them, they having made some beginning,' and in April, 1644, Plymouth saw, with a heavy heart, the more vigorous half of her population depart for Nauset. They had made suitable arrangements with the Purchasers and Old Comers, and their hopes were high as they began their fifty-mile journey; but they left something very like despair behind them. As Bradford puts it, 'Thus was this poore church left, like an ancient mother, growne olde and forsaken of her children. . . . Thus she that had made many rich became her selfe poore.'

The pioneers from Plymouth arrived at Nauset in time to plant corn and beans, and had the spring before them to build their houses. The soil came up to their expectations, and they were happy in their new location. But freedom from the immediate vigilance and restraint of the Old Colony seems to have gone to their heads, for they hacked down the forests in such a wanton fashion that the generations which followed found the soil blown bare. The 'blackish and deep mould' which Bradford had seen there twenty years before had become dry and sandy waste, blown this way and that with no forests to break the force of the wind. Almost literally, when the Nauset forests were demolished, the surface of the soil was blown away, and the loose sand which lay below it was laid bare, an easy prey to every gale.

However, for some years the crops were good and the town prospered. The land had been 'legally' bought from the Indians, as it had been in the earlier Cape towns, but it is hard to take such transactions seriously or to see anything but the mere letter of the truth in the proud boast of Governor Winslow, who proclaimed that 'The English do not possess one foot of land in the Colony but was fairly obtained by honest purchase from the Indian proprietors.' The traders who give Congo

natives glass beads for ivory have never been lauded for their
ethics, yet their practices differ in no way from the dealings of
our ancestors who gave a hatchet for a square mile of land.

At Nauset the settlers showed themselves even more avari-
cious than usual, and the Indians more than usually compliant;
for when they were asked who owned Billingsgate, they replied
that it belonged to nobody. 'In that case,' said the settlers, 'it
is ours'; and the Indians believed them. Perhaps the men from
Plymouth quieted their consciences with the reflection that they
had paid George and Mattaquason, the sachems of Nauset and
Monomoyick respectively, something (they prudently refrain
from saying how much) for most of the territory that is now
Eastham and Orleans.

When the settlement was two years old, and the watchful eye
of the Old Colony officials saw that it prospered, they consented
to its being incorporated. Five years later, in 1651, its name was
changed from Nauset to Eastham, though the old name is still
used for the beach, the lighthouse, and the life-saving station.

On these four solid pillars — Sandwich, Yarmouth, Barnstable, and Nauset — rested the early civilization of the Cape.
From these sprang all the other towns, sometimes by gradual
segregation, sometimes by a deliberate exodus, until, like Plymouth, they had made themselves weak to make the Cape
strong. And by a curious chance, which the devout Plymouth
fathers would have called divine retribution, Eastham, whose
inhabitants had so weakened Plymouth by their departure, was
the town that herself suffered worst from such losses.

What manner of men were these who started civilization on
the Cape? They were, first of all, men to whom Democracy, as
a theory of government or as a way of life, was unheard of. No
royal parent ever scanned the eligibility of the suitors for the
hand of his daughter with greater care than the Plymouth
Government scanned the applicants for admission to its towns.
Before any man might own land or build a house in these new
settlements, he must pass inspection by the General Court or its
local representatives. This law was no dead letter in the statute
book — it was vigorously and unceremoniously enforced. Every
town appointed a couple of substantial citizens to the unpleasant duty of ejecting undesirables. If a newcomer, whether

through ignorance, arrogance, or mere thoughtlessness, failed to consult these officials and began to build his house unsanctioned, he was promptly 'warned out of the town,' regardless of his desirability, and was obliged to leave his house unfinished until he should have complied with the law.[1] Such was the fate of Richard Child, of Yarmouth — a worthy character who subsequently was admitted and allowed 'to enjoy his cottage.' In 1639, the committee on personnel took exception to 'Old Worden (dead), Burnell, Wright, and Wat Deville.' Two early guardians of Barnstable's exclusiveness — William Crocker and Thomas Huckins — found themselves called upon to perform the same ruthless duty. If the town official proved too tolerant in judging applicants for admission, the watchful eye of Plymouth detected the weakness and promptly let the town know of its displeasure. In 1639, some recruits slipped by the local authorities in Sandwich and established themselves as landowners in the town. Instantly Sandwich was complained of for having admitted men who were 'unfit for church society.' The Colonial Court was entirely arbitrary in making decisions of this sort. Every man must have the 'leave and liking' of the Governor and his assistants, or out he went.

Such an apparently hostile attitude toward strangers took deep root in the Cape soil. In fact it never entirely disappeared. As late as 1810, the selectmen and town clerk of Brewster remonstrated against the appointment of Edward O'Brien as postmaster, 'he being a foreigner a catholik and, in the opinion of the town, an alien.' Even to-day the old suspicion lives, and appears in the instinctively critical way in which every newcomer is scanned by the townspeople. The fact that their ready censure is often justified does not make the phenomenon less interesting. It is a direct inheritance from the old days — a ghost of the former vigorous practice of 'warning out.'

There was nothing democratic, either, in the first assignments of land. The town of Yarmouth affords a good illustration of the aristocratic fashion in which this was done. Anthony Thacher and a number of associates were chosen as a committee to apportion lands there, but the Colonial Court stipulated that they should assign them in accordance with each man's 'estate

[1] See note 1 to Chapter IV.

and quality.' This close scrutiny of strangers and particularly the 'to-him-that-hath' principle for dividing land, were direct inheritances from Plymouth, where lands were apportioned according to each man's ability to contribute toward paying off the Colony's debt to the Merchant Adventurers who had financed the Mayflower's voyage.

There were other good reasons, too, for all the anxiety which the settlers showed in regard to the quality of the men they admitted as householders, for the communities were alarmingly small and surrounded by a wilderness where Indians skulked and wolves howled. Under such conditions it was imperative for the safety of all hands that the inhabitants of each town should stand together. Plymouth had already had in 1624 a bitter experience with newcomers in the persons of John Lyford and John Oldham, who, as soon as they had established themselves in the new settlement, set to work to undo the very thing the Pilgrims had come for; they tried to start a 'reformation in Church and Commonwealth.'

Titles on the Cape were bestowed even more charily than citizenship; and consequently they meant something. Not every Tom, Dick, or Harry was dignified with a 'Mr.' before his name. This was a distinction reserved for a very few — the minister and perhaps one or two more. 'Reverend' was seldom used in the early days of the settlements; John Lothrop was commonly called 'Mr.' Lothrop. 'Goodman' or 'Yeoman' was the extent of dignity usually ascribed to ordinary citizens. As for 'Squire,' it was a title that carried with it something not very far removed from the awe with which European vassals used to look up from their cluster of wretched huts at the castle that crowned the hilltop. There was never more than one squire in a town. Wealth was the usual foundation of his glory. Ability and unselfishness, though they were no obstacle to a man's achieving the honor, were not in themselves sufficient. Titles and rank followed men to church, where they were seated according to their quality. Planning the proper arrangement was a ticklish business, and the men whose duty it was to allot the pews gave long and earnest thought to the problem. The method varied somewhat between town and town. Harwich at one time adopted the prudent scheme of allowing the richest

man to have first choice of pews, the next richest the second
choice, and so on. Truro showed a little more democracy by
placing the town officers in the front row, the military veterans
next, and the highest taxpayers behind them. In the rear sat
the soldiery, the strategic position in case of an Indian raid.
Another method that was suggested at Truro was to allow every
man to build his own pew after whatever fashion and at whatever cost he saw fit. This was an entertaining scheme, though
the results may have been architecturally unconventional; however, it seems not to have been practiced widely or for very long.
Perhaps, indeed, it remained only a suggestion.

The women sat by themselves on one side of the meeting-
house, while across the center aisle were the men, perhaps forti-
fying themselves against the hour-long sermon by a glance or
two into forbidden territory. If the year was 1696 or later, and
the town was Eastham, the young bachelors may have thought
of the number of blackbirds they were required to kill annually
as long as they remained unmarried, for by such expedients did
the town authorities encourage an increase in population and
at the same time help to save their corn. A man's pew in church
was as much a part of his real estate as his barn or his woodlot,
and had a pretty definite cash value. Sometimes he sold it, in
which case regular papers were passed and the transaction was
encumbered with as much legal phraseology as if it had been a
farm.

An unpleasant sequel to the aristocratic principles of the
early Cape men was their ownership of slaves. This subject
may as well be disposed of now as later, for the settlers brought
a belief in slavery with them from Plymouth and the Bay
Colony as part of their social background. It is no great shock,
therefore, to find them cheerfully owning slaves in such numbers
as they could afford. Here again Plymouth, that stern disciplinarian and pattern for all things good and bad, led the way by
declaring as early as 1646 that it was her intention, as a last
resort, to sell Indians or exchange them for Negroes in punishment for offenses — real or fancied. The fact that the Governor
of the Massachusetts Bay Colony some ten years before had
sold captives taken in the Pequot War into slavery in Bermuda
is no excuse for Plymouth, any more than Plymouth's per-

formances are any excuse for the Cape. The old adage, 'the Plymouth saddle is always on the Bay horse,' seems to have worked both ways occasionally. At all events, from 1640 until well after the Revolution, slaves were common in all parts of the Old Colony, and if there were fewer on the Cape than elsewhere, it was only because there were fewer rich men or extensive landowners.

Not even white men were safe. In 1640, at the very beginning of the history of Barnstable, Henry Coggin rented his servant, James Glass, to a Plymouth man for five years. The price was fifty shillings and twenty bushels of corn. Obviously Glass was an indentured servant of some sort who had even less to say about his disposal than a professional ball-player has to-day. In 1678 three Indians, Canootus, Symon, and Joel, stole twenty-five pounds from Zachariah Allen, of Sandwich, and spent the money. The Court immediately decreed that they should be made perpetual slaves, and empowered Allen to sell them for as much as he could get. After King Philip's War, Jonathan Hatch, of Falmouth, bought an Indian family, father, mother, and son, from Captain Church. The parents were subsequently ransomed by their native friends for three pounds apiece, but their boy was to work for his freedom until he was twenty-four. In 1697, Mr. Cotton, the Yarmouth minister, allowed the church to employ his Indian slave, Saxuant, as janitor, and pocketed the proceeds, one pound a year, for himself. At the same time that Mr. Cotton was profiting by Saxuant's labors in Yarmouth, the Hinckleys of Barnstable were dying and leaving slaves and tableware in their wills, as items of the same list. Joseph Hinckley, who lived at Great Marshes and died there in 1753, bequeathed to a daughter his slave girl 'Sarah, bought of Hopkins, and his biggest silver porringer.' Ebenezer Hinckley, his brother, who lived in Barnstable, left to his wife all the property which she brought to him 'excepting her clock and negro woman.'

Wills are, in fact, the most fertile source of our information on this subject; few of them, however, contain such whimsical disposition of slaves as John Bacon's, of Barnstable, who looked far into the future in his desire to control other people's destinies. The will was registered in 1731, and contains among other chattels the following bequest to Bacon's wife: '... she shall have the whole use of the negro Dinah and Calash during her life and after her desease, if said Dinah be living she shall be sold by my executors and all that she is sold for shall be improved by my executors in buying Bibles and they shall give them equally alike unto each of my said wives and grandchildren.' John Gorham, who died at Barnstable in 1769, lists along with sundry 'indoor moveables and provisions,' his Negro girl Peg and half the use of the man 'Cezer.'

Truro was never a very wealthy community, yet the town records for February 8, 1753, refer to a bill of sale for 'Old Moll,' a Negro woman about whom 'there has been so much controversy.' A few years earlier, a distinguished citizen of Truro, Jonathan Paine, sold his Negro Hector to Benjamin Collins for thirty pounds. Hector, we are told, lived to be an old man and became something of a local celebrity — his name being given to such places as Hector's Nook and Hector's Stubble, spots which were once well known to Truro men. Paine had a less happy experience with another slave, a Negro named Pomp, who was kidnaped from the Congo by the crew of a Truro whaler and sold to Paine at the end of the voyage. The poor fellow never became reconciled to his new way of life. The bleak shores of Truro supported no vast plantations where a hundred darkies worked by day and found solace in singing wild melodies together at twilight. Pomp suffered silently until loneliness conquered, and he hanged himself to the limb of a tree.

This tragedy undoubtedly hastened the abolition of slavery on the Cape. Faint streaks of light had already begun to appear in the east. As far back as 1719, Chief Justice Samuel Sewall, of Boston, had written an eloquent letter on the subject to Judge Addington Davenport, who had asked his advice in regard to a difficult case which he with some other judges was about to hear in Sandwich. A certain Samuel Smith of the town had killed his slave and was held for trial, and Davenport, before rendering a verdict, consulted the Chief Justice. A few lines of Sewell's letter will suffice to indicate the tenor of the whole: '... the poorest Boys and Girls in this Province, such as are of the lowest condition; whether they be Indians or English or Ethiopians: they have the same Right to Religion and Life, that the Richest Heirs have. And they who go about to deprive them of this Right, they attempt the bombarding of Heaven, and the shells they throw, will fall down on their own heads.'

The records that could have told how Smith fared in the trial are lost. In theory he was punishable by death; but it would have taken a courageous judge to render such a verdict in 1719. However, a beginning had been made, and little by little the sentiment against slavery on the Cape grew. James Otis, the West Barnstable patriot, struck a blow at slavery in his great Writs-of-Assistance Speech in 1761. In this oration he included the Negro along with white men in his vehement assertion that all persons should be free. That Otis was ahead of his time in this respect, as in all others, is shown by John Adams's comment. Adams heard the speech and 'shuddered at the doctrine he taught ...'

A dozen years later, the town of Sandwich continued the good work by voting to instruct its representative to work for an act which should prohibit the importation of slaves to the Colony and should free at the age of twenty-one the children of those who were already slaves. To be sure, the act was not passed, but it shows the growing tendency toward abolition. Sandwich, indeed, has a better record in regard to the treatment of slaves than many of the New England towns. The Reverend Abraham Williams offered his slave, Titus Winchester, his freedom, but Titus was so devoted to his master that he refused to leave him. Not until Williams's death in 1784 did his slave depart to become a sailor. When he died, he left money for a clock in the tower of the First Parish Church of Sandwich. In Falmouth at about the same time, another slave named Titus was virtually free, though nominally the property of the Reverend Samuel Palmer. This clergyman was an enthusiastic though inexperienced farmer, and showed his wisdom by meekly obeying Titus in all agricultural activities, just as indoors Titus accepted the spiritual guidance of his master. Thus the two lived on a coöperative basis that bore little resemblance to slavery in its accepted sense.

But the evil continued in Massachusetts until well after the Revolution, and not until March, 1788, was the selling of slaves in the American market prohibited in Boston. In fact, no records of the buying or selling of slaves on the Cape are found after the Revolutionary War, but this is undoubtedly owing to the impoverished condition of all the towns rather than to any sudden access of humanitarianism on the part of the citizens. Nothing is more dangerous, however, than ascribing single motives to the actions of human beings. It is entirely possible that, with the enjoyment of their own hard-won liberty, the Cape men saw the indignity of bondage more clearly than ever before, and were therefore less inclined to enslave others. The last faint echo of this once common practice died away on the Cape about 1840 with the vanishing of a few elderly Negroes who were still vaguely referred to as 'old slaves.'

Our country has always been given to extremes, even before it became a separate nation; but only once in their history have our ancestors tried to embrace simultaneously two ends of social organization so far removed from each other as Slavery and Communism. The one period when they did try it came during the early days of Plymouth, and Plymouth's experiment was of course forced upon the Cape. By the time it reached there, it had taken on a greatly modified form, to be sure. Slavery had won, and Communism had pretty much vanished. Yet there remained enough of it in certain departments of life to cause an apparent incongruity. But this, like most of the incongruities in human nature, contained a certain strange reasonableness, and appears, on examination, to be not entirely incongruous, after all. The origin of this communism, at any rate, was sensible, and since it began in Plymouth, it must be examined there first, before the remnants of it on the Cape are discussed.

Up to April, 1623, no man in Plymouth had owned any land privately — it had all been held and harvested in common, and the produce justly divided. But in the spring of this year there was an alarming shortage of food. The settlers argued that if they were given land of their own, and each man was allowed to keep all that he raised, the crop would be greater than it was under the existing arrangement. This was not the first time that such suggestions had been made. They had been already so numerous that in 1621 Robert Cushman preached an eloquent if unconvincing sermon in reply. Bradford, though he heard with concern the citizens' complaints, could not help being impressed with the force of their arguments. Like Winslow, he had begun to realize that even in this chosen band of pioneers egotism endured. To put it in another way, the Plymouth men, though they were zealots and idealists, had not ceased to be human beings; the Governor's dream of a Utopia was shattered by 'that self-love wherewith every man in a measure more or less, loveth and preferreth his own good before his neighbors.' He yielded to the importunity of the citizens, and in April, 1623, assigned to each man his parcel of land for one year to be planted and reaped for the owner's own private benefit.

The result was a revelation and a delight to Bradford. At the end of the year a far larger supply of corn was stored in the houses than any of them had dared to hope. In view of this success, each man was given an acre for his own.

Such in brief was Plymouth's experience with Communism, and such was the inheritance that the Cape settlers took with them to their new towns. Thus it happened that a communistic tendency appeared there, but it manifested itself only in the form of common lands. This does not mean that private ownership was tabu, but that in addition to every man's personal allotment of land, there was in every town a large area reserved for the benefit of all. Usually this tract included both marsh and woodland, so that the citizens might cut salt hay for their cattle and chop wood for the winter hearth. Such an arrangement was natural enough. It would have been silly for a dozen or twenty men to have had exclusive titles to the miles of hay grounds in Barnstable, or to the hundreds of acres of standing timber. Sometimes, too, there were particular reasons for declaring certain pieces of land to be common property. At Yarmouth the best place to watch for whales was a strip of upland along the north shore of the town close to what is now the Dennis line. This land was therefore quite properly thrown open to the free use of all citizens, and was called the 'Whaling Grounds.' When the rest of the common lands in Yarmouth were divided, this area was kept as public property, and has remained so ever since. Shanties were built there for the use of those who were watching for whales, and men often lived in them for considerable periods of time.

A similar reservation was made in Barnstable on the outer beach of Sandy Neck. The whole Neck was common land until 1715; then it was divided among the heirs of the Proprietors, with reservation of four spots where any citizen of the town who was engaged in whaling might erect a try-house and have room enough for his blubber barrels, lumber, and other gear. A part of Sandy Neck is still called the 'Try Yard,' although no one knows exactly where it is. These four 'spots or pieces' have never been divided. Neither has a wide strip of the outer beach running the whole length of the Neck; this strip was reserved at the same time as the 'Try Yards' for the use of any citizen of the town who wished to put up fish houses there, and it may still be legally used by them for that purpose.

For two generations the plan of having common lands in each town worked well. Abuses occurred, but that was to be expected. Cattle were turned loose 'to range the Commons'; the minister's winter supply of wood was cut on the public woodlot and delivered to him in his own back yard; salt hay was boated ashore or stacked on staddles in the marshes. Chatham, about 1670, even had a whaleboat that was common property. But as the towns grew, complications began to arise. Experiments can succeed in small communities where the citizens' interests are largely the same; but they are doomed as soon as the settlements grow large enough to include many trades and professions. A cattleman finds common pasture land very convenient; a miller has small use for it; a lawyer, none at all.

And so it happened that, beginning about 1700, dissatisfaction with the arrangement began to be heard. Nobody had any objection to the division, but the question was, exactly who owned the common land and was therefore entitled to make allotments. In theory it belonged to the Proprietors. The Proprietors were originally the men to whom the Plymouth Government had granted the land in each town to make settlements on; but by 1700 these dignitaries had two generations of descendants; many newcomers, besides, had been admitted to full citizenship and consequently to rights in the commons. The citizens of Barnstable held a town meeting in 1701 on purpose to solve some of these conundrums. 'Does the bare admission of a man to the state of *townsman* give him a share in the Commons?' they asked. 'Has all the Common Land been already divided?' 'Do rights granted in the Commons extend to the grantees' heirs?' The men who attended this famous meeting would have grown old in debate (since they could not send to heaven for Miles Standish) had they not wisely chosen a committee of fifteen to work out answers to these questions. The committee girded up their loins and went valiantly to work, with the result that after another town meeting in 1702, in which it was decided to divide the commons, a new committee was chosen and the grand division was made in 1703 on as fair a basis as could be devised. In this way town after town unsnarled the tangle into which the public ownership of land had involved it and started afresh, each man the richer for the division. In 1713, after three years of hard work deciding who were the proper persons, Yarmouth handed over to the heirs of the Proprietors and other qualified persons most of its common lands except the whaling grounds. The Proprietors of Truro, indignant at the wanton way some men cut more wood than they could use and left it to rot on the commons, put an end to the practice in 1715 by ordering further division of common land. Eastham began to divide its common upland the same year.

So vanished the last substantial traces of the Pilgrims' valiant experiment with Communism.[1] The name 'Common Fields' is still used for a good-sized tract of land bordering Barnstable Harbor, though it has been in private hands for generations, and a few barren regions that the towns have forgotten remain still undivided — a strip of sand hills somewhere in Barnstable and the still unclaimed whaling grounds between Yarmouth and Dennis. In truth we are a young country!

[1] See note 2 to Chapter IV.

CHAPTER V

HOW THEY LIVED IN THE EARLY SETTLEMENTS

THE first generation or two of settlers on the Cape were no
freer to choose their occupation than they were to choose their
religion. They had to be farmers or starve, even if they came
from London and had never drawn a furrow. It must have been
hard for some of them — men who like Robert Linnel came to
Barnstable with Lothrop without ever having cut down a tree
or hauled a stump. But there were compensations; the land
was their own; and there is deep satisfaction in toiling over
one's own acres. Furthermore, when once cleared, it yielded
a respectable crop; there was no need of cultivating big tracts
either, for hay grew wild on the marshes, and a small cornfield
and a patch of onions sufficed for a good-sized family. Every
man had some cattle and sheep, which were immensely profitable and required no pasturage, for they were turned loose to
roam at will, branded as Western cattle are to-day. Some of
these brands showed originality, but no one had a saltier device than Jonathan Weekes, Jr., of Falmouth, who marked his
'creatures' with a mackerel-tail in the top of each ear. Pigs also
were allowed to root about at large, provided their noses were
ringed to prevent their doing damage.

The large numbers of cattle brought tanners and cobblers at
a very early date, but even these specialists laid aside the tools
of their trade in spring and followed the plough until October.
In this way every family was self-supporting. There were at
first no local markets for food or clothing. The men sheared
their sheep, and the women spun the wool and fashioned it into
garments which made up in durability what they lacked in
grace. Our ancestors sometimes eked out their wardrobes with
deerskin coats, after the Indian fashion. Good food was abundant. If a man grew tired of corn and beans and onions, he had
only to dig a 'dreener' of clams or pick up a bushel of lobsters.
Herring were so plentiful that they were spread on the ploughed
land for manure — another practice which the settlers learned

from the natives. Every now and then they killed a pig. There was little time for hunting, but who can doubt that many a haunch of venison found its way to a hook in the back shed, where it hung frozen until its duty was done? It would be strange, too if the old flintlock in the corner was not sometimes put to a livelier use than waiting for the Indian raid that never came, and brought down a backload of ducks or geese in the course of a windy afternoon. Add to this gamey diet an abundance of home-grown beef and mutton, and it will appear that there was no need for the first Cape-Codders to be vegetarians.

Corn was their principal crop. Corn was, indeed, the very backbone of their existence. It was not only food, but money, and remained for years the standard measure of value. No one had any money to speak of — it has been stated that in 1675 there was not five hundred pounds in the whole Plymouth Colony — but every one had corn, which passed current in any sort of transaction, from buying a farm to paying the minister. But the settlers were experimentalists, and tried other crops, too, with varying success. They planted wheat, which did tolerably well for a time, but about 1670 it was attacked by a sort of mildew, and since then has never been raised in any quantity on the Cape. Rye proved to be a better investment, and there has always been more or less of it for local consumption. From the very first, the Cape men set out orchards from seeds imported from the old country; but it took generations of cultivation to make the apples good for much. Pears were as poor as apples until years of toil brought them up from hard and gnarled excrescences to their present mellow excellence. Some cherry trees were planted as well, but though they were hardy, the fruit would pucker any but the most robust palate.

As the years passed, the Cape farmers grew more prosperous and more ambitious. Each season they converted a few more acres of woodland into arable fields, and thus they began to produce more corn than they needed. The days of struggling for existence — incomparably less severe on the Cape than they had been at Plymouth — were over. The settlements had gained momentum, and steady industry took the place of heart-breaking toil. By 1700, half the citizens had farms of thirty acres or more, a pair of oxen for ploughing, a horse or two for occasional

visits to a neighboring town, besides an appropriate number of
cattle and sheep. While the sons of the family were growing, a
slave or two helped the farmer with the heaviest work. The
families were large. One reason that has been suggested for
this phenomenon is that, according to the old idea, every son
was worth a hundred pounds to the family and every daughter
fifty pounds! This explanation need not be taken with undue
solemnity.

It was one thing to raise corn, however, and another to grind
it. Except for what little was pounded up at home in hand mortars, all the corn had to be ground at a mill, and there were no
mills nearer than Plymouth. Even Sandwich had a long haul
overland to reach the Old Colony headquarters, for boats were
as scarce as mills. The plight of the towns farther down the
Cape can be imagined. Half the pleasure of a good crop was
spoiled by the difficulty of getting it ground. The remedy was
obvious — to construct local mills; but the art of the millwright was second only to that of the shipbuilder in difficulty,
and few had mastered it. But the need of mills was so urgent
that the inhabitants spared no pains to find the men who could
build them. The easiest type to construct was that operated by
water-power, and, although there is some truth in the statement that the scarcity of water-power on the Cape forced the
settlers to build windmills, which were far more intricate and
expensive, yet it must not be supposed that no running water
was to be found on the crooked peninsula. Falmouth, Bourne,
Sandwich, Barnstable, Yarmouth, Brewster, Eastham, and
Truro all had streams which were set to work soon after the
towns were settled, and some of these water-mills were still
grinding away within the memory of men now living. So, even
without the aid of wind, the Cape was not powerless to grind
its own corn and full its own homespun.

Useful as these water-mills were, they were not the type that
attracted the eye of early Cape travelers or inspired the pencil
of such graceful artists as Miss Amelia Watson. For pictur-
esqueness, the long-armed old windmills stand alone; but the
difficulty of finding men who could build them was so great that
capitalists who wanted a mill found it easier to scour the Cape
for an old one, and move it to the desired location, than to hunt

up a millwright who could start work on a new one in less than
six months or a year. Half the windmills on the Cape ended
their days on new sites.

The most celebrated millwright was Thomas Paine, of Eastham. This overworked craftsman was kept traveling from one
town to another all the way from Barnstable to Truro. First,
in 1683–84, with proper loyalty, he put up two windmills for his
fellow citizens in Eastham. Then he was called to Barnstable,
where in 1687 he erected the first windmill that town had ever
seen. Not to be outdone, Yarmouth ordered one from him
immediately afterwards, and Paine complied. He returned to
Eastham and appears to have enjoyed a well-earned breather,
until the citizens of Truro assured him that they, too, must have
a windmill, and held out flattering inducements if he would
build it for them. 'A man must go where his trade calls,'
thought Paine; and he liked Truro so well that he never left it;
subsequently he became one of her leading citizens. The first
mill in Truro was not built so easily as the last one, however,
which appeared about 1800, long after Paine was in his grave.
Every stick of lumber used in it came ashore from wrecks, most
of it landing as a single windfall when a lumber schooner piled
up on the outer beach; it would not have been surprising if the
corn ground at this mill had had a salty flavor — the more so
as Freeman Atkins, the miller, was a retired shipmaster.

Another family of millwrights won such distinction that they
were celebrated in verse; they were Thomas Baxter and his two
sons, of West Yarmouth, who put up two windmills near Parker's River. Their success was crowned by the following ballad:

> 'The Baxter boys they built a mill;
> Sometimes it went; sometimes stood still;
> And when it went, it made no noise
> Because it was built by the Baxter boys.'

Close behind the builder in prestige, came the miller. His
task was no sinecure, and was so essential to the prosperity of
the towns that great inducements were held out to any man
who would undertake it. Just as the mill itself went untaxed,
so was the miller exempt from military duty, and he was a
privileged character in other ways besides; he need not hold

office, his social position was assured, and he was often given a good-sized piece of land adjacent to the mill. His pay was in kind; from every bushel of corn he ground he was authorized to take a stated quantity, known as the miller's 'pottle'; and it was well earned. At the beginning of each day he had to mount to the top of the mill and scale the long arms to set the sails, which were rigged in nautical fashion with halliards; at night he must climb out again and furl them. If it blew hard, he had to shorten sail by twisting up the lower part of each sail. In a gale the mill scudded under bare poles, the surface of the slats across the arm offering sufficient resistance to the wind. Unlike the master of a ship, however, the miller had no crew of nimble acrobats to carry out his orders aloft. He was his own crew, and was perpetually short-handed. The clumsy rigging and primitive mechanism of his command made the work not only hard but dangerous. But for the fact that many of the millers were retired seamen who had learned agility at the mastheads of fishing schooners, casualties would have been more frequent than they were. If Henry Hall, for example, who at the age of seventy operated a mill in Dennis, had not been a sailor in his early days, he never could have extricated himself from the very ticklish position in which he once found himself. He had stopped his mill to shorten sail, but had neglected to make the arms fast with the huge iron chain which was used for that purpose. When he was halfway out on one of the arms, a free flaw caught the sails, and the arms began to turn. With amazing activity Hall worked his way back along the revolving arm until he reached the shaft, which, of course, was also revolving. Here he perched, three stories above the ground, straddling the shaft and maintaining an upright position by hitching himself clear of his seat as it turned under him. Luckily assistance arrived before the old mariner was exhausted.

Blow high, blow low, millers must turn out each man's corn with as little delay as possible, for the farmers were impatient and, if the truth is to be told, not a little envious of this privileged specialist. Their envy took the form that envy usually takes — criticism. Sometimes they declared that their corn was only half ground; sometimes they accused the miller of stretching his pottle and taking more than the law allowed.

There was right and wrong on both sides, of course. Human nature, alas! is not always proof against temptation, nor were millers more righteous than other men. One at least, Philip Dexter of Falmouth, was thought to be a pottle-stretcher, and the townspeople put up a rival mill. But envy is a commoner sin than avarice, and the citizens were probably jealous oftener than millers were dishonest.

Of the scores of windmills that once spread their sails to the Cape breezes, only a few are standing to-day — sole survivors of a high art and a dead industry. A few channeled millstones are in use as doorsteps; a few more may be seen lying abandoned and half buried beside creeks alongshore. 'Nothing beside remains.'

The early Cape houses varied greatly, according to men's means, and became more elaborate from generation to generation as building improved. The first hasty structures that some of the pioneers erected were never intended to be more than makeshifts to provide temporary shelter until the owner had a chance to draw his breath and contemplate something better. These early buildings, sometimes called 'booths,' were not frame houses at all; the walls consisted of two parallel rows of saplings stuck in the ground, and the space between was filled with clay and stones. Slanting poles covered with the longest marsh-grass formed the roof, and the fireplace, which often backed into the side of a hill for convenience and support, was crowned by a chimney built cob-house fashion of green sticks smeared with clay inside. Oiled paper covered the windows. There was no floor — unless dry thatch spread on the ground can be called a floor. The only virtue of such structures was that they could be thrown together in a very short time and without any expense; but one winter in such quarters was usually enough to persuade the owner that he must have a real house.

Not all the original settlers lived in such flimsy contrivances, of course. Some of them had frame houses from the first. Mr. Hull, for example, was living in one when John Lothrop and his flock arrived in Barnstable, and some of Hull's parishioners had followed his example. These dwellings, though anything but elaborate, were durable and snug. They were nearly square, one story high, with walls and floors made of planks sawed by hand and a thatched roof sharply pitched. The cracks between the boards were daubed with clay.

The 'great room' was usually in the southeast corner. Its bare wooden floor was sanded and thereby scrubbed smooth. One side of the room was chiefly occupied by a stone fireplace eight feet wide and high enough for the goodwife to walk into easily and reach the door of the brick oven, which opened out of one corner of the back. Across the whole breadth of the fireplace ran an iron bar festooned with trammels for the pots. The swinging crane is a comparatively modern contrivance. The whole structure was wide enough to allow for the traditional seats in the chimney corner, favorite places for the youngsters, who perched there happily on dye-tubs or empty beer-kegs until bed time. At one end of the room stood the big dining-table with stools for the children and chairs for the man of the house and his wife. Near it was placed the corner cupboard, a tall semicircular piece of furniture containing shelves for pewter or glassware. A big wooden chest against one wall held the family valuables — the deed for the farm, what money the man happened to have on hand, and in summer some of the extra bed 'furnishings.' If the children were not all grown up, there would certainly be a cradle in the room, and near it a loom where the wife could weave woolen cloth and keep an eye on the baby at the same time. A few chairs, either home-made or else the product of a local artisan, a couple of candles in iron candlesticks on the great mantelpiece, an hourglass, and a brass warming pan hanging beside the chimney completed the furniture of this room. No paint or paper adorned its walls (plaster was rarely used except by the rich until after 1700), but it was homelike and comfortable, and for several generations the Cape farmer of moderate means wisely regarded it as sufficient for his needs. The cost of building such a house complete, 'latched, thatched and daubed,' was twenty-five dollars. The inhabitants of the temporary 'booths' were therefore very soon able to build one and live in comfort.

Snug as they were, these one-story cottages were beneath the dignity of the wealthy, who wanted something more elaborate and were willing to pay as high as one hundred dollars for their ambition. In the seventeenth century this sum would produce a big two-story house, like that which Nathaniel Bacon built in Barnstable in 1642. Bacon was a prosperous tanner and could afford to live in style. His house was set on enormous hand-hewn oak sills which projected into the rooms and made convenient ledges for the children to sit on. When, after more than two hundred years, this structure was torn down, the timbers were still as hard as iron. Some of the walls may have been plastered. There was a spacious though low-studded bedroom on the second floor, with a couple of smaller ones at the rear and plenty of space for the servants in the garret.

The houses that have been mentioned — either as types or individual specimens — were built during the fifty years or so after the settlers arrived. The biggest and most elaborate of them were very plain, and from the modern point of view unfinished in many ways. The turn of the century, however, saw the beginning of the era of fine houses, with more rooms, a wider variety of types, and some handsome interiors. Skilled artisans began to take pride in their creations and produced houses whose pleasing proportions and easy lines made them look like natural objects in the gently rolling landscape. They presented no high, flat surfaces to challenge the northeasters; the rule was 'a short hoist and a long peak' for one-story houses, and a broad enough foundation for two-story structures to make them look lower than they were. The story-and-a-half style, called 'salt-boxes,' was always popular, too, rising to two floors in front with a short slope to the ridgepole and a long, easy slant down almost to the ground on the other side. A fine specimen of this type is the Isaac Dillingham house in Brewster. Gambrel roofs made their appearance, like that of Captain James Baxter's house in Barnstable, the most beautiful model yet devised for applying the virtues of a short hoist to a two-story house. With it came the well-known hip-roofed type, another scheme for relieving the boxlike appearance of the second story by slicing down both ends of the roof on a slant from a short ridgepole.

Inside, these eighteenth-century houses were finished with plaster and paneling, the latter sometimes covering the walls from floor to ceiling, as in the old Hinckley house in Barnstable.

CAPTAIN JAMES BAXTER'S HOUSE, BARNSTABLE
Burned about 1898

SEARS HOUSE, DENNIS
Built about 1750

Thus the Cape builders advanced, adhering in the main to a few approved types, but ready at any moment to experiment with some new design, until, at the beginning of the Revolution, Squire Edward Bacon wrote from Barnstable that he had a mansion with twenty rooms, a striking contrast, indeed, to the humble booths of 1639.

In addition to their dwelling-houses, our ancestors built two kinds of fortified structures to defend themselves from attacks by Indians. A blockhouse of the traditional type, built of hewn timbers placed one on the other, was put up in Yarmouth very soon after the town was settled. The upper story of this fort projected over the lower, and the whole was pierced with narrow loopholes. At Great Marshes — then a part of Barnstable — two stone forts were built; the first one disappeared very early, but the second was not taken down until after the War of 1812. Its lower walls were of rough stone, but the upper story, which was built with a three-foot overhang like that in Yarmouth, was of wood. Another method of defense was for a man to build the lower walls of his house out of broken stone and mortar. This type of construction was very much like that of the primitive booths. Two rows of holes were bored in the sills, with saplings stuck into them to serve as studding. The plate-beams were similarly bored to admit the upper end of these poles, and the space between the two rows was filled with stone and mortar — a rudimentary sort of concrete, with saplings taking the place of modern board 'forms.' Houses built in this fashion were almost indestructible. John Crow's house in Yarmouth, built about 1650, was of this type and stood for two hundred years, its stone and mortar walls being concealed by clapboards that had been nailed on by a subsequent owner. Some men surrounded their houses with palisades of sharpened poles; but it was soon obvious that the last thing the Indians wanted was a fight; the blockhouses were therefore converted into dwellings, and no more palisades were put up.

It would be a temptation to pursue the history of architecture on the Cape further, were the prospect not spoiled by the looming horrors of the Victorian epoch and the serviceable but unsightly bungalows of the Finns. High courage alone can confront undaunted these dreary examples of modern taste; it is pleasanter to take comfort from reflecting that our ancestors built, not for decades, but for centuries, and that their houses may yet be sound when the amorphous outrages of their descendants are dust.

The simplicity of life in the early days appears in the importance which the settlers attached to trifles. Robert Eldridge, of Chatham, was a prosperous farmer who died in 1682 possessed of an estate valued at three hundred and sixteen pounds. Yet the inventory of his possessions mentions such items as a pair of pot hooks, an hourglass, a gridiron, and a toaster. About a half-century later, the inventory of Kenelm Winslow, of Harwich, contains among other things two wool shirts, mittens and garters, a 'line,' part of a land compass, two forks, and a brush and two combs. Yet Mr. Winslow was wealthy enough to be the owner of several slaves. Almost a hundred years after the settlement of Barnstable, one of its richest citizens, John Bacon, left his best hat and wig to his son Nathaniel, and bequeathed to his youngest son, Judah, the whole family orchard, but with the stipulation that the other children should have the *fruit of five trees each for seven years.* Andrew Hallett, of Yarmouth, died in 1684 the wealthiest man in town; but his executors particularize such trifles as a knife, a spit, 'and other small things.' In 1669, a stolen shirt caused the Sandwich authorities grave concern, and received the attention of two sittings of the Court. As for the value of a cow, one could not be bought in the first years of the settlements for less than the price of a good-sized farm.

Such painstaking particularity in keeping close track of all possessions — even the smallest — needs no comment. Our ancestors found it easier to buy a woodlot than an hourglass. Because all manufactured articles had to be imported from England, the value was disproportionately high. Food and land were cheap; tools and kitchenware were very dear, and were handed down from one generation to another with the same care that our own age takes in bequeathing diamonds.

Farmers after a day's work in the cornfield or onion patch are not ordinarily inclined to spend the evening in conviviality. They are more likely to be in bed by nine o'clock. Since most of the Cape men in the early days were farmers, it is natural that after an April day with the plough and an hour by the fireside after supper, when they perhaps received a call from a neighbor, broached a keg of home-made beer, and smoked a leisurely pipe, they were ready for bed. But in winter the evenings were longer, and work on the farm was a mere round of chores. The farmer puttered about, mending his tools and getting ready for spring. At night he was as fresh as a lark. However exemplary a husband and father he might be from seedtime to harvest, in winter his thoughts began to wander from his own fireside to the group gathered at the tavern. The Cape had its share of cotters, to be sure, who could spend as pious a Saturday night as the dourest Scotsman, but its shores produced some Tam O'Shanters as well, and the company and the liquor both beckoned from the tavern hearth. Home-brewed beer did very well as a steady diet, but there was a quality in the landlord's rum that could not be reproduced on the premises. Innkeepers must live, and away went the happy farmer.

It was quite right for him to do so. When a man went to the tavern for an evening, his horizon was broadened, at least enough to include other farms besides his own, and often so much that he gained a bird's-eye view of the policies of the entire Colony. For the group gathered in the taproom was very different from George Eliot's assemblages of ignorant yokels, presided over by a portly host as ignorant as they. Raveloe and Colonial Cape Cod had nothing in common but the King. The landlords of all the taverns from Sandwich to Eastham were leading citizens and had been carefully chosen by the selectmen of the town. They were intelligent and public-spirited. Well versed in the doings at Plymouth, they were able to steer town activities in a course consistent with the grim court there. A glance at a few of them will show their quality.

About 1700, Ebenezer Hawes was the proprietor of a tavern in Chatham. He was a man of intelligence and honor, a foe to bigotry, and a valuable citizen for any town. The esteem in which he was held by the townspeople was shown by their choosing him as selectman, an office which he filled with ability, and he was also captain of the military company. His taproom became the rendezvous for the best men of the village; many a bushel of corn and barrel of tar was bargained for over a friendly glass before his fire. His one enemy was Mr. Adams, the parson. This gentleman took exception to Hawes's public house, not because it was improperly run, but because it was a public house, and he took up arms against Hawes, not because the latter was an undesirable character, but because he sold rum. Parsons were formidable men, but when Mr. Adams attacked Hawes, he was opposing a man who was quite as formidable as he and just as strongly entrenched in respectability. The battle went through two Courts, with the tavern-keeper victorious both times. Not until the case was carried to Plymouth for a third hearing did the minister get the meager satisfaction of seeing Hawes fined ten shillings. Public sentiment, however, was too strong for Mr. Adams, and he was forced out of town. The contest between Adams and Hawes was a contest between mighty opposites — not a one-sided skirmish in which armed Virtue routed slinking Vice.

Nor was Chatham any more fortunate than other towns in its selection of a man to run the tavern. In 1663 and earlier, Thomas Huckins was bringing rum to Barnstable in his own packet, and selling it to the citizens from his own tap. And Huckins was seven times chosen selectman and was for eight years a deputy to the Colonial Court. If the conversation of such a man failed to lift his patrons out of petty policies and narrow-mindedness, the case was hopeless. An evening in his tavern was an evening of liberal education in affairs of state, and the townsmen who went there returned home better citizens than they had come.

Another dignitary was the captain of the militia company that every town was ordered to maintain. Although these companies were very small, the citizens would certainly have resented having to spend valuable time in drill had not the fear of Indian attacks hung over them like a cloud. This fear, as unnecessary as it was natural, kept the townsmen drilling vigorously. The trouble and expense of maintaining these military organizations was partly justified in 1675 by the outbreak of King Philip's War, to which every town was required to send its quota of men. No doubt the drill they had received was of some value to them at this time as discipline, though the tactics which they had been taught can scarcely have been adapted to fighting Indians. The great service of these companies, however, was in creating a sense of security in the minds of the population.

And now it is time to take a look at the government of the Cape towns. As has already been suggested, the new settlements could not roam far afield in any direction without being brought up short by a tether that reached to Plymouth; so in order to form an intelligent conception of their government, it is necessary to hark back to headquarters, from which all government was derived, and see how things were done there; for the Cape, though geographically quite distinct from Plymouth, was bound to that stern autocrat by ties of kinship, loyalty, and fear.

The highest authority in the Colony was the Governor, who was elected annually by the 'freemen' — those who were members of the orthodox church and whose estate was not less than twenty pounds. With him was elected one assistant; but it soon appeared that one was not enough, so in 1624 the number of assistants was increased to five, and in 1633 to seven. At this figure it remained until the Plymouth Colony merged with Massachusetts Bay in 1692. The Governor and his assistants comprised the General Court, or Legislature. The first function of the General Court was to make laws, and this function it performed without hesitation. As the Colony grew, the General Court grew with it by the addition of more assistants, and when the Cape was settled as part of the Colony, the Court was still further enlarged by the addition of two deputies from each new town.

Sandwich, Yarmouth, Barnstable, and Eastham elected such deputies as soon as they were incorporated, and the men thus honored went to Plymouth and became part of the Government, with full right to vote on new laws. But Plymouth kept matters under her control in two ways: first, by entitling herself to four deputies besides the Governor and assistants, and secondly by reserving the right to dismiss the Cape deputies if she saw fit, and demand new ones in their place. Each town paid its deputies with money raised by taxing every householder — whether or not he was a freeman. It seemed only

proper, therefore, to give all these householders a vote in electing them. This was done, and forms a unique exception to the
rule that none but freemen should vote. It looked like the
Cape's first reluctant step toward universal suffrage; but it was
not, in fact, for this extension of franchise was withdrawn in
1671.

Such, then, was the composition of that grim abstraction, the
General Court: the Governor and his assistants, four deputies
from Plymouth and two from each of the other towns; its duties
were primarily duties of legislation. Its most startling performance, which it executed in 1636 before the addition of any Cape
deputies, was the Declaration of Rights, which announced to
the world that thereafter the colonists would recognize no laws
made for them without their full consent and approval. This is
really something like a declaration of independence, and it is
not without significance that it was made the same year that
the last installment was paid on the debt to the Merchant
Adventurers.

The Plymouth law courts at first were composed of the Governor and his assistants, supported by a jury of all the freemen
in the town. But as the population increased, this rudimentary
arrangement gave way to grand and petty juries — like those
of to-day — with the Governor and assistants as judges. As
all cases anywhere in the Colony must be heard before this
tribunal, the Court soon found itself overworked. So in 1641
certain men in the outlying towns were authorized to constitute
themselves as a court for deciding cases that involved not more
than twenty shillings. By this arrangement the citizens of
Sandwich, Yarmouth, and Barnstable could take their minor
troubles to a court of three men — Edmund Freeman, of
Sandwich, Thomas Dimock, of Barnstable, and John Crow,
of Yarmouth — who were empowered to settle such disputes.
The fact that Mr. Freeman was one of the Governor's assistants
lent prestige to the tribunal.

This was the beginning of local courts on the Cape, and they
developed in prestige and power until the establishment of Circuit Courts in 1811. This very early court was also important
because it was the germ from which, twenty years later, developed the now time-honored custom of choosing selectmen to

guide the destinies of each town. As an interesting step, the Court in 1651 designated four men who were authorized to call town meetings in Sandwich whenever they thought it necessary, and a dozen years after this, the regular election of selectmen for every town was established. These selectmen originally had powers which, owing to the more intricate organization of modern government, they no longer retain. They might even act as an impromptu court and judge cases of debt up to forty shillings. A great part of their work consisted in settling differences between the townspeople and the Indians. In short, they were created, to quote the words of the Plymouth Court, 'for the better managing of the town's affairs.' They were elected by the freemen of their town, subject always to the approval of Plymouth.

Another factor in local government on the Cape — the Proprietors — were at first far more important than the selectmen. It is easy to define the title 'Proprietor,' but by no means easy to explain what authority it carried with it, for the authority varied greatly, diminishing as the years passed. The Proprietors were in a very literal sense the fathers of the town, for they were the men to whom the General Court granted the land on which the earliest settlements were made. This gave them control of the important question of dividing land and admitting newcomers as townsmen and owners of property. The committees formed in each town for this purpose were composed exclusively of Proprietors — naturally enough, because of their strategic position as titleholders to the land. The number of Proprietors was at first small in every case, sometimes no more than three or four; their first concern was to induce others to join them, and the bait they offered was land, for they had more of this than they knew what to do with. They held themselves responsible also for building roads, for subdividing all land that was suitable for tillage, and for seeing to it that, for the time being at least, woodland and marsh were held as common property for the benefit of all.

Their heirs and assigns, together with others whom for one reason or another they chose to admit, became Proprietors as well, so that their numbers grew rapidly. At first they held the reins of all the town's activities, both political and economic;

a town meeting was a Proprietors' meeting. But later, when town governments were organized, the Proprietors' duties were restricted to apportioning land to newcomers — for they still held title to the hundreds of acres that they had not been able to give away. When finally everything had been divided — even the public woodland and marsh — the usefulness and prestige of the Proprietors came to an end. Their title vanished, and they became ordinary citizens. The dates of their disappearance depended, of course, on the speed with which they divided the land in their town. The Proprietors of some towns got rid of their commons very promptly. Others never quite got rid of it.

But in spite of selectmen, Proprietors, and local courts, no town was allowed to forget that Plymouth was in command. To enumerate all the little privileges which Plymouth forbade the Cape to enjoy, and which to-day we regard as the inalienable rights of freemen, would be too discouraging altogether; it is pleasanter to let a few of them indicate the nature of the rest. Smoking on Sunday within two miles of the meeting-house was an offense that could be expiated only by paying twelve pence to the General Court. Jurors might not smoke while trying to reach a verdict. Stocks, a pound, and military drill were all required for the welfare of the citizens, and any towns which were delinquent in these respects were 'presented,' reprimanded, and fined. If a youth, be he never so respectable, paid court to a maid without first asking her parents' permission, he was punished by a fine or corporal punishment or both. The Court did not approve of driving sharp bargains except when its own members wished to buy Indian land, and the records are full of cases where men were fined for charging too much either for their work or for their wares. Swearing was punished by a three-hour sojourn in the stocks, and when the supply of specific human errors gave out, the Court in desperation passed an act in 1640 'to prevent idleness and other evils.' Whatever charges may be laid at the door of the Plymouth legislators, lack of ambition cannot in fairness be included among them.

Annoying as these edicts must have been, none of them so far has struck deep at the roots of self-government in the towns.

But Plymouth had no hesitation about interfering with even this important privilege. Some of the people whom the Sandwich committee on personnel had allowed to settle there were displeasing to the General Court; the committee was therefore promptly taken to task and 'forbidden to dispose of any more land.' This was in 1639, and it must have very thoroughly shattered any hopes that the citizens had of being allowed to decide town matters for themselves. To be sure, the Cape sent representatives to this Court, as we have seen, and it may therefore be said that this strict surveillance was practiced on each town, in part at least, by its own citizens. But it should be remembered that the Governor and his assistants reserved the right to reject the representatives that the town elected — and thereby kept the control of the Colony in their own hands. If the representatives were courageous and tried to oppose the Plymouth faction, they were replaced. If they were weak, they voted as Plymouth voted, and kept their positions.

Such, at least, was the autocratic theory on which the General Court based its government. In practice, however, things might have been much worse, because, though the principle had no virtue, the men themselves had a great deal. Such a scheme in the hands of modern politicians would result in a corrupt oligarchy. In the hands of our ancestors, it was an oligarchy, but it was not corrupt. The real trouble with Plymouth was that she had not learned the great secret of leadership, which is to refrain from meddling with subordinates when they are making the mistakes of inexperience in carrying out general principles which you have laid down for them.

Whatever suffering the Cape towns endured, therefore, came not so much from any actual restrictions that Plymouth placed on them, as from hurt feelings when the General Court interfered with their honest attempts to manage their own affairs. As far as restrictions went, their own town meetings abounded in them. The local authorities in Eastham fined a man for 'lying about a whale,' and Sandwich punished two maidens for laughing in church at the attempts of the tithing man to chase a dog out of the building.

CHAPTER VI

CIVIL AND MILITARY HISTORY TO 1775

THOUGH the Cape's influence in legislative matters was not at first so great as its citizens would have liked, the days of its weakness did not last long, for by 1650 Plymouth had shot its bolt and was beginning to decline in population, business, and wealth, whereas the Cape, its feet firmly under it, was stretching forward with vigor and assurance. An indication that the tide had turned was the election of Thomas Prince, of Eastham, as Governor of the Colony in 1657. From this point on, the Cape was a bright spot in the political map. Prince was a man of experience in Colony affairs. He had recently moved to Eastham from Plymouth, where he had already served two terms as Governor. The last thing he wished now was to go back to Plymouth, where the Governor was expected to live while he held office. Prince held out so firmly for remaining at Eastham that the Court consented, and to the delight of all the citizens, the new Governor began his third term with his residence on the Cape. He was reëlected every year for the next seventeen years, with Thomas Hinckley, of Barnstable, as his assistant, and died in office in 1673.

The years of Prince's régime were not years of tranquillity. The Quakers were making themselves obnoxious and were in turn outrageously treated by the magistrates. These troubles will be discussed more fully in another chapter. Suffice it for the moment to say that the Governor's inflexible hostility toward the antics of this sect did nothing to remedy a situation which would have tried the abilities of the most seasoned diplomat. The difficulties increased instead of subsiding, and the blame may be divided about equally between the Governor and the Quakers.

But Prince's years as chief magistrate were marked by more profitable activity than anti-Quaker demonstrations. Two of the original Cape towns, Yarmouth and Barnstable, became parents during this period, the former under picturesque circumstances. William Nickerson, a citizen of Yarmouth, and the greatest speculator in wild lands the Cape ever saw, had the soul of a pioneer and the tenacity of a bulldog. He needed both in his undertaking — which was to buy a great tract of land at Monomoyick (now Chatham) and start a new settlement.

He began cheerfully in 1656 by purchasing about a thousand acres from Mattaquason, the sachem of the region, giving him a boat in payment. But here his troubles began, for he had neglected to obtain the Court's permission to make the purchase, and was haled to Plymouth for trial. He pleaded ignorance of the law, and the Court, anxious to have a settlement started, but reluctant to let one man hold so much land, and determined always to uphold its authority, first disfranchised Nickerson for furnishing Mattaquason with a boat, then fined him five pounds for each acre bought, and finally gave him a title to a small tract of land. There was not money enough in the whole Plymouth Colony to pay such a fine as this, as the Court well knew, and for some time no attempt was made to collect it. As for the disfranchisement, that seems to have worried Nickerson very little; if it was ever put into effect at all, it was only for a short time. But the loss of most of his purchase grieved the pioneer deeply. He temporarily abandoned his attempt to settle in Chatham, went instead to Boston, took a flier in Roxbury real estate, and was back in Yarmouth in 1661.

Here his proximity to Chatham made him think again of his great plan, and he petitioned the Court for a title to all the lands he had purchased. The Court then perpetrated the one joke in its history by replying that if Nickerson would pay the fine of five pounds per acre on all the land that he had bought illegally, he might have a title to it. Nickerson's answer was to move to Chatham with six sons, three daughters, three sons-in-law, and all their families. He arrived there about 1664. It was now Plymouth's move, and without delay the Court ordered the Chief Marshal to collect two hundred pounds in money or goods from this troublesome speculator. The Marshal did his best, but found nothing worth taking. Nickerson then appealed to the Commissioners of the Crown, a group of royal inspectors who turned up in Plymouth about this time in the course of a tour of the Colonies. These dignitaries thought that he wanted too much; but the Court, tired of the whole affair, and wishing to appear generous in the eye of the King's minions, remitted Nickerson's fine, and gave him title to one hundred acres, assigning all the rest to a group of very distinguished citizens, including Thomas Hinckley, the Governor's assistant.

Nickerson was furious and was foolish enough to put his fury on paper, accusing Hinckley of using his position to influence the Court. For this, and for another written invective against the colonial authorities, the luckless settler was summoned to Plymouth and fined again. This last encounter with the law convinced him that opposition was useless. Instead of continuing the losing battle, he approached Hinckley and the other grantees, and for ninety pounds succeeded in buying out all their interest, thereby at last acquiring title to the tract of land on which his heart had been set for sixteen troublous years. The deed was dated 1673. This, and other large purchases made from time to time during the next ten years, made him the proprietor of four thousand acres — a domain princely enough to compensate him for the bitter years he had spent in acquiring it. His settlement grew slowly and after being first placed under the jurisdiction of Yarmouth and later under that of Eastham, it was finally incorporated as the Town of Chatham in 1712.

Governor Prince died the year after Nickerson's great purchase, and for the first time in seventeen years the two chief executives of the Colony were not Cape men. Prince and Hinckley had guided its affairs so long that their repeated elections had become matters of routine. A contested election was still unheard of. The problem was not for a man to get himself elected, but for the electors to find a suitable man who would consent to serve. With the death of Governor Prince, Hinckley withdrew from public life for several years and lived quietly in Barnstable.

While Nickerson was in the midst of his legal troubles, a group of men and women moved quietly from Barnstable and started a new settlement at Succonessitt, now called Falmouth after the English town. The first detachment arrived in 1660. The Court had given its consent the year before. The reasons for this enterprise are not entirely clear. There was no land-greedy Nickerson among the emigrants, to establish himself first and then sell lots to newcomers. They could not have felt cramped for pasturage with Great Marshes close at hand. Probably there were Quakers in the group who wanted to get away as far as possible from the established church. But though freedom to enjoy their Quaker meetings unmolested was apparently the principal motive of the settlers at Succonessitt, their removal did not exempt them from attending the regular church at Barnstable; and whatever services they may have held at home, they were obliged every Sunday to travel twenty miles through the woods to the meeting-house at Barnstable. For the first twenty-five years of its history, Succonessitt remained under the jurisdiction of Barnstable; finally in 1686 it was incorporated, and in 1693 its name was changed to Falmouth.

Up to this time, the South Side of Barnstable had remained virtually a wilderness. Hyannis, which to-day acknowledges itself to be the business center of the Cape; the Port, which boasts the summer residences of as many millionaires as are good for any community; Centerville, the most quietly prosperous and dignified village on the South Side — all were forests of virgin pine, and the whole region was known as the South Sea. A Barnstable trader, Nicholas Davis, was the first man to put up a building there, which he used as a warehouse for goods received from Rhode Island, Connecticut, and New York. This outpost of progress was at Lewis Bay, and Davis's shed stood on land which the Sachem Yanno 'gave' him in 1660; but no houses were built in Hyannis for another twenty years. By the end of the century, about a dozen families, attracted by the abundance of oysters, had settled alongshore between Hyannis and Cotuit. A few years later, the Indians had been done out of the ownership of Oyster Island and Cotuit Neck, and all was marching smoothly for the whites. Though handicapped by this comparatively late start, the South-Siders have done well, and their villages have grown into prosperity.

Meanwhile, the lower Cape had not been idle. The region lying north and west of Chatham, and now comprising the towns of Brewster and Harwich, was thinly settled at about the time when Nickerson was beckoning recruits to his domain at Monomoyick. By 1694 the inhabitants of this anomalous territory, which in theory was under the jurisdiction of Eastham, had become numerous enough to form a town of their own, and the Court authorized its incorporation that year. The new town was called Harwich, after the famous English seaport.

As early as 1689, a group of Eastham men had begun negotiations with the Pamet Indians for purchasing land at Truro, and, calling themselves the Pamet Proprietors, were allotting farms to newcomers. They appointed one of their number — Thomas Paine, Jr., son of the millwright — as agent for all their purchases. In this way they avoided the risk of trouble from any who might develop land-grabbing propensities, and at the same time protected themselves against the chance of the Indians' selling the same property twice. By 1700, enough land had been bought to furnish each proprietor with a good-sized tract, and the settlers left Eastham and established themselves at Pamet. Five years later, under the name of Dangerfield, the community was granted municipal privileges, and in 1709 it was incorporated as the town of Truro.

Dangerfield, apparently, was not thought to be a name likely to attract newcomers, so the settlers wisely changed it; and Truro it has remained ever since.

Provincetown, the first place on the Cape to be visited by white men, was one of the last to be dignified with the title of town. Its geographic situation is responsible for both facts: an explorer, groping his way in New England waters, could hardly fail to stumble over the tip of the Cape, and Provincetown Harbor was pretty sure to tempt him to anchor. The settlers, on the other hand, making their way overland from various parts of the Bay Colony, found plenty of good sites long before they reached the sand spit that is Provincetown. If they had been seafarers from the outset, instead of farmers and herdsmen, there would have been a different story to tell. But they were looking for hay grounds and arable fields, and took small interest in harbors.

Other Europeans had been interested in Provincetown Harbor, however, long before the Mayflower found shelter there — long before the Concord skirted its outer shore, carrying Gosnold and Archer. Landlords of sixteenth-century fishermen's taverns anywhere along the coast of Brittany or the Bay of Biscay had heard all about Provincetown from the picturesque villains who dropped in to drink brandy and sour wine of an evening between one fishing season and the next. They told tales of lurid sojourns ashore where a sickle-shaped arm of sand made a harbor in which their vessels could ride out storms from any quarter, and where natives gave them venison and strange corn for rum; tall trees stood close to the water's edge; all day great flocks of wild fowl flew about the marshes; they could fill their holds with fish without going a mile from shore. This was better than facing the rigors of the Grand Banks to the north; here they lived in houses, and the savages were their friends. 'An island, perhaps?' the landlord suggested. An island, perhaps; perhaps a cape; of that they knew nothing. So the conversation drifted along, and by and by the fishermen went to bed.

With a history like this behind it, Provincetown smiled at the earnestness of the Pilgrims. Incorporation was an amusing detail to a region whose fame had reached Europe a hundred years before. Moreover, the grandsons and great-grandsons of these first merry Gallic buccaneers, following the family tradition, continued to make free at Provincetown even after 1700, when the first staid Britishers had built their houses there. Vessels of other nationalities likewise dropped in for one purpose or another, greatly to the concern of the permanent population. One pious settler, William Clap, recorded his indignation in a letter to Governor Dudley dated 1705:

SQUIER DUDLEY;
... Very often hear is opportunity to seas vesels, and goods which are upon a smoglen acompt. i believe had i had a comishon so to do i could have seased a catch this last weak which had most of thar men outlandish men i judge porteges. she lay hear a week and a sloop i believe did thar bisnes for them ... one thing more I make bould to inform your honor that hear are a gret many men which goes fishing at this harbor and som times the french comes hear and then every one runs his way because they have no one to hud them. i myself have been a souferor since i lived hear, being cared away by a small sloop and hear was 130 men and several brave sloops and no hand, a capt. about 12 miles distant, but we may all be tacken at the Cap and he no nothing of it ... your homble and unworthy sarvont
WM. CLAP

This picturesque document reflects in a curiously exact fashion the random work at Provincetown. Miscellaneous smug-

glers, 'Portege' whalemen, French privateers, and colonial
fishermen who camped for the summer, all plied their trades
with as much freedom as if Provincetown had been a remote
island of the Spanish Main. The town was living up bravely to
the wild days of its youth. Echoes of riotous doings reached and
shocked the ears of the General Court, and resulted in an act,
passed in 1714, which put the unruly settlement under the jurisdiction of Truro and decreed that all visiting fishermen — of
whatever nationality — should pay four shillings a week during
their sojourn. Truro had no desire to act as mere disciplinarian
for a lawless gang of polyglots, and promptly petitioned the
Court 'that Cape Cod [that is, the tip end of the Cape] be
declared either a part of Truro or not a part of Truro, that the
town may know how to act in regard to some persons.' At the
same time Truro demanded an explanation from its troublesome protégé why it 'did not entertain a learned orthodox
minister of the Gospel to dispense the word of God to them as
required by law.' In 1727, Provincetown petitioned to be incorporated. The Court granted its request, and Truro was
released from the burden that it had borne dutifully for twelve
years. By degrees, as the new town learned respect for law, the
gay French freedom that had marked its early days gave way
to more decorous walking. The town became a dignified and
subsequently a very prosperous member of the community.

Shortly after Provincetown was incorporated, the lower Cape,
on the strength of its growing population and the new towns
that were being incorporated there, petitioned the Court to be
made a separate county, with its headquarters at Eastham.
The reason for the request was that the distance to Barnstable
Courthouse was a great inconvenience to jurymen and others
who had lawsuits on their hands. The Court, however, wisely
refused. In 1763, Billingsgate, which had always been under
the jurisdiction of Eastham, set up for itself and became the
town of Wellfleet. In the act of incorporation the Court christened the new town Poole, perhaps after the English town of
that name. But the citizens preferred Wellfleet and Wellfleet
it became. Clearly this is not a fancy name. Its origin was
for many years a mystery. Various conjectures were made —
among them the suggestion that the name was a corruption of

'Whale fleet' — appropriate enough in view of the town's
activity in this business, but hardly convincing. The late
Everett Nye, postmaster and historian of the town, suggests
that it was named for the celebrated Wallfleet oysters, which
came from Blackwater Bay in the English Essex; and quite
recently an alert antiquarian, in glancing over a sixteenth-
century broadside, came upon the line 'Wallfleet oysters be very
good food.' The riddle was answered — oysters had lain thick
on Billingsgate flats from time immemorial; nothing was more
natural than that the men who lived there should name the
town for these famous oyster beds of England.

In 1797, Eastham was shorn of still another great district,
Orleans, that lay along her western border. The incorporation
of this town completed the ruin of Eastham. Originally she had
controlled — nominally, at least — all the territory below Yarmouth. One by one, as her forests fell and her soil was blown
thin, Chatham, Harwich, Truro, and Wellfleet had been lost to
her. Now, with the independence of Orleans, the old mother
town of the lower Cape experienced the same feelings of deser-
tion that Plymouth had undergone when half her men left home
to settle Eastham in the wilderness. Her prestige was gone; like
Plymouth, she must from now on rest content with a small tax
list, a modest acreage, and a proud past.

Minor troubles like these, however, are of no importance when
compared with a very real disaster that the Cape met with during this period. Prosperity, in spite of Quaker troubles, had
marked the long régime of Prince and Hinckley. Prosperity
continued, after Prince's death, under the tolerant leadership
of Josiah Winslow, who served as Governor until his death in
1680. The helm was then once more put into the hands of a
Cape-Codder, and Thomas Hinckley, after seven years of retire-
ment from public life, was elected Governor. He was sixty-two
years old, and no man in the colony had a more intimate knowledge of its affairs. He had come to Barnstable with Lothrop in
1639, had fought in the French and Indian War, and afterwards
had served for seventeen years as Prince's assistant. Thus he
had had experience as pioneer, soldier, and magistrate. Hinckley was progressive, and under him in 1685 the Colony, for convenience in administration, was divided into three counties,

Plymouth, Bristol, and Barnstable, the last including the entire Cape, with Barnstable as the shire town. A courthouse was built, and appropriate officials were appointed.

But the great disaster lay ahead. In 1686, while Hinckley was serving his sixth term, the notorious Edmond Andros came from New York with a commission from James II, and not only supplanted Hinckley as Governor, but completely abolished the now long-sanctioned government of the Plymouth Colony. This amazing magistrate operated on the theory that the colonists were not Englishmen. The titles to their farms, which the settlers had earned by the sweat of their brows, and had hewn with their own hands out of the wilderness, Andros declared worthless. Indian deeds he characterized as 'a scratch with a Bear's paw,' and he demanded that the colonists pay quit-rent for land that had been theirs for two generations.

Nothing can more effectively destroy a man's peace of mind than to be told that his house is built on quicksand; he may not believe it, but his tranquillity is at an end. Such was the effect of Andros's proclamation. Hinckley was powerless to oppose this royal representative, who came armed with the majesty of the British Empire, but his long training stood him in good stead. He kept his head, bowed though it was to the inevitable, and, realizing that he could best serve the interests of the Colony by quiet work from the inside, he accepted a seat in Andros's Council. While he held this position — which he soon discovered to be an empty honor — Hinckley did his best to relieve the sufferings of the citizens. He repeatedly petitioned a deaf King for justice, he stalwartly opposed a scheme that Andros devised whereby the colonists should be taxed for the support of the Church of England. But all was in vain. During 1687 and 1688, the Colony was paralyzed. The withering tyranny of Andros taxed men into poverty and killed their ambition. Cornfields were knee deep in weeds. His administration was a fine example of belated severity. Wisdom has her own opinion of the parent who, after giving his son free rein for years and shutting both eyes to his errors, suddenly calls him to account in the woodshed and then locks him in his room. This was precisely what the British Government, in the person of Andros, was doing to New England. There is no doubt that in some cases freedom had gone to the colonists' heads and affected them as old wine affects an abstainer. Charters had not always been obeyed; the settlers had more than once taken the law into their own hands. At such irregularities Parliament had winked for seventy years; but now, suddenly aroused to irrational severity, it acted as though the colonists were a penal settlement instead of a group of earnest experimentalists.

Happily, in 1689, James, who was no more successful in England than his agents were here, was forced to flee for his life, and with the accession of William and Mary, Andros, who had been jailed in Boston at the first whisper of the King's flight, was officially deposed. The Plymouth Government immediately resumed its activities, with Hinckley in command. The New-Englanders learned much from their experience with Andros; the old country nothing. Almost a century later, Burke was laboring to make a stubborn House of Commons understand that a wise neglect was the only way for an empire to hold remote possessions; and the colonists, having experienced once too often the tyranny that only ignorant governments are capable of, were storing up powder and molding bullets for the Revolution.

The last year of Hinckley's régime, 1692, was marked by an event of great importance — the merging of the Plymouth Colony with its younger neighbor, the Massachusetts Bay Colony. This step was taken in spite of the strong opposition of the Old Colony, whose citizens petitioned in vain for a separate charter. William and Mary remained obdurate and would give but one charter for both Colonies, uniting them into the 'Massachusetts Bay in New England.' Furthermore, the Crown from now on insisted on appointing the Colonial Governors, refusing to allow the practice of electing them to continue. In 1692, Sir William Phipps (the only successful treasure-seeker outside the pages of fiction) arrived with the new charter and with his own commission as Governor. The Old Plymouth Colony was entitled to four Councilors, and promptly sent Hinckley as one of them. Two of the others also, John Walley and Barnabas Lothrop, were or had been Barnstable men; so the Cape was well represented in the new government.

There was much speculation throughout the Colony as to

how far Hinckley had aided the unwelcome union, and his
firmest friends had to confess that he had at least done nothing
to oppose it. What his real feelings were in regard to this important transaction cannot be known, for he was wise enough to
keep them to himself. If, as many believed, he favored it, he
showed himself a statesman. Any one who was not blinded by
sentiment could see that the days of the Plymouth Government
were numbered. On the north, the Bay Colony outnumbered
its population more than four to one. On the west and south,
New York had already begun to angle for its annexation. The
Old Colony was living on the unsubstantial basis of its past, and
men of vision saw clearly that it must soon be absorbed by one
or the other of these prosperous neighbors. It is more than likely
that Hinckley was among this number. No one knew better
than he the impoverished condition and the growing weakness
of the Colony, and he was honest enough to admit that hope
for future prosperity unaided was a will-o'-the-wisp. In such
circumstances any conscientious Governor would work for a
powerful alliance, even if it sacrificed the identity of his government and cost him his own position.

The Cape, during the hundred years or so following Governor
Prince's death, was at war with some one or other a good part
of the time. First came King Philip's conspiracy in 1675. After
this had been crushed, there followed the long, intermittent
French and Indian wars, which for want of better names have
been called after the King or Queen who happened to be reign-
ing at the time. Thus the 1690 fighting was known as King
William's War; when this was prolonged after the Treaty of
Ryswick, it became Queen Anne's War. Hostilities ceased for
a time with the Peace of Utrecht in 1713, but twenty-five years
later England and Spain were at each other's throats, and a few
Cape men — who took about as much interest in the quarrel as
the Madagascar Negroes did in the World War — died of fever
in Cuban swamps. In 1744, the English and French were at it
again, and the Cape in consequence embarked on the celebrated
Louisburg Expedition. The Peace of Aix-la-Chapelle, which
followed the capture of Louisburg, was a bitter pill to the victorious Cape soldiers, but they took up arms again in 1755 and
marched against the French at Fort Duquesne, Niagara, Crown

Point, and in Nova Scotia. The Peace of Paris, which was signed in 1763, came just in time to give the Cape a chance to draw breath for the Revolution.

It must not be supposed that the Cape was much exercised by these wars. They were too frequent and most of them too remote to be regarded as anything more than nuisances by men whose interests were in raising good crops of corn and catching as many fish and harpooning as many whales as they could. None of the fighting took place on Cape soil, and although at one time or another a good many Cape men were in the service, their casualties were not heavy. The only conflict that touched them nearly was King Philip's War, and even then all the fighting was off the Cape. However, the effects of such prolonged hostilities were marked, and two or three of the outstanding military figures were Cape men.

The nominal cause of the war against Philip was the supposed murder at Middleboro of an educated Indian named Sausamon. The Plymouth Court, with characteristic zeal, arrested three Indians — one of whom was a councilor of Philip — charging them with the murder; they were tried and executed, whether justly or unjustly nobody knows. Here was the pretext that Philip had been waiting for. He assembled his warriors, and the fight was on.

The ins and outs of the Sausamon affair remain mysteries. It has been alleged that he was bringing or had brought to the whites news of Philip's hostile preparations, and that this treachery was the cause of his murder. It may very well be so. Far more doubtful is the question whether or not the Court hanged the right men as his assassins. However, these matters are of no importance. A conflict was inevitable, murder or no murder. Whenever civilized men invade the domains of savages, a fight is bound to follow, sooner or later. Philip had long been restless and alarmed; the settlers had never felt easy since their arrival more than fifty years before. Anything might have served as a spark for the inevitable explosion; Sausamon's death was more than adequate.

The unnecessary but perfectly natural apprehensions of the Cape villages during this war have been sufficiently discussed in another chapter. Surrounded as they were by Indians who might turn hostile at any moment, it is no wonder that the townspeople felt anxious as they watched their quotas march off to Rhode Island, the departure of every detachment weakening their own defense to an alarming degree. Sandwich, Barnstable, and Yarmouth each sent about one hundred men in all; Eastham about fifty. Happily for the peace of mind of those who stayed at home, these soldiers did not leave at the same time; each town sent its quota in several installments, and many of the enlistments, following the old custom, were for very short periods of time. Even so, a wide breach was left in the Cape's defenses, and boys who were too young to enlist were drafted into the home guard.

Owing to the cheerfully unscientific fashion in which our ancestors conducted wars, it is almost impossible to trace exactly the campaigns in which Cape-Codders were engaged. A letter from Captain John Gorham, who commanded the Yarmouth detachment, has been preserved, and indicates that he and his men were having the same experience that has been shared by many fighters of Indians: they had spent fourteen weeks in a vain attempt to find the enemy. Subsequently, Gorham succeeded in joining forces with the main body of the colonial troops, and took part in the most important battle of the war, that of Swamp Fort, near North Kingston, Rhode Island. This was not an attack against Philip but against the Narragansetts who were supporting him. This powerful tribe had withdrawn to a fortified plateau surrounded by a swamp and further protected by a rude palisade. Here were assembled not only their warriors, but their families and all their possessions as well. The Colonial Headquarters decided that this stronghold must be taken, and troops consequently set out from Wickford before daylight on a December morning, marched twenty miles through the snow, stormed Swamp Fort in a four-hour fight, killed or wounded about a thousand Indians, burned their lodges, and started back to Wickford through snow and darkness. Thomas Hinckley was in charge of the commissary department on this expedition, and managed to supply the troops with food enough to keep them going, but when they arrived at Wickford next morning, their condition may be imagined. Captain Gorham, who during this attack was in command of half the Plymouth Colony's battalion, with Sparrow, of Eastham, as lieutenant, was struck by a bullet which shattered his powder horn and drove the splinters into his side. He died two months later but no other Cape men were lost.

The Narragansetts were now out of the running, and the Colony was free to concentrate on Philip. The only other engagement that affords any record of Cape troops was at or near Seekonk (Rehoboth). Here in the early spring of 1676, Captain John Pierce, of Scituate, with a small command of about fifty whites and twenty Indians from the friendly Cape tribes, was led into ambush by the same trick, that birds employ to lead enemies away from their nests — feigning injury. Too late Pierce saw his predicament; almost the entire company were killed; their lives were not thrown away, however, for the Indian losses were still heavier. The Cape casualties in this disaster numbered twenty-one. It is easy to criticize Pierce for his folly in being deceived by so ancient a trick. In fact, however, like most of the tactical errors of colonial officers, it was the result of impetuosity and zeal. The settlers knew little of the science of warfare. They distrusted the unorthodox methods of their one inspired commander, Captain Ben Church, and tied his hands so often that he resigned and was induced to take the field again only by a conscience which was powerful enough to overcome his righteous indignation. If his advice at Swamp Fort had been followed, the nightmare march back to Wickford would have been avoided, and the weary soldiers would have slept in the warm Indian huts which their commander's folly had prompted them to burn. No group of men were ever educated at a higher price than the early New England army officers.

Philip, his allies falling away and his own tribe scattered, finally returned to Mount Hope with three hundred warriors who remained faithful to him. Church, who had resumed command, with a little band of forty men, half of whom were Indians, harassed the luckless Philip in repeated skirmishes and finally bottled him up in his stronghold. While trying to sneak away from this last entrenchment, the notorious savage was shot by one of Church's Indians. After a few more false flashes, the settlements were again at peace.

The happy situation of the Cape during the war becomes more striking when compared with the experiences of settlements near by. A part of Plymouth called Halifax was burned; Bridgewater, Taunton, and Scituate were raided, some of them more than once; houses were destroyed in Middleboro. At Eel River, three miles on the Sandwich side of Plymouth, a fortified house that sheltered the property of a number of neighboring settlers was plundered and burned and a dozen women and children tomahawked while the garrison were at church. At such atrocities the Cape shuddered, but was safe. Even the casualties among its troops were insignificant. To set the total at fifty would be putting it high.

When it came to paying the bill, however, the case was different, and justly so. The war debt of the Plymouth Colony had reached the staggering sum of £27,000, and of this amount the towns of the Cape were naturally called upon for their full share. Every spare shilling that could be wrung out of the soil or pulled out of the sea went into taxes; frugality, always the rule on the Cape, became now an absolute necessity, and with a fortitude equal to that which their fathers had shown in paying the Merchant Adventurers, the settlers paid this huge sum to the uttermost farthing.

Scarcely were they relieved of this burden when another war cloud began to roll up ominously in the north. As early as 1631, Plymouth traders had had trouble with the French in the neighborhood of Penobscot Bay, and the skirmishes that took place then indicated clearly enough that serious trouble must come when the colonies of the two old rivals began to spread. It is not the purpose of this volume to rehearse in detail the well-known story of the long struggle which did come, and which, though broken from time to time by a series of inadequate treaties, left the Colonies small time for profitable pursuits between 1689 and 1763. Omitting all references to causes and effects, except in so far as they were reflected in the fortunes of Cape-Codders, the present narrative will confine itself to the exploits of Cape men in these French and Indian Wars.

Of these exploits the most picturesque was that of the whaleboat fleet commanded by Lieutenant-Colonel John Gorham, of Barnstable, son of the renowned Indian fighter. Shallow-draft

boats of some sort were needed for carrying troops up the rivers
to the settlements which the French, with a proper respect for
the British navy, had established far inland. Whaleboats were
the very craft for this sort of enterprise, and since the Cape was
the home of the most experienced whalemen in New England,
it was only natural that Captain Ben Church should look to the
Cape for the man to command this branch of the expedition.
These unique fleets made their first appearance in 1690, early
in King William's War, and continued to be used during Queen
Anne's War. Church in a letter to Governor Dudley gives a
good description of them: he called for forty or fifty 'good
whaleboats, well fitted with good oars and twelve or fifteen good
paddles to every boat. And upon the wale of each boat, five
pieces of strong leather to be fastened on each side to slip five
small ash bars through; so that, whenever they land the men
may step overboard and slip in said bars across, and take up
said boat that she may not be hurt against the rocks.' Each
carried its own camping equipment and provisions, and when
turned bottom-up furnished adequate shelter at night. On
a pinch, five hundred men could be floated inland on forty or
fifty boats.

Young Cape whalemen, who could be dragooned into any
other branch of the service only with the greatest difficulty,
consented to embark in this flotilla with less reluctance. They
felt more at home swinging an ash oar in a whaleboat than
trooping through the woods with a musket. So the whaleboat
fleets were very largely Cape Cod ventures, and to the Cape
men who commanded and manned them belongs the credit for
such success as they achieved.

At first this success was not great. The Canada expedition of
1689–90 ended in disaster, and Gorham's whaleboats had to
retreat as well as the land forces. That Church in no way ascribed his failure to the 'fleet,' appears from the fact that in
subsequent expeditions the Barnstable Captain was promoted
to the rank of Lieutenant-Colonel and was second in command
of the entire campaign. But in spite of his advancement he
stuck to his whaleboats, and led several fleets of them against
French settlements before the Peace of Ryswick was signed in
1697.

This peace, though it put a stop to hostilities for the moment, by no means settled the differences between England and France. The respite lasted six years. Then, in 1703, Queen Anne's War began, and the Indians, at the instigation of the French, sacked Deerfield. Again Church was given command of the New England troops, and again Gorham assembled the whaleboats. The expedition sailed north, where it ingloriously pillaged the Acadian coast. The French retaliated by sending an occasional privateer to loot the unprotected fishing village of Provincetown. Port Royal fell in 1710, but the English forces shattered themselves in vain against the natural bulwarks of Quebec. The Peace of Utrecht in 1713 came nearer being permanent than any preceding cessation of hostilities, and gave the Colonies a generation in which to recuperate.

During the lull, Church and Gorham died, but the latter handed the torch to his son Shubael, who, when the next phase of the century of warfare began, was on hand at the capture of Louisburg in 1745, with his two sons John and David. Louisburg was the headquarters of armed French vessels that for years had made fishing on the Grand Banks risky business for British subjects; and, forsaking northern waters, had even seized our merchantmen as they plied between New England and the West Indies. The Cape had money invested in both these branches of maritime enterprise, and many of her sons were in command of the ships. It was with altogether unwonted zeal, therefore, that Cape men girded up their loins for the reduction of this stronghold.

Forty recruits immediately enlisted from Yarmouth under Captain Joseph Thacher, and the other towns were equally prompt with their quotas. The freedom of the sea was a cry that touched these sailors nearly. Shubael Gorham commanded the first company of the Seventh Massachusetts Regiment, and his son John commanded the Second, and had charge of the whaleboat fleet, which had become a family tradition. Shubael's other son, David, also served under his father. All three had the title of Colonel, and were citizens of Barnstable. As usual, numbers of friendly Indians were included in the Cape detachments. The whaleboat fleet went through the hardest fighting of the entire siege, and, though its attacks were repulsed, John

Gorham and his men lived up to the reputation for valor that his ancestors had established. Tradition has it that one of the Yarmouth Indians in Thacher's company risked his life for a bottle of brandy by crawling into the fortress through an embrasure and opening the gate to the invaders. At any rate, the stronghold fell, and in June, 1745, the city of Louisburg surrendered to Sir William Pepperell's New-Englanders.

For the next three years, Cape-Codders, though they did little fighting, were kept in a state of apprehension by the report that a French armada was under way to avenge the fall of Louisburg by plundering the New England coast. If such a fleet had actually arrived, the Cape would certainly have been the first to suffer, for its unprotected shores were an invitation to any invader. Happily, storms and sickness took the teeth out of the expedition, and in 1748 the Peace of Aix-la-Chapelle put an end to the Cape's anxiety. But it was a bitter pill to all New-Englanders, for by its terms the fortress that they had bled to reduce was handed back to the French. This amazing piece of folly looked to the colonists like treachery pure and simple; but it was only another of the many instances in which statesmen have undone the work of soldiers.

War came again in 1755. Great Britain accused France of violating the terms of the treaty of Aix-la-Chapelle, and sent over a force of regulars to show colonial troops how campaigns should be conducted. Expeditions against Fort Duquesne, Crown Point, Niagara, and Nova Scotia met with varying success, but the British were at last the inglorious victors, and Canada, which for a century had been the bone of contention between the two powers, passed into their hands by the Peace of Paris in 1763.

Early in this phase of the war, the Cape was bewildered by the arrival, on the south shore of Sandwich, of seven boatloads of 'French neutrals' with their families. These wanderers said that they were on their way from Rhode Island to Boston, and asked to have their boats carted across to the Bay shore. Instead of granting the request, the Sandwich authorities seized the boats and sold them, and held the Frenchmen under arrest — distributing them among the neighboring towns, where they were detained until the end of the war. This was the only band of exiled Acadians whose wanderings brought them to the Cape.

The result of sending British troops to this war was very different from what the King and his Councilors had anticipated. Instead of furnishing the undisciplined local talent with a splendid example of military acumen, the regulars, who knew less about Indian warfare than the settlers did about dress parades, marched to destruction under the valiant but hidebound Braddock, while the colonial troops, watching from the shelter of tree-trunks and rocks, discovered that these invincibles were frail creatures after all. Cape-Codders who limped home after these fights brought astounding news to their fellow citizens: The British regulars were men of straw; they knew nothing of warfare as it was waged in the wilderness; their valor served only to lead them into close range of hidden muskets; a young Virginian had reassembled the remains of Braddock's command and shown a flexible leadership that made the officers of the old country stare in amazement. Great Britain, indeed! What had she to enforce obedience with? Such was the comment of veterans at the fireside, while James Otis, the young West Barnstable orator, was preaching Independence in high places. Revolution was only twelve years away.

The wars had reduced the Colonies to financial chaos. New England had been wading through campaigns for three generations, and there was not money enough to pay for them all. Men had had small experience with money in the eighteenth century, and wise ministers of finance were too few to prevent the inflation of currency — a resort which has proved fatal as often as it has been tried. The Colonies were deluged with paper money that had nothing behind it; on the Cape the depreciation was not only tremendous, but shifted with the disconcerting unexpectedness of a feather before random zephyrs. Fishermen could not tell what their fares were worth until they had reduced the fabulous sum of paper pounds to a basis of hard cash, and in the process the profits shrank almost to invisibility. In 1707, the citizens of Falmouth, in calling a new minister, furnish an illuminating bit of evidence as to the value of a shilling. 'We ... are ... agreed,' they write, 'to give you £160 in money, at weight and value it now usually passeth at, which is 15 pennyweight at

six shillings.' At that rate, a shilling had shrunk to a quarter
of its normal value. Ten years later, it was worth even less.
Jenkins, the historian of Falmouth, reckons that in his town in
1718 a pound was worth forty-four cents. In 1749, the Yarmouth minister was poor with a salary of £625 beside the usual
perquisites of wood and salt hay. Such was the result of repeated issues of bills of credit; they served only to increase the
depth of the water in which the Colonies were already floundering.

The Cape had by this time become largely a maritime region.
Fishermen, whalers, and small West India trading vessels, commanded, manned, and in many cases owned, by Cape men, sailed
from all the harbors alongshore. The growing commerce, however, had been seriously interfered with by the wars and was
now hampered almost as badly by the chaotic state of the currency. Furthermore, whales began to be scarce in local waters;
cod-fishermen wanted to be nearer the Grand Banks; Quakers
wanted to be farther from the General Court; restlessness and
discontent — infallible visitors of civilians in time of war —
descended upon many Cape families, and exoduses took place
with disturbing frequency. The emigrants offered various ex-
cuses for their departure, but behind them all lay the war with
its apparently never-ending series of renewals. Besides those
who actually left — and only one degree less unsettling to the
rest — were the men who kept talking about moving away, but
never went. Such malcontents, who lacked the courage to prove
their complaints sincere, were abundant. In 1739, a group of
Provincetown whalemen announced that they would depart
with their families for Casco Bay the next spring and talked of
little else throughout the winter; but as far as can be discovered
from the records, they grumbled on to their graves in the old
town.

Of those who did little talking and quietly sailed away bag
and baggage, in search of a new Utopia, the Gorhams of Barnstable are the best known. Colonel Shubael Gorham, the same
who took part in the capture of Louisburg, spent all his money
and many years of his life in founding the town of Gorham,
Maine. With him went some of the best citizens of Barnstable,
Yarmouth, and Eastham, with a few from Sandwich. Among

them were his brother John and other members of the family. None of these newest pioneers had the enterprise so much at heart as Colonel Shubael, however. His perseverance was largely responsible for securing grants of land from the Legislature as pensions for the descendants of the soldiers in King Philip's War. A township called Narragansett No. 7 was assigned to old Captain John Gorham's heirs, and Colonel Shubael, as his grandson, had an indisputable right in it. In 1736, he assembled the other claimants, chief among them his fellow townsman, Captain John Phinney, who acted throughout as his right-hand man. Some who received grants in the new township had no desire to go. The Colonel bought their shares without ever having seen the ground, and like many another land speculator, went bankrupt as a result. His command in the Louisburg Expedition switched his energies from Gorhamtown, as the settlement was usually called, and turned out to be the last act of his life, for he died the next year, 1746. The town of Gorham to-day stands as a monument to his perseverance.

Other scattering emigrants settled in various parts of Maine and Canada, but the majority of those who had no warring ancestor to justify them in claiming land at Gorham set sail for Barrington in Nova Scotia. The history of this township is inextricably interwoven with the narrative of the Cape men who left their homes for newer pastures. Such Cape names as Doane, Crowell, Knowles, Sears, and Nickerson are scattered all over the early records of Barrington and are still common there to-day.

Among the earliest Cape men to settle there were Thomas Crowell and Solomon, Jonathan and Archelaus Smith, fishermen who had grown familiar with the region on their annual voyages north. In 1761, they decided to stay at Barrington instead of wasting time on the long voyage home. They put up log cabins and were joined by their families, who made the trip with Captain Eldad Nickerson, another Cape fisherman and a veteran of Nova Scotia waters. He stayed, too, and became a prosperous trader.

Edmund Doane sailed from the Cape with the timbers of his old house lashed on deck, though he had to cut them shorter in order to get them on board. Doane also carried his furniture and live stock, but, owing to storms and exposure, most of his cattle died before the vessel reached Barrington. In 1762, the little settlement welcomed another group of newcomers from Nantucket and the Cape.

Though Barrington was the first permanent settlement that Cape men made in Nova Scotia, other Cape-Codders were scattered here and there throughout the Province before Crowell and the Smiths decided to move. Governor Lawrence, in a report dated 1760, writes: '... Transient fishermen from Marblehead and Cape Cod, who have put in there [Liverpool, N.S.] out of curiosity, are so taken with the promising prospects of those people that they have all solicited strongly to be admitted into their township.'

Governor Lawrence, in fact, did everything in his power to make things pleasant for New England fishermen, and his many inducements reached the Cape at the psychological moment. Taxes were high, whales scarce, and the Grand Banks too far away for convenience. It looked like a fine chance to change a Province that was at swords' points with the King for one that basked in the sunshine of the royal smile. The combination of circumstances was too strong for a good many Cape families. They sailed north and became pioneers once more.

Meanwhile, in spite of taxes, wars, and emigrations, the wheels of progress ground on. Schools were started; churches were full. Even before King Philip's uprising — as far back, indeed, as 1670 — the Plymouth Colony farmed out the Provincetown fisheries to pay for a free school at Plymouth. This was all very well for Plymouth, but it was small help to the Cape children. Plymouth apparently thought she had done her duty by outlying towns seven years before when the General Court recommended that each settlement give the question of schools 'serious consideration.' A more generous step was taken in 1687 under Hinckley, when the Court, instead of spending all the revenue from the fisheries to support the Plymouth school, let it be divided among the more important towns. The sum thus supplied was only half enough to pay a teacher, however, for five pounds was the most that any town might receive.

When the two colonies merged, the Cape tried a different scheme, called the 'Squadron System,' whereby the school went to the pupil instead of the pupil's going to the school. It was out of the question for children who lived far out on the fringes of thinly settled towns to make long daily trips to school; it was hard enough to get them all to church once a week. The schoolmaster, therefore, following the example of the peripatetic philosophers, moved from one part of a township to another and kept school for a stated time in each. At first only one shift was needed to cover a whole town; but as the settlements grew, the pedagogue's wanderings became more frequent, until in 1730 it took him six moves and three years and a half to make the rounds of Harwich, allowing on an average six months for each group. When he had finished the cycle, if his courage was still good, he began again and worked his way round the town once more.

The curriculum consisted of the three R's, good measure considering the salaries the towns paid the teachers. In 1700, Eastham paid ten pence per week per child; in Sandwich, the devoted James Battersly labored from 1701 to 1704 for ten pounds a year. But for the custom of 'boarding round' with the families of their pupils, it would seem that schoolmasters must have starved; but Deacon Joseph Hawes, who taught in Yarmouth and Barnstable just after the Revolution, received seven dollars a month and boarded himself.

The Deacon has left an illuminating account of his experiences as a pupil in the pre-Revolutionary schools of Yarmouth. He says that the teacher

was generally placed in a great chair, at a large table before a large fireplace. When he entered, every scholar must make a bow. The master would make a short prayer, (this was held sacred by the good old women). The Bible class was then called out to read one chapter, standing in a half circle behind the master. He would meantime be employed making pens etc., while each scholar would mention the number and read one verse, while some might be playing pins and others matching coppers. Then the Psalter class read in the same manner.... The master would be writing copies, setting sums, making and mending pens, etc., while nearly all the scholars would be playing or idle. The most forward in Arithmetic might do one or two sums in a day, if they could do them without the master's assistance; — he gave me one sum in the Single Rule of Three, which I could not resolve for two or three days; after requesting him a number of times to inform me, he would reply he had no time, and I must study the answer....

ISAAC DILLINGHAM HOUSE, BREWSTER

WALTER DILLINGHAM HOUSE, BREWSTER

As soon as the master retired from the school, every instrument of correction or torture would by the scholars be destroyed. At this time I lived with my aged grandfather, who had a liberal education but in low circumstances. I could learn more in his corner with my pine candle, in one evening, than I could at school in a week.

Apparently Ichabod Cranes tarried in other regions besides Sleepy Hollow, but some discount should be granted the Deacon's narrative for the unfailing exaggeration that every adult male allows himself when recounting his youthful exploits at school. Time is a magnifier that turns snub-nosed youngsters into gigantic malefactors; with the passing of the years, a single unruly episode is seen as habitual rebellion. Some muscular discipline must have been called for at times, however. Who can doubt, for example, that Nathaniel Dill, of Wellfleet, who for years taught a school for youthful Provincetown whalemen between voyages, relied on something more primitive than knowledge to inspire awe in his Herculean pupils? Our ancestors, in fact, were convinced of the beneficial effects of the rod. The citizens of Truro paid two men to act as 'boy whipers' when youth profaned the Sabbath, and they would certainly have supported their schoolmaster in the same robust style. But not even methods of discipline in schools can be standardized. There remains always the individual to upset the profoundest generality. While Dill with his fists was pounding obedience into lads who had harpooned whales, the widow Sarah Spencer, mindful of Satan's delight in idle hands, gave her Barnstable pupils cotton to pick the seeds out of as they learned the Bible by heart.

CHAPTER VII

THE REVOLUTION

CAPE-CODDERS were not exempt from the limitations that an All-Wise Providence has seen fit to place on human nature. Like the rest of mankind, they had their frailties and went to their graves with all their imperfections on their heads. But though there was no alchemy in the Cape soil to make its sons infallible, there was much in its geographical situation to explain their conduct during the Revolution. And though some Cape-Codders, by their loyalty to the King, helped to prolong the war, another Cape-Codder hastened its coming by a speech made fifteen years before the Declaration of Independence. He was James Otis, Jr., the West Barnstable Patriot. Since he was the first man to plant the seed of Independence, not only in the minds of Cape-Codders, but in the minds of all the northern colonists as well, and since nothing that had been said or done on the Cape before his time has any immediate bearing on the Revolution, he becomes a proper person to be discovered as the curtain rises.

Otis is no local figure; his influence was not confined to Cape Cod, or for that matter to Massachusetts. His words were heeded in New York and New Jersey as well as in Watertown and Barnstable, and his doctrine was the doctrine of patriotism in a sense that it had never had before; for with him patriotism, for the first time in our history, meant, not loyalty to the British Crown but separation from it. Otis's eloquence was based on a self-confidence and intolerance that were almost sublime. Anger is as frequently an incentive to eloquence as it is an impediment to it, and Otis, in the course of his speeches, always became angry. He was clear in his views, sure that he was right, and consequently impatient of stupidity or chicanery. On such sure foundations was his eloquence based. He fetched his doctrine from the first principles of the rights of mankind — the right of the individual to hold property; from this sure hypothesis, he developed and proved the theorem of his statesmanship, and justified the liberation of the Colonies from unjust taxation by Great Britain.

But he did more than justify Colonial Independence; he created the idea of it — sowed the first seed that was to grow, through the thorns of Toryism and the barren ground of selfishness, into Revolution. The power of his mind reduced complex problems to their simplest terms, and then solved them. On one occasion he sent to a member of Parliament a message Byronic in its impudence: 'I shall transmit to your lordship by the next mail,' he wrote, 'a simple, easy plan for perpetuating the British Empire in all parts of the world.' Otis was a Cape-Codder and had a sense of humor. Though he could have fulfilled the promise of this letter at least as well as the British Parliament, his tongue was certainly in his cheek when he wrote the lines and a twinkle in his eye as he fancied the noble lord's outraged sense of importance when he read them.

Otis sprang into political prominence in 1761, when he delivered his celebrated speech against the Writs of Assistance — those extraordinary documents — universal search warrants that authorized any official to enter any house for any goods at any time. But the ultimate significance of this speech stretched far beyond the blocking of any particular measure. It created a permanently suspicious state of mind in the colonists, that caused them, from 1761 until the outbreak of the war, to scrutinize every act of Parliament with the greatest care; to 'snuff the approach of tyranny in every tainted breeze' and to challenge much legislation that would previously have passed without suspicion. It was by creating this state of mind in the Colonies that Otis engendered the germ of Revolution. He opened their eyes not so much to particular outrages as to the outrageous point of view in Parliament that gave birth to them; and herein lies his contribution to our Independence.

The effect of Otis's Writs-of-Assistance speeches on the Cape was immediate and violent. Not every one there, by any means, was ready to declare himself for Independence, and the citizens found themselves divided into two camps — Loyalist and Patriot. Not content with this, each camp split into two factions, moderate and extreme. Thus four clearly defined political parties can be distinguished. There were the extreme

Loyalists, 'peace-at-any-pricers,' who, from whatever motives, regarded war with England as equivalent to suicide or treason. There were the moderate Loyalists, who wished to avoid war, not because they believed Revolution was treason, but because they thought it unnecessary and continued to hope, or to pretend to hope, that the unhappy state of affairs was only temporary and would be remedied by Parliament. The Patriots were similarly divided into two wings, the firebrands and the calmer spirits. The extreme Patriots regarded the moderates as hardly less evil than Tories; and the feeling was reciprocal and lasted throughout the war. This furious animosity appeared with startling intensity in the course of an evening's conversation in a Barnstable tavern between Colonel Nathaniel Freeman, of Sandwich, one of the leaders of the extreme Patriots, and Captain Samuel Crocker, a dignified and intelligent member of the conservative branch of the Patriotic Party. Captain Crocker declared that routing out tea from old women's larders was a procedure unworthy of a high cause. Freeman replied that such a statement was toryism. Others of the violent Patriots agreed with Freeman and showed their patriotism by pulling up the fence in front of Crocker's house.

Another incident that shows the heights which political hatred reached at this restless period occurred when the Barnstable militia were parading on the village green. Colonel Nathaniel Freeman and Colonel Joseph Otis, brother of the Patriot, were present, and Captain Samuel Crocker was putting the company through its drill. As the two Colonels passed the lines, the soldiers instead of presenting arms, clubbed their muskets. Otis, like a flash, turned on Captain Crocker and accused him of being the instigator of the insult. Crocker hotly, and probably truthfully, denied the charge, whereupon Otis struck him with his cane. Crocker retaliated, and there followed the spectacle of two distinguished citizens and officers — both Patriots — both espousing the same great cause — engaged in something very like a street brawl. The gentlemen were pulled apart, and their differences were eventually reconciled. The incident was closed, but remains a clear indication of the violence of the feeling between factions of the same party.

Some sensitive souls have catalogued the next patriotic demonstration that took place on the Cape, among the villanies of the Tories. But there is small doubt that its authors were Patriots, though, fortunately for their memory, their names are not recorded. A widow named Abigail Freeman kept a little grocery store in Barnstable. This lady, like many of her kind, was outspoken; she was an ardent Loyalist and took no pains to conceal her views. She said quite frankly what she thought about Colonel Freeman and his friends, and flatly refused to allow her stock of tea to be confiscated. For these reasons a band of Patriots waited upon her one night, dragged her from bed to the center of the village, smeared her with tar and feathers, and rode her on a rail until, beside herself with terror, she promised to keep her political views to herself. She was then allowed to make her way home. Not even the tension of the times or the justice of the cause can excuse such a performance as this. If the truth were known, it would doubtless appear that Medford rum, not patriotism, was at the bottom of the outrage, and this hypothesis does not add to its respectability. It was another of those unfortunate incidents which, as President Adams remarks, 'were more lamented by the Patriots than by their enemies.'

It is pleasant to turn from such atrocities to the legitimate and laudable activities of our ancestors in their fight for freedom; the first of these was a demonstration which, quite as truly as the battle of Lexington or Concord, represents one of the first bold steps that any of the Colonies took toward freedom. Its immediate cause was a change which King George saw fit to make in the method of selecting juries for the superior courts. Instead of being drawn from the box by the selectmen, as formerly, they were now to be appointed arbitrarily by the sheriff. Such a manifestation of absolute authority was intolerable to men who were determined to govern themselves and had learned by experience that they were able to do so successfully. The question was, what should they do? Very deliberately, with a full realization of the seriousness of the step, they decided on direct action. They would prevent the King's courts from sitting; they would prevent it by force if necessary; they would begin at Barnstable.

They well knew that this was treason, and they were ready to take the consequences. Accordingly, in September, 1774, six months before the Concord fight, the leading citizens of Rochester, Wareham, and other towns near by, assembled and started an orderly march down the Cape to Sandwich. There was no blowing of bugles or flashing of muskets, but in spirit this 'Body of the People,' as they called themselves, was as truly an army as the grim patriots who a little later faced the British regulars on the slopes of Bunker Hill. Perfect orderliness and absolute decorum marked their progress. They had drawn up rules and regulations for their conduct, and the keynote of these regulations is worth quoting. 'We are,' they said, 'neither friends to mobs nor riots.'

They spent the night at Sandwich, where they were joined by a considerable number of the male population, and early the next morning, under the leadership of Colonel Nathaniel Freeman, they set out down the Cape for the Barnstable Courthouse. Patriotic citizens joined them on the march at various stages of its advance, falling in at the rear of the column, while at its head rode Freeman, a superb figure in his snow-white wig, wearing his hat tilted jauntily to one side. In Barnstable they were joined, as at Sandwich, by patriotic citizens, and by the time they had drawn up in front of the Courthouse door, they were fifteen hundred strong.

They were in plenty of time. It was ten o'clock in the morning, and the Court had not yet arrived for its opening session. A committee was chosen, with Freeman as its spokesman, to state to the Court, when it should appear, the purpose of the gathering. They had not long to wait. The bell was rung, announcing the opening of Court, and along the road came the Chief Justice (the venerable Colonel James Otis, father of the Patriot) and the other dignitaries, among them, as clerk, Joseph Otis, his son. They halted close to the outskirts of the crowd, and Colonel Otis demanded the purpose of the assemblage. Freeman, from his position on the steps of the building, answered him over the heads of the crowd. His words are recorded by an eye-witness; 'May it please your Honor,' he said, 'we have directed this movement to prevent the Court from sitting or from doing any business. We have taken all the consequences into consideration. We have weighed them well and formed this resolution, which we shall not rescind.'

The Chief Justice was a wise man and a good patriot. He was merely doing his duty by conducting His Majesty's Court until the war, for which he fervently hoped, should break out. The old gentleman continued, even now, to do his duty, and pointed out to Freeman and his associates that this was not a Superior Court and that its jury had been drawn from the box in the traditional manner by the selectmen of the town. But another son of the venerable Chief Justice, James Otis the Patriot, had taught the colonists to see through such statements as this, even as the old gentleman had known they would when he spoke the words. Freeman replied without a moment's hesitation: 'We do not apprehend,' said he, 'that if you proceed to business you will do anything that we could censure. But, sir, from all decisions of this Court an appeal lies. An appeal to what? To a Court over which we have no control or influence. And *there* the jury will be appointed by the sheriff. For this reason we have adopted this method of stopping the avenue through which business may otherwise pass to that tribunal.'

Judge Otis must have chuckled at this reply. His conscience was clear. He had done his duty in trying to open the King's Court, and had met with determined and intelligent opposition. After withdrawing for consultation, he returned a statement to the Body of the People, saying that the Court consented not to sit. So far the success of the Patriots was complete, and they might well congratulate themselves not only on the outcome of their bold move, but quite as much on the dignity and propriety with which they had carried it out.

But the Patriots' duty was not yet done. Though the Court had agreed not to sit this time, there was no guaranty that it would not resume its activities on a more propitious occasion. Committees were therefore chosen from the Body of the People to extract written promises from the various officers of the Court to discontinue all anti-colonial activities in the future. One of the justices that signed such an agreement was Edward Bacon, Esq., an eminent Loyalist, whose exertions in the King's cause will be mentioned later. Another Court official was his bitter enemy and one of the most energetic Patriots the

Cape ever produced, Joseph Otis, son of the old Chief Justice and brother of James the Patriot. Clearly the Body of the People were taking no chances and were forcing Patriots to sign as well as Loyalists. Other Loyalists were then routed out from among the crowd, and various promises and recantations were obtained from them. Committees were chosen for towns farther down the Cape, 'to desire of the militia officers that they would no longer hold commissions under the present Capt. General, who is appointed to reduce us to obedience to the late unconstitutional acts.' In Barnstable, the Edward Bacon aforesaid was thus obliged to resign his militia commission.

At about this point in the proceedings, Colonel Freeman resigned as leader of the movement. The Body of the People promptly elected Joseph Otis in his place, and from this moment forward Otis was unsparing in his exertions in the cause of Independence. So, although this great demonstration did not originate on the Cape, a large percentage of its members were Cape men, the entire scene of its activity was on Cape soil, and both its leaders were Cape-Codders, one from Sandwich, the other from Barnstable.

The assemblage next erected a liberty pole in Barnstable and marched back to Sandwich, where they found that the Tories had taken advantage of their absence to cut down the Liberty pole there. Before disbanding, the Body of the People extracted from these enthusiasts apologies for their behavior, and the price of the pole. These Liberty poles, by the way, were a picturesque feature of the pre-Revolutionary landscape, and one of the favorite pastimes was for the Patriots to set them up in the daytime and for the Tories to cut them down by night. Most of the Cape towns had them; some had two, and lively scenes were enacted around them. Whether any unfortunate Tories on the Cape were ever hoisted to the top of the poles amid the derisive hoots of the Sons of Liberty, is doubtful; but a bit of doggerel from Trumbull's 'McFingal' describes such a performance so whimsically that it would be pleasant to believe it had been practiced once or twice. The poet sings as follows:

> 'There from the pole's sublimest top
> The active crew let down a rope;
> At once its other end in haste bind
> And make it fast upon his waistband;

Till like the earth, as stretched on tenter,
He hung, self-balanced, on his center.
Then upwards, all hands hoisting sail,
They swung him like a keg of ale,
Where looking forth in prospect wide
His tory errors he espied.'

The Tories bided their time and waited for revenge. The most spectacular instance of this revenge took place at Sandwich a few days after the proceedings of the Body of the People just described, and was directed against Colonel Freeman.

This gentleman's patriotic activities had not prevented him from continuing his medical practice, and late one night he was aroused by a call to the bedside of a sick friend. Freeman promptly set out, though he felt little confidence in the authenticity of the summons, and was not surprised as he passed Newcomb's Tavern, a favorite resort for Sandwich Loyalists, to be accosted by a small group, who came out and announced in ironic tones that they were a Committee from the Body of the People, and that they had orders to bring him before that assemblage to answer for his conduct as leader of the recent demonstration at Barnstable. Freeman replied that he would have nothing to do with them or their tavern. They then fell upon the Doctor, knocked him down, and might have killed him but for the arrival of some Patriots who came running to his support. He was carried home, his wounds were bandaged, and a warrant for the arrest of his assailants was immediately issued. This was a lucky thing for them, for it alone prevented what would have looked very much like a lynching party with the Patriots on the lower end of the rope. But the law took its course, and the Court, which was convened at West Barnstable with the venerable James Otis as Chief Justice, fined the ruffians £100 and forced them to give bonds for their good behavior in the future. The fury of the Patriots was partially allayed by this action, but it was not satisfied. They erected a platform in Sandwich, marched the Tories from the Courthouse to it, and compelled them to subscribe to the following apology and recantation:

Whereas the subscribers did attack and cruelly beat Dr. Nathaniel Freeman with such unparalleled cowardice and barbarity as would disgrace the character of a ruffian or a Hottentot, for no other reason or provocation than that he, uninfluenced by hope or fear, has dared to stem the tide of tyranny and corruption ... we sincerely and heartily ask forgiveness of Heaven, whose sacred laws we have so shamefully violated, and of Dr. Freeman, a gentleman to whom we are indebted for the most important services done this Country.... And we do solemnly engage for the future religiously to regard the laws of God and man and conduct ourselves in all respects as becometh friends to society and good government.

Sandwich, Oct. 10, 1774.

But the Loyalists were not all conciliatory, nor would they always recant. Benjamin Percival, of South Sandwich, has this pithy entry in his diary for February 25, 1778: 'Went to town to see the tories take the oath of Allegiance but they all refused it.' Even those who grudgingly apologized for their behavior were by no means convinced of the error of their ways, any more than a Fiji Islander, who, for the sake of expediency, assures the missionary that the Christian religion is the only religion, becomes thereby a pillar of the Church.

Sandwich and Barnstable were not the only Cape towns that were troubled by Loyalists. There were enough of them in Truro to make things very uncomfortable, personally and professionally, for Dr. Adams, the town physician and a staunch patriot. They contemplated storming his house, but were prevented by some of the cooler heads among their number. They did succeed, however, in seriously curtailing his practice by establishing a tabu on consulting him professionally. They preferred to remain sick, or to go elsewhere for a physician whose political sentiments were closer to their own. Misery loves company, and Dr. Adams found a congenial spirit in the Reverend Mr. Upham, the patriotic clergyman of Truro. This gentleman entertained at his house a group of citizens whose patriotism, like his own, burned hot and strong, and Dr. Adams, in a letter dated December 5, 1774, says that the minister was slandered outrageously by certain Loyalist members of the parish, and was refused admission to their houses.

Nowadays, when it is the fashion to point complacently to a pirate or two or a witch among the branches of the family tree, there is no need of repeating the stock justification for Loyalists. But Loyalists on the Cape had more than the stock justification. In the first place, the British navy was the best and largest in the world, and the Cape consisted entirely of unprotected shore line, with the crooked finger of Long Point beckoning the British fleet into the shelter of Provincetown Harbor. Most of the Cape money was by this time invested in shipping of one kind or another, and many of the inhabitants were sailors. In case of war, the former would be ruined and the latter idle. The only chance of protecting the shores was by a large and well-equipped home guard for every town. Instead of being allowed to maintain such home guards, the Cape towns would certainly be called upon to furnish their full quota of men and material for the Continental armies. Their families and homes would thus be left defenseless.

Here, then, was a situation that might well give pause to the stoutest Patriot and lend color to the pretexts of the most craven Loyalist. Brave men who were willing to fight for freedom might well think twice if they lived on the Cape; and cowards in search of escape from the thunder of the guns that sounded closer and closer in their ears, found in these reflections a highly respectable refuge. Remember, then, in considering the question of the Cape's patriotism, that every one of her citizens who first voted for Independence and then marched off to fight, knew that, though a committee would try to see to it that his family did not starve, his house stood on a shore that was unprotected against landing parties, and his family had only an insignificant home guard to protect them.

Events showed that these fears were prophetic. The British were quick to realize the strategic value of Provincetown Harbor as a base for naval operations, and promptly sailed in with a fleet of frigates — the celebrated Somerset among them — and dropped anchor just off the town. This gave them control, not only of Provincetown, which, consisting of only a score or so of dwelling-houses, was of itself of no great importance, but of Truro as well, and Truro was a far more considerable settlement. That the enemy never attacked either town is explained quite simply by the fact that no attack was necessary. So completely defenseless were the shores, and so inadequate was Truro's home guard, that the Britishers were free to go ashore as they pleased and help themselves to fresh water and provisions. They did, it is true, indulge in a little minor raiding alongshore, in small boats, but for the most part their coming and going was peaceable, and as month followed month, their relations with the townspeople became almost friendly. Before the end of the war, a chaplain from one of the British frigates was preaching in the Truro church, though the record does not add that he was entertained after the service at the homes of the townspeople! That the British officers were not insensible to the charms of the Cape girls appears from the fact that Dr. William Thayer, a surgeon on one of His Britannic Majesty's frigates that was anchored in Provincetown Harbor, married Lucy Rich, of South Truro, and after the war settled there with his wife and practiced medicine until he died.

Such instances of fraternizing and affection were, however, exceptional. Provincetown and Truro were hostile to the fleet, and the fleet was hostile to the towns. There is the story of a comic maneuver executed by the captain of the little Truro home guard. He saw a raiding party push off from the fleet in small boats and head for shore. He promptly mustered his handful of recruits, marched them to a convenient rise of ground at the water's edge and kept them marching round and round it until the British from their boats concluded that a large armed force was at hand to receive them, and returned to their ships without more ado. This yarn smacks of local jingoism, but is quite in accord with the Cape Cod sense of humor and with the British tactics at Truro and Provincetown. They were not looking for a fight, and doubtless landed somewhere else quite unmolested the next day.

But it was warfare all the same. If the townspeople ventured outside the harbor for a mess of fish, there was danger of being picked up by the enemy, as David Snow and his father were. They were fishing off the back side of Truro in a small boat, were captured by one of the British vessels, and did not see home again for seven years. Always, too, the inhabitants had to endure the humiliation of helplessness. They never forgot that the Englishmen could sack the town at any moment. With this emergency in view, they had a committee ready to discuss terms of capitulation if it should be necessary. Exactly what form this capitulation was to take does not appear from the intentionally non-committal language of the record. Probably they would have bought exemptions from bombardment.

The British squadron did not confine its attention to Provincetown and Truro. Hardly a day passed but the sails of His Majesty's frigates cast gray shadows across some Cape town and kept them all in a state of vigilance and alarm. Militia detachments were detailed to watch the shore even in villages as well protected by nature as Sandwich. If these militia companies had been left intact, they would have furnished considerable security; but they were no sooner formed than orders came from headquarters directing them to march off to Cambridge or Providence to join the Continental forces. The staunchest Patriot resented withdrawing troops from his scantily guarded shores to go to the aid of towns that were safely tucked away inland among the hills. Colonel Joseph Otis (now a general) writes in 1778, 'There is scarcely a day that the enemy is not within gun shot of some part of our coast, and they very often anchor in our harbors.' Again he writes, in reply to an order for fifty men to go to Providence, 'As the enemy are around and threaten danger here, it is like dragging men from home when their houses are on fire. But I will do my best to comply.' Once more he says, 'Highanos is much exposed; and to draw men off to Falmouth causes much uneasiness.' A little later a whole militia company was ordered from Barnstable to Boston. Colonel Hallett, of Yarmouth, replied, 'The general opinion that prevails among the people here is that this county is so much exposed on both sides to the enemy that it would be very dangerous to send off those men.' Again, two months after the signing of the Declaration of Independence, twenty per cent of all the Cape militia was ordered to New York, and sixty whaleboats assembled at Falmouth to transport them.

But the constant demands for men were not all that was required of the Cape. Boots, beef, and blankets in a steady stream poured out of its towns until it looked as if nothing would be left. The situation was desperate. The citizens looked from the rotting hulls of their fishing schooners to the sails of the British fleet that hung ever in the offing, and wondered what the end would be. The strain became too great for some of the weaker spirits. They flew the white flag and petitioned to be allowed to move their families to Kennebec or the Provinces, in spite of the embargo that the Government, partly to forestall this maneuver and partly to prevent their falling into the hands of the enemy, had placed on outgoing vessels.

But desperation more often engendered reckless and in fact illegal valor, and for every man who begged to be allowed to go to Kennebec, there were a dozen who resolved to defy the embargo, run the British blockade, and trade with New York or Rhode Island. Sometimes these adventurous traders succeeded for a voyage or two. More often they failed, as did two little vessels that in October, 1779, set sail from Hyannis for Stonington. One was captured; the other driven ashore. This disaster was the harder to bear because it was effected by Loyalist refugees who had established themselves in considerable numbers on Nantucket and Martha's Vineyard, where their knowledge of Cape waters proved of great value to the enemy. A more insidious practice of the British was to issue propaganda encouraging deserters. Notable among these propagandists was one Leonard, who is picturesquely described as head 'of the Loyalist gang in the Sound.' This worthy suggested to the desperate Patriots that they were fighting against their will, and promised protection and comfort to all who would come over to the enemy. Some no doubt yielded to the temptation, but strange to say their numbers were offset by a trickle of returning Loyalists, who, through the dark days of their indecision, had finally seen the light, and now avowed their allegiance to the cause of Independence.

The skill of the British in holding up blockade-runners led indirectly to the only real engagement between the local militia and His Majesty's troops that occurred on Cape soil — the attack on Falmouth in the spring of 1779. The situation of Falmouth was in one respect the most precarious of any of the Cape towns. It was close to the Elizabeth Islands, and these islands formed a very convenient base for British naval operations. Tarpaulin Cove in particular was a point of concentration for the King's ships, and from this snug anchorage a series of raids along the Falmouth shore provoked the citizens to retaliation.

The British in their raids used a type of boat called shaving mills. These were good-sized sailboats of light construction and shallow draft. They usually mounted a single gun forward. The largest of them had three masts which could be easily unstepped and stowed with their sails, so as not to be in the way. They could carry twenty-five men and still leave room for as much beef and mutton as they were likely to capture in a single raid. If they were so lucky as to pick up an unguarded Yankee schooner moored alongshore, so much the better; they had men enough to sail her off. Equipped with these craft and sometimes piloted by renegade Patriots, the British succeeded in diminishing the food supply of Falmouth until the inhabitants were at their wits' end. Their fury was increased when the enemy on one occasion captured a schooner that had run the blockade and was returning to Falmouth with a cargo of corn which she had procured on a voyage to the Connecticut River. This was the last straw, and Major Joseph Dimmock determined to recapture the schooner. He manned three whaleboats and rowed off by night to Tarpaulin Cove, where the vessel lay. As soon as it was light enough to locate the schooner and her captor, Dimmock and his three boats rowed up to them at top speed, boarded the schooner, retook her, and sailed out of the Cove. After further adventures and more fighting, he finally got her safely into Woods Hole.

A few such exploits stung the British into planning an elaborate attack on Falmouth with the object of burning the town. They assembled a fleet of about ten vessels, and on April 2, 1779, anchored close to shore and began to send off landing parties under the protection of a barrage from their heavy guns. The townspeople had received warning in time to get reënforcements of two militia companies from Sandwich to bolster up their own home guard. While they were waiting for these reenforcements, the Falmouth men improved their time by entrenching themselves alongshore. The Sandwich companies arrived before daylight and established themselves beside their Falmouth brethren in the new trenches, so that the British landing parties, as they rowed toward shore, were confronted by a force more than twice as large as they had ever seen there before, and by proportionally brisk volleys of musketry. This gave the attack a different complexion; so instead of trying to land, they returned to their vessels — no doubt for further orders — and they did not again disembark. The cannon balls did some damage, but as they were aimed chiefly at the breastworks instead of at the town itself, most of the buildings escaped without injury, and the fleet soon after sailed away. One result of this repulse was particularly gratifying — the trickle of returning Loyalists increased to a stream.

Yet the situation of the Cape was critical. Her shipping was ruined; the shores infested by hostile warships; the militia ordered inland; the cattle either requisitioned or taken by the enemy. But though they foresaw these consequences, most of the Cape towns had voted for war. One, however, Barnstable, stands out as an exception, and failed to instruct its Representative to vote in favor of the Declaration of Independence. The fact is of particular significance, for Barnstable, as the county seat, should have set the pace for her neighbors up and down the Cape. That she failed at this critical moment in the Nation's history is a serious blot on her patriotism, and was so regarded by many Barnstable citizens, who protested that the action of the town failed to represent the wish of the majority of the townspeople.

The meeting at which this unpatriotic decision was reached took place on June 25, 1776. The language of the resolution is a little guarded, though its intention is clear enough. It reads: 'Voted not to give any instructions to the Representative with regard to Independence.' Colonel Joseph Otis and twenty-two other indignant Barnstable Patriots immediately published a protest. Sturgis Gorham, who had been present at the meeting and had voted with the majority, answered the protest in language that makes it look as if the phrasing of the resolution had been made purposely non-committal in order to leave a loophole in case of just such an attack as Otis's. Gorham said that there was nothing in the language of the resolution to indicate that the town *did absolutely refuse to support the cause of Independence if such a course seemed necessary.* This kind of hedging reflects no more credit on the town than the vote itself does. Weathervanes have their uses, however, and Gorham's reply at least shows the strength of Otis's patriotic blast. What actually happened at this famous town meeting was this.

The Loyalist camp, headed by Edward Bacon, Esq., ably seconded by Nymphas Marston, the moderator, so intimidated the meaner spirits that out of a total of one hundred and forty, only sixty-five dared to vote at all. Of these, thirty voted in favor of instructing their Representative for Independence; thirty-five voted against it. General Otis's contention was that if the silent seventy-five had not been bullied out of voting, the town would have gone patriotic. Whether he is right or wrong is a matter of no consequence. The fact remains that of those who had the courage to vote in spite of Squire Bacon, five more were against the Declaration of Independence than were for it; and little confidence can be put in the patriotic zeal of men who let themselves be beaten into silence on such a question, even by so impressive a figure as the Squire.

Surely the seed of Independence has flourished mightily in a century and a half! To-day, if the wealthiest man in a Cape town rises in meeting and declares that the town should do thus and so, it is regarded by the citizens as a pretty good reason for voting in the negative. Feudalism has gone out of style since the days of Caleb Williams. But it was feudalism, or something very like it, that prevented Bacon from being arrested and his property sold. Throughout the Revolution he never wavered in his loyalty to the Crown; yet, far from being molested or ostracized, he was in 1778 elected a Representative to the Legislature. Thanks to another protest by Joseph Otis, however, Bacon was excluded from a seat in the House and returned to Barnstable. But his political prestige did not suffer from this rebuff, for in 1780 he was a member of the General Court, a position which he had already held several times before, notably in 1774, when he had been forced by the Body of the People to resign his commission in the militia and abandon his office as justice. He died at his home in Barnstable in 1783.

The Cape's best efforts in the war, naturally enough, were on the sea, where many of the citizens had earned a living before the war began. Twenty-one vessels — ranging all the way from shaving mills to ships — were commanded by Cape-Codders, and carried in all one hundred and twenty-six guns and more than six hundred men — not a bad showing for an impoverished region. Besides these twenty-one captains, a good percentage of the crews of other privateers were Cape fishermen or traders. The General Arnold is a case in point. In December, 1778, she sailed out of Boston on a cruise to harass Britishers off the Southern States. In trying to weather the Cape, she was driven back by a northeast gale, and anchored off Plymouth Harbor in a temporary lull which Captain Magee mistook for the end of the storm. With the renewal of the storm, the Arnold dragged, pounded her seams open on the flats and filled with water almost to the main deck, driving the men from their shelter below. They stayed on deck, exposed to a blinding snowstorm and smothered with flying spray, from Saturday afternoon until Monday morning. Of her crew of one hundred and five, seventy-eight froze to death. Of these, eleven were Barnstable men and one came from Falmouth. Another disaster gives us significant figures. In the fall of 1780, the British captured the American privateer brig Resolution and sent her crew to the Old Mill Prison. Among them were sixteen Cape men, chiefly from Wellfleet and Truro.

The Yankees were quick to see the effectiveness of shaving mills for coastwise raids, and these extraordinary craft, manned by Americans, cruised along the shores of the British Provinces, plundering towns exactly as the British plundered the Cape. A party landed in a shaving mill near Barrington, Nova Scotia, intent on raiding the sheep-pen of one Hezekiah Smith. Some of them went to the door of the farmhouse and looked in. Among them was a young Cape-Codder, who, as soon as he got a good look at the inhabitants of the house, cried 'Hello, Aunt Nabby! How are you?' Aunt Nabby, it appears, was one of those with whom the Cape air had not agreed, and who had emigrated some years previously to this secluded spot in search of peace. She must have realized the futility of her flight when she recognized, in this cheerful Yankee raider, a nephew whose family had been made of sterner stuff and had stayed on the Cape. The conclusion of this yarn is the standard one and has been told of both sides in every war in the world. Aunt Nabby took a gun from the corner and announced that she would shoot the first man who stole a sheep. The invaders returned shame-faced to their boats without any mutton!

Here is a more creditable privateering exploit, and one that was conceived and carried out entirely by Cape-Codders. In 1779, two English vessels, one of them the General Leslie of twelve guns, lay in Old Town Harbor, Martha's Vineyard, guarding some recent American prizes. Captain Joseph Dimmock, of Falmouth, whose previous exploits have been described, determined to attack them. He collected twenty-five fellow townsmen and fitted out a little sloop with two three-pounders. Thus equipped, he set sail for Old Town Harbor, boarded the General Leslie amid a brisk fire of musketry, forced the crew below, battened down the hatches, and brought her into Hyannis along with his own little vessel.

Benjamin Franklin and John Adams, Commissioners in France, give in their communications some important information as to the numbers of Cape-Codders the British found on the American privateers they captured. Adams writes, 'Whenever an English man-o'-war has taken an American vessel, they have given the whalemen among the crew . . . their choice either to go on board a man-o'-war and fight against their country or go into the [British] whale fisheries.' So much by way of introduction. The joint communication from the Commissioners follows: 'The English last year (1777) carried on a very valuable whale fishery . . . off the River Plate. They have this year about seventeen vessels in this fishery. *All the officers and almost all the men belonging to these seventeen vessels, are Americans from Nantucket and Cape Cod,* . . . excepting two or three from Rhode Island and perhaps one from Long Island.'

Sometimes Fate took a hand in the fortunes of the Colonies and delivered a British ship to them free in their back yards. The outer shore of the Cape is about the most dangerous spot on the Atlantic Coast, and it was not to be expected that the Britishers, with all their skill, could cruise there off and on for seven years with impunity. The Cape's long, exposed coast line paid its inhabitants back from time to time for the anxiety it cost them. One such payment was the wreck of His Majesty's transport Friendship, which came ashore on the back side of Truro late in the winter of 1776, and furnished General Washington's army with paint, canvas, and other marine stores, as well as cannon and small arms. A year or so later, another British vessel, the Cumberland, found her grave on the Yarmouth flats.

But the enemy's most serious loss was the ship-of-war Somerset in November, 1778. The Somerset mounted sixty-four guns and was one of the vessels that had been sailing in and out of Provincetown Harbor at will since the beginning of the war. It was, therefore, a happy day for the townspeople when she struck on the outer bar near Dead Man's Hollow, not far from the Highland at North Truro, pounded over with the rising tide, and hit the beach helpless. The home guard took four hundred and eighty survivors in charge, and they were marched by Captain Enoch Hallett through a chain of jubilant villages to Boston. Two months later, the General Court directed the sheriff to sell the contents of the ship — a somewhat naïve order, for though Colonel Doane, of Wellfleet, had been officially put in charge of the wreck, by the time the sheriff's sale took place she had been picked clean by local mooncussers. This, no doubt, is what General Joseph Otis, a master of racy phraseology, refers to as 'wicked work at the wreck'; or perhaps he refers to what was bound to happen if a Truro and a Provincetown man got hold of the same coil of ratline-stuff at the same moment.

Another wreck — the most picturesque of them all, though important only for what it shows us of the Provincetowners' state of mind and morals — occurred very early in the war. In March, 1776, Jolly Allen, a prosperous Boston shopkeeper and a staunch Tory, deciding, like many of his ilk, that a change of scene was indicated, chartered the sloop Sally and engaged a captain to sail him with his wife and family and all their possessions to Halifax. The Captain, who did not know one end of a vessel from the other, soon had the Sally pounding on Peaked Hill Bars behind Provincetown, with her sails blown to ribbons. He did not even know how to take them in; a halyard and a bobstay were one and the same thing to him. Allen was justly indignant, and to add to his troubles, one of the party, Mrs. Wezzle by name, came down with smallpox.

It did not take long for news of the Sally's predicament to

reach Provincetown. A couple of citizens who had had small-pox rowed off and brought all hands ashore. Allen was put in a wretched hovel, through which wind and weather blew with perfect freedom; here his wife died. The Sally was floated high and dry on the beach, and the selectmen sent a message to the General Court stating that in their opinion her company were 'some of those vermin which have been so destructive to the peace and good order of the Colony,' and asking what they should do with them.

Up to this point the Provincetown men had behaved with commendable propriety. But while they were waiting for a reply from headquarters, they improved their time by looting the Sally with the thoroughness and dispatch of which only experienced mooncussers are capable. Under the pretext of saving the cargo for the colonial authorities, they began carting it across the sand hills to town; but so small a fraction of each wagonload ever reached the village that it was laughable. Pious citizens took pleasure in visiting Allen in his shanty and regaling him with graphic accounts of how he was being robbed. 'A gentleman of veracity came to me,' he writes, 'and ... said he had seen one of the completest battles he ever had in his life, and all on my account. About fifteen or sixteen men and women was fighting battle royal in the fields, and condemning one another, and each saying the other had taken more of my property than they.'

Allen had need of the vein of whimsical philosophy with which he seems to have been blessed. He saw that there was nothing for him to do but grin and bear it, and began making friends with some of his callers. To convince them that he was no stranger to misfortune, he related how he had been deceived by the pseudo-captain of the Sally. This tale elicited instant and genuine sympathy from his seagoing captors, for sympathy was cheap, and Allen's goods were all safely in their possession. To quote again from the unhappy merchant's narrative, 'the people, as incensed as they was against the government and their friends, when they heard my case, how I had been used by the Captain, ... they was ready to tear him to pieces. They called him a fresh-water captain; that they should not choose to hang a salt-water Captain, but a fresh-water Captain, it would

give them all the pleasure imaginable.' It looks as though a
strain of the old wild blood still ran in the Provincetown veins!
To crown their impertinence, they sent the General Court a bill
for one hundred and fifty pounds for their exertions in saving
the sloop's cargo. No wonder Allen was glad to be rid of Cape-
Codders and to try his luck, as he soon after did, with the
authorities in Watertown instead.

A few days after the wreck of the Somerset, James Otis, the
venerable Chief Justice, died. This gentleman's advanced age
prevented him from taking any part in the Revolution that
called for great physical exertion. He was not able, like his son
James, to start a war or, like his son Joseph, to command a
brigade; but he had worked himself to high places in affairs of
state. He started life as a mechanic and ended as Judge of
Probate, Chief Justice of the Court of Common Pleas, and
President of the Council, which meant that he was the chief
executive magistrate in Massachusetts after the departure of
General Gage. These honors he achieved with no education
beyond the grammar school. He was repeatedly elected to the
Provincial Legislature and was twice Speaker of the House. He
remained throughout his life a level-headed Patriot, respected
even by his enemies, and the head of a family that has brought
much honor to Cape Cod.

An anecdote will show the extraordinary way in which Otis
kept matters in their proper perspective, even through the trying times when perspectives were frequently lost. One day as
he stood with some friends in the doorway of his house, a certain Bill Blachford, a deserter from the army, came hobbling
along the road on his way from camp, bent almost double with
rheumatism. As President of the War Council, it was Otis's
duty to arrest deserters. 'Hullo!' said one of his friends;
'there's Bill Blachford!' Otis instantly turned his back to the
road and entered the house. 'Where is the rascal?' he cried.
'I can't see him.'

Far more tragic than the death of the old Chief Justice was
the death of his son James, who was struck by lightning and
instantly killed in the spring of 1783. Though he lived to see
the triumphant end of the war for which he was so largely responsible, it meant nothing to him. His mind was gone, and the

orator, whose eloquence twenty years before had electrified the colonists, now babbled of green fields and blinked at the sun. There was mercy in the lightning that killed him.

The condition of the Cape at the end of the Revolution was, in fact, nothing to cheer any man who contemplated it. The constant calls for men and material had drained the towns dry. Their commerce was gone; their fishing vessels were hauled out and the daisies grew rank between their seams; what little money they had was worthless through depreciation. The most eloquent proof of their poverty is found in the bald phrases of the report of a committee sent by the General Court in 1782 to investigate the condition of the Cape towns: 'We have fully and critically attended to the service and are satisfied that the several towns in said [Barnstable] County have complied with the utmost of their abilities with the requisitions made upon them by the General Court for beef and men, and that said towns are incapable of complying therewith any further.' The committee further reported that 'all deficiencies of beef or men due from any of the towns in the County of Barnstable should be abated to them and that all fines for said deficiencies should be remitted.' In the following spring (1783) the State Treasurer was directed 'to recall the executions issued for taxes and to stay in the future, until further ordered, executions for two-thirds of the taxes.' This order applied to the towns of Eastham, Harwich, Yarmouth, Barnstable, Sandwich, and Falmouth.

It is not the custom of governments to excuse requisitions or to remit taxes. The fact that the General Court of Massachusetts did both these things is evidence enough of the impoverished condition of the county. The Cape weathered the storm and emerged, shattered but triumphant, with plenty of searoom to refit.

CHAPTER VIII

FROM THE REVOLUTION TO THE CIVIL WAR ASHORE

THE surrender of Cornwallis was followed by six years of black
bewilderment and depression, during which New England
tottered, regained her balance, and tottered again; always on
the brink of disaster. Too many readjustments had to be made
— too many unprecedented and unimagined situations confronted her. Before the war, the salt tang of the winds from the
sea had been the breath of life to all New England. Nowhere on
the Atlantic Coast had whales or codfish been safe from New
England harpoons and handlines. British wharves were piled
high with casks of colonial whale oil, and the West Indies
bought all the salt fish that home ports rejected. But now, with
the white elephant of Independence on their hands, Boston
merchants found the traditional European markets closed.
Winds from the ocean still piped to them, but they could not
dance. Their vessels lay rotting from disuse or had been captured during the war. Bewildered by the complete change in
their economic universe, and hampered by wagonloads of worthless colonial currency, the Bay State shipowners floundered in
the doldrums while England laughed.

But there was enough vigor and virtue in the blood of our
ancestors to carry them through these six years of blind man's
buff. Strong wine lay underneath the bubbles of confusion and
brought long thoughts into the heads of youthful merchants,
who rightly concluded that Europe was not the world, and that,
if European churlishness saw fit to bar its gates to American
vessels, they would head westward instead and knock at more
hospitable doors across the Pacific. The Cape, which was the
saltiest corner of this salty community, was well represented in
these wildly speculative voyages. The experiences of some of
her shipmasters will be told in another chapter. Less spectacular but quite as useful was the unrecognized resumption of the
West India trade, which began to flourish again even in the
islands that were English possessions. The arm of British law,

for all its length, could barely span the Atlantic; the islanders felt none of the bitterness toward the new nation that the old country did. Yankee fishermen, by hook or by crook, swapped cargoes with Jamaica traders on forbidden docks, and thereby managed to keep the turnover of exports and imports brisk at home during the long absences of the Canton merchantmen.

The Napoleonic Wars gave Yankee enterprise a fine chance for neutral trade, which was carried on in a brisk and miscellaneous fashion; even British ports were sometimes opened just wide enough to let a Yankee vessel slip in if she carried a useful cargo. To cut a long and intricate story short, maritime New England, after a few years of post-Revolutionary doldrums, had got its sea legs once more and was squared away on what looked like a long and prosperous tack.

Ashore, too, prosperity returned quickly, and as business gathered headway, the Cape divided its stock, as it had done when it prospered before, and created two towns for one. Yarmouth in 1793, by an almost unanimous vote, allowed the eastern part of the village to incorporate independently as Dennis, so named for the Reverend Josiah Dennis, a former pastor of the West Parish. Four years later, Orleans became a separate town, instead of continuing as a part of Eastham. These divisions were achieved amicably; but when, in 1803, Brewster split from Harwich, as Harwich had split from Eastham, there came near being a diminutive civil war. However, the transaction was put through, and Brewster, named for the pious Elder of Plymouth, is to-day one of the proudest towns on the Cape. These were among the last incorporations that took place. The settlements were now at last divided enough to satisfy every one's passion for independence, and the towns have remained pretty much *in statu quo* ever since.

But as the European wars continued, they became grimmer and more ruthless. Napoleon's navy made no bones about seizing American merchantmen that were carrying cargoes to British ports, and the British on a few occasions picked the crews from Yankee vessels and impressed them into His Majesty's service. In the face of such outrages, Jefferson had to do something. If he had been a prophet, he would have declared war in 1807. Instead he tried to avoid further trouble by keeping American sailors at home. His Embargo of 1807 forbade our ships to engage in trade with any foreign port. Even China came under the ban, because a large part of every cargo from the East was exported to Europe after a sojourn on New England docks.

The Embargo knocked Massachusetts' feet from under her just as she had got back into her stride. Yankee sailors were thrown into a state of rebellious idleness. They must either submit and become farmers or break the law. No part of the State was harder hit than the Cape. Her fishermen could no longer carry their fares to foreign ports, and half their vessels lay rotting once more at abandoned wharves. The villages were filled with idle men who spent their days in vehement and not always very intelligent invective against the Administration. Others, though they felt no less hostile toward the Embargo, chose a more sensible method of trying to remedy it. They called town meetings and petitioned Jefferson to have it lifted.

Still others showed an active instead of an oratorical rebellion by trading in spite of the Embargo. A group of Brewster merchants fitted one of their vessels for a voyage to Surinam out of Plymouth. She was hardly clear of the land when a Government boat seized her and took her into Provincetown, where she would have shared the fate of the fishing fleet and perished at the dock if the Brewster owners had not sent a crew across the Bay to recapture her and resume the voyage. This raid was so unexpected that it succeeded. By the time the United States Marshal arrived, the vessel was well on her way, and no one in Brewster or Provincetown could give him any information about her.

But in spite of occasional flashes of the old fire, the Cape, with its small vessels, small capital, and small fleets, suffered severely — far worse than the merchant princes of Boston and Salem, who had ships abroad that continued to trade without coming home, and who had money enough in the bank to tide them over a few lean years. With the Cape it was small investments and quick returns, or nothing. Since this was precisely the sort of trade that the Government could most effectively stop, it is no wonder that hostility to the Embargo blazed even hotter on the Cape than in the larger seaports.

True, Jefferson, after turning a deaf ear to scores of petitions, finally raised the Embargo in the spring of 1809. Massachusetts deep-sea voyagers became neutral traders once more, and a few Cape families cheered up for the moment. But the Embargo had lasted long enough to ruin most of them. They were not the minions of merchant princes with a command awaiting them; they were their own capitalists, and recommissioning their schooners was slow work. They had no more than begun to gather headway when they were held in irons once more by a new embargo which was the preface to war. The declaration of war sunk them as surely as a torpedo from a submarine. No wonder they regarded it as the crowning folly of a treacherous Administration.

Under such conditions it is not surprising that the Cape's part in the War of 1812 was an inglorious one. Throughout the hostilities, most of her towns shared the sullen and defiant attitude that was reflected in the resolution which the citizens of Yarmouth drew up in a town meeting of 1814:

Voted unanimously, that as this town have ever expressed their decided disapprobation of the present ruinous and unhappy war, and have hitherto refrained from engaging in the same; we are still determined not to engage in, encourage or support it any further than we are compelled to do, by the laws of the country of which we are citizens.

Except for their state of mind, this war was for Cape-Codders a short and diluted repetition of the Revolution. As soon as vessels could be spared from European waters, the British sent a fleet across to begin operations along the Atlantic Coast. The frigates Majestic and Spencer established themselves in Provincetown Harbor, where their officers passed the time agreeably enough, going ashore, strolling about the towns of Truro and Provincetown, purchasing whatever the townsfolk had for sale, and smiling gayly at the girls, for whom the arrival of a bargeload of young Britishers from the Majestic was no hardship.

Commodore Ragget, of the Spencer, had a more unpleasant assignment, albeit a bloodless one. It was his duty to sail along the shores of the Cape, threatening to burn the towns unless they paid him ransom. Naturally enough, in view of the citizens' attitude toward the war, Ragget met with considerable success. Eastham and Brewster dug up $1200 and $4000 respectively, and their citizens slept peacefully in consequence. Truro had a 'Committee of Safety' whose exact function is shrouded in darkness. Nobody could blame them if they, too, decided to pay the price of security, but the town records are non-committal on this delicate subject, just as they were at similar critical moments during the Revolution. In Wellfleet the Committee of Safety had instructions not only to be ready to negotiate for exemption from attack, but also 'in all cases and at all times to so conduct as to keep in as much friendship with the said enemy as possible, making the Constitution and laws of the United States and the Constitution of Massachusetts their guide as far as they can with safety to the particularily exposed position of the said town of Wellfleet to the enemy.' Sandwich considered what course to follow if threatened and valiantly decided to defend herself 'to the last extremity.' Without wishing to detract from the staunchness of her citizens, it may be observed that Sandwich was far less accessible to an attack from the sea than the towns on the lower Cape. A narrow neck of beach, with an expanse of salt marsh inside it, stretches almost the whole length of the shore line. A handful of militiamen, strategically hidden at the edge of the upland, could have made life very unpleasant for a landing party that had to pick its way between the salt holes and flounder through the muddy creeks of this marsh. Such a shore front reduced to one or two the number of points at which the British could land in Sandwich, and Ragget might blaze away with all the cannon the Spencer carried without landing a single shot in the town, so remote were its houses from deep water.

Barnstable was similarly protected from cannonade, and so was Yarmouth. The fact is that the whole Bay side of the Cape presented a singularly uninviting prospect to invaders, whether it was their intention to stand off and bombard the towns or send landing parties ashore in small boats. The buildings did not line the water's edge, but stood well back, leaving a wide belt of rough country for the assailants to cross before they reached the villages. Salt works were the only valuable objects near shore. These might, indeed, have been destroyed without much trouble and they formed the most telling item in the British threat.

That Ragget realized these difficulties and was therefore bluffing the towns into paying the money appears from his dealings with Orleans, the only town on the lower Cape that refused to pay up. The Commodore could hardly ignore the indignant rejection of his offer; so he went through the motions of sending off a landing party, and a small group of the enemy actually came ashore. But they had no intention of fighting if they could help it; some musket shots from the Orleans militia were enough to turn them back. By this demonstration the town showed that it was ready to stand behind the vote it had cast in the last two elections, when in 1813 it had returned a large majority for Varnum, the war candidate for Governor, and a still larger one for Dexter the next year.

But the troubles of Orleans were not over. History repeated itself when the British frigate Newcastle went aground in December, 1814, on the flats off the Bay side of the town. This ship was luckier than the Somerset, however, for by stripping her of some spars and rigging, the crew managed to work her off. The spars went ashore, but these were thin pickings in comparison with what the citizens had hoped for when they first saw the Newcastle aground. Nothing so completely destroys a seaman's temper as to get his vessel into trouble in the sight of spectators. When the spectators are men with whom he is at war, his exasperation is all the greater. The captain of the Newcastle, therefore, vented his wrath on Orleans by sending a barge into Rock Harbor and seizing a small schooner named the Betsy and three sloops, the Camel, Washington, and Nancy. Two of the vessels lay on the mud, and so were set on fire. The others, the Betsy and the Camel, were manned by prize crews and headed for British headquarters in Provincetown Harbor. The young midshipman who commanded the Betsy ordered an Orleans man, who had been acting as ship-keeper at the time of her capture, to pilot her out; but he loyally ran her on the beach near Yarmouth, where she fell an easy prey to the citizens, after a sojourn of only a few hours in hostile hands. The British had better luck with the Camel, which arrived safely at Provincetown and was never retaken.

Meanwhile, there had been lively doings farther up the Cape. Falmouth, like Orleans, had voted for war and was called upon to stand to its guns. The citizens had taken pot-shots from time to time at British cruisers that passed within range of their two field pieces, and had quite properly seized the Nantucket packet on the ground that the islanders were aiding the enemy. This charge was probably true, for Nantucket men, faced with the alternative of declaring themselves neutral or starving to death, had wisely declared themselves neutral. It was a short step from this position to piloting British vessels in the Sound, and the chances are that some Nantucketers could have been found thus employed. At any rate, the Englishmen regarded them as friends, and the captain of the British brig Nimrod demanded the surrender of the field pieces and the packet.

Captain Weston Jenkins, commander of the Falmouth Artillery Company, replied that the British were at liberty to try to get them. The invitation was accepted; word came back from the Nimrod that the citizens had two hours in which to move their non-combatants out of range; then the town would be knocked to pieces.

Two hours proved to be adequate. When the first cannon ball landed, the houses were empty, and the militia safe in trenches alongshore. The Nimrod blazed away for several hours, but made no real attempt to set a landing party ashore. Nobody was hurt, and after the bombardment ceased, the inhabitants returned to inspect the damage. One house had been badly smashed, a few others had received a shot or two, and some salt works had been struck, but otherwise it was the same old town. This incident occurred in January, 1814.

The following months saw some random plundering along the Falmouth shore with Captain Jenkins swapping raid for raid with the British. The chief offenders in plundering were the crew of the privateer Retaliation, Captain Porter. During the spring and summer his men had given the citizens little peace. Finally, in the fall of 1814, Jenkins decided to capture the vessel while she lay in Tarpaulin Cove, a favorite resort of British cruisers. He assembled about thirty volunteers, embarked on the sloop Two Friends, and set sail for the Retaliation. His crew had to row most of the way and finally arrived in broad daylight near enough to be seen from the enemy's deck.

Captain Jenkins then anchored and ordered all but one or two of his men to get out of sight. The trick worked well. A boat filled with British sailors immediately bore down on the Two Friends like a duck coming to decoys. When she was alongside, the Falmouth volunteers stood up and pointed their muskets in the faces of the Britishers, who surrendered without more ado. Jenkins now outnumbered the enemy about two to one; it was therefore no very desperate enterprise for him to sail up to the Retaliation and demand her surrender. The whole maneuver went without a hitch. The Britisher was taken into harbor by a prize crew, and the Falmouth shore was left in peace.

At intervals during this random war, the Cape harbors received visitors more welcome than the British. Late in 1812, the ship American Hero with a cargo from India slipped into Barnstable Harbor on a high tide and drew her first free breath for weeks. There must have been busy evenings at Crocker's Tavern when her officers came ashore to stretch their legs. If Mr. Madison's port ear did not burn after these sessions, it was because that organ was already callous to Cape sentiment. Hyannis, which at this time was little more than a trading post, was much excited by the arrival in June, 1814, of the schooner Kutuzoff from Savannah, which put in under fire from a British privateer. Her cargo of rice and cotton was unloaded on the beach, where the militia prepared to defend it if necessary against a landing party. But the British, following their sensible custom, kept the sea, rightly concluding that the small quantity of goods which slipped through their blockade was not worth the lives it would cost to recapture it.

Blockade-running on this side of the Cape, where a bold foreshore and deep water enabled the British to sail close in, was almost hopeless business; but the Bay shore, with its wide fringe of flats, which at certain stages of the tide were covered with only a foot or two of water, was just the place for small boats to skirt alongshore trading. A brisk traffic with New York grew up, carried on in whaleboats, of which there were plenty in every village. The route was from Truro or Wellfleet or Orleans to Barnstable; from there a quick dash took them past the long arm of Sandy Neck to the safety of Scusset Creek, in Sandwich.

From there the boats with their cargoes were hauled overland by oxen along the present Canal route to Monument River and launched again for the last leg of the voyage to Providence, New Haven, or New York, where they swapped their salt fish for flour. 'It was no unusual thing,' says Frederick Freeman, 'for those who had commanded first class merchantmen, being now out of employment, to sail these small boats on such adventures.' One of the most conspicuous of these blockade-runners was John Collins, of Truro, a lad of eighteen who afterward commanded, among other vessels, the Roscius of the celebrated Dramatic Line of Liverpool packets. Ephraim Sanford, of Falmouth, by using red sails for night work, ran the salt that he made into New York to the tune of one hundred dollars' profit per trip.

The voyages of the whaleboat fleets were not always successful. On one occasion Captains Winslow Knowles and Matthew Mayo, deep-water shipmasters from Eastham, embarked on a private speculation, carrying a boatload of rye to Boston. On the return trip they were scooped up by the Spencer. Knowles was sent to Boston to collect three hundred dollars' ransom, and thereafter faded from the picture. Mayo's fun had just begun, however. Commodore Ragget made him pilot of a captured Duxbury pinkie, whose commander had orders to patrol the Bay. This suited the Eastham sailor nicely. A northwest gale sprang up and brought with it a string of adventures for him that reads like a boy's yarn of the Spanish Main. Kegs of rum, drunken sailors, picked locks, pistols, dragging anchors, and cut hawsers all figure in the tale, the scene of which was the stretch of salt water between Billingsgate Island and the Eastham flats. The climax came when Mayo got the schooner hard aground and, slipping over the side, notified the militia of his own town, who marched off at low tide and took her. It was after this exploit that Ragget collected $1200 from Eastham as the price of keeping his hands off the town.

A good many fishermen tried to run the blockade and make voyages to the Labrador grounds, but very few of them succeeded. Most shared the fate of Timothy Hallett, of Yarmouth, who with his schooner Victory was captured before he was clear of the Bay. He saved himself a long term of imprisonment by sharing his knowledge of Nova Scotian waters with the grateful British commander. These services earned for him safe conduct back to Yarmouth with his schooner. Such adventures served only to break the monotony of life at home; they almost always ended in disaster. The whaleboats were the craft that kept fresh provisions in Cape kitchens.

So far all the Cape's activity in the war had been selfish. Her citizens had rested content with protecting their own shores, either with money or the home guard, and running the blockade in the hope of replenishing their own larders. What little damage they had done to the British fleet had been incidental to carrying out their own narrow programme, it had consisted, indeed, of little more than recovering captured vessels. They had undertaken no enterprise with the desire of helping the Government of which they were a part. Only four of the thirteen Cape towns favored the war: Sandwich, Barnstable, Falmouth, and Orleans. The rest were more than willing to let Madison and his party stew in their own juice. What support the Administration received from the Cape, therefore, had to be furnished by the loyal minority.

These, quite naturally, took to the sea in privately armed vessels because the Government had no navy worth mentioning. Long-sparred topsail schooners were the favorite rig for the business of privateering, which called for a maximum of speed and no carrying capacity to speak of. Fleets of these lean and graceful craft which put out from the ports of recalcitrant New England did much to offset the depredations of His Majesty's navy. One of them, the brig Reindeer, was commanded by Captain Nathaniel Snow, of Truro, who had several other Cape men in his crew, among them Captain Matthew Mayo, whose early adventures with the Spencer have been mentioned above. Snow had orders to intercept the fleet of returning East-Indiamen that was due in the English Channel. They appeared on schedule time, to be sure, but were accompanied by so strong a convoy of warships that the Reindeer sheered off and contented herself with picking up six scattered prizes in a five months' cruise. Though some of the captured vessels were retaken by the British, all hands retired at the end of the voyage with money in the bank.

Captain Reuben Rich, of Wellfleet, was the quickest Cape money-maker, however. Sailing in a vessel that he and two others had fitted out at their own expense, he returned to Boston almost immediately with a British East-Indiaman under his wing and put $17,000 in his pocket as his share of the prize money. Apparently Captain Rich knew when to stop, for no further record of him as a privateer appears. John Collins, of Truro, was still too young to vote when, tired of running the blockade to New York in whaleboats, he took to deep water and sent back his share of prizes. The youthful impetuosity of the Truro lad finally brought disaster, however, for mistaking a British sloop-of-war for an East-Indiaman, he sailed in, dazzled by visions of another rich captive, only to be met by a fire that outweighed his own. He hung on for an hour, but found too late that he had bitten off more than he could chew. Collins emerged from an English prison at the end of the war with more wisdom and as much enterprise as ever.

A handful of Cape-Codders appear here and there on board the few vessels that comprised the regular navy. John Cook, of Eastham, served under Perry at the battle of Lake Erie; two Harwich men were on board the Constitution when she beat the Guerrière. Local historians have done their best to turn these few loyal Cape-Codders into a multitude, but no alchemy can distort the truth. Too many men spent the three years of war at home, stoutly proclaiming that they would not fight for a Southern Administration, or trying to quiet a troublesome conscience by sporadic activity in the local militia. They were not lacking in bravery. What they lacked was vision. A house divided against itself had no terrors for their political inexperience. Blinded by sectionalism, veterans of the Northwest Coast, like Captain William Sturgis, joined with veterans of the European ports, like Captain Elijah Cobb, in trying to scuttle their nation. Luckily peace came before they succeeded. Just as no part of the country had done less than New England to bring about the peace, so no part of the country was quicker to profit by it. Cape shipmasters, once more in demand, sailed forth to trade with the nation they had refused to fight.

Ashore, too, the end of the war marked the beginning of a period of energy and prosperity for the Cape that has never

CAPTAIN JOHN COLLINS   CAPTAIN JOHN ELDRIDGE

been equaled. Men of all callings, from reformers to bridge-builders, sprang into violent activity. A branch of the Boston Temperance Society spread as far as Yarmouth, where in 1817 a group of righteous townsfolk decided to check the drinking of hard liquor, which in those robust days was as universal as swearing. The old custom of 'a tavern to a town' no longer sufficed. Like other good things, drinking was being overdone, until it took seventeen grogshops to quench the thirst of the men who lived on the Bay side of Yarmouth. No doubt as many more catered to the drought of the unregenerate South-Siders. A number of the worthiest citizens joined the new Temperance Society and some of the taverns went out of business.

The slings and arrows of righteousness were leveled at tobacco as well. Societies against its use were formed in many towns. A peripatetic reformer, the Reverend Charles S. Adams, of Boston, visited the Cape in 1837 and 1838, and delivered an original poem before the Temperance Society of Orleans and the Anti-Tobacco Societies of South Wellfleet and Harwich. There is no doubting the author's conviction, nor can it be denied that he pays a fitting tribute to the power of his antagonist:

> 'Popes, kings, and legislatures all combine
> By excommunication, threats and fine,
> To stay its march, to break its iron rod —
> It conquers still, and triumphs like a god:
> This nauseous weed, despite of all their laws,
> Still holds its throne within the human jaws';

and so on for twenty-four ferocious pages. Certainly the Cape was doing its share toward discouraging frailties of the flesh.

The Cape men — now essentially a seagoing population — fancied, among other things, in this period of hectic energy, that they were manufacturers as well. They began to build factories and operate them. Wellfleet, having given up the attempt to renew whaling, incorporated what was known as The Wellfleet Manufacturing Company for making cotton and woolen cloth. Sandwich, the same year that the war was declared, showed her nonchalance by putting up a cotton factory near Wolftrap Neck. Sandwich's chief shore activity, however, was its glass works, which were started in 1825 and ran with increasing prosperity until 1888. The recent demand among collectors of antiques for pieces of Sandwich glass has lent a fictitious value to the products of this factory, and has shed a glamour over the old concern that makes it seem like a much greater industry than it really was.

The Chatham and Harwich Manufacturing Company was established in 1827 for making cotton and woolen cloth. The year 1829 saw a savings bank incorporated in Barnstable; the Duck Harbor and Beach Company started at Wellfleet, the Union Wharf Company at Truro, and the Skinnaquits Fishing Company at Harwich.

And so it went. To judge from their activities on shore, one would suppose that the Cape-Codders' only hope for immortality lay in what they could achieve on dry land, instead of in what they were doing for the nation at sea. Wharfs appeared like mushrooms to accommodate the fishing fleets, and riggers and sailmakers and caulkers had their establishments near by. These industries must be taken more seriously than the factories, for there is propriety in them. A Cape-Codder who makes cloth for print dresses is a misguided victim of an age of contagious energy. He is a temporary figure, and will disappear when the pace drops back to normal. But a Cape-Codder who makes sails and blocks, or who pounds oakum into the seams of fishing schooners, is a proper picture for his setting; he may go on as long as schooners continue to sail, and the world will not tire of watching him and praising his wisdom.

So it was with the shipbuilders. It is impossible to say when the first vessel was launched on the Cape — not very early, at all events, for farming took all the time and energy of the settlers for three or four generations. Occasionally, to be sure, a man would build himself a sloop large enough to sail round the Bay, and there is some evidence that a few scattering craft of this sort were built by amateurs as early as 1675. Thomas Bourne, of Sandwich, built the sloop Charming Betty for Simeon Dillingham in 1717, to be used as a Boston packet. But the first professional builder of whom any record exists was Thomas Agrey, who, about 1750, began the business at Barnstable, and trained his young assistants so well that they continued after he moved away to Maine. Once sown, the seed took root and spread up and down the Cape; Shipyards appeared like mushrooms beside every creek from Buzzards Bay to Provincetown. Immediately after the Revolution, the Brays at Hockanom launched a fleet of fishing schooners and sloops running from fifty tons to three times that size; and before the Revolution, the Wellfleet whalemen pursued their calling in big local schooners, built by fellow townsmen.

The most active builder on the lower Cape was Anthony Thacher, whose headquarters were at Harwich, but who, like the early millwrights, went where business called. About 1845, he laid the keels for a small fleet of vessels in Harwich and Chatham. Some of them were for a wealthy Harwich merchant, Job Chase, and were framed from timber growing on his own land. Meantime, at Truro, Henry Rogers and Nathaniel Hopkins were building brigs and schooners at their yard near the mouth of Pamet River. Barnstable did not rest on her early laurels, but immediately after the War of 1812 resumed the activity she had shown before the Embargo. On the south side of the town, Richard Lewis was launching schooners at Hyannis, and Crocker Marchant had a yard at the Port. At Osterville, Horace Crosby and his brother, C. Worthington, started boatbuilding in the thirties, and the business still flourishes in the hands of their descendants, Wilton, Herbert, and H. Manley. West Dennis was represented by Elisha Crowell and Luther Studley. Provincetown, during these busy years, built more small vessels than any other town and even after the Civil War, John Whitcomb launched a number of whaling schooners there.

The names of some of the Cape vessels show that the spirit of independence had spread even to the shipyards. Men christened their craft according to their fancy, scorning names that were traditional and trite. Even when they named them after real persons, a custom which usually indicates the last resource of an exhausted imagination, Cape-Codders injected a note of whimsical familiarity, like Willie Swift and Freddie W. Alton, two of Whitcomb's whalers. But the most original names occurred when owners gave free rein to their fancy and drew down parts of speech at random from the sky. Two of the schooners that Anthony Thacher built were called the Ostrich and the Emulous. Captain William Handy, of Bourne, was too old to have been serious when he christened one of his vessels Love. Chatham proclaimed a religious toleration which she did not practice, by painting Jew and Gentile across the broad stern of one of her schooners; two others were dubbed Exit and Philanthropic. Job Chase, Jr., and his associates luxuriated in Hopes. Among his fleet appear such names as Superb Hope, Royal Hope, Hope Mary Ann, Hope's Lady, and Lady Hope. Thacher selected creeks with strange names, too, to build his craft on. He launched several from a place called No Horns, a corruption of the Indian Nauhaught, and others from the Snake Hole.

Few of the vessels that have been mentioned measured more than seventy feet over all; many of them were much smaller, for the Cape's fame in shipbuilding depended on the number of yards it supported, not on the size of its vessels. But there were exceptions. At Sagamore, Benjamin Burgess and Abner Ellis built two barks, the Franklin and the Lysander, for the West Indian trade. These were launched in 1837 and 1842 respectively at the very peak of the boom. A little earlier, Captain William Handy, after retiring from the sea, launched, besides various brigs and schooners, the full-rigged ship Rebecca on the shores of Buzzards Bay.

But the men who really saved the Cape from having nothing but small craft to its credit were the Shivericks. Asa Shiverick, Sr., was born in Falmouth, but moved to East Dennis, where, after learning his trade in the shipyard of Jeremiah Crowell, he began to build brigs and schooners on his own account. His son Asa was born there in 1816, and before he was twenty-one he had considerable experience in shipbuilding off the Cape. He worked for a time in Boston in Lot Wheelwright's yard, and later in the shipyards of Maine. When he returned to East Dennis in 1837, therefore, he was a valued ally to his father, who had more than he could do to supply the demand that the boom had created. The old gentleman had never tried his hand at ships, but had been content with turning out small craft like the other Cape builders. He took the goods the gods provided, and when the Atlantic came ashore at Sesuit, near his house, he used her planking and timbers for the topsail schooner Atlas that was then on the stocks. The arrival of his son Asa, fresh from the Maine coast and with experience in Boston as well,

THE WILD HUNTER

brought new life and larger ideas to the business. His other sons, Paul and David, also joined forces with their father, and the old man's troubles were over. If the boys wanted to build big ships, well and good; he was glad to let them try it. He retired a few years later, and the firm, with Asa, Jr., as its leading spirit and his brothers as staunch supporters, constructed a new and bigger yard farther down the creek, where they began in 1850 to build a fleet of ships that would have done credit to any yard in the country. They were in close relations with the local capitalists and merchants, Christopher Hall and Prince Crowell, retired shipmasters whose financial backing gave the young builders confidence and a free hand. By 1862 eight full-rigged ships and barks took the water from their ways. The first was the Revenue; she was followed by the Hippogriffe, Belle of the West, Kit Carson, Wild Hunter, Webfoot, Christopher Hall and Ellen Sears. Two of these, the Belle of the West and the Wild Hunter, were extreme clippers with all that the phrase implies. Another, the medium clipper Hippogriffe, was hardly less graceful. She was a lucky ship, for though, in 1858, while working her way across the China Sea, she struck an uncharted rock, Captain David Sears, by a piece of expert seamanship, got her clear and arrived safe at Hongkong. Here it was discovered that a large fragment of the rock had come away and was lodged in her planking, completely filling the hole that it had stove. The rock was subsequently charted under the name of Hippogriffe Rock. Toward the end of the Civil War, while she was lying in Calcutta, her owners — Hall and Crowell — decided to sell her rather than risk a lop-sided encounter with the Alabama; so, like many another American clipper, she ended her days under the British flag.

The Wild Hunter, though she made no record runs, proved to be a good investment and — after a checkered career, which included the California trade, guano-carrying from the Pacific, and China voyages — the yards were stripped from her mizzenmast in the seventies, and bark-rigged she faded from sight in the decade that followed.

The Belle of the West was the sharpest of all the Shiverick ships. Her designer was Samuel Pooke, of Boston, the same man who designed the celebrated Red Jacket. She was towed to

Boston to be rigged in 1853, a year when the harbor was full of clippers from the yards of the greatest builders in the country. Surrounded though she was by such rivals, her appearance excited admiration, and on her maiden voyage to San Francisco the newspapers of even that clipper-surfeited port found space to praise her saucy lines. Thomas F. Hall, of East Dennis, who sailed on her for four and a half years, thus pays tribute to the excellence of the Shivericks' workmanship and the beauty of the Belle:

> The *South American* . . . was often said in shipping circles to be the best built wooden ship afloat. The first opportunity I had, I visited her in East Boston. I think that if the *Belle of the West* and the *South American* could have been placed alongside each other, that the *Belle* would by competent judges, be said to be the most excellent. The beauty of the *Belle* was never exploited. She was always commanded by William F. Howes, who cared nothing for such publicity. He rather abhorred it. She was not extensively known.

Christopher Hall sold her after ten years to Glidden and Williams, and from these owners she passed into Eastern hands at Calcutta. Loaded with rice, reduced in rig, and under a foreign commander, she foundered in the Bay of Bengal in 1868.

The decline of our merchant marine, which began in the late fifties, silenced the busy hammers of the Shivericks, as it silenced the din in the other shipyards of the country. Asa Shiverick moved to Woods Hole, where he spent the latter part of his life. His name does not appear in the history of the Nation for the same reason that the names of Donald McKay and Samuel Hall and Paul Curtis do not appear: they never sought office. But these shipbuilders, by displaying the finest sailing vessels that have ever been launched, did more for the Nation's prestige than many of its Presidents have done, and created a respect for our flag that could not have been achieved by an army of polished diplomats.

The next great industry on the Cape was, like shipbuilding, carried on close to the water's edge. Until a few years ago a man who stood on the edge of the upland and looked out across the level expanse of marshes, might have seen, in one or two places, a lone timber, bleached like a huge bone, slanting up against the dark green background. If he was interested enough to make

his way out to it, he would have found the splintered stumps of
three other uprights hidden in the thatch and forming, with the
one left standing, the corners of a square. This was all that remained of the salt works that once kept hundreds of Cape-
Codders busy and prosperous, and dotted the shore-front with
the sails of windmills.

Of course Cape-Codders made salt long before they invented
salt works. The primitive method was to boil sea-water in great
iron kettles and scrape out what little salt remained after the
water had boiled away. But this was slow business; incidentally,
it helped to destroy the forests, for the amount of fuel needed
was prodigious. Yet it continued for more than a century, until
1776, in fact, when Captain John Sears, of Dennis, his wits
sharpened by the high price that salt was beginning to fetch because of the British blockade, tried the experiment of letting the
sun do the work of evaporation.

He built a big shallow trough — one hundred feet by ten —
which could be covered in case of rain by a clumsy contrivance
of shutters. His apparatus was crude, the vats leaked, and the
labor of filling the trough was prodigious, yet it was a great improvement over the old method; and though the Captain's
ingenuity was rewarded by only eight bushels of salt the first
year, he was confident that further improvements would make
his invention practical.

Encouragement was given to his energies by a bounty of
three shillings per bushel which the Court offered on all salt
locally manufactured from sea-water. Captain Sears brought
his nautical training to bear successfully on the problem of
making his vats tight; but still the labor of filling them was
great, in spite of experiments which he tried with hand-pumps.
This obstacle was finally removed by Major Nathaniel Freeman, of Harwich, who, after the Captain had been racking his
brains in vain for ten years, suggested a windmill. The success
of this device was immediate. Meantime, other improvements
had been made. In 1793, Reuben Sears, of Harwich, invented a roof that could be rolled off on wooden sheaves that
ran on narrow ways built out beside the vats. Hatsell Kelly, a
fellow townsman of Captain Sears, contrived a still more in-
genious scheme, which made it possible to cover or uncover two

vats at a time. He placed them corner to corner in pairs; at the point of contact was a huge upright with a stout peg protruding from its upper end. On this peg was pivoted a long horizontal crane that supported the roofs of both vats. The roofs were left clear of the sides of the vats, so that by swinging the cranebeam horizontally on its pivot, both vats could be covered or uncovered as desired.

Such facilities as these encouraged so many men to become at least part-time salt-makers, that in 1802, James Freeman reports 136 separate establishments on the Cape, producing a total of over 40,000 bushels of salt and 182,000 bushels of Glauber salts a year. Even these figures look small when compared with the output a generation later, for the War of 1812 gave a fillip to prices, and still more works appeared, until, when the peak of the business was reached in the thirties (the same decade that saw industry of all sorts booming on the Cape), the number of salt works reached a total of 442, the annual output of which was well over half a million bushels, exclusive of Glauber salts, which were at that time a drug on the market.

Loring Crocker's works at Common Fields, in Barnstable, represented the last word in salt-making. To avoid having to lay his log pipes all the way down to low-water mark, Mr. Crocker built big wooden reservoirs on the ridge of the beach where the ground was highest. From these the water was run through 'falls' into sets of seven vats, placed on ground that sloped gently down from the level of the reservoirs, so that when the falls were opened, the water ran through automatically. The vats were eighteen feet wide, from fifty to sixty feet long, according to the lay of the land, and not quite a foot deep. The first three were called the first, second, and third water-rooms respectively; the next three, the pickle-rooms; and the last was the salt-room. Each played its part in the process of evaporation. The gunwales, or sides, of the first water-rooms were left festooned with ropy vegetation by the evaporating liquid; in the next two, a thick slime was deposited on the bottom. In the pickle-rooms a substance called lime was precipitated, and remained on the bottom when the brine passed through the last falls into the salt-room, where the crystals of salt formed and were shoveled out and stored in sheds to dry.

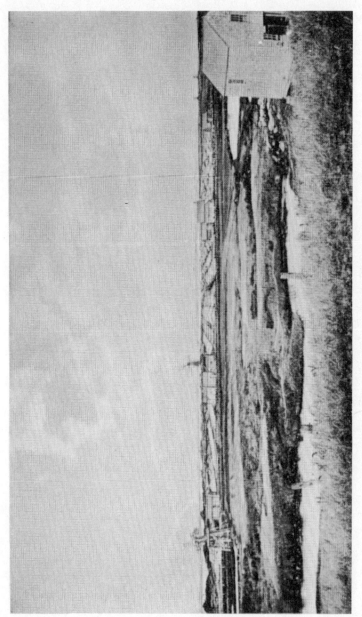

LORING CROCKER'S BARNSTABLE SALT WORKS IN 1870

The whole process took at least six weeks, but of course varied with the weather.

The 'bitter water,' which was the name given to the liquid that remained after all the ordinary salt had been extracted from it, was still valuable for making Epsom salts. The manufacture of these salts was a process apart, and could be done only in cold weather, when crystals of crude Epsom salts formed in the bitter water. For this reason the bitter water had to be stored in separate vats until winter. As soon as the crystals appeared, the liquid was drained off into a cistern, and fresh water was poured in on the crude salts until an expert could tell by feeling it that the right strength had been reached. The solution was then heated to about blood temperature by a special stove (though the process was called 'boiling salts,' the liquid was never allowed to boil) and was left standing overnight. In the morning the windows of the shed were thrown open to chill the air, the water was drawn off, and Epsom salts lay four or five inches deep on the bottom of the vat. By adding a little fresh water to the old bitter water, it could be made to produce crude salt crystals three or four times, but those that appeared after the second time were of an inferior quality. Even then the bitter water had commercial value; it was used for making a special cement for cornices and filigree work, and Mr. Crocker sold it for a dollar a barrel. Another by-product of the business was Glauber salts, which formed before the water reached the salt-room; they were removed and refined in much the same way as the Epsom salts, and were sold to tanneries, where they were used to prevent the hides from drying stiff. A cloth wrung out in a solution of Glauber salts might hang on a clothes line all summer and still be wet.

Thus had the crude trough of Captain Sears been elaborated into an intricate system of reservoirs, falls, vats, and boiling rooms, that extracted the last ounce of salt from the sea-water. Such an improvement in apparatus speaks for itself; the business paid in spite of spells of bad weather and a fluctuating market, which sent the price all the way from forty-two cents a bushel before the Civil War to eighty-two cents after it. Hundreds of men prospered with salt-making as their chief business, and many a building on the Cape was stored to the eaves with salt for months on end, like whale oil on the New Bedford docks, waiting for a rising market. This business, in flush times, paid upwards of twenty-five per cent on the investment. Since $2,000,000 of Cape money was invested in salt works throughout the thirties, one reason for the great prosperity of that period becomes clear. About 1840, the business began to decline for various reasons. The price of soft pine from Maine — which was used almost exclusively in building the vats—was going higher, and foreign salts became cheaper as mines were developed. By degrees the vats were broken up, and some of the lumber was used for building barns, sheds, and even houses, to the despair of carpenters, whose tools were red with rust in a few days from contact with boards that had been pickled in brine for years.

The growing economic importance of the Cape justified quicker communication with Boston than the stage-coaches or packets provided, and in 1848 the first train puffed its way from Middleboro to Sandwich. For six years this remained the end of the route. Then rails were laid as far as Hyannis. The next notch in the progress of the railroad down the Cape came in 1865 with the building of a line from Yarmouth to Orleans, whence it advanced jerkily the rest of the way, reaching Wellfleet in 1869 and finally stretching to its goal at Provincetown in 1873. The Chatham Branch was not built until the late eighties.

The arrival of the first train in a town aroused varied emotions among the citizens. Packet-owners and riggers were hostile, of course, and cursed the railroad in picturesque style, while fishermen, rejoicing in the quicker transportation of their fares, were whole-hearted supporters of it. The Reverend A. J. Church was inspired to compose the following lines, to be sung at the celebration which was held when the directors decided to open the road to Wellfleet:

> 'The great Atlantic Railroad for old Cape Cod, all hail!
> Bring on the locomotive; lay down the iron rail;
> Across the Eastham prairies, by steam we're bound to go,
> The railroad cars are coming, let's all get up and crow.
> The little dogs in Dogtown [1] will wag their little tails;
> They'll think that something's coming, a-riding on the rails.'

---

[1] Dogtown was the name given to the region between Wellfleet and South Wellfleet.

'All hail, hell!' muttered the packet captain. But no progress can be made without treading on somebody's toes, and even the dourest conservative had to admit that, as a means of reaching Boston, the train was a great improvement over the stage-coach.

Stage-coaches had begun to lumber their way to various parts of the Cape about 1800. Before that, unless a man was lucky enough to pick up a coaster, he had to hire his own horses and carriage, as James Winthrop did in 1791. This young man was engaged to survey a route for the proposed Cape Cod Canal, and his account of the journey to Sandwich gives a good picture of travel on the Cape at that early date. He writes in part as follows:

Thursday 12th May 1791, at 1 P.M. set out from Cambridge to survey Sandwich neck. . . . Miss H. a lovely girl of eighteen, was polite enough to take this opportunity to visit her Barnstable friends, and rode in the chaise with me. . . . Oated at Bracket's in Braintree . . . lodged at Cushing's in Hingham twenty-three miles from home. Well accomodated for horse keeping and victuals, but bugs in the bed. Friday 13th, after breakfast set out for Plymouth; soon began to rain but got to Kingston to dine, put up at Beal's, accomodations good but people slow. Saturday 14th, Rain. After breakfast the storm inter-mitted. Rode into Plymouth by 9 o'clock, introduced Miss H. to General Warren and lady, and put up at their house, proposing a friendly but early dinner with them. Storm renewed and held till to-ward night. Sabbath 15th. Attended meeting, drank tea at Mrs. Winslow's. Two agreeable and pretty daughters, both amiable. In the evening Major Thomas and Lady, the Misses Winslows, Miss Gorham and Miss Barr came to see Miss H. all the young ladies about her time of life. We had an agreeable evening. Monday 16th. After Breakfast rode to Ellises in Plymouth Woods where we dined in Company of the Supreme Court as they were returning from Barns-table. Afternoon rode to Sandwich, put up at Fessenden's, deposited Miss H. at Rev. Mr. Burr's. He has a very handsome and agreeable wife. Spent the evening at General Freeman's. Capt. Allen & Major Williams & Rev. Mr. Burr spent an hour with us at Fessenden's.

Thus did young Winslow reach his goal. He sent Miss H. the rest of her journey to Barnstable in the chaise in charge of his assistant, Mr. Henry Parker.

Even after stage-coaches appeared, no one used them if he could help it, except travelers from the city, like those hardy voyagers Dwight and Kendall, who made the trip overland to

Provincetown early in the century. The wheels buried themselves in sand above the rims; for miles on end the horses had to walk. Yet these vehicles somehow paid their way, and the proprietors did what they could to make the journey agreeable. Some of them painted their coaches with gaudy yellows and reds, and employed festive philosophers to drive them. Their greatest allies, however, were the tavern-keepers along the route. If these public-spirited gentlemen had shut up shop, the stage-coaches could hardly have survived. Even after the Temperance Movement breathed its arid breath on the Cape, there were always one or two hosts in each town who were glad to provide a glass or so to cut the dust of the journey from the throats of passengers and drivers; and these oases were not far enough apart to allow a very heavy gloom to settle between taproom and taproom. It was a short jog from Fessenden's at Sandwich to Howland's at West Barnstable, and a shorter one still from there to the Crocker Tavern in Barnstable. A scant four miles, and the stage stopped in Yarmouth under the swinging sign of Sears; there was balm for the tired traveler after all.

From some parts of the road, too, the view was striking. Dr. Dwight, as his coach climbed the old highway that used to lead over the top of Scorton Hill in West Barnstable, was properly impressed by the broad sweep of Great Marshes, threaded with creeks and bordered on the north by the seven lean miles of Sandy Neck, which he describes with appropriate eloquence as a 'long, lofty, wild and fantastical beach, thrown into a thousand grotesque forms by the united force of winds and waves.' Beyond lay the Bay, and if the day was clear, the low, white shore of Wellfleet and Truro could be faintly discerned on the horizon. A less reverend man than Dwight might well have been moved by such a prospect.

Post-riders also helped to keep the Cape in touch with what was going on in other parts of the State. Before the Revolution, letters had come and gone in the pockets of chance travelers, but in 1792 the Government took charge of the mail and employed John Thacher, of Barnstable, to carry it between that town and Boston. He made the round trip once a week, leaving Barnstable Tuesday morning and returning Friday night. His pay was one dollar for each day spent on the road. His budget of letters was never too big to be carried in a saddle-bag. The lower Cape got on as best it could for another five years; then a rider was put on the Yarmouth–Truro route and made a round trip weekly. The War of 1812, obnoxious as it was to all Cape men, furnished so much interesting news, particularly to families who had sons or fathers on privateers, that the mail began to run twice a week as far as Yarmouth, and beginning in 1820 it came three times. This proved to be often enough until the very height of the Cape's prosperity in 1837, when a daily mail was established, which lasted until the opening of the railroad.

The citizens did not allow the business and commercial prosperity that they were enjoying to interfere with intellectual pursuits. Besides the churches, which, thriving though they were, represented centers of emotion and controversy rather than of intellect, the townspeople started lyceums, over the graves of which monuments still stand in the shape of dreary buildings, with 'Lyceum Hall' written large above their doors. Yet in their day these organizations were centers of light and leading. The Preamble to the Constitution of the Barnstable Lyceum, organized in 1829, gives a good idea of the motives of its founders:

Being desirous of witnessing, in the community around us, a development and expansion of mind and a refined and elevated taste; it is our wish that a society for the advancement of these purposes, may be established in this town.

The objects of this Lyceum shall be the improvement of its members in useful knowledge and the advancement of popular Education.

These societies were also rudimentary museums and libraries. Curators were elected who were authorized to collect any specimens of minerals, natural curiosities, and books which they thought would be useful for children as well as for adults. The lyceums worked hand in hand with the schools, and encouraged children to become non-voting members by admitting them for one half the annual fee. They allowed teachers to use the society's collections for the benefit of their classes. Their scope was broad, and freedom of debate in meetings was encouraged. Only one exception to this policy was made: no religious or political question was allowed to come up for discussion. But there was fruitful ground for discussion outside these forbidden realms, and the President had it in his power to regulate the temperature of debates by designating the men who should support respectively the negative and the affirmative side of each question. Further interest was guaranteed by the fact that the debaters usually spoke extemporaneously. The exercises were by no means confined to debates, however: 'Lectures, Readings, Illustrations of the Sciences, and Conversation' all found a place in the meetings. The precise character of the topics discussed is given in an entertaining style by a member of the Brewster Lyceum who had a talent for verse, and who read the poem from which the following extracts are quoted, at a meeting of the society in 1836. The first lines allude to a address on 'Curiosity' which had recently been delivered by the Reverend S. Williams:

> 'On the 23rd day of the last month, December,
> In a *curious* address, if I rightly remember,
> In a *curious* way, too, I truly believe,
> We were all introduced to our Grandmother Eve,
> A *curious* feeling 'twas said we possessed,
> Which dwelt in her bosom, — which burnt in her breast,
> And led her to wander and stand by the root
> And pluck from the branches and eat of the fruit
> Of the tree of the knowledge of evil and good,
> Which she was forbidden to visit for food.
> And 'twas said her fair daughters possess the same trait,
> Which leads them to bite at the old serpent's bait.'

In the same happy vein the writer reviews the rest of the address, and then turns to a lecture that had been delivered by the Reverend Nathaniel Simpkins, of Yarmouth:

> 'Again we heard from a father — a sage —
> The wisdom, advice and experience of age.
> He stated the good that a rational use
> Of the means we enjoy would most likely produce.
> Lyceums, he observed, are most wisely designed
> To call into action the powers of the mind,
> To waken ideas that latently sleep,
> That one from another advantage may reap.
> . . . .
> And as a good steel and a flint produce fire,
> Our minds by collision raise intellect higher.'

Another clergyman had favored this lyceum with a discourse on 'Phrenology,' to which our poet alludes as follows:

> 'But I leave this and hasten to give a few thumps
> At the well-known address, Sir, the "Lecture on Bumps."
> .   .   .   .
> This science, it seems, has commenced quite a rage
> With many good people of this wondrous age;
> And it is an employment by no means so dull,
> To lecture on brains and examine the skull.
> Pursuing the way that some others have trod
> This doctrine has journeyed *quite down to Cape Cod.*'

Leaving the lecturers, the poet continues:

> 'But again. In reviewing our doings of late
> I shall notice the questions proposed for debate.
> We have agreed and voted that riches have more
> Influence than knowledge in towns along shore.
> .   .   .   .
> The next we contended to ascertain which
> Enjoyed the most pleasure, the Poor or the Rich.
> .   .   .   .
> Again we debated. A great deal was said
> About hanging bad people until they were dead;
> And after advancing what reasons we could,
> Concluded that hanging produces most good.
> We must all behave well, then, according to that,
> As we wish to avoid a new hempen cravat.
> .   .   .   .
> But while on this subject I must, by the way,
> Observe that strict justice requires me to say,
> That since this debate we have read a report
> And given a vote of a different sort.'

Not every town could boast of a poet like this nameless Brewster bard, but they all had lyceums, which succeeded in giving the citizens something besides business and prosperity to think and talk about. Yarmouth was regaled with lectures on subjects ranging from 'The Genius and Poetry of Lord Byron' to Nat Atwood's sterling comments on fish. Even Province-town, which has become an intellectual center only very recently with the arrival of summer scriveners from Greenwich Village, boasted a lyceum, but had something more important to occupy its attention in another direction: the wind began to blow sand into East Harbor until it became almost useless, and there was danger that the main harbor would be ruined in the same way.

The danger to Provincetown was twofold: first to the village itself; second to the harbor. The houses all border a street which runs along the water's edge. Behind to the north stretches a wilderness of sand hills which, when the Mayflower band arrived, were for the most part held stationary by trees and shrubs. But from the earliest times the inhabitants, following the example of visiting fishermen, fell upon the trees until the sand lay bare, a prey to the four winds of heaven. The captains of fishing schooners were allowed to take sand ballast from these hills, and, not content with this, the citizens turned their cattle loose to graze on what clumps of vegetation still struggled for existence on the denuded sand hills, with the result that the grass was demolished as fast as it grew. The sand was free to blow down upon the unprotected village with every northwester, threatening even to bury the houses.

The danger attracted the attention of the Colonial Government as early as 1714, when an act was passed to preserve the trees. In 1727, Provincetown was incorporated, and a dozen years later another act forbade the pasturing of cattle on the sand hills. The Court might as well have forbidden the winds to blow or the sun to shine. Provincetowners cared nothing for laws, and continued to cut wood and turn cattle loose for the next hundred years; in short, until the danger, instead of threatening, actually arrived. The sand buried a house or two, and was advancing toward the town, salt works, and harbor at the rate of fifty rods a year along a four-and-a-half-mile front. In 1825, another commission was sent to study the situation and suggest remedies. This time they found the citizens so frightened by the marching sand that they were ready at last to obey the laws. They planted beach grass on the barren dunes, kept their cattle in the pound, and stopped cutting down young pine trees. Thus was the sand anchored and the town saved.

But the harbor, without which the town could not exist, was still imperiled from two directions. The chief cause for alarm came from East Harbor, which had been filling up for years with sand blown into it from the north and washed down through its entrance into Provincetown Harbor, which was being gradually silted up by this constant deposit. Furthermore, the strip of beach that separated the marshes at the head of East Harbor from the open ocean was so low and narrow that any northeaster might send the sea tearing through it. At one point it was only four or five rods wide at high water. If the sea ever should break through, it would sweep tons of sand down into Provincetown Harbor, from both banks of the new channel, doing damage that it would have taken the blowing sand a century to accomplish. This danger was in no sense chimerical. One storm had already sent a trickle of water across the frail barrier. To add to the danger, this narrow beach was the only road for vehicles, and much of its beach grass was thereby ruined.

Various makeshifts had been tried to offset this menace. In

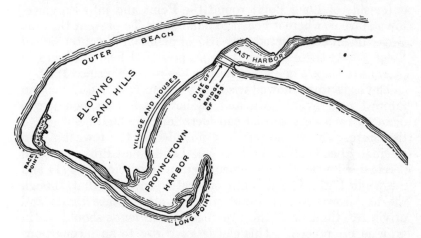

1854, a legislative committee recommended building a bridge across the mouth of East Harbor so that the traffic might be switched from the beach and allow grass to grow on it, in the hope that it would then build itself higher. A fence of posts and brush was also suggested to help the process. The bridge was built, but the danger was not removed, for the beach remained as low as ever. Two years later another committee, wiser and more daring than any of its predecessors, came out flat-footed with the statement that the only guaranty of security was to throw a solid dike across the mouth of East Harbor below the bridge. They agreed that this harbor was ruined, anyhow, and, that if a dike were built, the sand from the upper reaches of the harbor would lodge against it, and thus be prevented from filling Provincetown Harbor.

The drastic nature of such legislation staggered the lawmakers. It would cost five times as much as the total of all the money that had previously been spent on Provincetown Harbor. They thought about it for ten years; then in 1868, work on the dike was begun, and was virtually completed in 1869, at a cost of $131,770. It was 1400 feet long, 75 feet wide on top, and rose 6 feet above high-water mark. It was built chiefly of earth and planted with beach grass.

Meantime, there was cause for anxiety from the opposite direction. The tides carried sand from the Race Run and the outer side of Long Point round the Point and into Provincetown Harbor, where it began to build flats. To prevent this, the Government constructed bulwarks of plank on the outer side of Long Point; these served their purpose and held the sand in place; the Cape's one great harbor has been safe since 1869.

The legislature showed wisdom, to be sure, in taking such an interest in Provincetown and its harbor; but its policy was dictated by a very special consideration: the land belonged to the State. The whole territory included in the township had originally been called the Province Lands; and Province Land it remained when the settlement became a precinct in 1714 and a town in 1727. The act of incorporation specified that, though the new town was invested with all appropriate rights and privileges, the title of the Province to said lands should be 'in no wise prejudiced.' This clause gave rise to an incongruous situation. The inhabitants had heard in a general way that the land was the State's, but the information in no wise affected their actions. They bought and sold property with complete freedom; they staked out and fenced lots in the wild land, and received warranty deeds for them from the selectmen. Opinion was divided among them in regard to the State's title. Some wanted the State to surrender its rights. Others preferred to leave matters as they were, being satisfied that their title would never be questioned. Still others refused to believe that the

State owned the land at all; and as far as any outward or visible sign went, they were right. The only evidence of State ownership was the model way in which the Legislature kept its eye on the blowing sands and provided money to check their advance. Whenever the State's title was in danger of lapsing, it was renewed; it still exists, in fact, for most of the territory, though in 1893 the Legislature surrendered its rights to the strip of shore on which the town is built; but the wild land that lies behind remains Province Land to this day.

CHAPTER IX

WHALING

Bold, hardy men, with blooming age,
Our sandy shores produce;
With monstrous fish they dare engage,
And dangerous callings choose.

From a 'Whaling Song,' by Dr. John Osborn, of Sandwich

WHENEVER a man speaks of whaling nowadays, he is pretty sure to mention New Bedford in the same breath; and naturally enough, because New Bedford, by almost exclusive devotion to killing whales, brought the business to a degree of perfection that stands unsurpassed. But New Bedford learned the art from Nantucket, and Nantucket learned it from Cape Cod. The fame of the Cape whalemen had reached the ears of the Islanders and excited their admiration as early as 1672, for they held out flattering inducements to one James Lopar if he would move from the Cape to Nantucket and teach them how whales should be killed. For some reason the scheme fell through; but another Cape-Codder, Ichabod Paddock, of Yarmouth, answered a second call about 1690, and carried the light to the Island.

It was a dim and feeble ray, however, compared with the subsequent science of New Bedford, for never has an art developed more brilliantly — or for that matter more logically and inevitably — than the art of whaling. The first Cape-Codders to profit by whales never left dry land; they were in fact not whalemen at all, but farmers, who, quite by chance, found dead whales washed up on the beach, and stripped them of their blubber. Attending to whales of one kind and another that came ashore on the Cape was a pleasant diversion from clearing woodland and cutting salt hay; it was a more frequent pastime, too, than one would suppose, for whales were incredibly abundant. A school of them, it may be remembered, nearly drove Captain Jones out of his senses by playing about the Mayflower as she was standing in for Provincetown Harbor, for he had no harpoons and was in the tantalizing position of the man without a gun. Fall and winter were the best seasons for whales, and by a happy chance these were the off months for farmers, who were able to reap the full benefit of this peculiar crop without neglecting their farms. After the Cape was settled, few whales, gallied at finding themselves in the shoal water of either the Sound or the Bay, ever thrashed themselves to death in vain.

Frequently, instead of a single specimen, a whole school of blackfish (a species of small whale) was stranded on the beach, and then there was need of lively work if all the blubber was to be boiled down before the air became too fragrant for human nostrils. But sanguinary as the job was, the townspeople looked upon it as a lark, particularly since the profits were immediate; and before long some began to wish that whales would come ashore often enough to provide steady work in trying them out. At this point the seed was sown that was to turn the Cape-Codders into whalemen.

The disputes that arose over the dead bodies of stranded whales were many and bitter. Riparian rights at their simplest have always been a Sargasso Sea for lawyers, and when this intricate question, instead of being allowed to drift along in the usual state of uncertainty, was brought to an immediate issue by the arrival of a school of blackfish on a particular stretch of beach, the fat was in the fire with a vengeance. The man who found them said, 'Findings are keepings; if it hadn't been for me, nobody would have known they were there.' The town authorities said, 'The oil is the town's, because the shore where the fish stranded is within the town limits.' Plymouth said, 'The profits belong to the Colony, for without our consent you would never have had any town.' The King said, 'You are all my subjects; — therefore the oil is mine.' [1] Here, indeed, was work for lawyers; but there were no lawyers, and there was no time to argue, for such donations of the tide do not improve with age. If the townspeople were wise, therefore, they first tried out the oil and then sat down to see if they could find out whose it was.

The various towns reached different solutions. In 1653,

[1] See notes to Chapter IX.

Sandwich, basing its argument on the fact that the beach was common land, decided that the proceeds should be divided equally among the householders of the town. This Utopian solution was too good to last, for Plymouth soon decided that so much liberty was not good for young towns, and demanded one hogshead of oil from each whale. There was a vague idea in the Plymouth brain that this oil was the property of the Crown; but how much of it ever went to lubricate the wheels of government in England does not appear. As a matter of fact, the proceeds from almost every drift whale were disposed of differently. In 1682, for example, a school of blackfish dotted the Sandwich beach, and Jo Holway and some others began immediately to strip them and boil down the blubber. The town then woke up to what was going on and voted to allow Holway and his friends to buy from the town what oil they had already made; the rest was to be sold to others for the benefit of the town. The next year four men were granted a monopoly on all drift whales in Sandwich for ten years, provided they gave half the oil to the town, and deducted from their own half the barrel per whale that must go to Plymouth. Eastham and Truro decided that drift whales were blessings sent by the grace of God, and so dedicated a part of the proceeds to help pay the minister. Each town made up its mind for itself what to do with its share of the proceeds of these valuable carcasses and changed its decision as often as it saw fit — which was about as often as a whale was stranded.

As long as whale oil had any market value, and long after the Cape was sending elaborately equipped whalers to all the seven seas, drift whales continued to be prized and were welcomed ecstatically by the amateur whalemen at home. The cry 'A whale in the Bay!' was enough to empty the hall during a town meeting; every able-bodied man rushed to the beach with the same speed that citizens to-day show in leaving church at the alarm of a forest fire. There is a story of a Truro youngster who abandoned some cows he was driving to pasture and, unaided, captured and killed a porpoise that he saw floundering about on the flats. The boy held him by the tail to prevent his thrashing his way into deep water, and then, after dispatching him with a knife, stripped off the blubber with the skill of a professional.

All was fish that came to the townsmen's net provided it contained a gallon of oil, and every chance prize — from the lone porpoise of the Truro boy to the record school of two thousand blackfish taken at Provincetown in 1884 — was drained to the last drop. By 1850 findings were keepings; in that year Captain Daniel Rich cut his mark in the sides of a school of seventy-five blackfish on the beach between Wellfleet and Truro and thereby established an indisputable claim to them. Within twenty-four hours he had sold them as they lay for $1900. That the Standard Oil Company has not altogether changed the Cape-Codder's attitude toward drift whales was illustrated in July, 1928, when eighty blackfish came ashore at Eastham. The lucky man who found them collected twelve dollars apiece from parties in New Bedford, who hurried to Eastham and took the 'melon' from the head of each blackfish. Since the 'melon' contains oil which, when properly tried out, brings upward of sixty dollars a gallon, it is safe to say that New Bedford lost nothing by the transaction. On the other hand, a lone dead finback, sixty-five feet long, which drifted into Barnstable Harbor in the autumn of 1928, had to be towed to sea at the town's expense lest he pollute the water and spoil the clams.

Not every school of blackfish, however, or every lone whale that was sighted offshore, was unlucky enough to be stranded on the flats. More than once the citizens who lined the beach, waiting for the prize to blunder into shoal water, were chagrined to see it turn seaward and vanish. One or two such experiences changed the townspeople from watchful waiters into pursuers. Their tactics at first, at least as regards blackfish, were not very aggressive, for most of them were farmers and more dexterous with a pitchfork than with a harpoon. Their method was to surround the fish in a fleet of small boats and, by beating the water with the flat of their oar blades, to drive them ashore in a panic. This maneuver was an exciting one to execute and it produced good results. It is easy to imagine a fleet of dories half a mile off shore, spread out fanlike beyond a school of blackfish, and slowly closing in with yelling and splashing until the fish struck the sand. Then the fun was over and the work began, the proceeds usually being divided equally among the boats that had taken part in the pursuit.

It must be clearly understood that these men were in no sense of the word whalemen. They were not professionals but amateurs. None of them owned any whaling gear, or would have known how to use it if he had owned it. To them a harpoon was a dangerous weapon — not a tool of their trade. They were no more whalemen than a man who shoots a skunk in his henyard is a hunter. But some of the youngest had the makings of whalemen in them. They had tasted the wine of pursuit, and it was an insidious vintage; it urged them to try a deeper draught by cruising round the Bay and harpooning whales.

This was called shore-whaling, and though the men who practiced it never went on long voyages, and though the Cape-Horners who came afterwards regarded them much as deep-water shipmasters regarded coasting skippers, they were nevertheless real whalemen, and experienced the same thrills of pursuit and capture as their successors who cruised to Davis Straits or the South Pacific. Furthermore, they had the advantage of being able to operate their farms in spring and summer. The tactics of the shore whalemen were simple. They watched from the shore until they saw a spout or the rounded backs of a school of blackfish. Then they shoved off in clinker-built cedar whaleboats, and the chase began. If they came up with the monster and succeeded in planting an iron, they played him in the regular way, paying out line around a post in the bow of the boat as long as they could, and, as a last resort, heaving overboard a drag — or heavy buoy — with the end of the line made fast to it. When finally they came close enough to the exhausted whale to reach 'the life' with a lance, the excitement was over and the toil began, for the carcass had to be towed ashore — sometimes a distance of a good many miles. When their boat grounded, they dragged the carcass up the beach with heavy tackle rigged to a capstan. There the blubber was boiled in the try-yard near by, and the bone was scraped and cleaned.

As long as the supply of local whales held out, shore-whaling on the Cape was profitable and immensely popular. Barnstable, Yarmouth, and Truro reserved whaling grounds for the use of their citizens. No doubt other towns made similar pro-

BLACKFISH ASHORE AT PROVINCETOWN

SANDY NECK AND THE HAY-GROUNDS, WEST BARNSTABLE

vision. Chatham, at any rate, offered to exempt the Reverend Daniel Greenleaf, of Yarmouth, from all taxation if he would settle somewhere in Chatham and follow shore-whaling. But the minister apparently decided that empty souls in Yarmouth were more important than empty oil casks in Chatham, for he did not move.

Most of the young men, after a taste of this sport, found farm work dull, forsook the plough for the harpoon and lance, and lived in whale-houses alongshore. Two hundred Barnstable men were shore-whalers in 1715 for three months of every year. And no wonder, for sometimes stranger creatures than blackfish challenged their skill. In 1719, a sea-monster appeared in Provincetown Harbor and defied the combined efforts of a whole fleet of shore-whalemen; B. Franklin (uncle of the celebrated Benjamin) has left a racy account of its appearance:

Boston, Sept 28, 1719. On the 17 Instant there appear'd in Cape-Cod harbour a strange creature, His head like a Lyons, with very large Teeth, Ears hanging down, a large Beard, a long beard, with curling hair on his head, his Body a bout 16 foot Long, a round buttock, with a short Tayle of a yellowish colour, the Whale boats gave him chase, he was very fierce and gnashed his teeth with great rage when they attackt him, he was shot at 3 times and Wounded, when he rose out of the Water he always faced the boats in that angry maner, the Harpaniers struck at him, but in vaine, for after 5 hours chase, he took to sea again. None of the people ever saw his like befor.

Provincetowners, it would seem, were still fond of strong waters! Captain John Thacher, whose duty it was to draft recruits for the French and Indians Wars, had great trouble in rounding up the young bloods who were shore-whaling. In a letter to Governor Stoughton he says: 'All our young and strong men are employed in whaling and mostly have their rendivous remote from the towns, and if they see any man coming towards them, presently mistrust; make a shout and run into the thickets.'

So jealous was each town of its whaling rights that trespassers were instantly detected and either warned off or forced to pay for the privilege of fishing the local waters. By 1711, the barren stretches of Sandy Neck in Barnstable had caught the eye of strangers as being a good base for whaling stations. Some of them squatted there, to the displeasure of the Proprietors, who promptly voted that 'every stranger, both English and Indian, that shall come and settle at Sandy Neck to go on whaling voyages... shall pay for their fire wood each person three shillings, at entry.' The amount of fuel consumed in the try-houses must have been enormous, and this was one of the many factors in the demolition of the Cape forests.

Not content with challenging strangers who came poaching whales, the authorities of the various towns kept a sharp eye on the activities of their neighbors. Thus, in 1758, Eastham considered measures for preventing Harwich enthusiasts from pursuing whales at Billingsgate. Drift whales, too, were still bones of contention, particularly when they came ashore near town lines. A contemporary jingle states the situation exactly:

'Down on East Harbor bar there lays a cow and a calf;
Provincetowners swear they'll have the whole;
Truroers swear they shan't have but half.'

But such difficulties were easy to settle compared with the disputes that arose over whales that had been wounded in the Bay by men from one town, had escaped, and had afterwards died and been washed ashore within the limits of another. Did the oil belong to the boat's crew that struck the whale; to the town where the body had been found stranded; to the man who found it, or to the owner of the strip of beach where the carcass came ashore? Here, for example, is an affidavit signed by a Barnstable man who found himself trying to harpoon a whale off Truro:

Dec. 7th, 1725; The declaration of John Lewis in Barnstable. — I, being at sea near a place called Hogg's Back, with the boat's company, I then and there struck and wounded a whale fish, she lying soothing under water; — my iron took her upon the rising of her bulge, but she drawing my iron made play, and was soon struck and wounded by James Bearse, and after awhile drawing his iron, she still making play, was in a few moments struck by Thomas Thatcher, and they and we soon killed said whale.

JOHN LEWIS

Attest, JOHN SNOW — *Town Clerk*

Clearly this affidavit was connected with a dispute over the ownership of the whale, and Lewis and his friends were indeed in a dilemma. It was out of the question to tow the carcass all the way to Barnstable; if they brought it ashore at Truro, the townsmen would probably warn them off or charge rent for the beach. And Lewis's predicament was only one of many like it. The only solution in such cases was to equip boats with casks to hold chunks of blubber that could be cut up at sea and carried home to be tried out in the local try-yards. This practice was followed for a time, and from then on it was only a step to the last stage in the development of whaling. Men went farther and farther from shore in bigger and bigger vessels that carried try-works built into their decks, until at last cruises of four years were not uncommon. Scarcity of whales now drove men to sea oftener than disputes. The constant activity of hundreds of shore-whalemen had chased the monsters out of the Bay so effectively that by the middle of the eighteenth century only an occasional whale was sighted. Shore-whaling was a thing of the past — it was now a question of deep water or nothing. The Cape chose deep water.

But the vanishing of the shore-whaleman's livelihood must not be taken lightly. It was a very real disaster to scores of Cape families, some of whom had neither the capital nor the courage to follow the whales to sea. In 1739, only about half a dozen whales were taken in Provincetown waters, and a number of families decided to move away. Ten years later, the citizens of Yarmouth were so impoverished by the failure of the whale-fishery that they were barely able to give the minister an increase in salary they had promised him. It was only by the titanic exertions of the wealthiest and most energetic citizens on the Cape that money was raised in each town and fleets equipped for deep-sea whaling.

Truro was the pioneer in this hazardous business. In 1758, one of her citizens, Captain Henry Atkins, cleared from Boston for Davis Straits in the ship Whale, and filled in the gaps between whales by trading with the natives. He soon found that this was by far the quickest and cheapest way to get bone, for in return for ten shillings-worth of trinkets they gave him whalebone valued at one hundred and twenty pounds! Other Truro whalemen cruised along the shores of Africa, and two of them, Captains David Smith and Gamaliel Collins, won fame that reached the ears of the British Parliament when in 1774 they pursued whales as far south as the Falkland Islands. Not content with this bleak outpost, others soon rounded the Horn and pursued sperm whales in the uncharted waters of the South Pacific.

Wellfleet, during the years preceding the Revolution, devoted almost her entire energy to whaling. Nearly every man in town was a whaleman — and the result of thus putting all the eggs in one basket was that the declaration of war in 1775 and the immediate blockading of the Cape ports utterly prostrated the town. The citizens could not pay the Provincial tax and, in a petition to the General Court for exemption, they declared that nine tenths of the townsmen had been engaged in whaling and were now left with no source of income. Exaggerated as this statement may appear, it is borne out by statistics, which show that four hundred and twenty men and twenty or thirty vessels were thus employed at Wellfleet up to the beginning of the war. The local honors were divided about evenly between Captain Jesse Holbrook, whom the British employed to teach them the art, and Colonel Elisha Doane, who, having learned in his youth how to handle a harpoon, spent the latter years of his life financing the voyages of others and reaping the profits — with such success that he died one of the richest men in Massachusetts. After the war, Wellfleet tried to launch her fleet again; but none of the citizens had capital enough to build new vessels, and the old ones had perished during the seven years of disuse. In 1802, her fleet had shrunk to five schooners, and these set sail half-heartedly; they lacked the confidence that is necessary for success, and were quite as much fishermen as whalers, carrying salt and fish lines as well as whaling gear.

Taken by and large, Provincetown has done most for Cape whaling. Provincetown, indeed, ranks with Truro as a pioneer in the business, and continued it long after the last Truro whaleman was in his grave. The town was virtually depopulated when, in the middle of the eighteenth century, twelve whalers were equipped and manned in its harbor and set out simultaneously on long voyages. The Revolution gave the Provincetown whalemen pause, but did not stop them altogether, for after the war, they started out again with a determination unequaled anywhere else on the Cape, and succeeded in bringing the business back to a prosperous basis. The Civil War dealt it another blow; several of the whalers burned by Confederate cruisers were owned in Provincetown. But even this — a heavy loss for so small a town — did not kill the business. With high courage, the citizens began once more to sharpen their harpoons, and in 1876 they had seventeen whaling vessels at sea. Thanks to the energy of such men as Captain John Cook, the Cape flag was flying on the whaling grounds until 1916. During the last century about one hundred and seventy-five whaling vessels have hailed from Provincetown.

The history of these three towns, Truro, Wellfleet, and Provincetown, comprises the bulk of the history of the Cape long-voyage whale-fishery. But no town was immune. Eastham was represented until the eighties by Captain Edward Penniman, who commanded half a dozen different barks out of New Bedford, and, on retiring, handed the torch to his son Eugene, who continued until the business died. Falmouth has a goodly list of vessels and commanders to her credit, the most celebrated of whom — Captain Silas Jones of the Awashonks — will demand further attention presently. Barnstable now and then sent out a whaler, and was credited with two at the beginning of the Revolution. During the Civil War, Semmes burned one of Sandwich's two representatives, the brig Ocean.

But not even Provincetown and Wellfleet, in their palmiest days, were in a class with Nantucket in its time. Long before the Revolution the pupil had far outstripped his teacher, and the men who a century before had sent to the Cape for a whaling instructor were now in a position to instruct Cape-Codders. Forty men left Harwich for the new whaling headquarters in 1760.

Yet the Cape whalemen, before they yielded the palm to Nantucket, and afterwards as well, were leading lives of adventure in remote seas that made them something more than mere killers of whales. They were not always successful, either. Captain Solomon Sturgis, for example, who sailed his sloop out of Barnstable on a whaling voyage in 1741, was no match for a Spanish privateer who seized his vessel but let the chagrined Captain escape. Then there was the question of storms. As a matter of fact, whalemen were better off in bad weather than their more aristocratic brethren of the merchant service, for their barrel-bottomed, apple-cheeked hulls, built for capacity and without a thought for speed, were as good dirty-weather sailing vessels as have ever been built. Unlike the clippers, they were not heavily sparred; the crew had no towering sky-sails or moonrakers to struggle with, and the Captain never hesitated to snug down at night, for there was just as much danger of sailing past a school of whales in the dark as there was of not coming up with one. So the whalers rode out in comfort many a storm that would have brought the overcrowded spars of a merchantman crashing down on the heads of the overdriven crew.

But no ship is safe at sea, and even the stout barks of the blubber-boilers were sometimes in trouble. In 1881, Captain Caleb Hamblin, of Sandwich, commander and half-owner of the brig Henry Trowbridge, was returning from a combination whaling and sealing voyage below Cape Horn. In the tricky latitudes of the West Indies, a hurricane tore down on his vessel and swept her decks clean, carrying both masts over the side. When the storm was over, Captain Hamblin rigged jury masts, set what sail they could carry, and worked his way to the Azores — a distance of about a thousand miles. This achievement is important, not because it is unusual — hundreds of shipmasters have done as much — but because it answers an accusation that is sometimes heard, to the effect that whalemen were not sailors. If this means that they did not spend their time making Flemish eyes or hoisting coach-whip pennants, the statement is true. But such frills were refinements of the sailor's art, not essentials of it. When it came to sending down a sprung spar, setting up new shrouds, or reeving off running rigging in a high sea, the whalemen were as good as any British East-Indiaman. They had to be, in fact, for their cruises took them for months at a time to unfrequented corners of the world far from any ports where they could put in for repairs. The best they could hope for was the shelter of an atoll where the natives were friendly and would let them work in peace. At worst they could set up new spars and rigging at sea — as Captain Hamblin's crew did in the South Atlantic. Resourcefulness beyond the usual resourcefulness of sailors was the prerequisite for the captain of a whaler; and it is fair to say that resourcefulness is as valuable an asset to a sailor as knowing how to make a Flemish eye.

Like many of the wives of whaling captains, Mrs. Hamblin, herself the daughter of a shipbuilder, went several voyages with her husband, and after the two came ashore for good and settled in Falmouth, she had something more interesting to talk about than the outrageous behavior of the neighbors. She had been round the world, had had one child born at sea in the cabin of the Eliza Adams, another in New Zealand, and a third in Australia. Hers was the horizon that bounds the seven seas; she liked Falmouth, but she knew that Falmouth was not the world. Captain Hamblin, too, was more than a seaman. Early in his career, while second officer of the Congress, he found himself half in and half out of the mouth of a sperm whale that was fifty feet under water and headed for the bottom. The whale had a harpoon in his side, and before the monster had carried out all the line, Hamblin managed to take a couple of turns with it around his hands. It jerked taut; the whale was captured; and the young whaleman, half drowned, his arms pulled almost out of their sockets, and with a wide gash the length of one leg, was hauled into the boat — ready for the next encounter. It is dangerous to generalize about human nature, but it is a reasonable guess that such a man, when he retires and settles down at home, is not likely to go to law if an overenthusiastic young marksman breaks his henhouse window with a stone.

Silas Jones, of Falmouth, was twenty-one years old when, in 1835, he started on a four-year cruise as third mate of the whaler Awashonks. After the ship had been a year or two at sea, Captain Coffin hove to in a squall in the lee of Baring's Island in the South Pacific. It has not been his intention to trade with the natives of the island; in fact, according to the chart it was uninhabited. But as soon as the squall blew over, a number of canoes put off from shore and headed for the Awashonks. The chief, followed by a group of naked savages, clambered over the rail, and the crew began to barter with them for cocoanuts and breadfruit while the Captain and Mr. Gardiner, the first mate, went below for dinner, leaving Jones in charge. Scrap iron was the currency the natives chiefly desired; soon they had turned over all their fresh fruit for some bits of this metal, and with the usual curiosity of primitive peoples, were nosing about the deck examining everything with the greatest interest. The gleaming blades of the cutting-in spades, neatly ranged in their racks, seemed to fascinate them particularly; they tried the edges with their thumbs, their eyes wide in admiration.

The Captain, who had finished his dinner and come on deck, good-naturedly showed the natives how they were used on whales. Their excitement and wonder grew; they began to jabber in their outlandish dialect and more canoes appeared alongside. Some of the newcomers were armed, and young Jones, who felt vaguely uneasy, gladly obeyed the Captain's orders to disarm them before they came on deck. While he was thus engaged, he heard a whoop from behind, and turned to see the natives making a rush for the spades. They got most of them and in the twinkling of an eye had sliced off the Captain's head, killed the first mate, and were starting operations on the crew. The second mate dived overboard and was never seen again. This left Jones in command. He jumped into the midst of the fight, grabbed a spade from one of the islanders and thrust at him with it so hard that the blade was embedded in the woodwork of the deckhouse, and he was left unarmed. He attacked one native with his fists, but was confronted by three more, one of whom had a spear. Realizing that in another second it would be lodged in his breast, Jones leaped down the open hatchway into the forehold. Here he picked up one or two recruits, and they made their way aft below decks and forced an entrance to the cabin.

Here there was a moment's respite, which was used in loading all the firearms the ship carried, and from the shelter of the cabin Jones and his followers, one of whom was desperately wounded and another useless from fright, directed a musket fire that for a moment silenced the yells of the savages, who were now masters of the deck, with their chief standing in childlike pride at the helm, though he knew as little of its use as a baby at the wheel of a motor-car. He was invisible from the cabin, but, realizing that some one was monkeying with the steering-gear, and alarmed lest the ship might go aground,

Jones and one of the crew fired at the same moment through the cabin roof in the direction of the wheel, and by great luck killed the chief. This was the turning-point of the fight. Some of the natives took to the canoes; others stood undecided, their thirst for blood still unquenched. It was the strategic moment for a sally, and Jones led the way on deck with a loaded musket. He found that the battle was over. The last of the savages had gone over the side and was swimming for shore in the wake of the departing canoes. The vessel was promptly headed away from this 'uninhabited' island, and Jones, keenly aware of his new responsibility, divided his time between sewing up the gashes of his men and navigating his ship. After fifty days he dropped anchor in Honolulu Harbor and turned the Awashonks over to the American Consul.

This bloody experience did not discourage Silas Jones. He continued to go on whaling voyages and commanded various vessels out of Falmouth until after the Civil War. One of them was the Commodore Morris, whose figurehead — a grim representation of this maritime celebrity — at present occupies a prominent position in Mr. Hutchinson's bookstore in New Bedford. Jones himself, after leaving the sea, directed the fortunes of his native town of Falmouth with the same resolution and vigor which he had shown as a lad in shooting the Baring's Island savages off the deck of the Awashonks.

Another Cape-Codder from the opposite end of the peninsula came within an ace of having his vessel, the bark Parker Cook, stove and sunk by a fighting whale. This was Captain Cook, of Provincetown. In 1850, while cruising in the Atlantic, he lowered for a whale, and two irons were planted in the monster. Like a flash he turned, rising almost out of water, and capsizing the boat. In the mêlée, a turn of line caught the boatsteerer's leg and almost cut it through. The whale then attacked the Parker Cook, and rushed straight for her bow, hitting the cutwater with such violence that it was driven deep into the creature's head. The impact knocked the men on deck flat, and the vessel staggered from stem to stern as if she had struck a derelict. The whale suffered more than the bark, however, and though he tried another charge, his ardor was quenched, and Captain Cook dispatched him with three shots from the bomb-lance. The crew of the wrecked whaleboat were picked up, and all hands took savage satisfaction in extracting one hundred and three barrels of oil from this ferocious old bull. The Parker Cook put in to Fayal for repairs to her cutwater, and here the injured bo's'n received more skilled treatment than was to be had on board.

Whaling captains had to turn surgeon oftener than other shipmasters, for their voyages were measured in months instead of in weeks, and they spent those months in the most hazardous business that has ever been followed by man. Irrespective of what injuries whales themselves might inflict, the constant use of formidable weapons like cutting-in spades, harpoons and lances in the crowded quarters of pitching boats and rocking decks, produced frightful wounds with a frequency that even the unluckiest merchant mariner was spared. And when it came to Arctic cruises for bowheads and bone, the Captain was obliged to treat frozen hands or feet so often that it became almost a part of the routine.

Arctic whaling was, in fact, a separate science, and a grimmer calling it is hard for a steam-heated generation to imagine. It combined all the dangers of sperm whaling in southern latitudes with the perils of polar exploration; and it was besides the bitterest test that human patience can be put to, for the voyages sometimes lasted four years, and of this time only about six months could be spent in whaling; the remaining forty-two consisted of living aboard a vessel frozen fast in an ice-bound harbor and trusting to native hunters to supply venison. Captain John Atkins Cook, of Provincetown, whose book describing his northern whaling voyages has been recently published, is the last of the Cape-Codders who has followed this calling. What can have induced this indomitable whaleman to make voyage after voyage to the Arctic it is hard to imagine. Not the hope of riches, certainly, for a man of Captain Cook's abilities could have made more money in any one of a dozen callings at home. The only explanation that suggests itself is that the love of encountering and overcoming hardships — of succeeding where many fail — perhaps, too, the lure which the very desolation of the North exerts on some men, kept Captain Cook's vessel headed time and again for the frozen latitudes of Bering

Strait. In addition to his other troubles, the Arctic whalemen had problems of navigation to solve, of which the merchant sailor knew nothing. Here is what Captain Cook himself says on this topic:

These voyages in the Arctic seas present to the master some of the most intricate problems of navigation that the world has ever known. As the Arctic navigator, leaving San Francisco in February looks to the eastern horizon and sees the last blink of the Farallone Light (off Golden Gate) he realizes that in his lonely watch at night or when steaming along among the loose ice off the coast of Alaska, and in search of whales in the Far North among the icefields, that light is the last guide he will have, and that no beacon by night or buoys by day are to be seen by him to warn of treacherous shoals or other dangers. No: he must sail without them and depend upon his past experience to bring him out safely.

Captain Cook had his full share of surgery to perform during his many Arctic voyages. On one occasion a Provincetown boy, Fred West, sailed with the Captain and was soon made third mate. During the winter at Herschel's Island, West obtained the Captain's permission to go inland on a hunting expedition with another member of the ship's company. While he was taking a loaded gun from the canoe, the trigger caught, and young West got both barrels in the upper arm. He was brought back senseless and almost dead from pain and loss of blood. Captain Cook and the captains of three other whalers took him to a hut on shore and gave him a tumblerful of raw whisky and a whiff of chloroform. Then they amputated the arm so successfully that, in spite of its loss, West continued to follow the sea in command of coasting schooners until 1923, when he was drowned off the Delaware Capes.

In 1908, Captain Cook turned his attention to sperm whaling in Southern waters, and had the brigantine Viola built for the purpose. In this graceful vessel — which looked like a yacht — the Captain and his wife set sail for a two years' cruise, and made successful voyages in the South Atlantic and along the African Coast until 1916. This business, strenuous though it was, seemed child's play to Captain Cook after the rigors of the Northern icefields, and his voyages for sperm were more like pleasure cruises than work. In 1916 he retired for good — the last of the Cape Cod whalemen.

It is easy, dazzled by the glamour of far voyages to palm-fringed islands, to be deceived into false sentimentality toward this great dead industry. Many an up-state farmer's boy, lured by the will-o'-the-wisp of romance, left his plough in the furrow and went whaling — to end his days a beachcomber, disillusioned and beaten. It was a grim game, with the dollar always at the helm. But the financial side of it, with all its ruthlessness and with all that it led to — hazing men into deserting with money due them; overcharging for shoddy clothing from the slop chest and underfeeding until the hungry crew looked greedily on slices of broiled whale meat — all this was not more destructive to men's fiber than herding together in a forecastle, compared to which the forecastles of clippers were palatial, a miscellaneous crew composed of round-eyed lads from the Vermont hills and crime-hardened degenerates who ought to have been in jail. Men were not made to live by themselves; wherever circumstances force them to do so, they seek, like water, the level of the lowest and most vicious among them. The forecastles of whaling barks produced these circumstances as perfectly as they have ever been produced in the world, and our fresh-cheeked youngster, who embarked on a voyage as immaculate as a man can be, stood a fine chance of emerging from his four years' association with the dregs of the water-front, as hardened a character as they.

> 'She'd a crew of blacks from the Cape Verde Isles
>   That spoke in Portagee,
> With men from Norway, Finland too,
>   And the shores of the Irish Sea.

> 'She'd whites from the rocky Yankee farms
>   Mixed up with Sandwich brown,
> With a skipper who hailed from New Bedford,
>   And a mate from Westport Town.'

Beside learning vice, the young whalemen learned violence. A three months' voyage from New York to San Francisco in a clipper ship, with a ventilated deckhouse for the crew, was enough to beget frequent mutinies; what, then, can we expect from a forty months' cruise in a bobtailed blubber-boiler? Mutinies there were aplenty, and not without good reason did whaling captains sometimes sign on five mates to help them hold the lid on. Cook went through one Arctic winter with a mutinous crew—the only wonder is that crews in those latitudes ever refrained from mutiny. The sperm whalemen opened the petcock from time to time by calling at Honolulu, or Tahiti, or Guam, where men might desert instead of killing an officer, and where natives could easily be procured as replacements. But captains often neglected this safety valve, and stayed at sea as long as there was an unbroached barrel of salt horse in the hold, or a gallon of ropy water in the butts. Under such conditions, is it surprising that Captain Nathaniel Burgess, of Bourne, who made his last voyage with a crew that represented nine nationalities, called discipline the whaling captain's most serious problem?

Time has blurred the sharp and cruel outlines of life on a whaler. In our enthusiasm over those who returned victorious, we are likely to forget the many who were left behind, broken and polluted, to drag out the last years of their lives on the beach of a coral island. To-day there are those who lament the passing of this undoubtedly picturesque, though certainly ruinous industry. But the world is a better place without long-voyage whaling than it ever was with it. Keenly as we appreciate the skill and self-reliance and valor that it taught some of the men who practiced it, we cannot forget the merciless malignity with which it shattered the rest. The wreck of the Wanderer, New Bedford's last whaler, in the summer of 1925, was a happy event for the march of civilization.

CHAPTER X

FISHERIES

THE story of the Cape fisheries begins and ends at Provincetown, but the midships section of it finds Provincetown nowhere. The beginning came in what, from the point of view of
this volume, were prehistoric days — prior to 1620, that is —
when wild European fishermen squatted in shacks along the
Provincetown shore and drank rum with the Indians. During
the early 'historical' period, when the rest of the Cape was
farming, Provincetown was hardly in existence: it had not even
been officially settled. A little later, when the other towns were
merrily catching cod, the cluster of shanties on the beach way
down below High Head was wondering whether or not it was
ever going to achieve the dignity of a town. But finally, when
the demand came for larger vessels and longer voyages, the
creek harbors of the upper Cape became worthless, while a fleet
of schooners swung easily at anchor inside Long Point, and
fishermen flocked to Provincetown as deer to a salt-lick. Later
still, capital concentrated the fleet at Gloucester and Boston,
and Provincetown was once more abandoned. Such, in a
nutshell, are the stages in the development of fishing on the
Cape.

It is pleasant to grope back into the prehistoric age — that
dim, enchanted era of the sixteenth century, where the labored
quill of no town clerk has left records of fact to clip the wings of
fancy. Provincetown had no written records to tell of the com-
ings and goings of adventurers on her shores. The best we can
do is to pick up the story in the middle, and even there our
information is so meager as to be of little historical value.
One thing, however, is certain; phantom ships of nameless fishermen entered Provincetown Harbor before 1600, and

continued to do so, unrecorded and often unobserved except by Indians, for the next hundred years.

Then in 1714, the Court, judging that the time had come to snatch the brand from the burning, put the untamed community under Truro's jurisdiction. Here its importance comes to an end for the time being. A life of captivity seems not to have agreed with it. No longer could outlandish crews enjoy the license of a wilderness, and so exposed were its shores to French privateers that all but three families moved away during the long wars that followed.

Meantime, fish had become an important factor in the lives of the settlers farther up the Cape. Of course they had always caught fish enough for their own tables, but they had been too busy farming to go fishing for a livelihood. The thrift of the Old Colony, however, could not bear to let great schools of cod and mackerel swim about the Bay without bringing so much as a shilling into the treasury. But the Plymouth settlers were such unskillful fishermen that, in spite of the abundance of fish, they usually returned empty-handed. Realizing the limitations of its children, the Court frankly surrendered, farmed out the fishing rights to more expert persons, and used the revenue to support a school.

Among the first Cape men to hire these rights was Thomas Huckins, of Barnstable, an enterprising man of business whose manifold activities had made him amphibious as early as 1660 — perhaps earlier. Aside from various public offices which he held from time to time, Huckins kept the tavern, whose cellar was well stocked with rum which he brought from Boston in his own packet. As he was his own rum-carrier, so was he his own fisherman. In those days men did not hire others to do what they were able to do themselves. Even if he had wished to employ some one else to do his fishing, it is doubtful whether he could have found any one without going far afield, for Huckins was very early for a Cape-Codder in the fish business. In his day the soil was still good, and most men were exulting in the ownership of their fields and houses.

By degrees, as the novelty of possession wore off and the soil grew thin, others began to follow Huckins's lead and, looking out over the Bay, decided to try their luck afloat for a season.

Early in the eighteenth century, John Gorham, of Barnstable, a member of the fighting family that distinguished
itself in the French and Indian Wars, was starting in as a trader
with a place of business on the wharf at the foot of Scudder's
Lane. Before long — perhaps as early as 1730 — he had cod-
fishermen making voyages to the Grand Banks for him and
carrying their fares to the West Indies, whence they returned
with cargoes of rum and molasses. Eastham at this time was
busy not only fishing but also taking measures to prevent the
destruction of fish by porpoises — which apparently were as
great a pest as the seals in Barnstable Harbor are to-day. The
town offered a bounty on porpoise tails, and was called upon
to pay for a good many of them. Elisha Young seems to have
been the most successful man at the business; he turned in some
five hundred tails between 1740 and 1742, all of them duly recorded by the town clerk. Other Cape fishermen, notably Eldad
Nickerson, of Chatham, found their way to Nova Scotia waters
well before 1760. Some of them, it will be remembered, were
so taken with the convenient location of Barrington, so encouraged by Governor Lawrence's inducements to settlers, and
so tired of wars and taxes at home, that they left the Cape for
good and became inhabitants of Nova Scotia before the Revolution began.

The Cape fishing fleet — for the number of vessels had in the
late colonial period grown large enough to be dignified with this
term — by degrees established a well-fixed routine over the
triangular course which Gorham's schooners had navigated
fifty years before: from Cape Cod to the Grand Banks, where
they filled their holds with cod, which they salted and dried on
whatever beach lay closest at hand; thence to the West Indies,
where they traded their salty cargo for rum and molasses, and so
back home with a handsome potential profit under the hatches.
Those who could not afford large enough vessels for the West
Indian voyage, and for whom the rugged water of the Grand
Banks was too great a risk, fished closer to the Newfoundland
shore, salted their catch just enough to keep it during the run
home, finished 'making' it on their own beaches, and sold it in
Boston. Harwich, Chatham, and Barnstable were at this time
the chief fishing ports of the Cape.

It was a miscellaneous-looking flotilla that went codfishing in the colonial days from the creeks and harbors of the Cape. Standardization had not yet produced one-design vessels like the fleet which was owned in Provincetown a hundred years later, or that which keeps Gloucester on the map to-day. Men used such boats as they had or could afford to build. The largest of them were round-bottomed, two-masted schooners, measuring not more than seventy tons, but able to carry their fares from the Grand Banks across the Atlantic to Spain, if the West India prices failed to attract them. But these vessels called for more capital than most Cape fishermen could raise. The best the majority could do was to hug the shore in tubby sloops and put in at some cove at the first sign of weather. Always, too, there were the boat fishermen — the humblest and poorest of them all, but by no means the hungriest — who would hoist a spritsail in a whaleboat and spend the day hand-lining for cod on the ledge off Barnstable, or outside Long Point if they hailed from Provincetown. These unambitious citizens kept a supply of fresh fish in town for local consumption while the Grand-Bankers were away. As often as not they were half-farmers, with a patch of corn to be hoed if they felt like staying ashore. Altogether the boat fisherman lived as independent and irresponsible a life as men are likely to achieve in this existence. He had no money tied up in large vessels, to send him fishing whether or no; his table was well supplied with the produce of sea and shore; when northeasters howled in from the Atlantic, he smoked his pipe beside a six-foot fireplace and thanked God that he was not shortening sail on the Grand Banks. Wise men, if not admirable, were these boat fishermen of colonial days.

Then came the Revolution, sweeping banker and boat fisherman, whaleman and merchant, from the seas more completely than all the storms of a generation. Chatham's experience is typical. When the war began, she had a fleet of twenty-seven cod-fishermen. In 1783, four or five were all that remained. It was a costly victory which the citizens had won, and clearly it was the moment for the government which they had fought to create to lend them a helping hand.

This the Administration was not slow to do. In 1789, Congress voted to pay a bounty on all exported codfish; in 1792, another bounty was granted to cod-fishermen who were busy at their calling four months in the year. Cape-Codders, like the rest of New England, began to rebuild their fleet, but they headed more often for new fishing grounds — the Bay de Chaleur and the Labrador Coast — where small craft were adequate and where miles of desolate beaches lay close at hand on which they could salt their catch enough for the voyage home. The Grand Banks were not abandoned; but the ease of the new waters and the fact that they could be reached in inexpensive vessels, appealed to all but the richest and hardiest.

This shifting of the bulk of the tonnage to short-voyage work covered the shore-front of the Cape villages with fish flakes lying gray to the sun, for the small size of the new vessels made even a West India voyage too risky. From now on, the bulk of the catch was cured at home. The process of making fish which was followed at this early date never changed, so long as there was a schooner in the business or a quintal of codfish to be sold. As soon as a homeward-bound vessel dropped anchor, the fish were boated into shallow water in dories, washed clean of their salt, and rolled up to the flakes in wheelbarrows. The flakes were low platforms, with slats instead of planking; on these the fish, split, washed, and again salted, were laid to dry in the sun — in much the same manner as one broils a steak. They had to be turned every now and then, and in rainy weather were stacked and covered with tarpaulins.

This trend in business brought Provincetown into her own. She had long since grown accustomed to law and order, but was still numerically insignificant. In 1755, ten houses sheltered her entire population. Apparently discouraged by the long detour around East Harbor Creek, the census-taker of 1764 ignored the town altogether. But now that the impoverished condition of the young country was setting the fashion for home-cured fish, Provincetown began to flourish.

Beaches? She was all beach, with her houses strung along just far enough from the water's edge to leave room for sheds and flakes between. As for her harbor, the whole New England fishing fleet could have anchored in it with room to spare. Drawn into codfishing by pre-war habit and government bounties, and to Provincetown by its facilities for the business, men who up to

PART OF PROVINCETOWN'S FISHING FLEET A GENERATION AGO

PROVINCETOWN FISH-FLAKES WITH SCHOONER FREDDIE W. ALTON
AT THE DOCK

that time had regarded Provincetowners with scorn, now migrated eagerly to the sandy tip of the Cape to share in her growing prosperity. In 1790, Provincetown had 20 vessels that went codfishing to the Grand Banks, the Labrador Coast, and the Bay de Chaleur. A dozen years later the number had grown to 33. This branch of the business alone gave employment to 225 Provincetown men and boys, besides 75 from neighboring towns. They brought home on the average 33,000 quintals of cod a year, worth $3.50 a quintal. Half these were salted on Labrador beaches, half at home. But this was not all. From October to December — off months for the cod-fishermen — they shipped more than 5000 barrels of herring at $4 a barrel. About the time that the fleet set sail for the Banks in the spring, boat fishermen began to catch mackerel in local waters, and it was a poor season when they did not ship 300 barrels pickled to Boston before the fish struck off. Some of the mackerel-catchers used seines, of which there were 50 in the town worth $100 apiece. And five vessels were kept steadily at work carrying lobsters from both sides of Long Point to New York.

All this business called for kindred industries ashore. Ten salt works made 8000 hogsheads of salt a year, every pound of which was bought by the cod-fishermen and mackerel-catchers; five buildings were used for smoking herring and ninety for storing fish. The population jumped from 812 in 1800 to 946 in 1802. All this Provincetown achieved during the twenty years that followed the Revolution. From being an inconsequential, half-civilized settlement before the War, and the headquarters for sea-weary Britishers during the War, Provincetown by 1840 had grown to be a famous fishing port with a larger fleet than any other town on the Cape.

Meantime, the rest of the Cape had not been idle. The shore-front of every village was a scene of healthy activity. In 1802, Wellfleet, in addition to five whalers that went to the Straits of Belle Isle and Newfoundland waters equipped for codfishing if whales were scarce, had four vessels engaged in offshore cod- and mackerel-fishing, four oyster-carriers with a capacity of thirty tons apiece, and a dozen smaller craft that kept busy hand-lining within sight of Billingsgate. Orleans had no harbor suitable for a fishing fleet of her own, yet 'the flower of the people' from twelve to forty-five years old sailed on cod-fishermen out of Provincetown, Chatham, Duxbury, and Plymouth. Eastham, never a great fishing town, had only three vessels in the business, but Chatham owned twenty-five, half of them Grand-Bankers; the other half divided their time between the Nantucket Shoals and Nova Scotian waters. Two hundred men and boys were thus employed, and their annual catch of cod was some 17,500 quintals — about one half Provincetown's average. Harwich had the same number of fishermen, most of whom went on small vessels of forty tons or so to the Nantucket Shoals, though four good-sized schooners sailed regularly to the Straits of Belle Isle. A tidy little fleet of twenty Dennis vessels was moored in Bass River or tied up alongside the three wharves; but they were all small — none being over forty tons. On the Bay side of the town a half-dozen more wintered in the Bass Hole and Quivet Creek. Yarmouth had ten fishing vessels as well as a good-sized fleet of coasters. One hundred men in Barnstable pulled a living from the sea. If the reader is not utterly bewildered by these statistics, he will have gathered that by 1802 almost every village was baiting a good many hooks once more.

But the years that followed the Revolution were not plain sailing for the fishermen of the Cape or anywhere else. England, chagrined by her defeat, not only closed her doors to American traders, but tried to keep New-Englanders from fishing Canadian waters as well. By the treaty of 1818, which grew out of the repeated encounters between Yankee fishermen and the King's ships, Labrador, the Bay de Chaleur, and adjacent waters were — theoretically at least — closed to American vessels. Though northern cod still found their way to the Boston market, repeated unpleasantness and occasional confiscation of their vessels considerably dampened the ardor of Cape fishermen. They began to look again at the dangerous tide rips that criss-cross each other on the Georges Banks, only a little more than a day's sail from home.

These waters had always been held in an almost superstitious terror. Strange things happened on them. Men said that they had seen the water run off, leaving the banks bare for gulls to feed on. Fishermen had visited them for years, but the currents had swept them off so fast that it was an unsatisfactory business. To anchor in the rips was held to be suicide — the staunchest vessel would be pulled under like a buoy in a tideway. Nobody had ever tried it, though men tantalized themselves by imagining the fares of fish they could catch there if they did. Finally, in 1821, a hardy Gloucester skipper, tired of running the gauntlet of the royal fish patrol, and tired of being carried out of reach of the fish by the Georges currents, took a chance. Boldly he sailed to the Georges; boldly he anchored; safely he sailed home. A new era in New England fishing had begun; Georges Banks, where the churlish veto of British legislation could not be heard, was open for business.

To the Cape fishermen this discovery meant as much as striking oil in his cattle range means to a ranch-owner. It brought the source of wealth hundreds of miles nearer than it had ever been before. Provincetown, the closest of all to the Georges, became busier than ever; but Truro and Wellfleet were not far behind; while Chatham, Harwich, and later Dennis, were well in the running. Codfish and halibut were the staples of the Georges fishermen; quick voyages and quick profits were their reward.

But meanwhile and always — treaties or no treaties, Georges or no Georges — the Grand Banks, with their inexhaustible supply, furnished the steady background of drumbeats in the Cape's piscatorial orchestra. It must not be supposed, either, that the Grand-Bankers rested content with the old methods. Hazardous as their calling was, even when all hands stayed on board and fished over the side, these progressive fishermen devised a yet more hazardous practice, justified in their own minds, if not in their families', because it caught more cod. They began in the late fifties to carry dories with them and to fish in pairs from these instead of from the schooner. It was believed that the quick motion of these little boats kept the bait dancing more conspicuously than the slower rise and fall of the schooner. Theoretically the dories did not venture too far away for safety, but fog and wind are unstable elements; a sudden blow, coming while the fish were biting, would often go too long unheeded by the dorymen. The schooner could no longer ride at anchor; the nicest handling could not keep her in sight of all her scattered dories. Some would get back to the safety of her deck; others would never be heard of again. Thus did the fearless Bankers add another hazard to their already hazardous calling.

Not content with running these risks, they employed another new device which took them still farther from the safety zone around their vessels. A Cape Cod fisherman conceived the idea of setting trawls — heavy lines anchored close to the bottom with short lines carrying baited hooks made fast to them at intervals. Sometimes there were a thousand hooks on a single trawl. The whole contrivance was buoyed and left, and the fisherman moved on to set the next one. Trawls had to be set and hauled from dories. If the men were reluctant to stop handlining when bad weather set in, what must have been their reluctance to abandon a half-hauled trawl with a codfish or halibut on every other hook? More fishermen were lost than ever, but there was no scarcity of volunteers to fill the gaps in their ranks.

What induced them to follow such a laborious, dangerous, and above all unprofitable business, it is hard to say. The Honorable Zeno Scudder, of Osterville, has calculated that a fisherman's earnings for four months for the decade between 1841 and 1851 were sixty-three dollars. The Government bonus brought the figure up to seventy-seven dollars but there is still nothing Crœsan about it, even if a wide margin is allowed for statistical inaccuracy. The old jingle,

'Sailor lads have gold and silver,
Fisher lads have nought but brass,'

sums up the situation. The gambling element — which would account for much — was reduced to a minimum with the Grand-Bankers. They were almost certain to return with a full fare if they returned at all. The best explanation is that the life itself appealed to a certain type of man. Discipline on board a fisherman was as elastic as it could be made without actually removing the skipper from command. It could hardly have been otherwise, indeed, for crews were composed for the most part, not only of men who had been friends from boyhood, but of brothers and fathers and sons. In 1789, a fishing vessel was lost on Nantucket Shoals with a crew of eight Yarmouth men, six of whom were named Hallett. The schooner Primrose of Yarmouth, which was lost in the great gale of 1841, carried two Brays, two Matthewses, two Halls, and two Wheldens. Of the twenty Dennis men lost in the same storm, twelve were named Howes.

These crew lists, selected at random from the scores that sailed from the Cape, suggest another answer to the question, 'Why did men spend their lives fishing?' It was an hereditary calling. The sons of Cape Cod fishermen were foreordained to the decks of schooners. It was taken for granted that a boy would step on board his father's vessel as automatically as the son of a business man nowadays steps into his father's office. Brothers and fathers fished side by side. The Dalmatia of Truro carried Gamaliel S. Paine and his fourteen-year-old son, Henry. The Altair, of the same town, was commanded by Elisha Rich, aged twenty-six, and sailing under him were his two brothers, Joseph and William. Boys whose parents to-day would think them too young to be sent to boarding school went to sea as cooks on fishermen, and all hands fared accordingly. Joseph Wheat shipped as cook on the Cincinnatus, of Truro, at the age of thirteen. Thomas White was twelve when he sailed in the Arrival, another Truro vessel, and he was not the youngest member of the crew, either. Charles Nott was only eleven, and Dick Atwood was fourteen. But these lads look like grown men when compared with Ambrose Snow, Jr., who in 1842 at the age of eight sailed with his father from Wellfleet for the Bay de Chaleur on the pink-sterned schooner Mariner.

An important result of this family grouping on board fishermen, where brother was often in command of brother, was to unfit men for the navy or merchant service. Fine sailors they were, but savage commands, such as issued from the brazen throat of the mate of a clipper ship, were not their style. Discipline disagreed with them. If brother 'Lisha was shaving Monomoy too close or was slow in giving the order to shorten sail in a blow, Joe and William were there to tell him of it — captain or no captain. More informal, free-and-easy crews never sailed the sea. The ship's company of a Cape Cod fisherman was a floating democracy where freedom of speech was the order of every day, and democracy sorted ill with the routine of a deep-water merchantman. Coming up with the fishing fleet off Highland Light and tearing past with skysails set, the fore-mast hands of a lordly clipper looked with contempt at the tiny schooners and wondered how men could live on board them. The fishermen cocked an eye at the towering canvas of the clipper, spat over the side, and ejaculated, 'Monkeys on a stick.' So each went his way.

In the thirties and forties, mackerel-catching first assumed the dignity of a serious business on the Cape. Of course men had caught mackerel since the earliest days, but these whimsical fish were looked on as too frivolous to warrant more than an occasional voyage. For years, while luring the humble, necessary cod from his dark lair in the crannies of some submerged ledge, skippers had watched the merry mackerel sporting in schools on top of the water — watched them and caught them, too, from time to time, as a gamey relaxation from the monotonous tug of the cod. But men in quest of bread and butter have small leisure for caviar. They were sure of their cod, whereas the mackerel would come one day, and the next would be gone like the swallows in winter. The cod-fishermen were not gamblers, but plodding sailors who preferred a long voyage with sure re-turns to the off chance of filling their holds in a single day with-out losing sight of the Hog's Back meeting-house.

But mackerel-catching was just the game for livelier spirits. It meant following the fish wherever they led, cruising about with a man at the masthead, watching for the peculiar shimmer and ripple on the surface of the water that betrayed the pres-ence of a school. Sometimes the fleet would cruise for weeks without so much as a smell of fish; but finally, by the forties, experts believed that they had found the route which these wily fellows followed. By cruising off the Virginia Coast in the spring, the fleet usually picked up the mackerel headed north, and stayed with them, marketing their catch at convenient ports on the way, until the fish disappeared somewhere off Nova Scotia.

The laws that govern the actions of fish are past finding out. One season the mackerel vanished completely. The fleet sailed as usual, but sailed in vain, returning as light as it set out. For ten years the fish remained lost. Rumor had it they had been seen off the African Coast. Captain Josiah Chase, of Provincetown, who was responsible for the report, crossed the Atlantic in pursuit, but died during the voyage. Then, as suddenly as they had vanished, the fish reappeared and resumed their old route northward along the coast. If the fancy struck them, they would play about for weeks in Cape Cod Bay, giving local fishermen plenty of sport and plenty of profits. In 1861, the schooner Bloomer, which after a useful career was left to drop to pieces plank by plank in a mud berth at Barnstable, sailed into port with 5700 mackerel, which her crew of ten men had caught with hand-lines in four hours.

For years hand-lining was the only way men knew of catching mackerel. Blithe spirits like mackerel-catchers gave no thought to improved methods; the old way was too much fun. Every man stood at the rail, throwing and pulling his lines as fast as he could move his arms, while the barrel at his elbow was filled with shining fish. No time was wasted baiting up between throws. The lead jig, scraped until it shone like silver, served as bait and sinker combined, a far more dazzling lure than the minced menhaden that had been thrown broadcast on the water to attract the school within reach. Fun enough in this game, even without the profits, to make up for weeks of cruising without wetting a line. There was need of frantic hurry, too, for the fish might stop biting at a moment's notice and for no imaginable reason. More than once tantalized fishermen have been forced to lean idly against the rigging and watch the mackerel swim about smelling at the jigs without once offering to take hold — this, too, in the midst of a spell of furious biting that had kept the men hauling and slatting as fast as their arms could move.

A few such experiences, combined with the mackerel's habit of traveling in schools on top of the water, suggested a bright idea to some inventive fisherman — tradition says to Captain Isaiah Baker. In 1853, he went mackerel-catching off Chatham with a purse seine — a huge light net, the lower edge of which could be pursed up by puckering-lines to form a pocket. When a school was sighted, a longboat very much like a whaleboat was lowered with the seine carefully piled amidships. The crew quietly rowed round the fish, letting out the net as they went. When the school was completely surrounded, the skipper gave the command, the bottom edge of the seine was pursed up, and the fish were trapped. The whole maneuver, from start to finish, was a ticklish one, demanding the utmost speed, skill, and caution, for at any sudden noise the fish were off like fleeting shadows. But when it succeeded, anywhere from one hundred to three hundred barrels of mackerel could be caught in a single cast of the net.

This method was a marked improvement over an earlier style of net which had been used with some success in shallow water. No puckering line was attached to this seine; it was a long straight net, deep enough to reach from the surface of the water to the bottom; it was dragged along by dories until the fish were swept into it; then the two ends were brought together, enclosing the school. Baker's purse seine was not only a more artistic contrivance than this, but also a surer way of getting the fish. Hand-lining, however, was never abandoned; it was too much fun, and called for no capital to speak of. Boat fishermen remained true to it; so did some of the schooners that followed the fish offshore. Wellfleet as late as 1889 had a fleet of thirteen 'seiners' and eight 'hookers,' which may be taken as a fair proportion for the other towns.

However they were caught, mackerel all received the same treatment ashore, a treatment very different from that which was shown the cod. Instead of being dried on flakes, they were salted and barreled under the eagle eye of a State inspector, who saw to it that they were graded as number one, two, or three, according to size and quality. 'Number ones' were the finest fish, fair and fat; the 'number threes' were small and poor, 'about as nourishing as a spruce shingle,' but good enough for the West India niggers, who would tackle even an oily menhaden.

What with its fleets of Grand-Bankers, Georges-Bankers, mackerel-catchers, and boat fishermen, Provincetown Harbor from the thirties to the fifties came nearer being crowded than ever before or since. Her cod-fishermen alone numbered one hundred sail, stout schooners of ninety tons or so that could ride the North Atlantic graybeards like a flock of ducks. Besides these she had a mackerel fleet that filled Marblehead Harbor, even when the Marblehead fishermen were away on the Banks. Nor was there anything deserted in the appearance of the shore-front. Wharves and packing-houses, salt works and fish flakes, riggers' yards and ship chandlers shouldered one another for a bit of beach. The 'city in the sand' had outstripped the older towns of Sandwich, Barnstable, and Yarmouth in activity, if not in wealth and self-esteem, and was growing every year. In 1845, Provincetown cod-fishermen were catching 20,000 quintals a year, a little more than a third of the Cape's total. Ten years later, they were catching 79,000 quintals, somewhere near double the total of all the other towns. This increase came with her own growth rather than with the decrease in the fishing industry on the rest of the Cape, for though such a decrease is recorded, it was so slight (6000 quintals in all) as to affect the statistics very little.

Other towns, notably Wellfleet, specialized in mackerel-catching and barreled more of these fish annually than Provincetown did. Wellfleet's three meager harbors were taxed to the utmost to accommodate her fleet of mackerel schooners (supplemented by a smaller number of cod-fishermen) that lay gunwale to gunwale in Herring River, Duck Creek Harbor, and Blackfish Creek, like Ægean melon-carriers in the Piræus. After the Civil War, a fleet of a hundred vessels slid out round Billingsgate, most of them in search of mackerel. Caulkers and riggers had plenty of work the year round; salt-makers found a ready market for their product. Although in the words of a local historian, 'the largest portion of the male inhabitants' went fishing either for mackerel or cod, there was no reason why a man who preferred to stay ashore should not prosper.

The most important of all the establishments alongshore was the outfitter's. The proprietors of these emporiums were business men with broad and elastic ideas. They sold everything from molasses candy to chain cable, owned shares in many of the vessels, and furnished the fishermen's families with provisions on credit while the head of the family was away. Some of them, notably the Union Wharf Company of Provincetown, were virtually bankers as well, lending money, receiving deposits, and paying moderate interest; in short, they coöperated with the fleet in every way. Without the facilities offered by these broad-minded men of affairs, the difficulties of making a voyage would have been enough to discourage half the fishermen on the Cape.

The free-and-easy way in which these establishments were sometimes run is well illustrated by the crash of the Union Company's store in Truro. Throughout the flush times of the fishing business, this store had been the great business house of the town. Most of the citizens owned stock in it, and received their ten per cent as regularly as the years rolled around. The Company was both borrower and lender, merchant and store-keeper, but never thought it necessary to incorporate. An earthquake could have been no greater shock to the complacent shareholders than the announcement, shortly before the Civil War, that the Company was bankrupt. The town never fully recovered from this blow. It was the beginning of the end of the busy days alongshore at Pamet Harbor, where Georges-Bankers and a fleet of more than sixty mackerel-catchers had huddled between voyages; where the caulker's mallet had sounded busily from the local shipyards, while the ubiquitous State inspector saw to it that no number twos from the mackerel fleet found their way into the number one barrels.

In the end it was Provincetown's unrivaled harbor that kept her in the fishing game long after the upper Cape had coiled its lines for good. After the Civil War, the genial days when a man could make money with a single small vessel yielded to the power of concentration. By degrees the business centered in Gloucester, Boston, and Provincetown, where big fleets and big vessels could be accommodated. The little fellows could no more compete with these great fishing centers than an old-fashioned corner grocery store can compete with the Great Atlantic and Pacific Tea Company. Little by little they gave up trying, went into other business, and watched Provincetown and Wellfleet go it alone.

The Yarmouth 'Register,' in reporting conditions in its own town in 1857, might have been speaking for a dozen others as well; here in part is the item. 'Not more than two or three vessels have been sent from this port the present season, where formerly 20 or 30 sail were employed. Our citizens have turned their attention to foreign commerce, or the coasting and packet-ing business, which pays altogether better than with our poor facilities for carrying on the fisheries compared with Province-town, Gloucester, Wellfleet and other places on the coast.' The same periodical says in 1863, 'The last of the fishing fleet has been sold.'

Until the nineties Provincetown was well in the running. Aside from her fleet of mackerel-catchers and Grand-Bankers, the town had developed a special type of vessel for the nervous work on the Georges — a schooner more graceful than the big cod-fishermen, faster than the mackerel-catcher, long-sparred like a yacht, and able to spread canvas that set the old-timers' heads wagging. With clipper bows, clean run, and tapered sterns, these schooners were, in the opinion of the local experts, the most beautiful craft that ever entered the harbor. But beauty, in the minds of designers, was incidental, for the Georges was as dangerous a fishing ground as ever tempted a crew to destruction. The water was so shoal in places that it broke in every easterly blow, and even where there was depth enough to prevent breakers, an ugly sea could get up in a few minutes. Furthermore, the fleet carried dories, like the Grand-Bankers, and fished from them instead of over the side of the vessel. This meant delay in getting off in case of dirty weather. The only solution of the problem was a schooner that could sail fast, would go to windward under shortened canvas, and yet was stiff enough to survive the fearful beatings they sometimes took while rounding Race Point in a northeaster. Hardy as they were, and fearless as men who live in danger become, the fishermen had no desire for another calamity like that which overtook the Georges fleet in '41. They wanted something better than the blunt-nosed schooners that had gone under in that memorable gale; and they got it in the lines of the new Provincetown fleet.

Another reason for speed in this branch of the business was that fresh fish had for a long time brought higher prices than salt fish. Halibut and cod were iced as fast as they were caught, rushed to port under a cloud of canvas, and transshipped to Boston with nothing but ice and their native salt to preserve them. The way the lean schooners cut the water in a fresh breeze, as they raced home with their perishable cargo, was enough to gladden the heart of the dourest skipper in Provincetown.

The beauty of these vessels was brought out more sharply by

contrast with some of the other hulks that still thrashed their way alongshore in pursuit of mackerel or anchored exhausted in a Labrador cove. A fleet still sailed to the Grand Banks, where sterner stuff was needed — speed giving way to seaworthiness, beauty to capacity. Labrador and the Bay of Chaleurs remained popular, too, and anything would do for these trips. The T. Y. Baker, for example, built in Wellfleet about the time of the Civil War, is described by one of her crew as being 'so blunt at the nose she would butt a sea about twice and then fall back and go around it.' Nor was she alone in her class. A small fleet of Bakers was launched at Duck Creek, with lines like those of the T. Y.

It has been argued that the danger involved in the fisheries is one reason for their decline, and that 'the toll of manly life taken in these dangerous seas was so terrible that young women hesitated to marry seamen.' If this is so, it is the only time in history that danger has prevented men from pursuing excitement, or that the glamour of a perilous calling has failed to fascinate the fair. The real reasons why the Cape abandoned deep-sea fishing were economic, not sentimental. All the villages except Provincetown were pretty much squeezed out when the demand came for larger vessels that needed good harbors. Wellfleet hung on for some time, but even there the fleet of the seventies and eighties was no match for the glory of the hundred sail that had been hers. As for Provincetown, capitalists were few and far between, and it took capital to float a fleet of purse seiners. In the old days of hand-lining, a boy of fifteen could catch as many fish as his father; but no boy was strong enough to shoot a seine or pull a trawl; so the rising generation, instead of being headed for a career with the codfish or mackerel, began to seek their fortunes somewhere else. After the Civil War the whole drift of Cape enterprise set shoreward, and fishing took the form of tending traps instead of sailing to the Banks.

From the middle of the century, when the first local weir was tried as an experiment at Chatham, until the present, this method of fishing has been followed persistently, through lean years and fat, all along the Bay shore. In 1890 a dozen weirs were in operation off Truro alone. Others appeared in Provincetown waters; at present three are operated outside Sandy Neck,

Barnstable; and so on all alongshore. Like every other sort of fishing, this business is uncertain. From three hundred to four hundred barrels of mackerel were taken from one of the Truro traps soon after it was set out; Captain Ed Pierce made another big haul in 1897, when he shipped thirty tons of cod and pollock taken from his weir in one day. But such records are rare; a commoner story is that told for the season of '95, when whiting and pollock were thought hardly worth shipping: 'The fish weirs that dot the coast from Wood End to Sandwich have experienced a most disastrous season. The first part of the year they were full of worthless whiting most of the time, and when they struck off the pollock struck in and hung on until cold weather started them southward. Some of the weirs hardly paid expenses.'

Quite recently — within a dozen or fifteen years — cold-storage plants have been built in a number of towns to handle the hauls of the fish traps. These fish-freezers are by no means fastidious; all is indeed fish that comes to their net. Not only the 'worthless whiting' but the still more humble squid are shoveled into the omnivorous maw of the freezers. The squid have some value as bait and are eaten by certain of our foreign population. The whiting do well enough for chowders. Yarmouth erected at great expense a very elaborate cold-storage plant at the head of a little creek that comes wandering inland through the marsh. A channel was dug through the flats. A gasoline boat and attendant dories plied in and out with commendable optimism. To-day the establishment has been torn down; weeds grow tall between the planks of the dock. The channel — what there is left of it — is handy for rum-runners and lobstermen, whose boats are the only ones that follow it, and whose trucks are the only vehicles that now make their way through the lane that joins the creek with the highway. It is rumored that some of the Provincetown freezers are making money. *Gaudeamus igitur;* that is as it should be. The harbor that sheltered the wild cod-fishermen from Europe, the Pilgrims in the Mayflower, the British in the Revolution, and the finest fishing fleet on the coast in the flush days of the high-liners, that harbor is the one that should still be making money for the freezers.

A man cannot spend his life catching fish without learning something about their habits. One citizen of Provincetown, at least, Captain Nathaniel Atwood, found something interesting about them besides their market value. Captain Atwood lived in Provincetown all his life and died there in 1886 at the age of seventy-nine. He thus watched the fisheries from their infancy, was in the prime of life during the boom, and passed his declining years abreast of the declining years of this great industry. Many another man had done the same, but though Atwood had no more education than any other fisherman, he had marked powers of observation and inference and a lively curiosity in all that pertained to fish. He became an authority on his chosen subject — one of the most intricate and baffling in the whole realm of natural history. His fame spread to Boston and Cambridge, where such scholars as Agassiz and Storer were glad to supplement their theoretical knowledge with first-hand information from a man who had spent his life watching the fish. During Atwood's two years as representative in the State House, the Legislature heard less rhetoric and more truth about the fish business than at any time before or since. He was a member of the Essex Institute at Salem and of the American Academy of Arts and Sciences; but the crowning honor came when he was asked to deliver a course of lectures at the Lowell Institute in Boston — an invitation which he accepted with enthusiasm, to the delight of his audiences, and to the amusement of his contemporaries in Provincetown, where he was regarded, as all prophets (and particularly all Cape Cod prophets) are regarded by their neighbors, with humorous skepticism, not altogether free from envy nor quite unmixed with pride. The Captain's achievements form a picturesque chapter in the long history of Cape Cod fisheries. 'Let his name,' says Dr. Storer, 'be indelibly associated with the science to which he is an honor.'

There was hard work but considerable excitement in the deep-sea fisheries; racing and risk added spice to the Georges; mackerel-catching, whether with jig or purse seine, was a sporting business; even the trap fishermen had the fun of an occasional record haul. But what can be said for the clam-digger, that slave of the tides, who turns up a living between low water and high and knows to a peck before he starts out how many clams he will bring home? Yet there have always been men in every town on the Cape whose chief occupation was clamming. A hundred years ago, the clam-digger was usually a veteran of the Banks who had grown too old for livelier work. But clamming for a livelihood nowadays is no work for old men. Digging must be hard and fast if a dory is to be filled before the flats are covered, and the best efforts of the shellbacks of the early days were no match for the record of ten barrels a tide which was made a few years ago by a Barnstable expert in the prime of life. Yet taking it all in all, the old people dug an enormous number of clams. In 1802 more than one hundred men in Orleans were glad to earn seventy-five cents a day digging clams for the fishermen, and a thousand barrels was the annual average for the town. Laws were made to protect the Eastham flats from the inroads of 'strangers'; and with good reason, for it has been estimated that a bushel of clams in the shell was worth in those days about half as much as a bushel of corn, and could be procured much more easily.

For the past twenty years clamming has been the chief and — except for the fish traps and a few strings of lobster pots and eel-cars — the only industry in Barnstable that has taken men off dry land: but it has taken them by scores. To encourage the business, the selectmen of the town, about 1906, granted sections of flats for the exclusive use of any citizen who applied for them. The response was the same as that of the Plymouth settlers in 1623 when the Court granted them land of their own. The most enterprising began to propagate clams on their grants, while the less ambitious citizens, and Finns who had not yet taken out naturalization papers, found as much work as they wanted digging for their more energetic or fortunate neighbors. From 1910 to 1925, the business was in its heyday. Hundreds of acres of flats were dotted with clam-diggers and dories, to the despair of the duck-hunters. 'Barnstable cultivated clams' appeared on the bills of fare in Boston and New York hotels. Foreign citizens who lived on the South Side and didn't know a clam from a quahaug took grants and rented them to those who did. The peak of the boom was reached in 1925, when an open season was declared the year round instead of only through the winter. Trucks backed down to the water's edge to meet the dories as they returned on the flood tide loaded to the gun-wales. All summer the roads to Boston were crowded with trucks full of clams. No time was wasted in packing them in barrels. They reached market in the same 'dreeners' in which they had been dug.

The selectmen, realizing the danger before it was too late, clapped a closed season on again in 1927, and started a tempest in the harbor by refusing to renew grants that had expired. The result is, at present, some hardship to the men with money invested in the business; but the measure protects the supply, which was melting fast before the unprecedented ardor of the former grantees.

Quahaugs — hardly inferior to oysters in flavor, euphe-mistically styled 'little necks' or 'cherrystones' on metropolitan menus, and persistently called clams by untutored inlanders — are well worth the effort involved in their capture. That this effort is great will be instantly apparent to any one who watches a Wellfleet quahauger at work. He chugs out to the west side of the great shallow Bay in a converted catboat equipped with a gasoline engine. There he anchors, and drags the bottom with a long-handled rake supplemented by a pouch made of netting. Beginning well aft, he hitches his way forward, pulling the heavy drag after him by its twenty-foot handle with a series of jerks that give him the back and shoulders of a Hercules. When he has reached the bow, he hauls his rake up and culls out the quahaugs from the mixture of sand and eel-grass with which its net-basket is filled. Then he shuffles aft again and repeats the process for hours on end, coming up a boat's length on his hawser as soon as he has exhausted all the bottom within reach of his rake.

In Wellfleet this work is done largely by Finns, who on smooth days between April and October make as high as ten dollars. Upwards of two thousand barrels of these shellfish leave Wellfleet every year; a fleet of about thirty boats is engaged in the business. Nowhere it seems is there safety for the quahaug. At Orleans he is dredged from apparent security in sixty feet of water. Eastham shows him no mercy. Twenty years ago there were plenty of native quahaugs in Cotuit waters.

A man could dredge up thirty or forty bushels a day, and enough of them were taken to keep Carleton Nickerson and his schooner, Luella Nickerson, busy carrying them to New London, eight hundred bushels at a time, as fast as he could make the trips. To-day if a man can rake up two bushels on a tide he is lucky. In spite of their scarcity, the advance in price keeps men dredging to the tune of twenty-five hundred barrels a year — though many of these are quahaugs which wise men have planted on grants and allowed to grow.

This business in Wellfleet is to-day on a par with the famous oyster industry, though ten years ago it was of nowhere near the same importance. And truly the oysterman has a proud history. Native oysters made life easy for the Billingsgate pioneers as they had for the Indians before them. Oysters gave Wellfleet its name when the town grew big enough to be incorporated; oysters were the subject of laws and restrictions a hundred years before the Revolution, and when a mysterious epidemic attacked the oysters in 1770, the citizens turned diseases to commodity and by vigorous protective measures achieved greater prosperity than ever. Various guesses have been made as to the cause of the epidemic. Some said it was a ground frost; others believed that a great school of blackfish, left rotting on the shores of the bay, so polluted the water that no oyster could live. The soundest theory is that the oyster shells on which the seed catches were removed and broken up to make lime, but the superstitious averred that the Almighty slew them as a punishment for the wicked quarrels between Wellfleeters and Easthamers. Whatever the cause, most of the oysters died, and with them went an important fraction of Wellfleet's prosperity.

The citizens promptly took measures for protecting and propagating those that remained. They could do no more for the moment, because the Revolution was upon them, but after the war they went further and as early as 1793 had begun to transplant seed oysters from the south. The change in climate agreed with the imported bivalves so well that not even the most fastidious could tell them from real Wellfleets.

Wellfleet, in fact, had a strangle-hold on the New England oyster business. From the thirties to the seventies she supplied the State. The best schooners that could be built were none too good for this trade. They were the only fishing vessels that could match the Provincetown fleet of Georges-Bankers in speed and beauty. Two of them, the Express and the Telegraph, were designed by the great Samuel Hall, of East Boston.

Before and after 1870, forty schooners, from eighty to ninety feet long, the smallest of them with a capacity of 1750 bushels, were busy carrying young oysters from the Potomac to Wellfleet, and from Wellfleet to Boston and Portland. The firms of J. A. Stubbs, H. & R. Atwood, D. Atwood, and R. R. Higgins Company were as well known along Atlantic Avenue as they were in Wellfleet; but about 1900 the proprietors of the Southern oyster-beds found other uses for their seed oysters. This marked the beginning of the decline for Wellfleet. Her dealers bought some from Long Island, to be sure, and bedded them down as of old; and after 1914 an occasional schooner slipped quietly through the Canal with a cargo of oysters from Wellfleet destined for a sojourn in Cotuit waters; whence they emerged with the 'Cotuit flavor,' and a higher market value.

The last ten years, however, have seen the greatest falling off in the business. In 1916, operating with a fifty-foot power boat and a gasoline dredge that held three barrels, the Wellfleet oystermen shipped sixteen thousand barrels at an average price of $7.50 a barrel. This total was double what it had been the year before — the increase being accounted for by the improved methods. But in 1926, this gratifying figure had shrunk to eighteen hundred barrels, partly because the management of the business changed and partly because putting power against the oysters did not agree with them. Chiefly for these reasons, then, and only in very recent years, has the Wellfleet oysterman been caught up with and passed by the plebeian quahauger. The fact that his oysters to-day fetch from twelve to eighteen dollars a barrel instead of seven or eight dollars, gives him but cold comfort.

But what of Cotuit — the name that is synonymous with oysters in every city from El Paso to Portland and as far west as Denver? In the days of the Indians, Cotuit, like Wellfleet, had native oysters thriving in the shallow waters of its harbor. Oysters, indeed, were the magnet that first drew settlers to the South Sea, a name which covered the whole shore-front from

Bass River to Poponesset. Jonathan Hatch, who left West Barnstable for the vicinity of Oyster Island about 1655, was among the earliest pioneers of that region, and he undoubtedly sold oysters, which he found growing thick on the beds close to his farm, to Nicholas Davis, who a little later had a trading post on the shore of Lewis Bay in Hyannis. Davis, at all events, included oysters in his miscellaneous business; though the method of handling them was at that early date very different from the present. They were opened and pickled in brine instead of being shipped fresh — the process being known as 'making oysters.' For years the shells supplied the community with lime. Another early South Side oysterman was Benjamin Bearse, who died in Hyannis in 1748. In his will he left his real estate to his younger sons, but stipulated that his oldest son, Augustian, should be allowed a convenient way to the landing 'where I make oysters.'

From such beginnings grew the now celebrated Cotuit oysters. The business is still the chief industry of the village, although not so many oysters are raised there as formerly, because of the advance in the price of seed oysters from Long Island — whence the Cotuits are transplanted. Lack of capital, therefore, the same cause which signed the death warrant of the Cape fishing fleets, has forced a good many Cotuit men out of the oyster industry. The half-dozen or so that remain send an annual total of about eighty-five hundred barrels of the finest oysters in the world to the markets of Boston and New York. This crop is the result of a yearly planting of about thirty-two thousand bushels of seed from Long Island. For some reason, in spite of repeated experiments, the spawn refuses to catch anywhere in Cotuit Harbor, though small oysters thrive splendidly. This phenomenon is what forces the local oystermen to import their seed and let the alchemy of the harbor turn it into full-flavored Cotuits. The importance of the Cotuit shellfisheries will be brought home to lovers of statistics when they learn that after all shipping charges have been deducted, about $100,000 a year comes into the village from the combined sale of oysters and quahaugs.

'I don't care much for fish,' said an old lady in a Barnstable boarding-house, as a smoked herring was placed before her.

'What!' exclaimed the old gentleman who sat opposite; 'don't you like a herring? Everybody likes a herring.' And so they did when the old gentleman was young; but fashions change, and the herring, once the subject of complex and ever-changing laws, may now come upstream to spawn in comparative safety. It is dangerous for so optimistic a philosopher as Thoreau to lapse even for a moment into pessimistic prophecies. 'There are many Herring Rivers on the Cape,' he writes. 'They may soon be more abundant than herring.' But the herring have survived with the rivers they have named. Every spring the waters of these narrow creeks are dark with them as they shoulder one another in their eagerness to reach a pond. A few men on the lower Cape whose houses are near a herring river, take some in dip nets either to eat fresh or to smoke and hang in their barns, a dozen skewered together with a stick through the gills, but the upper Cape (Mashpee and Bourne in particular) is the only region where the business thrives to-day.

The middle of the last century, however, had a different tale to tell. Citizens of every town were jealous of their rights in the herring fisheries, for at first the General Court, and later the selectmen, allowed every taxpayer free access to the rivers. Sometimes, if they saw fit, the towns would rent these fisheries to the highest bidder, reserving to every inhabitant the privilege of buying what he wanted for his own use at the minimum price. Even mills — the construction and maintenance of which were encouraged in every way — were not allowed to interfere with the precious alewives. When it happened that a mill was so situated as to obstruct the spring run, it was closed until the spawning season was over. Incredible as it may seem, the citizens of the South Side about 1740 dug a canal from Nine-Mile Pond to the sea in order to bring more herring into the village. And just such a passage was dug in 1917 to let the herring pass from the newly constructed Cape Cod Canal into Monument River and so to Great Herring Pond.

Mashpee is the herring center to-day. Within a few years a thousand barrels have been shipped in a season from the streams of this little town. Salted and sunbaked, these fish yet fetch prices which warrant the small effort involved in taking them with nets, curing them and heading up the barrels. In 1890, the selectmen of Bourne rented the Herring River fisheries for a thousand dollars — reserving two barrels for every 'Indian' family and one barrel for every white family. Perhaps after all the old gentleman was partly right, and some still like a herring!

CHAPTER XI

STORMS, WRECKS, AND WRECKERS

IT has been said that if all the wrecks which have piled up on the back side of the Cape were placed bow to stern, they would make a continuous wall from Chatham to Provincetown. This is a picturesque way of putting what is substantially the truth, for Peaked Hill Bars and the Monomoy Shoals are to sailors of to-day what Scylla and Charybdis were to Æneas. Nauset Beach, which stretches along the whole coast line of Orleans and Eastham, holds in its fatal sands the shattered skeletons of vessels from half the seaports of the world; while farther north, the outer shores of Wellfleet and Truro have gathered in the hulls of a thousand ships, driven helplessly upon them by northeast gales. Even the comparatively sheltered waters of the Bay have had their share of shipwrecks, though there the hulls are not usually pounded to pieces as they are on the outer shore. It is not idle curiosity that makes the Cape-Codder a keen observer of the weather; it is habit inherited from ancestors who antedate lighthouses and life-saving stations, who have weathered typhoons and outguessed the fog.

Great storms become, like wars, points from which each generation dates events. The gale of August, 1635, marked an epoch in the lives of the Pilgrims, who in the intensity of their religion, were torn two ways in trying to interpret its significance. One half thanked God on their knees for not having obliterated their settlement entirely; the others anxiously scrutinized their past actions to discover wherein they had offended. It was well for Plymouth that she had no fishing fleet at sea when this storm hit the coast. If we can believe Bradford, it was of such fury as to frighten men from the sea forever — if men could stay frightened by memories. It seems to have been a vicious swing of the tail of a West India hurricane, like that which visited the coast in August, 1924. A building at the Manomet trading post lost its roof; many thousand trees were uprooted or snapped off, and a twenty-foot tide flooded acres of upland on the Cape.

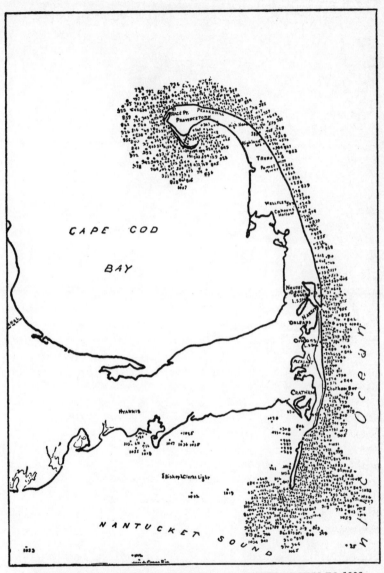

APPROXIMATE LOCATIONS OF CAPE COD WRECKS DOWN TO 1903

'The wrecks of it,' says Bradford, 'will remain a hundred years.'

The lower Cape had a close call in September, 1815. Its towns lay along the edge of a hurricane which wrought havoc on the shores of Buzzards Bay but which did no damage to speak of farther east. A few small vessels came ashore — among them a brig at Hyannis. The tide in Buzzards Bay, backed by a furious gale from the east and later from the southwest and south, all but made the Cape an island: a rise of another foot would have done the trick. As it was, salt works were carried away, vessels torn from their moorings, and trees uprooted. Salt houses on the Elizabeth Islands, lifted bodily from their posts, came to anchor in the Wareham woods. Coasting vessels were swept inland and deposited in the front yards of houses alongshore; thousands of dollars' worth of crops were ruined; wells and springs became brackish; sand was deposited thick over hayfields.

But though the Cape towns, with the exception of Falmouth, suffered little from this gale, they made up for it ten years later in the succession of storms that raged along the coast in 1825. Between January and June, three distinct gales sent a fleet of fishing vessels and their crews to the bottom. Truro was especially hard hit. The names Snow, Atkins, and Collins, all of them familiar in the town, were conspicuous on the long list of casualties which her fishermen sustained between Province-town and the Grand Banks.

Grim as the records of this disaster are, they become a mere preface to the October gale of 1841, which brought death to so many Cape fishermen and poverty to their families. Truro alone lost seven vessels and fifty-seven men. Ten men of Yarmouth perished, and upwards of twenty from Dennis. The storm caught most of the fleet on the Georges Banks, and, coming as it did from the northeast, made the passage home a beat to windward in the face of a sea that swept the decks from stem to stern. Of the Truro fleet only two crews survived: Captain Matthias Rich brought his schooner Water Witch safe round the Cape and anchored in Herring Cove under the lee of Race Point, having spent twelve hours lashed to the wheel. Captain Joshua Knowles lost his vessel Garnet, but saved the crew. No better picture of the storm or of the valiant fight that the young fishermen put up against it can be had than Captain Knowles's account of his experiences.

We left Provincetown Saturday, second; at sunset were off head of Pamet, one league East. Soon after spoke the Vesper of Dennis direct from Georges, bound home; reported good fishing. For Georges we shaped our course setting all sail. Wind light from the northeast but soon began to breeze. At ten took in light sails. At twelve took in mainsail, the wind now blowing a gale. At four Sunday morning took in the jib. Had thirty-four fathoms of water. Judged myself on the southwest part of Georges. At six double-reefed the foresail, which soon after parted the leachrope and tore to the luff. We cross-barred the sail, and put on a preventer leachrope as soon as possible, and set it close reefed. The gale increased every moment. At ten a heavy sea took the boat and davits. By sounding found we were fast drifting across South Channel, and knew the shoals were under our lea. Determined to carry sail as long as it would stand, to clear the shoals, if possible. To the close-reefed foresail, set a balanced-reefed mainsail and reefed jib, and, blowing as it was, she carried it off in good shape; and had our sails stood, I have little doubt we should have carried out clear.

The foresail again gave out, was repaired and set; as soon as up, it blew to ribbons. Mainsail soon shared the same fate. We had only one jib left. It was now about eight o'clock Sunday evening. We could do no more. Sounded in fifteen fathoms of water and knew we were rapidly drifting into shoal water. The next throw of the lead was six fathoms. As the sea was breaking over fore and aft, advised all to go below but brother Zack. We concluded to swing her off before the wind, and if by any possibility we were nearing land, should have a better chance. Put up the helm. Just as she began to fall off, a tremendous sea or a breaker completely buried the vessel, leaving her on her broadside, or beam ends. Brother Zack was washed overboard but caught the mainsheet and hauled himself on board. The foremast was broken about fifteen feet above the deck, the strain on the spring-stay hauled the main mast out of the step, and tore up the deck, swept away the galley, bulwarks and everything clean, and shifted the ballast into the wing. I thought at once of a sharp hatchet that was always kept under my berth, which was soon found. A lanyard was fastened to the hatchet and a rope to Brother Zack, who went to the leeward, and when she rolled out of water, he watched his chance and cut away the rigging. I did the same forward, cut the jibstay and other ropes, so we got clear of spars, sails and rigging sheet anchor and chains. The men got into the hold through the lazaret, and threw ballast to windward, so that she partially righted. We were now a helpless wreck. I had noticed that immediately after the great breaker the sea was more regular. With a few of the waist-boards left, and a spare

STORMS, WRECKS, AND WRECKERS

old canvas, we battened the hole in the deck, and with the remaining anchor out for a drag, we made a pretty good drift considering the circumstances, though mostly under water. It was now nearly daylight, and the gale unabated. As soon as fairly day, I saw by the color of the water that we were off soundings, and had a fair drift. During the afternoon the wind moderated considerably. Tuesday morning, the fifth, the wind was more moderate. Saw a schooner under reefs standing by the wind to the northwest; made every effort to attract their attention, but as we lay so low on the water she did not notice us, and soon passed out of sight.

We put a stay on the stump of the foremast, set the staysail for a foresail, and the gaff topsail for a jib, so we could steer.

At ten A.M. the weather was fine. We opened the hatches, found some potatoes floating in the hold — fortunately the teakettle was in the cabin when the galley went overboard. The boys built a fire on the ballast and boiled potatoes, the first mouthful of food since Sunday morning the third. Just before sunset discovered a sail approaching from the East. Our flag on a long pole served as a signal and we used every effort to get in her track, lest we should not be discovered. We were soon satisfied she was steering for us, and that there was great interest in our behalf, as the yards and rigging were full of men on the watch.

As soon as within hailing distance, the Captain inquired what assistance he could give. I had before determined to abandon my vessel and so replied. A quarter boat was soon alongside; the crew and luggage were mostly taken in the first boat; during her absence with the same hatchet that had done such good work, I let in the blue water and stepped in the boat, leaving the Garnet, which had been my home for several years, to find the bottom. Never was rescue more fortunate. I found myself and crew of ten men on board the New York and Liverpool packet ship Roscius, the first merchant ship of her day, commanded by John Collins, a Truro boy, and formerly my nearest neighbor, and a connection by marriage. One of the officers was Joshua Caleb Paine, a Truro young man, and a nephew of Captain Collins. I need not say we received every attention and were regarded by the passengers, of whom there were four hundred in steerage and cabin, with much interest. We were two hundred miles from the highlands of Neversink, which we sighted the next day, landing at New York on the seventh, receiving the most generous offers and kind attention, and in good time all arrived safely in our homes.

So much for the survivors. The fate of the rest of the fleet will never be certainly known, with the exception of the Pomona, of Truro (Captain Solomon H. Dyer, aged twenty-three), which drifted bottom-up into Nauset Harbor with three boys drowned in her cabin. But in the opinion of experts, notably

Captain Eldredge, of Chatham, who has charted the whole region, they perished in the breakers on Eldredge's and Rogers' Shoals, two dangerous outriders of the great Nantucket Shoals.

These are the epoch-making gales — the high spots of disaster in the story of the Cape. Others might well have been included, like the squall of December, 1853, which sent twenty-one vessels ashore between Highland Light and the Race; or the tidal wave which in 1871 rolled into Provincetown Harbor in front of a heavy gale and carried the ship Nina into the post office. The Portland storm of November, 1898, is still fresh in men's minds; wreckage from the unfortunate steamer came ashore not far from the Clay Pounds in North Truro. But if every great storm which has raged on this coast were to be mentioned, the end would be far to seek.

The same is true, but to an even greater extent, with the wrecks, for many a good ship has left her bones on the Cape beaches when no gale shrieked a requiem through the rigging. Fog is a greater foe to seamen than wind; it blinds pigmy and giant alike, and sends them groping their way through a strange, new element, where strength avails them nothing, where the old signs fail, and where science itself still falters at the threshold. It is a bewildering task, therefore, to try to select the most significant wrecks from such a list as is revealed by even the most casual research. Storm and fog have multiplied the tragedies; and sometimes the malice of man has contributed as well.

The first wreck on the Cape was probably contemporary with the voyages of French and Basque fishermen, somewhere in the fifteenth or sixteenth century. One may well ask one's self where the Indians got the Biscay shallop in which they sailed out to meet Gosnold a day or two before he sighted the Cape, or how the blond-haired skeleton that the Pilgrims found went to his grave beside Pamet River. The wreck of the Sparrowhawk on Nauset Beach, in 1623, has been mentioned in an earlier chapter. These ancient disasters are so remote that the details and sometimes even the names of vessels are conjectural; quite different is the story of Captain Rymer, of the George and Ann.

This vessel was not wrecked; but her voyage was a prolonged nightmare of four months and a half, hardly a day of which

passed without Captain Rymer's reading the funeral service
over the shrouded figure of a passenger. She sailed from Dublin
in April, 1729, her decks crowded with Irish emigrants whose
hopes were high for easy riches in the New World. Almost
immediately an epidemic set in, and burials at sea became daily
occurrences. Bad weather made progress slow, giving the disease plenty of time to take its full toll. Before its ravages were
at an end, fourteen servants, forty-two children, and about
forty-five other persons had died — a total of over one hundred
— and the end of the voyage was nowhere in sight. The survivors, weakened by disease, by short rations, and by fright,
were in no condition to work the vessel. Westerly gales blew
them off their course; week followed week, and still the westerlies prevailed. The end of their drinking-water was at hand;
provisions shrank lower and lower. Mutinous mutterings were
heard among what were left of the passengers. Rymer, they
said, was prolonging the voyage on purpose, waiting for them
all to die. Then he would seize their money and baggage and
sail home before the wind.

These whispers reached the Captain's ears, but with set teeth
he kept his vessel headed westward as the weeks crawled by.
Finally, one October day, with fifteen biscuit and a few pints of
water between them and eternity, the ghostly crew steered the
George and Ann into the waters of Nantucket Sound, and saw
a sail coming up on them from astern. Frantically they flew
signals of distress which were seen from the other vessel, a
Boston packet commanded by Captain Lothrop and bound for
Martha's Vineyard. As soon as he came alongside, the emigrants, pushing their captain aside, crowded to the rail, clamoring to be piloted to the nearest land. They threatened to throw
Rymer overboard if he tried to continue the voyage.

Lothrop sized up the situation in short order; obviously these
people were half crazy from suffering; the best thing to do was
to put them ashore as quickly as possible. There was Jo Stewart's tavern at Wreck Cove, not far from the end of Monomoy
Point. That would be a good place to land them. So he changed
his course, told them to follow in his wake, and led the way
round the long arm of Monomoy, where he gave them some
fresh water and provisions, pointed out the location of Stew-

art's tavern, wished them good luck, and squared away for the Vineyard.

Stewart made shift to put the forlorn company up for the night; the next day they were billeted for the winter in various houses about the village. The townspeople little realized what a service they were performing for the country-to-be. The head of the party, Charles Clinton, a native of Ireland but born of Scotch parents, proceeded the following spring to establish a colony in Ulster County, New York. Among his descendants are some distinguished names. His son, General James Clinton, had a fine record in the Revolutionary War; another son, George, became Governor of New York and was Vice-President under John Adams. James's son, DeWitt, served as Mayor of New York, Governor of the State, and United States Senator. Truly the hospitable folk of Chatham and Harwich, who sheltered the father of such sons, builded better than they knew.

A diligent historian has said that wrecks form no part of local history; and from one point of view he is right. Yet many wrecks that came ashore on the Cape presented the townspeople first with a problem in amateur life-saving, and second, with a more intricate problem in *meum and tuum*. On the whole, they had more success in solving the former than the latter, for the temptation of a rich cargo scattered along the beach is hard for a poor man to resist. So before passing on to the Cape-Codders' exploits as life-savers, it is necessary to glance at a few of their equally successful performances as mooncussers.

To be sure, the full significance of this picturesque term never applied to the Cape. Originally it meant the villainous practice of luring vessels to destruction by false lights in order to plunder them when the crews had perished. It went even further and included murdering survivors to give free play to the looting. A humorous Provincetown saying used to be, 'Don't get ashore on the back side of Truro; there's women waiting there on the beach with a brick in a stocking.' But nowhere on the Cape was there ever a case either of decoying a ship to its death, or of maltreating her crew. To-day mooncussing means no more than the pleasant and sometimes profitable practice of strolling along the beach looking for chance wreckage — a plank worth hauling home, an unbroken lobster pot, a vessel's quarter-board to nail over the barn door. But somewhere between the two extremes there exists a disagreeable truth, for unquestionably stranded vessels have been robbed of their cargo and gear by Cape-Codders; and who can say that mixed emotions did not sometimes exist in the breasts of men as they stood on the beach hills of Nauset and watched a ship pounding shoreward over the bars?

Laws there were, it is true, which from their very strictness, invited violation. Early in the eighteenth century the colonial authorities decreed that a man who found a wrecked vessel, any part of one, or any of her cargo on the beach, should report it to the town clerk, whose duty it was to salvage it and hold it safe until the owners should appear. This law subjected human nature to too great a strain. The rule that findings are keepings, though recorded in no statute book, is yet a principle so deeply rooted in men's minds, and so nearly in accord with a pleasant and informal kind of justice, that it is likely to take precedence over paper decrees. The Reverend Enoch Pratt, historian of Eastham, writing in the middle of the last century, faces the facts with commendable candor. After stating the law, he continues, 'The law requires that this should be done in all cases, yet it cannot be denied that it was frequently evaded, and the property found appropriated to private use, which has often been the case since.' A few of the most glaring cases of looting cargo will serve.

Early in the Revolution, the brig Wilkes was wrecked at Eastham, and her cargo was made away with by certain of the townspeople before an official could get to the beach. So much indignation, some of it envy, no doubt, was aroused by the robbery, that a committee was chosen to detect the culprits if they could, and bring them to justice. Whether or not the committee succeeded in its commendable task does not appear. It is hardly fair, of course, to take war-time conditions as a criterion for normal conduct. If Cape men had not often plundered cargoes when they had not the excuse of war and hard times, the Wilkes incident would not have been mentioned. Everything considered, however, it seems probable that her cargo would have met pretty much the same fate fifty years later.

Young Zachary Lamson, of Beverly, who was wrecked on Nauset Beach in 1802, left the Cape with mixed feelings toward the inhabitants. He was obliged to stay in Chatham for some time to make arrangements for the salvaging of his cargo. His diary contains interesting comments on his visit. After paying high tribute to the hospitality of the Chatham folk, he says:

I wish I could say the same of the Orleans people; they were detected in taking bags of coffee, and actually took one in defiance of the watch. Apparatus of the vessel was stolen, more or less, and deposited in an obscure outbuilding belonging to Mr. Timothy Blank, where it was to lie for division. This fact I detected by taking one of his party in a snowstorm with our effects in his possession, and as he candidly confessed the whole plan and who employed him, I had the satisfaction of deducting about one hundred and fifty dollars from Timothy Blank's account, which was very cutting to him.

The most sensational instance of pillaging a wreck in defiance of law occurred in the spring of 1717, when the pirate ship Whidaw was driven ashore on the back side of Wellfleet. It is a long story, but by no means a dull one; it involves, in fact, not one wreck but two. After a lurid cruise in southern waters, the notorious pirate, Samuel Bellamy, headed his ship Whidaw north to try his luck in Nantucket Sound. He was accompanied by a much smaller craft, a snow, which he had recently captured off the Virginia Coast. Between sunrise and sunset on April 26, Bellamy took two vessels near Nantucket Shoals. One of them was the Mary Anne, an Irish pink bound for New York with a cargo of Madeira; the other a Virginia sloop whose name is not recorded. Seven pirates from the Whidaw were put on board the Mary Anne; others took over the Virginia sloop, and the whole fleet of four vessels headed north into the night.

A gale came up from the northeast, and the pirates — none of them very sober — found themselves in trouble, driven off their course to the westward. The Mary Anne in particular made bad weather of it, no doubt because her crew had a larger supply of Madeira than the others, and toward midnight she got among breakers off Orleans and went aground. Not knowing what better to do, the pirates stayed on board. In the morning the Whidaw was nowhere in sight, but the snow and the Virginia sloop were riding it out at anchor in deep water.

Those two vessels soon slipped their cables and made an offing — vanishing forever from the sight of the Mary Anne and from this narrative.

Before long a boat with two men, John Cole and William Smith, of Orleans, rowed off from the mainland and took the crew ashore. Not until they arrived at Cole's house did the rescuers know that they were entertaining pirates, but here the fact was announced in no uncertain language by one Mackonachy, cook of the Mary Anne, who demanded their instant arrest. Seven to three was too long odds for Cole and Smith; they did not hanker for a knife between the ribs. So by the time the startling news reached Joseph Doane, Esq., of Eastham, who as justice of the peace was the nearest official, the seven pirates had made off over the road, headed for Rhode Island. Doane and a posse of volunteers overtook them before they had gone far and sent them to the Barnstable jail for safekeeping. The pink went to pieces where she lay — but not, it is to be hoped, until her casks of Madeira had found their way into Eastham and Orleans cellars.

Meantime, the Whidaw, flagship of the pirate fleet, was having troubles of her own — divine retribution if ever there was a case of it. She had thrashed her way as far north as the ocean side of Wellfleet, but there Bellamy, realizing that he could keep off shore no longer, let go his anchors and tried to ride it out. The seas ran so high, however, that the Whidaw threatened to go under. As a last resort he set a little sail, cut the cables, and tried to claw off into deep water. He might have saved himself the trouble. Before morning his ship had capsized and was fast going to pieces in the breakers about two miles south of Cahoon's Hollow. Bellamy and one hundred and forty-four of his men were drowned. Only two survivors ever reached shore alive. They were Thomas Davis, a Welshman, who had been impressed from a captured ship, and John Julian, a Cape Cod Indian.

Davis found his way to the house of Samuel Harding in Wellfleet early in the morning of April 27, and told him of the wreck. Harding scented rich pickings; he hitched up his horse and, accompanied by Davis and the Indian, salvaged several wagonloads of the most valuable plunder before any one else knew that the Whidaw was ashore. But before long the beach was black with carts, half the able-bodied men of the village being on hand to haul what they could from the surf. The great prize would have been the chest of gold coins which was supposed to have been on board when the ship struck; but, like most pirate gold, it has never been found.

News of the wreck reached Justice Doane while he was still busy with the crew of the Mary Anne, but as soon as he had started them on their way to the Barnstable jail, he hurried to Cahoon's Hollow, only to find that the bones of the Whidaw had been picked clean. He arrested Davis and John Julian, who joined the seven men of the Anne at Barnstable, whence all were marched under an armed escort to Boston and tried for piracy — all but the Indian, that is, who vanished soon after reaching the city. Davis was acquitted; the others were hanged.

As soon as word came to the ears of Governor Shute that a pirate ship was ashore at Wellfleet, he did two things, both of them proper and both futile. First he issued a proclamation to all His Majesty's subjects whom it might concern, to seize all 'money, bullion, treasure, goods and merchandises,' from the wreck, that they might swell the royal exchequer. Second, he ordered Captain Cyprian Southack to sail to the Cape, collect the loot, and return with it to Boston. No man ever tried harder to achieve the impossible than Southack did. He anchored in Provincetown Harbor five days after the wreck, searched the town in vain for a horse, dispatched a detail of two men to Truro with orders to hire a pair there and proceed overland to the scene of the wreck, where they were to post themselves as a guard over the valuables on board her! Meanwhile, he himself set out for the spot in a whaleboat (with which the town was better supplied than it was with horses), skirted the Bay shore as far as Boat Meadow Creek in Orleans, and made his way across the Cape to the outer beach via this waterway, Jeremiah's Gutter, Town Cove, and Nauset Harbor, a feat which could have been accomplished even at that early date only on the very top of the spring tides.

All that was left of the least value on the Whidaw had been taken home by the citizens. The men whom Southack had sent to watch over the treasure had found nothing but fragments of the hull to guard. The cold rains of May, for which the Cape is famous, did nothing to improve the Captain's temper. It was a dour mariner who began knocking at the doors of the Wellfleet inhabitants, most of whom had a barn full of plunder from the wreck, and demanding that they hand it over. He was greeted variously. Some, with expressions of blank astonishment, asked him to what wreck he referred — they had heard of no wreck. Others laughed and bade him try to get it. Samuel Harding, at whose door the angry minion of His Majesty knocked loudest — for it was he who with Davis had skimmed the cream of the cargo — assured Southack that he was holding the goods for Davis until after the trial. It would be a breach of trust to give them up, even to so well authenticated an official as the Captain. In short, Southack returned to Boston with nothing but some second-hand rigging for his pains, convinced that all Cape-Codders were villains.

From the official point of view he was right, for the law expects men to do what it demands of them. But from the point of view of the observer of human nature, who realizes that temptations are sometimes too strong for mere man to resist, these same Cape-Codders appear as average samples of our race. Many an honest man has robbed the Crown who would not take so much as a stick of firewood from a neighbor. One may sympathize with Southack, without being prepared to denounce the men of Wellfleet. Even so there is danger that the Cape beachcomber is beginning to look like a more desperate fellow than he really was. It is time to reverse the canvas and contemplate a few of his virtues. He often had to open his doors to shipwrecked men. In December, 1820, Freeman Doane, of Eastham, boarded and lodged the only three survivors of the ship Rolla for ten days and refused to take a cent. The wreck of this ship, which was a total loss, kept local treasure-seekers tramping the beach for weeks when it became known that a chest containing thirteen thousand dollars in cash had gone down when she went to pieces. Shipowners, it seems, knew rather more about human frailty than legislators did, for the owners of a Virginia coaster, which was wrecked on Nauset Beach in the winter of 1799, wisely offered one fourth of the cargo of tobacco to the citizens if they would salvage it.

Even allowing for an occasional illegal pipeful, this arrangement must have proved more profitable to the merchant, and was surely a lighter burden for Eastham consciences, than a less intelligent attitude on the owners' part would have been.

Again Easthamers showed restraint when the brig Java, on her way from the East Indies to Boston, was wrecked outside Nauset Harbor in the winter of 1831. Not content with bringing the crew safely ashore in dories, the citizens salvaged her cargo of coffee and nutmegs and were well paid for their exertions by the owners. The Java's hull soon went to pieces, furnishing, like the hulls of so many other vessels, legal spoil in firewood and building material for any one who would take the trouble to harness his oxen and drive to the beach for it.

Underwriters and owners usually found it more economical to employ Cape men as wreckers than to send crews of their own to the scene. In every town below Yarmouth experts were to be found whose principal occupation was salvaging cargoes, transshipping them to their own schooners, and sailing them to their destination. Sometimes, if there was a chance of floating a wreck whose hull was not badly damaged, the same men would patch her up, work her off the bar, and sail her to port, jury-rigged under her own canvas. The great difficulty in this business was the weather. As long as the sea remained calm, all was well, but a single blow often was enough either to smash the vessel to pieces or to drive her so hard aground that she could never be floated. A job of this sort, therefore, was gambling with the elements for high stakes, but oftener than not it succeeded.

In 1829, Messrs. Doane and Knowles, two well-known Eastham wreckers, took a contract to float the brig Creole, which had stranded near the entrance to Nauset Harbor, and sail her to Boston. The cargo of cotton was first lightered ashore, carted across the Cape, and transshipped to Boston. Then Doane and Knowles set to work on the hull, got her off by means of anchors and cables, and sailed her round the Cape to Boston, where they collected $1150. On another occasion the same two men landed a mixed cargo from the brig Massachusetts, hauled it across to their schooner on the Bay shore, and delivered it undamaged to the consignees in Boston. Provincetown wreckers were em-

THE WRECK OF THE CALEDONIA, JANUARY 1, 1863

WRECKERS PULLING OFF A BEACHED SCHOONER AT PROVINCETOWN

ployed to do the same with the cargo of the cotton ship Jenny
Lind, which was wrecked in 1857. 'Our village,' writes a re-
porter for the Provincetown Banner, 'has presented quite a
cottonish aspect during the present week, the cargo of the Jenny
Lind, which came ashore on the back side of the town, being
conveyed across to our port to be reshipped to Boston.' Between times the wreckers kept busy dragging for lost anchors
and cables, a steady industry until well into the eighties. Coasting schooners that lay at anchor waiting for a good chance to
sail round the Cape were often caught by a sudden blow and
forced to slip their cables and make an offing in a hurry. By
dragging for this lost ground-tackle in heavy sloops, the
wreckers made enough to keep them going between storms.

The only flaw in the character of wreckers was that they
sometimes forgot their humanitarianism in their zeal for a
profitable job. In this respect, indeed, they furnish the last
echo of the triumphant yells which in earlier and robuster years
had accompanied the plunderers of wrecks in their pell-mell
rush to the beach. Emerson writes under the date of September
5, 1854, 'Went to Yarmouth Sunday 5th, to Orleans, Monday,
6th; to Nauset Light on the back side of Cape Cod. Collins, the
keeper, told us he found obstinate resistance on Cape Cod to
the project of building a lighthouse on this coast, as it would
injure the wrecking business. He had to go to Boston, and
obtain the strong recommendation of the Port Society.' In
fairness to the Cape it should be said that in 1854 three quarters
of her best citizens were at sea as shipmasters, and could therefore have had no share in the business. It is certain, too, that
those who were at home between voyages would, as sailors, be
the last men in the world to object to lighthouses. For the
miserable remainder no defense is offered.

The statement was made early in this chapter that Cape-Codders were valiant amateur life-savers. A glance at some of their
exploits in this highly special form of Christianity will help to
obliterate the unpleasant recollection of the anti-lighthouse
faction. They had plenty of chances to practice it, too, for only
after wrecks had been coming ashore for years, did the Government see fit to establish a Life-Saving Service. In the mean
time the citizens had to make shift to get as many sailors off
wrecks as they could with a boat and a pair of oars.

Early in April, 1849, the British ship Josephus, bound for Boston, went aground at Truro in an easterly blow about a mile north of Highland Light. She was a wooden vessel and immediately began to break up. Most of the townspeople were on the beach, but they could only watch helplessly while spar followed spar into the surf and was whirled ashore. Two fishermen, Daniel Cassidy and Jonathan Collins, who had just arrived on the scene, caught sight of a dory which lay high up under the bank. Without a moment's hesitation they dragged it to the water's edge, where, heedless of their friends' protests, they performed the apparently impossible feat of launching it through the surf, and were off, rowing into the breakers toward the Josephus. For a few minutes all went well. Then a wave of such size tore in upon them that before the little boat could rise on its crest, they were buried under tons of water. The last that was ever seen of them was two heads — black dots against the foam — that appeared for an instant and vanished under the next wave. Cassidy, who had been married only a few weeks, left a widow who had already lost a father and a brother in the great gale of 1841. These were not the first men of Truro to perish thus. Fourteen years earlier Elisha Paine lost his life in the same way in an attempt to row off to the Russian brig Emeline Charlotte before she went to pieces.

The day after Christmas, 1873, brought with it a gale that at times approached hurricane violence and sent two vessels to their graves on Cape beaches. One, the American ship Peruvian from Calcutta to Boston, was doomed the moment she struck, for the Peaked Hill Bars off Provincetown held her a mile from shore where there was never a chance for her crew to be taken off, even if any one had happened to be on the beach in such a storm and had been able to see her through the snow. Bit by bit she went to pieces through the night; all hands perished, and only three bodies were ever washed ashore.

The other vessel fared better, at least as far as loss of life was concerned. She was the iron bark Francis flying the German flag, and had left Calcutta within a few days of the Peruvian. She came ashore about three miles south of Peaked Hill, where there was water enough to let her pound over the outer bar with hull intact; she fetched up not more than a couple of

hundred yards from the beach at North Truro. The rescue of
her crew by volunteers from the village was undoubtedly the
most laborious ever undertaken on the Cape. There was no
boat on the beach, none in fact nearer than the Bay shore.
Nothing daunted, the citizens dragged a whaleboat from the
Bay to a pond; skidded it across the pond on the ice; hitched
a pair of horses to it, and began the real journey across the Cape
to the point on the outer beach where the crew of the Francis
were wondering how long her hull would hold together.

Finally the rescuers topped the last ridge and rushed the boat
down the beach. She was safely launched through the surf,
but it took more than one trip to bring the officers and crew of
the Francis ashore. No one was lost except the Captain, who
had been sick for some time and who died in the Highland
House, North Truro, four days after being taken from his
vessel. The hull of the Francis, after remaining buried for half
a century, was uncovered by a freak of wind and wave during
the winter of 1927.

Again, in October, 1808, six Truro men whose names are
unrecorded rowed off in a storm to the schooner Active, Portland for Boston, which had capsized several miles offshore the
previous night. She had not struck, but was drifting helpless on
her beam ends in deep water. The great distance the rescuers
had to cover made their exploit a particularly hazardous one.
They took off Captain Danforth and three passengers, whom
they landed safely on the beach after a terrific row through a
rising gale. They had contemplated making another trip, but
it was too late. Darkness set in as they brought their first boatload ashore, and there was no chance of locating the drifting
wreck until the next morning. When daylight came, no trace of
the Active remained, but two months later, long after they
had been given up for lost, it was learned that her crew had been
picked up half frozen by the ship Alexandria, which had subsequently been dismasted and had put into Antigua under jury
rig, thus causing the long delay.

The next adventure occurred farther up the Cape. After
drifting dismasted for three days, the sloop Fox, which had
sailed from Boston, November 29, 1820, with twenty-eight
passengers, was sighted by some Chatham men. They put off

to her in a fleet of small boats and brought every one of the
passengers and crew ashore on Nauset Beach, half dead from
thirst and exposure.

Almost sixty years later, the schooner Sarah Fort was
wrecked in April, 1879, near Peaked Hill Bars. Government
life-savers smashed their boat while trying to launch it through
the surf. So Captain Isaac F. Mayo, of Provincetown, rowed off
in a whaleboat with a rough-and-ready crew of local volunteers
and brought a number of the schooner's men ashore. And so it
goes. Sometimes these amateur life-savers succeeded; sometimes they failed; but if there was the shadow of a chance for
success, they tried.

Valiant and expert as the rescuers were, they realized more
poignantly than any one else the need of an organized life-
saving service with suitable equipment on the spot. But 'the
march of the human mind is slow' — and it is particularly
slow in the case of legislative bodies when they are asked to
appropriate money for humanitarian purposes. Congress knew
little of the surf on Peaked Hill Bars or of the shoals that
stretch seaward from Monomoy. With comfortable philosophy,
Senators concluded that a shipwreck was a shipwreck and that
sailors must take their chance. Besides, were they not voting
money all the time for lighthouses and coast surveys? [1]

But Massachusetts men knew something about shipwrecks
and were ready to spend money to reduce the number of
fatalities. As early as 1786, they organized the Massachusetts
Humane Society — said to be the first of its kind in the world.
Its goal was to supply boats and equipment to be kept ready at
all times at dangerous points alongshore. They could not at
first afford to place lifeboats wherever they were needed, but
they did the next best thing. Relying for the moment on the
willingness of volunteers to continue rowing off to wrecks, they
began by building huts on remote beaches to shelter survivors
who might get ashore unaided. This was a much-needed measure, for a shipwrecked man's troubles had only begun when he
dragged himself above the reach of the surf. In March, 1872, for
example, John Silva, sole survivor of the wrecked schooner
Clara Bell, was washed ashore on a plank shortly after mid-

[1] See notes to Chapter XI.

night within two miles of Highland Light. A snowstorm hid the flash of the great lantern, and the wretched sailor wandered about until daylight, when he was found in a road, still on his feet, but unable to take another step or to utter an intelligible word. He finally recovered with some minor amputations.

Again, Peter Woodbury and John Low, of Beverly, after having dropped to dry land at Orleans from the bowsprit of their wrecked schooner, celebrated the early hours of New Year's Day, 1802, by wandering on Nauset Beach until they fell exhausted in the snow. They were picked up later in the day by citizens of Orleans and Chatham, whose wives thawed them back to life with hot blankets. Zachary Lamson, acting captain, and other members of the crew, after a futile attempt to find a way off the beach, went back to the vessel drenched as they were and turned in all standing. They were saved from freezing to death by the same men who found Woodbury and Low. This was the same wreck which resulted in Lamson's somewhat caustic remarks about Timothy Blank, of Orleans.

A hut with some dry straw would have been paradise to any of these frozen mariners, and if such huts were strategically located, there was a chance that shipwrecked men might stumble upon them. So, at any rate, argued the fathers of the Massachusetts Humane Society, and forthwith they set about raising the money to build them — no difficult task in a sea-going community like the Bay State. Before long, a scattering chain of huts appeared, oases in the bleak desert of the Cape sand hills. The first of them was put up in 1794, back of Provincetown, near the head of Stout's Creek, but, owing to faulty construction, it was soon demolished by wind and blowing sand. By 1802, six properly built shelters had appeared between Race Point and Monomoy. To aid survivors in finding them, James Freeman in 1802 wrote a careful description of the whole outer beach of the Cape, with instructions how to locate each of the six shelters. His pamphlet was distributed in shipping circles and may have helped a little. As early as 1804, for example, the three survivors of the burned schooner Farmer were saved from perishing, after being half drowned in the Orleans breakers, by finding one of two huts which the Society had put up on Nauset Beach. Captain Schott and his two men spent a tolerably comfortable night in this shelter, buried in straw and listening to the fourteen-foot surf which pounded the beach outside.

But, as may be seen from the experiences of Silva and Lamson, the remedy was anything but sure. The trustees of the Society, therefore, kept developing the equipment, until by 1845 the huts were supplied with boats, and with mortars for shooting lines across the decks of stranded vessels. At last the Federal Government began to take notice. They had already begun, in fact, by paying part of the Humane Society's expenses, as did the State Government as well. But when finally Congress took full charge, the result was appalling. The years between 1850 and 1870 were marked by waste and inefficiency, while as many wrecked men were drowned as ever. Not till popular indignation had been raised to the boiling point by repeated disasters along the coast with all hands lost, was the Government finally frightened into establishing an effective and disciplined service.

The Cape, for some reason best known to the politicians, was left till the last; but the year 1872 saw nine stations built and manned between Provincetown and Chatham. Four more have been added since. To-day they are models of comfort and efficiency, with sleeping-quarters for the crew, which in most cases consist of six or seven men and a captain, spare cots for rescued men, and the best and most complete equipment in boats and gear that can be obtained. Usually there are two surfboats. The crew live in the station and are on duty the year round. Telephone lines connect station and station as well as with the towns. Every foot of beach from Wood End to Monomoy is patrolled each night and, if the weather is foggy, by day as well. Throughout the week, drills of various sorts are held to keep the crews tuned up to concert pitch, and no more skillful or valiant boatmen can be found than those employed in this service. Until very recently nine out of ten were natives of the Cape, but within the last few years a Portuguese or two have been admitted to many of the crews. A few samples of their skill and courage will suffice.

The first rescue that suggests itself was in connection with the grounding of the old stone sloop Trumbull, that was sighted in distress by a patrolman from the Peaked Hill Bars Station on the last day of November, 1880. She was aground on the bar, with white water breaking all around her. Captain David Atkins, keeper of the station, took five of his crew with him in the boat, got safely through the first row of breakers, and arrived in due time close aboard the sloop. The sea was so rough in the shoal water that it was out of the question to bring his boat alongside; so he directed the crew of the Trumbull to jump overboard one at a time, that he might pick them up. The crew, three in number, obeyed orders and were promptly pulled into the lifeboat. The captain and mate, however, whether from lack of courage or from a proper desire to stay with the ship, refused to jump. It was not a time for argument. Captain Atkins swung his boat's bow toward shore, and all hands were landed safely on the beach.

His duty was done, but Atkins was not satisfied. He looked off again to the spot where the Trumbull, her boom slatting and her hull pounding, threatened to go to pieces at any moment. Again he ordered his crew to launch the boat through the surf, and again they rowed off to try to induce the captain and mate to come ashore. This time a wave carried him too close to the rocking hull; the slatting sheet of the sloop was caught under the surfboat's bow, a fierce gust carried the boom across to the other side, the sheet came taut with a jerk, and the lifeboat was capsized. Captain Atkins and two of the surfmen perished almost immediately. The three remaining men of his crew clung for a time to the bottom of their boat; then, kicking themselves out of what clothes they could, they struck out for shore. All three arrived and were pulled out of the breakers by John Cole, a surfman who had been detailed to stand by on the beach and help the boat in landing. The Trumbull floated clear of the bars on the next high tide, the wind moderated, and she continued her voyage to New York, manned by the captain and the mate. The quality of Captain Atkins and his men as exemplified on this occasion needs no comment.

If life-savers could count on intelligent coöperation from the crews of stranded vessels, a large part of the danger of their calling would be eliminated. So expert are they in handling their surfboats in all weathers, and so perfect is their discipline, that hardly a man of them need be lost even in the worst storms, if those whom they are trying to rescue keep their heads and obey orders. But too often they do neither. The Monomoy disaster of 1902 is a terrible instance of this sort. Like so many other tragedies, it involved no more impressive a vessel than the stump-masted coal barge, Wadena, which struck on Shovelful Shoal, south of Monomoy Station, on March 11 in a heavy northeaster. Captain Eldredge and his men of the Monomoy Station brought the crew ashore and supposed that the incident was closed. The barge lay intact during the next few days, giving Boston wreckers a fine chance to salvage the coal.

At the same time that the Wadena struck, another barge, the Fitzpatrick, stranded not far from her, and two Chatham wreckers, Captain Elmer Mayo and Captain Mallows, were engaged by the owners to float her. They planned to begin work on the morning of the 17th, and accordingly spent the night before on board, after making the final arrangements with her captain. Toward evening it breezed up from the southeast, but Eldredge and his men at the station felt no anxiety, because they supposed that a tug which the wreckers were using had brought all hands ashore from the Wadena. What was their surprise, the next morning, to see a distress signal flying from the barge's rigging. Their surprise was mingled with concern, for the wind had increased during the night until it blew a gale which turned the water around the Wadena into a chaos of breakers.

Immediately Captain Eldredge, who had walked down to the end of Monomoy Point to look the situation over, telephoned back to the station for the lifeboat. When she arrived, he jumped aboard, and the crew, shipping a little water on the way, pulled off through the breakers to comparative shelter under the high leeward side of the Wadena and made fast. They found that five men had been left on board, all of whom had lost their nerve and were clamoring to be taken ashore. Worse still, they were in no sense of the word sailors, as appeared when their captain let go his hold of the rope by which he was lowering himself into the lifeboat and fell crashing aboard to the accompaniment of a smashed thwart.

Eldredge, ordering the five men to lie down in the bottom of the boat, braced himself for the return trip, and his crew shot the boat out from under the lee as he leaned against his long steering oar to head the craft into the seas. It was a beautiful piece of boatmanship; some water came aboard, but not enough to be dangerous. As soon as the trembling cargo in the bottom of the boat saw the top of the wave slop in over the side, however, they gave themselves up for lost, jumped to their feet, and seized the man at the oars around the neck — doubtless for the same reason that a drowning man winds himself around his rescuer.

In a second the boat was bottom up, with all hands in the water. Even now the Monomoy crew were calm. Twice they righted her, only to have waves capsize her before they could pull themselves on board. They had no strength for a third attempt, but clung to the bottom, determined to hang on till the last gasp. One by one, benumbed and battered, they let go and vanished, until the only man of that crew left was Seth Ellis, number one surfman of the station. Finding himself alone, he managed to wrap one arm around the centerboard which had floated up and protruded like a shark's fin from the bottom of the boat.

Up to this point the whole disaster had been shrouded in fog. Mayo and Mallows on board the Fitzpatrick had not even seen the crew put off to the other barge. But at this moment a hole was blown in the mist and revealed to the Chatham men on the Fitzpatrick the white bottom of a lifeboat with a single black figure sprawled across it. Deaf to the protests of Mallows and the Captain of the barge, Mayo in an instant had stripped to his underclothes, got a twelve-and-a-half foot dory over the side, seized a pair of clumsy oars which he cut down to somewhere near the right size, and was pulling toward Ellis and the lifeboat.

For any man who had not spent his life alongshore, as Mayo had, the attempt would have been suicide. But Mayo had been cradled in dories, spent his youth as fisherman, anchor-dragger and wrecker, and had substituted from time to time at various life-saving stations on the Cape. Now, at the age of forty, he knew all that a man can know about dories and the Monomoy Shoals. He knew that the boat which carried him was a poor specimen of her class; but even an indifferent dory is a remarkable sea-boat when handled by an expert, and that is how this one was handled. Yard by yard he pulled her to the side of the lifeboat, where the most ticklish part of the exploit awaited him. If Ellis had been another Wadena wrecker, both men would have perished. But numb and exhausted as he was, Ellis made not a single false move while Mayo helped him into the bottom of the dory. Then he headed for shore, came through the surf with the help of the shore detail of one, whom Captain Eldredge had left there, and assisted Ellis to the station. Six weeks later, Ellis, who was soon as well as ever, became keeper of it. Mayo was given one medal by the Humane Society and another by the United States Government.

The disasters which have been mentioned are not those that involved the greatest loss of money; if such had been the intention, ships and barks would have taken the places of brigs and schooners. The famous triple wreck of the Crowninshield East-Indiamen, Volusia, Ulysses, and Brutus, which were lost at Provincetown in 1802, would have headed the list; the ship Confidence, Captain Isaiah Knowles, which in 1806 floated into the Bay on her beam ends without a living man on board, would have been a close second. The ships Franklin and London, both lost in 1849, one at Wellfleet, the other on Nauset Beach, would have been included. So would the ship Columbus, a total loss at Barnstable in 1851, and the Orissa, another full-rigged ship, which added her bones to the Nauset graveyard in '57. All these and many more were wrecks of the first magnitude. A list prepared in 1864 shows that from the year 1843 to 1859 about five hundred wrecks occurred on the Cape. In 1903, the United States Engineer's Office at Newport, Rhode Island, made a map showing the locations of five hundred and forty more between 1880 and 1903. But the disasters which have been recounted above are those which in one way or another revealed the mettle of Cape-Codders. And taken by and large these men have not done badly by the shattered ships and broken men that the northeasters of three hundred years have hurled upon their beaches. If there was looting sometimes, so was there heroism; if there was greed, there was charity as well; and it should be borne in mind that the community where all men are righteous must be sought for on some planet other than our own.

To-day, though storms still pound ships to pieces on the Cape as easily as ever, the Canal and the Life-Saving Service have made it possible for most honest citizens to remain potential heroes only. The wrecker, done out of his business by metropolitan firms, has thrown out a sheet anchor in the shape of a cranberry bog or a filling station; the mooncusser hugs his hearth or smuggles whiskey for a thirsty land.

CHAPTER XII

THE MERCHANT MARINE

A FULL account of the merchant marine of Cape Cod would require not a chapter but a volume. Its tentative beginnings, its gradual rise to the glory of the forties and fifties, and its inevitable decline, comprise too vast and varied a subject for a condensed narrative. So in this chapter no mention can be made of many names that in their day were great, or of many ships that spread their masters' greatness from sea to sea. No foreign voyage is insignificant; every captain is in a very real sense his country's ambassador. Especially was this true in the early days of our nation, when we were yet a people unknown and untested, with the world before us to antagonize or conciliate, and no one but our shipmasters to represent us. These men neither antagonized nor conciliated. Instead, by their shrewdness, resourcefulness, and vigor, they won for their country the reluctant and sometimes acidulated respect of the world.

The Cape has so long been associated in men's minds with the sea and with those that come and go in ships, so large a part of her population has until very recently been composed of master mariners, either active or retired, and such a wealth of salty tradition has clustered about her name, that the casual observer is deceived with false pictures. He sees the Pilgrim Fathers themselves sailing the Mayflower into Provincetown Harbor with their own hands, and shouting orders to each other in a language of tarry technicalities. He sees the very earliest settlements that our forefathers made on the Cape as busy seaports, their harbors white with sails, and the settlers themselves, whenever they happened to be ashore, walking with a nautical roll. But the facts — it cannot be too often emphasized — were very different. It was not until years later that, with their houses built, their mills grinding, and their crops growing, Cape men turned their attention to the two most intricate arts that they ever mastered: the art of building ships and the art of sailing them. The first vessels that they built — aside from fishermen and whalers — were packets to run between Cape towns and Boston and New York. And naturally enough, for the discomforts of overland travel in stage-coaches were so great that only philosophers, like Thoreau, or men of God, like Timothy Dwight, dared face them. Most wise men on the Cape knew the way to China by sea better than they did the way to Boston by land. The Cape-Codder who had once undergone this journey, and who again found it necessary to visit Boston, would wait, if necessary, a month until a chance lumber schooner or fisherman could carry him by water. One man, who by a ghastly accident had been harpooned on a whaler off Provincetown, was rushed to Boston in a whaleboat rowed by a double crew working in relays. It became (and this is a happier motive for the trip) a common practice for young Provincetown and Truro fishermen to carry their sweethearts to Boston in their schooners when the time came for selecting a trousseau. Another incentive for starting packet lines was the enormous quantity of salt that was being made everywhere on the Cape. Much of this was used by local fishermen, but there remained a surplus for export, and the water route was the only way to carry it. There were also occasional cargoes of onions and flax. Thus the appearance of packets was inevitable. They were needed for both passengers and freight, and, with the prospect of sure returns on their investment, local merchants began to build them and to operate them. Framed by townsmen from timber growing near by, commanded and manned by Cape men and boys, these craft were as complete and absolute products of the region as anything made by man can be. The inhabitants regarded them with far more than a business interest. They looked on them with a pride and affection that was curiously allied to the pride and affection that they felt for their husbands, brothers, and sons who sailed them.

There were often two or three packets hailing from a village, and they usually made, among them, three trips a week to Boston and back. One, the Northern Light, of Provincetown, about 1830, ran to and from Boston three times a week from March to December — a performance unparalleled by sail before or since. No vessels of their size were ever kept more immaculate or were more promptly refitted or discarded when they began to show signs of age. Their beauty and comfort were almost as important in their owners' eyes as their speed and safety. One in particular, the schooner Postboy, of Truro, has been called 'the finest specimen of naval architecture and passenger accommodation ever seen in Bay waters.' Her cabin was finished in solid mahogany and bird's-eye maple; her draperies were of silk. She was at once fast and comfortable, the pride of her captain, Zoeth Rich.

There is no keener rivalry than the rivalry between towns of any district, and no more exciting sport than boat-racing. When these two factors combine, when the men concerned are Yankees, and when the question of pecuniary investment is also involved, the cords of competition will be stretched extremely taut. This was the situation that existed between the Cape Cod packets, their owners, and their captains. No sooner did the Postboy appear at Provincetown than the merchants of Eastham would see what they could do to go her one better. If Truro appeared with a new flier, Wellfleet within a month was laying the keel of a bigger and faster craft. If local timber and local talent were thought unequal to the task, vessels were ordered from other places where it was supposed newer methods obtained, for it is with shipbuilders even as it is with prophets.

The best example of this sort of rivalry occurred between the towns of Barnstable and Yarmouth. Yarmouth, about 1840, had a sloop, the Commodore Hull, that was rightly considered the finest and fastest on the coast. There was not a packet captain on the Bay who had not been chagrined by having her boil up from astern, pass him to windward, and beat him to Boston by a margin that was measured in hours. Barnstable stood this as long as she could, and then two of her leading citizens, Captains Matthias Hinckley and Thomas Percival, went up the Hudson River to contract for a new packet that would beat the Yarmouth wonder. The result was the sloop Mail. On their first rival voyage for Boston, the two vessels crossed Barnstable Bar abreast, leaving behind them two villages wild with excitement, and many wagers between the inhabitants of each. The watchers from the shore could see no change in their relative positions; neck and neck they tore along before a fresh southerly breeze until they were hull down and lost to sight. The new Barnstable vessel, however, fulfilled her destiny and nosed out the Commodore Hull, sliding into Central Wharf a bare three lengths ahead of her rival. But the Yarmouth citizens were loyal and declared that the Mail's victory was an accident, or was perhaps due to the fact that both Captains Hinckley and Percival had sailed her; and that the Commodore Hull was still the faster sailer.

This famous packet had other rivals right at home — chief among them being the Eagle's Flight, commanded by Captain Ansel Hallett. The competition between these two Yarmouth vessels was almost as keen as that between the neighboring towns. No records exist to show which was the faster; but there was no doubt in the mind of the bard who composed this lively stanza:

> 'O! the Commodore Hull, she sails so dull
> It made all the crew look sour,
> While the Eagle's Flight was out of sight
> In less than half an hour.'

A trip to Boston by packet, even when there was no one to race against, was by no means a dull affair. For one thing, there was the uncertainty how long the passage would take; it might last anywhere from six hours to two days, and the passengers made the most of their holiday. High and low, rich and poor, were on an equal footing, for the crowded decks and cabins (there were anywhere from twenty-five to fifty passengers on these little vessels) prohibited all exclusiveness. There might be a deep-water captain on his way to Boston to take his ship out to China; he kept the ship's company entertained with tales of deep waters, while others talked of record fares of cod, great schools of stranded blackfish, of local politics and national policy. The meals were plain, but abundant, and cost twenty-five cents. The fare for a round trip was $1.50.

As soon as a returning packet was sighted at Barnstable or Dennis or Wellfleet, a flag was run up, on a pole perched inland on the highest available hill, to notify the South-Siders. Since oftener than not the vessel was bringing home a shipmaster who had left his vessel in Boston and who was returning to the Cape after a year's voyaging on the other side of the world, it is easy to imagine the excitement that attended the hoisting of this signal and the scenes that took place at the little wharves along the Bay shore. Joy and sorrow, comedy and tragedy they saw, and healthy activity and moderate profits.

The importance of the packets to the Cape, however, was farther-reaching than the mere profits to their owners and convenience to the chance traveler or salt-maker. To be sure, they kept business brisk alongshore with plenty of work for the rigger and ship-chandler and an active turnover for the general storekeeper; so much so that when the railroad finally stretched its way to Provincetown, and the packets by the same token vanished forever, the opinion of one longshoreman, who found himself idle and the wharves empty, was, 'George, the railroad is a cuss!' But their real importance was that they served as the primary school for seafaring, and that, unlike some schools, they furnished their pupils with incentive to fare farther and reach higher, until many a youngster who began his career coiling halyards on a Dennis packet, finished on the quarter-deck of a clipper ship, establishing a new record across the Atlantic.

Such a *cursus honorum* is neither theoretical nor imaginary. Captain Joseph H. Sears, of East Dennis, left the little packet Combine to command full-rigged ships on foreign voyages. So did Captain Dean Sears, of the same town. Mr. Edgar Jones, of West Barnstable, an ex-seafaring man who spent his last years sailing parties around Nine Mile Pond in a jaunty little sloop, and who was in his day first mate of such ships as the Radiant, Comet, and Royal Arch, told the author that his first desire to go to sea came to him when, as a boy, he watched the sloop Mail leaving her wharf in Barnstable for Boston. How could it be otherwise? What youngster could sail into Boston Harbor on the Mail or Modena or Young Tell, and there see the spars of tall ships cutting the sky with their intricate tracery of rigging, or watch the strange and varied cargoes derricked up through their hatches, without longing to join the ranks of the conquerors and command those towering ships that would carry him to the ends of the earth?

So the packets, before they died and became history, opened the eyes of the young Cape-Codders to the roadsteads of the world; and this, if it had been all, would have justified their existence. As to their death, it was inevitable, and was due in the main to two causes. Salt-making began to be abandoned, for salt mines supplanted the old way of evaporation. Then came the railroad, which reached village after village along the Cape until it came roaring into Provincetown and steamed out with everything, passengers and freight, that the packets had carried.

The little vessels themselves fared variously. Some became fishermen; others continued a losing struggle with the railroad until they grew old and were condemned. One, the famous Northern Light, of Provincetown, was sold to owners on the Pacific Coast and was wrecked on her way round, in the Straits of Magellan. Another was sold for a pilot boat in New Orleans.

But steam in another form had already cut heavily into the business of the pioneer packets. The steamboat Naushon in 1857 ran from Provincetown to Boston and touched at other points on the north shore of the Cape. The steamer Acorn, of Sandwich, followed a few years later and plied back and forth until she was sold for a blockade-runner in the Civil War and was sunk by accident off the Carolinas. The George Shattuck and the Longfellow continued until the eighties, when the silting up of all the Cape harbors except that of Provincetown, the increasing efficiency of the railway, and the general depression of all business on the Cape, sounded their knell.

The wider horizons that young Cape sailors had caught glimpses of from the decks of the packets lured them in increasing numbers into deep water. Even before the Revolution, a few had followed the gleam. Timothy Thornton had grown rich by foreign trade as early as 1671, and Chatham boasted a far voyager or two in 1740. But most of the colonial seafaring was for codfish or whales. After the Revolution, however, the case was different. As soon as the new country got her bearings, she started out with energy, tripped over the Embargo of 1807, stagnated through the War of 1812, and then started afresh toward the great decade of the fifties. And from 1815 to 1860, it is safe to say that no part of the Atlantic Coast prospered more mightily than Cape Cod.

One should realize at the outset of this period the fundamental difference so far as the Cape is concerned, between deep-water navigation and the point-to-point work of the packets. The packets sailed from every little creek and harbor along-shore. Such harbors were impossible to vessels of deeper draught; nowhere along the Cape, except at Provincetown, was there a harbor fit for sheltering big ships, nor were there any facilities for loading and unloading them. Our merchant captains, therefore, sailed from other ports — from Boston, New York, Philadelphia, and Baltimore — and returned to their homes on the Cape between voyages only. No Cape town ever saw the graceful hulls and rakish masts of clipper ships tied up alongside her wharves or swinging at anchor in her roadsteads.

On the other hand, the shipowners of every port on both coasts of the United States were eager to get Cape men to command their vessels and transact their business in the far corners of the world. From 1815 to the decline of American shipping in the eighties, her captains carried every sort of cargo to every sort of port; encountered everything that can be encountered at sea (mutinous crews, calms, typhoons) and every sort of trick-ery that can be encountered on land, from the barefaced shanghaiing of crews to the devious business practices of the Orient. And, to the credit of Yankee resource and valor, it may truthfully be said that they seldom came off losers. It will be worth while to follow some of them to sea.

One of the early long-voyage Cape-Codders was Captain John Kendrick, who was born in Harwich in 1740. He is a proper figure to begin with, not because he was an example of the best the Cape produced, but because he was active at the outset of American seafaring, and, in fact, had helped to create it by commanding the privateers Fanny and Marianne during the Revolutionary War. Four years after the war, a group of Boston merchants, fired by a chance remark of the celebrated Captain Cook, of South Sea fame, decided, since Britain had slammed her doors against us, to take a financial flier by open-ing a Northwest fur trade. The scheme involved gigantic dis-tances over a route much of which was uncharted. The first leg of the voyage was round the Horn and up to Nootka Sound off the Oregon Coast; thence the course lay across the Pacific to the China Coast, where the adventurers traded their furs for silk; then south and west through the China Sea and across the Indian Ocean, round the Cape of Good Hope, and northwest across the Atlantic to Boston.

The men who invested their money in so hazardous an enterprize naturally wanted the hardiest and most courageous seaman they could find to take command. They selected Captain Kendrick. He set sail from Boston in 1787 in a stumpy little ship, eighty-three feet long, named the Columbia; with him as first lieutenant, in command of the little sloop Lady Washington, sailed Robert Gray, of Boston. They beat their way round Cape Horn, with flooded decks, the crews rotten with scurvy, cruised north by the west coast of South America, skirted the long coast of California (San Francisco was not then in existence), and finally dropped anchor in Nootka Sound near what is now Vancouver Island.

Kendrick ordered all hands ashore, and built a big shack in which to spend the winter while trading for sea otter with the Indians. At this point the Captain's character began to disintegrate. He had not shown himself a 'nimble leader' (to quote Gray's phrase) on the way out, but had wasted a month at the Cape Verde Islands and ten days more at the Falklands. Having now at last reached Nootka, he stayed there in idleness all winter, allowing Gray to do all the cruising for skins. In the early summer, when enough had been collected to fill the Columbia, Kendrick, instead of sailing with his cargo to China, turned the command of the larger vessel over to Gray, who promptly set out across the Pacific, leaving the nominal commander of the expedition to his own devices in the Lady Washington.

Kendrick spent the summer pleasantly enough in exploring and trading, and went as far north as Barrell Sound in Queen Charlotte Islands, where the Indians stole some clothing from him. As punishment, he seized two of their chiefs, bound one leg of each down the barrel of a cannon, and pretended that he was about to set them off. The cruel bluff succeeded; the other Indians in terror returned the stolen goods, but the Captain was not satisfied. Realizing that he had burned his bridges so far as trading with these Indians was concerned, he demanded all the skins in the village, paid the usual trade price for them, and headed for China. He took his time, as usual, stopping at one of the Hawaiian Islands, where he found sandalwood growing wild. This suggested possibilities; he left three men there to cut enough for a cargo, and reached China in January, 1790.

Here he spent a year and two months disposing of his skins, and rerigged the Lady Washington as an hermaphrodite brig. Neither a fever which he contracted, nor the hostility of Chinese officials, who made things as hard as they could for him, can account for such a waste of time. Clearly he was becoming demoralized. When (in March, 1791) he finally did leave the China Coast, he was heavily in debt. He headed east and very foolishly visited Barrell Sound again, supposing that the two years which had elapsed had given the Indians time to forget his previous treatment of them. Under pretense of friendly trading, they sprang a surprise attack on his vessel and very nearly took her. But they were finally repulsed, and Kendrick, with wanton malignity, killed as many as he could even while they were retreating in canoes. That he had abandoned all idea of returning home appears from the fact that he bought a great tract of wild land on Vancouver Island from the Indians, and built himself a log house which he called Fort Washington. Here Gray, who again arrived from Boston via Cape Horn, found him living at ease.

After this the Captain made only one more voyage to China. He started another, but got no farther than the Hawaiian Islands, where he found life so agreeable that he spent the last half of the winter loafing about Kauai, where the sandalwood grew. Returning there the next fall, after another summer on the Northwest Coast, Kendrick met Captain Brown, of the British navy, at Oahu, and was killed in an exchange of salutes. The Englishman's cannon, by some ghastly accident, was loaded. So died a man who had left Boston seven years before a respected merchant captain, and had degenerated into little more than a South Sea trader.

Such was the beginning of the Northwest fur trade, one of the earliest branches of our country's maritime activity. Other Cape men were quick to follow the long wake of Kendrick — notably Captain William Sturgis, of Barnstable, and his mate and fellow townsman Daniel Bacon. Captain Sturgis forms the

sharpest contrast to Kendrick. At sixteen he sailed to the
Northwest Coast as foremast hand on the Eliza, of Boston, and
returned as third mate. A few years later, after bringing the
Caroline back to Boston from the Hawaiian Islands, he was
given command of the Atahualpa, one of Theodore Lyman's
vessels, and with Bacon as mate, he made another voyage to
the Northwest coast. In 1820, Captain Sturgis retired from the
sea to start the firm of Bryant and Sturgis, one of the oldest
and soundest Northwest trading houses of Boston. Captain
Sturgis's experiences with the Indians were always of the friend-
liest kind. He learned their language, and it is hardly an exaggeration to say that there was as much of the missionary as
of the trader in his dealings with them. Apropos of their occasional attacks on American ships, he writes: 'It would be easy
to show that these fatal disasters might have been averted by a
different treatment of the natives and by prudence and proper
precaution on the part of their civilized visitors.' But though
Captain Sturgis never had any trouble with Indians, he once
had a battle with a fleet of Chinese pirates that makes Kendrick's brush with the natives of the Queen Charlotte Islands
look like a cockfight.

It was the Captain's last voyage in the Atahualpa. She lay
one day in August anchored in the Macao Roads. Bacon had
been sent ashore on some business or other, and hardly had he
landed when a fleet of piratical junks — sixteen in number —
swooped down upon the ship. Sturgis, a cigar clenched in his
teeth, put up a terrific fight, for every merchantman went
armed, and the Captain, although short-handed owing to the
absence of Bacon and his boat's crew, had firearms aplenty
and poured out shot after shot from his howitzers, while the
crew peppered the decks of the pirates with musket balls.
Knowing well enough the character of his assailants, he placed
a barrel of powder on deck and announced to his crew that if the
pirates once got possession of the ship, he would touch it off and
blow them all to eternity together — yellow men and white.

Bacon heard the guns and rushed to the shore with his boat's
crew, where he shoved off, despite the advice of his friends, who
told him that it was suicide. How he got through the swarm
of pirates and reached the side of the blood-streaked Atahualpa

is a mystery; but he succeeded, and owing very largely to this reënforcement, Captain Sturgis was able to keep the Chinamen at bay until he had worked his vessel up to a place of safety under the guns of Macao forts. The commander of the pirate fleet was afterwards captured and executed by the Chinese process of hacking to death, known as 'the thousand cuts.' The moral effect of this episode on the pirates was as beneficial as its immediate effect was disastrous to their leader, and American vessels and American masters were from then on regarded with no small respect by the inhabitants of Canton and Macao.

Just before the turn of the century, European wars switched some Yankee shipowners, who were willing to take a long chance for big profits, away from the Northwest Coast, into neutral trade with France. Food was so scarce in that beleaguered country that a cargo of provisions was worth almost any price, but the difficulties involved were twofold — first, to get across the Atlantic without being picked up by a hostile frigate, and second, to collect from the starving Frenchmen. The business called for very different qualifications from those demanded in the Northwest and China trade. Open powder barrels had no effect on naval officers; patience and diplomacy were of more avail than cutlasses in extracting payment from revolutionary Frenchmen; and patience and diplomacy are attributes which we do not always associate with the American temper, least often of all, perhaps, with the temper of American shipmasters. But consider the account that Captain Elijah Cobb, of Brewster, gives us of his difficulties with the French Government and his subsequent visit to Paris.

Captain Cobb was born in 1768 in what is now Brewster, but was then a part of Harwich. At the age of twenty-six he sailed out of Boston in command of the brig Jane bound for Cadiz. This was during the Reign of Terror, when Robespierre was supreme. Cobb's vessel was captured by a French frigate and taken into Brest. His situation looked hopeless, for his papers had been seized, and without papers his claim to the ship was worthless. He appealed, as a matter of form, to the *chargé d'affaires*, and was told that he must exercise patience and that in time the Government would do the right thing. The officials were as good as their word, for in six weeks Cobb was allowed to

ELIJAH COBB   ASA SHIVERICK

sell his cargo, receiving payment in bills of exchange on Hamburg, payable in fifty days. He went to Paris to get back his papers, riding three days and nights without sleep, and passing the remains of a butchered courier strewn about the road, together with fragments of master, postilion, and horses. This was a mild prologue, however, to the scenes he was to witness, for he subsequently watched a thousand persons mount the scaffold to be guillotined.

But the young Yankee captain had something else to do besides standing round at executions. He had to recover his papers, and these were not forthcoming. He pestered the office of what was called 'the 23rd department,' until he was forbidden the premises. Then by chance some one told him to try the great Robespierre himself. Cobb, nothing daunted, followed this advice, explained his predicament to the great man, secured the papers, and reached Hamburg just before the French agent there stopped payment.

For the next fifteen years or so Cobb sailed various vessels to various ports, now and then smuggling Medford rum ashore on the Irish Coast, but meeting with no startling adventures until, one August morning in 1812, while returning from Cadiz to Boston, he was captured on the edge of the Grand Banks by an armed British schooner and carried to St. Johns. Here he found about twenty other American captains living in comfortable captivity, and twenty-seven American prize vessels. This was the first he knew of the War of 1812. In the course of a week an exchange of prisoners was made, and all the Americans sailed out of St. Johns, landing two days later in New York, whence Cobb made his way to Harwich and walked in on his wife at midnight. He found her sitting up in bed, reading his last letter and conjuring up in her imagination the horrors of his life in a British dungeon.

It is quite possible that during his comfortable sojourn as prisoner of war at St. Johns, Cobb fell in with another deep-water shipmaster from the Cape — Captain Isaiah Crowell, of Dennis. At all events Captain Crowell was held at St. Johns at about the same time, and, like Cobb, was soon released by exchange. Captain Crowell's exploits are worth telling, for they typify the sort of experiences that half the Yankee sailors met with during this frenzied epoch in our maritime history. The British Orders in Council, which declared any neutral vessel that cleared from a French port lawful game for His Majesty's navy, found Crowell and his ship in the harbor of Marseilles. To get out into the broad Atlantic through the bottle-neck of Gibraltar was ticklish work, but doubtless the Dennis captain and his crew enjoyed it — all the more so as they were successful in eluding the British frigates.

But troubles at home were almost as great as dangers abroad. In April, 1812, when Madison's Embargo was expected at any moment, Crowell was loading at Boston for Lisbon. If the paralyzing decree should arrive before he could clear, his voyage would be lost. Just before the blow fell, therefore, Crowell, with only half a cargo, slipped out of Boston with clearance papers coastwise for Eastport. He arrived there still one jump ahead of the Embargo, dropped across to Campo Bello in British waters, finished loading at his leisure, and set sail for Lisbon. While he was there, war was declared, and on his return trip an English cruiser made a prize of his vessel, and his voyage ended at St. Johns instead of Boston.

Such misadventures were part and parcel of seafaring at this unsettled period. Crowell's adventures were duplicated by a score of others, for profits were so great that Yankee sailors were determined to make voyages whether or no. They set sail, Madison or no Madison, Embargo or no Embargo. The adventures of Captain Rowland Crocker, of Falmouth, another neutral trader, furnish a good case in point. To call him a neutral trader is to do him scant justice, for in fact there were few experiences that he did not meet sooner or later in the course of his life. He was a whaleman, privateer, merchant captain, Liverpool packet commander, and State Representative; a musket ball had gone in one side of his body and out the other; he had shaken Napoleon by the hand; he had been captured by the French, and rewarded by Lloyds' for navigating a wreck through a gale. The exploit last mentioned took place in 1807. The ship was the Otis. She lay in the Downs ready to weigh anchor, with a cargo worth £100,000 under her hatches. A sudden gale sprang up; the anchors let go, and the vessel crashed into a frigate that was lying close aboard her. She was

badly shattered — so badly that the pilot and a good many
of the crew, believing her lost, took to the boats and went
ashore. Captain Crocker, with what was left of his crew, got
the Otis under way and, crippled as she was, worked her
through the gale into Dover. Lloyds' did not exaggerate when
they presented him with a silver cup inscribed with the motto,
'Forti et fideli nil difficile.' Perhaps the five hundred pounds
that accompanied this mark of esteem was as acceptable to
Captain Crocker as the Latin dictum. It was the Cape's misfortune that this energetic citizen, like many others of her sons,
spent most of his life away from his native town.

It is no wonder that the War of 1812, which clipped the wings
of our lusty young merchant marine just as it had learned to fly
far and fearlessly, was gall and wormwood to Cape-Codders.
But they forgot their resentment in the fresh activity that came
with the signing of the treaty of peace. To trace the courses
that Dennis, Barnstable, and Truro navigators pricked off between 1815 and 1850, would be to draw a network over all the
oceans of the globe. Apparently haphazard, these voyages were
in truth systematic and very rational, for though the Yankee
trader was as ready a gambler as any man, he never crossed the
sea on a fool's errand. Out of the tangled lines of trade that
followed the war, there emerged as early as 1816 the glorious but
grueling routine of the Liverpool packets. These vessels were
built especially for trans-Atlantic work in all weathers — stout
craft with more staterooms for passengers than any ships had
had before, ample stowage room below decks, and lines that
gave them as much speed as could be safely combined with these
prerequisites. Their captains were confronted with a task that
was new to seafaring men: they had to keep the passengers
happy and the line popular. One way to do this was by making
quick passages; another was by playing the genial host. There
were plenty of drivers to be had in every Atlantic seaport, but
to find a driver with the manners of a deep-sea Chesterfield was
not so easy. Any swaggering bully who was a good sailor would
do to carry cargo. But the commander of a Liverpool packet
had to be able to move gracefully among a ship's company,
leaving affability and serenity in his wake. And let no one suppose that the nicest seamanship was not also required of him.

If an ordinary merchantman held on till a topsail was blown from the bolt-ropes, nobody knew it except the owner. But if a Black Ball packet lost a sail or sprung a spar, a horde of eager passengers spread the glad tidings to wide-eyed folk on shore, who solemnly vowed that they 'would never book on a Black Baller, the captains were so reckless!' If, on the other hand, a cautious commander lengthened his passage by shortening sail, the tongues of the passengers were equally busy. None but the most expert and genteel were fit for the command of an ocean packet, and they must be men of iron as well, for their fore-castles were infested with the wildest crews that ever sailed under the flag of a civilized nation. The Liverpool 'packet rat' was the incarnation of all the toughness and evil and malice that have clustered throughout the ages about the reputation of sailors. True, the captain no longer donned knuckle-dusters or swung belaying pins himself; he had mates to do such work for him. But he had to be a graduate of the belaying-pin school, for on him rested the ultimate responsibility for the obedience of the crew. Only men of parts need apply.

Such men — to name a few among many Cape-Codders — were John Collins, of Truro, Rowland Crocker, of Falmouth, and Ira Bursley, of Barnstable. From Yarmouth came Allen Knowles and the three Eldridge brothers, John, Oliver, and Asa. None of these men rested content with the Liverpool run. The packet service was only one step in the giant's stride of their careers.

Bursley was a veteran of more lines than one. He commanded everything in the way of ocean-going packets, from the little Dover, built in 1827 for a short-lived Boston–Liverpool Line, to the Hottinger, of the New York Swallowtail Line, a ship of twice the size, which he was driving back and forth across the Western Ocean twenty years later. Crocker, as has already been seen, figured in every branch of maritime activity, from whaling to the New York–Liverpool trade in what a contem-porary newspaper calls 'the floating palaces' of the packet lines. He retired after having crossed the Atlantic a hundred and sixty-four times without the loss of a ship. Allen H. Knowles, who lived just across the street from the Eldridges, was given the command of the two-thousand-ton Chariot of Fame, one of Donald McKay's creations, built in 1853 for the Boston owner

ROWLAND R. CROCKER

Enoch Train. Captain Knowles received her as she left the stocks and took her on her maiden voyage to Liverpool. She remained his vessel for about ten years, the first two of which were spent in the packet trade, the rest as a general merchantman.

One of Captain Knowles's passages from Liverpool to Boston will give an idea of what a commander might expect in winter. He sailed on January 11, 1854, with a cargo worth half a million dollars and a passenger list of over eighty, most of them in the steerage. The first night out he lost his jibboom in a collision. Ten days later, in mid-Atlantic, the main topsail was blown from the bolt-ropes, and the main yard broken. Knowles had hardly got the yard lowered and the vessel snug when a sea came aboard which carried away four boats and a section of the bulwarks and flooded the cabin. The gale increased until it blew several furled sails out of their gaskets and raised a sea that carried away the figurehead. By Herculean efforts the crew got a new yard slung and new sails bent, but in spite of everything the Chariot made not a mile of progress westward from January 22 to February 7. Again, off Boston, a northwester carried off the last of her spare sails; but Captain Knowles piloted her through a terrific snowstorm into Provincetown, where he got his first night's sleep for six weeks.

Late in the thirties, E. K. Collins, a nephew of John Collins, of Truro, started the famous Dramatic Line of Liverpool packets. It is not surprising that he gave the command of his flagship, the Roscius, to his able and energetic Uncle John. Captain John showed himself worthy of his vessel. It was during his years in her that he effected the rescue of the fishing schooner Garnet, quite as dramatic as anything in the career of the celebrated actor for whom his ship was named.

Collins later took command of the Shakespeare of the same line, and Asa Eldridge received the Roscius, in which vessel he learned, as will appear presently, all there was to know about trans-Atlantic work under sail. His brother John was at the same time captain of the Liverpool, with Oliver, the third brother of this illustrious family, serving with him as mate. Thus had these men of the Cape — from Falmouth, Barnstable, Yarmouth, and Truro — reached what was then the pinnacle of maritime ambition, the command of crack Liverpool packets. They trod their quarterdecks the lords of creation, taking backwash from no man alive. To be sure, they admitted Captain Nat Palmer, the young Stonington sailor who was to become the dean of clipper-ship commanders, as an equal, albeit his ship, the Siddons, was not the vessel that the Roscius or the Shakespeare was. But this they did in recognition of Palmer's sheer greatness.

Mighty as they were, these Cape-Codders were to become yet mightier before they died. They were still unsatisfied and kept looking ahead for new worlds to conquer. They had long to wait, for the dawn of the clipper-ship era was at hand. Space is lacking to discuss the evolution of these wonderful vessels. Suffice it to say that they revolutionized the naval architecture of two nations, ourselves and the British, and became at once the envy and the despair of the other maritime countries of the world. The bows of the clippers, instead of being the bluff, apple-cheeked affairs of the earlier type, were sharp, tapering, and concave, and cut deep into the waves instead of beating flat against them. Then the flare of the hull at the fore-rigging lifted them over the waves and prevented them from being flooded too often. The sterns, too, tapered gracefully and no longer squatted flat in the water. The alterations in the design of the hull were hardly greater than the changes in rigging and top-hamper. The masts of the clippers towered to a height hitherto undreamed of, and spread one and in some cases two more courses of sails. These sails fitted as sails had never fitted before, with the result that the clippers, when it came to windward work, sailed like yachts, and would lie closer to the wind than anything of their size afloat. Supplied with such ships from the yards of New York and Boston by such builders as Webb and Westervelt, Hall, Curtis, and McKay, the American captains sailed forth in the fifties and in a year or two had captured the commerce of the world.

The clippers were the most beautifully finished and expensive vessels that had ever been built and were the pride of their owners' hearts — a pride nicely blended with anxiety when they considered the investment that each ship represented. Handling these wild beauties was ticklish business, requiring far more dexterity, nerve, and experience than was needful for the old-style barrel-bottomed craft that bobbed along comfortably under stumpy masts and seldom came to grief. Even the stalwart packets were eclipsed by these glorious vessels. The owners wanted the best men in the business for commanders, and they got them. Hence the clipper-ship captains became the aristocrats of an already aristocratic profession — the conquerors of the conquerors of the world — and scores of Cape men strode proudly in their ranks.

There was Baker, of the Flying Dragon and Shooting Star; Burgess, of the Whirlwind and Challenger; Kelly, of the Fleetwing; Sears, of the Wild Hunter; Jenkins, of the Raven; Crowell, of the Robin Hood; Sprague, of the Gravina; Dillingham, of the Snow Squall; Stevens, of the Southern Cross; Bearse, of the Winged Arrow; Hallett, of the Phantom; Baxter, of the Flying Scud; Hatch, of the Northern Light. The list might be doubled and trebled, and every name, whether of ship or master, would be of the first magnitude. And it must be emphasized once more that the first magnitude in this case means not merely first among Cape captains nor even among American masters. It means of first magnitude in the world — men who commanded the finest ships afloat — extreme clippers that could leave any other vessel of any other type hull down in half a day.

Before going into particulars about such men as Sears or Dillingham or Hatch, it will be interesting to follow a few of our friends of the packets — like Oliver Eldridge, Asa, his brother, and Ira Bursley — as they forsook the stormy Atlantic and drove their new commands, the clippers, through the wild waters of Cape Horn and into the balmy trades of the Pacific. Even before the full splendor of the era of clipper ships arrived, these men were pacing the quarterdecks of the early medium clippers, which ushered in the extremely sharp models of the fifties. Oliver Eldridge turned his energies to the China trade, and in 1844 was given the command of Russell and Company's beautiful clipper bark Coquette, built by Samuel Hall in East Boston. Captain Eldridge took her from Boston to Canton in ninety-nine days. Four years later he commanded Warren Delano's new clipper ship Memnon on her maiden voyage to

China. Owners, it seems, had a habit of entrusting their new vessels to Captain Eldridge, for in 1855 Daniel C. Bacon, the retired shipmaster of Barnstable and Boston and President of the American Navigation Club, invited him to take command of the big clipper Titan, which had just taken the water from the yard of Roosevelt and Joyce in New York. Clearly Captain Oliver had profited from his experience as mate of the Liverpool under his brother, Captain John.

Meanwhile, Ira Bursley, having learned as much as he cared to learn about the rigors of Atlantic packet lines, took command of the Maine-built clipper Alert and tried his luck in the California trade. She was a small vessel, and her owners, Crocker and Warren, realizing that Bursley was too good for her, gave him in 1853 a new and larger ship, the Archer. The fact that Captain Cressy, of the Flying Cloud, later commanded the Archer is sufficient indication of her quality. She was a fast sailer even for a clipper. Captain Bursley also commanded on her first voyages the Snow Squall — an extremely sharp little clipper, one of whose voyages will be mentioned anon, when she was captained by another Cape-Codder.

The last graduate of the packets who claims attention as a clipper-ship commander is Asa Eldridge — the most distinguished shipmaster that the Cape ever produced. His career is a varied one. As has been said, he commanded the Dramatic Liner Roscius for a time, and later (after a vacation in 1853, during which he piloted Commodore Vanderbilt's steam yacht North Star in foreign waters), he returned to this country in time to receive command of a new extreme clipper ship Red Jacket, one of the four fastest sailing ships ever launched. She was designed by Samuel Pook, of Boston, and built during the winter of 1853 by George Thomas at Rockland, Maine. Her owners were Seacomb and Taylor, of Boston. Sharp, lean, and rakish, the Red Jacket was a vessel worthy of Captain Eldridge, and it must have been with deep satisfaction that he stepped on board a real ship again after his profitable but inconclusive sojourn with Vanderbilt's toy steamer. He cleared from New York on January 11, 1854, for Liverpool, and drove the Red Jacket through rain, snow, and hail to a record passage of thirteen days and one hour from dock to dock. No ship has ever

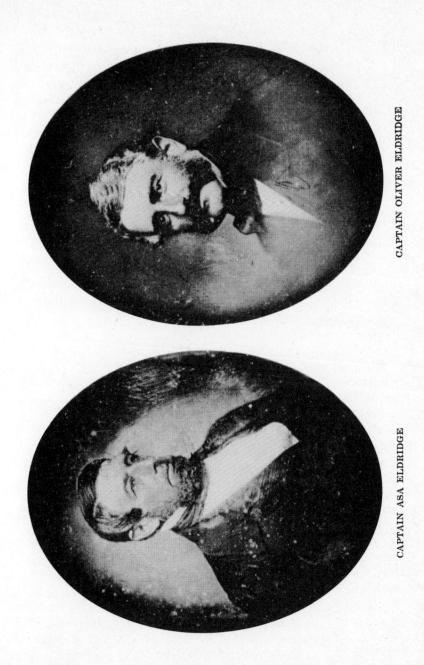

CAPTAIN OLIVER ELDRIDGE

CAPTAIN ASA ELDRIDGE

duplicated this run of Captain Eldridge's, but, as though this were not enough, he had logged four hundred and thirteen miles on one day of the passage, a distance which has been surpassed by only three other sailing vessels in maritime history, the Lightning, the James Baines, and the Donald McKay.

If the thirteen days during which the Red Jacket was crossing the Atlantic are epoch-making in the history of American sail, it may easily be imagined of what importance they are in the maritime annals of the Cape. They place Captain Eldridge at the very summit of his profession and put his name among the world's half-dozen greatest shipmasters.

Another distinguished commander of this epoch was James S. Dillingham, Jr., of Brewster. At the time of the Civil War he was Captain of the clipper Snow Squall, leaving Penang for New York. He made good time across the Indian Ocean, and, rounding the Cape of Good Hope, was on his way across the Atlantic when he sighted an American auxiliary bark, the Tuskaloosa, which sailed up to windward and partly blanketed him. The vessels lay so close that no speaking trumpet was necessary, and the captain of the Tuskaloosa called out, 'What ship is that?' Dillingham replied, 'Ship Snow Squall, Penang to New York; what ship is that?' 'Heave to,' replied the other, 'and I will send some one on board to tell you.' With that a row of portholes in the stranger's side flew open, presenting a line of cannon; at the same moment the Stars and Stripes was lowered and the Confederate flag run up in its place.

Captain Dillingham did some quick thinking. Without a moment's hesitation he sang out, 'Aye, aye!' but, instead of heaving to, he worked his ship far enough ahead of the Confederate to catch some wind in his forward sails; and, before the Tuskaloosa knew what was going on, the Snow Squall had squared away and was off at a speed worthy of her name and commander. Thanks to a rolling sea, the shots that followed her from the rebel went wild, and every minute increased the distance between the two vessels. The Tuskaloosa hung on till dark, firing all the time, but finally had to abandon the chase. The Snow Squall brought her cargo safe into New York Harbor.

It was for qualities like these that owners entrusted their finest ships to Cape-Codders; and such incidents, of themselves of no great historical importance, become significant for what they reveal of Cape character: a rare mixture of good judgment and daring, with experience and skill enough to carry through an apparently reckless maneuver successfully. It must be remembered, however, that seafaring was not all thrills and adventures, even in clipper ships. Much of it was steady, hard, and discouraging work — sometimes slatting about in the doldrums, sometimes trying for a week to get westward of the Horn when it blew so hard that vessels could not carry sail enough to make anything to windward. There is truth in the remark that Captain Joshua Sears, of East Dennis, made toward the end of his life to a young man who was just beginning his career at sea. 'Well, my boy,' he said, 'I am getting through, and you are just starting in. You have chosen a tough life, but it will make a man of you.' It certainly had made a man of Captain Sears, for he had risen to the command of the Wild Hunter, a beautiful little clipper that proved to be a gold mine for her owners. This vessel, it will be remembered, was one of those built by the Shivericks at East Dennis.

Another quality which helped to make clipper captains remarkable, was loyalty to their owners — a loyalty that induced them to run grave personal risk, and to perform with their own hands, if necessary, work that even the hardy breed of stevedores or wreckers refused to tackle. An anecdote regarding Captain Daniel Bacon will illustrate this point. He left the sea before the era of clippers began, but was among the first Boston merchants to become their owners when he ordered the famous clipper ship Game Cock to be built for him by Samuel Hall, of East Boston. One of the Captain's vessels came ashore on Nantasket Beach in a winter gale. Her hull was still sound enough to keep her cargo dry if it was unloaded quickly. Bacon tried in vain to find some one who would undertake the job. It promised to be too cold and wet a business. So he hired an ox-team and went to the beach himself, where he spent the day driving in and out of the water to unload the stranded vessel. The underwriters presented him with the traditional silver tea service.

But it will never do to conclude this account of the clippers and their captains on any such low note as is suggested by a hull

stranded on Nantasket Beach. The proper tune is that which
the brave westerlies sing through taut rigging, or the music of
the surge and swish of the sea as it leaps along a ship's topsides
in the roaring forties. Such was the song in the ears of Captain
Freeman Hatch, of Eastham, during his famous voyage from
San Francisco to Boston in the Northern Light in 1852. His
ship was designed by the celebrated Samuel Pook — the same
who had drawn the lines of Captain Eldridge's Red Jacket —
and she was built by the Briggs Brothers in South Boston. Her
figurehead was a full-length angel bearing aloft 'a torch with
a golden flame.' Captain Hatch made the voyage in seventy-
six days, a record which stands to this day. His epitaph, which
may still be read in the Eastham burying ground, is as follows:

Freeman Hatch, 1820–1889
He became famous making the astonishing passage in the
clipper ship Northern Light from San Francisco in 76 days
6 hours — an achievement won by no mortal before or since.

In fairness to the memory of Captain Hatch, let the reader reflect that it was the Captain who made the passage and his
relatives who composed the epitaph.

It may be asked why the name of Captain John Collins has not
been mentioned in connection with the clippers. The reason is
not that he lost interest in maritime affairs, but that, inspired
by his brilliant nephew, Edward K. Collins, of New York, he
was a whole generation ahead of his time. Foreseeing that the
days of sail were numbered, he jumped clear over the greatest of
our salt-water epochs and landed among the paddle-wheels and
side-lever engines of the early days of steam. Edward Collins
was a man of parts and imagination. Realizing before most
Americans that sailing packets would soon be out of date, he
turned his energies toward the organization of a line of passenger steamers that should eclipse the plodding Cunarders.
One of his first moves was to make his uncle, Captain John, a
partner, and these two were the guiding spirits of the enterprise. In 1847 they secured from the Government the contract
to carry the mails for $385,000 a year. Thus encouraged, they
proceeded to lay the keels for a fleet of steamers which were to
the Cunarders what the McKay clippers were to the sailing
packets. They were named appropriately for the oceans of the

world, The Arctic, Atlantic, Baltic, and Pacific. Captain Asa
Eldridge, whose performance in the Red Jacket was a byword
in shipping circles, accepted the Collinses' invitation to command
the Pacific, and all went well until 1855. Then came a series of
disasters. The Arctic was rammed in a fog by a Frenchman off
Cape Race and went to the bottom in a desperate attempt
to reach the Newfoundland shore. Next year the Pacific and
Captain Asa Eldridge met an unknown fate somewhere in the
North Atlantic. By this tragedy the Company lost a fine ship
and the Nation one of its greatest shipmasters. With half their
fleet destroyed, the Collinses set to work to rebuild. But a more
insidious blow was to come. Economic readjustments led Congress to withdraw part of the mail subsidy that had been keeping the line afloat. This was the thin edge of the wedge which in
the course of the next two years was driven steadily into the seafaring interests of the country until by 1858, it struck the heart.
The Collins Line went out of business, leaving Great Britain
supreme in the Atlantic.

The Collinses were not the only shipowners who, in the late
fifties, began to realize uneasily that economic changes were
taking place. The successful opposition of British steam, ad-
verse legislation in Congress, the opening up of the West and
the accompanying railway expansion that drew capital into a
new field where there was no foreign competition — all played
their part in driving the American flag from the sea. Our great
merchant marine was doomed before the sixties, and would
have vanished just as completely, though perhaps not so
quickly, if there had never been a Civil War, a Semmes, or an
Alabama.

The change crept slowly over the water-front like a long
twilight. Merchants and shipmasters alike were at first not
quite aware that their day was done. Cape men in particular
were incredulous and sailed away as bravely as ever through
the lengthening shadows into the sunset. Captain Banjamin
P. Howes, one of Dennis's many shipmasters, was in command
of Baker and Morrill's fine clipper Southern Cross when she was
burned by the Florida in 1863. After the war he decided to try
his luck in a smaller vessel. Accordingly, he had the little clipper brig Lubra built for him and sailed off with his wife to be-

come a South Sea trader. The Lubra was his last command. She was captured by Chinese pirates in 1866, and Captain Howes was murdered in his own cabin.

Another Cape man, Captain Edmund Burke, of Truro, commanded the bark Azor most of the time from 1854, when she was built, until 1870, when she was sold. This vessel, the most beautiful of Charles Dabney's Azores packets, sailed back and forth between Boston and the Western Islands with great regularity, carrying passengers, oranges, and wine. A large part of her popularity was owing to Captain Burke, for he was always ready either to crack a joke or to heave to and rescue passengers from a vessel in distress, as he did those of the sinking ship Gratitude in 1865. The maneuver meant trans-shipping three hundred and twenty people in a high sea; to make room for them, Captain Burke threw overboard a large part of his cargo of oranges.

In 1869, when Donald McKay launched the Glory of the Seas, the last of his great fleet of clippers, Cape men were on hand again to command her. Josiah Knowles, of Eastham, was her first captain; Elisha F. Sears, of Brewster, had her for a time; but another Brewster man, Captain Joshua Freeman, Jr., has the record of eighteen years as her commander. As long as there was a living in it, Cape-Codders followed the sea. Scores of them might be mentioned as commanders of the capacious barks and occasional ships that sailed to Calcutta or Hongkong in the lean decades between 1870 and 1890. Captain Frank Hinckley, of the ships Star of Peace and Leading Wind, and Captain Ansel Lothrop, of the Pilgrim, Conqueror, and Agenor, were both Barnstable men. So were John Turner Hall, of the ship Abelino, and Joseph Bursley, of the Victory. Not long ago Captain Howard Allen, who still lives in Hyannis, made six consecutive voyages round the world in his ship the Importer. Even as late as 1897, during the rush to the Klondike, his fellow townsman, Captain Ezekiel C. Baker, took the steamer City of Columbia from New York to the Yukon gold fields. But it is idle to continue; one is overwhelmed by sheer force of numbers. Captain Lothrop, who died in 1927, recently compiled a list of the captains whom he could remember from Barnstable village alone. This list, which is in the author's possession, contains sixty-three names, including both deep-water voyagers and coasters. Similar statistics could undoubtedly be procured from half a dozen other towns on the Cape. Enough surely has been said to show that, as long as it could be made to pay, Cape men continued the losing battle against British steam and sail.

Each year brought them fewer and lighter cargoes. The wealth of the West was making itself felt more and more in Congress, and the Westerner had no interest beyond the fences that bounded his own farm. We ceased to be a maritime nation, and one by one the Cape commanders furled their sails and squared their yards for the last time, left their vessels to the mercy of the ship-breaker, and came home to live. Here, though retired, their influence was almost as beneficial to the Cape as their remoter activities had been. One such man could make village affairs hum, and there used to be not one but scores in most of the Cape towns. Town meetings in those days were handled in quarterdeck style. Narrow-mindedness found barren soil in a district where two houses out of every three belonged to men who knew half the seaports of the world and had lived ashore for months at a time in foreign countries. They had gained a perspective that measured matters against far horizons, and they kept the Cape mentally alert as long as they lived. When they died, they bequeathed it a salty tradition that has not yet quite lost its savor.

CHAPTER XIII

THE CIVIL WAR

THE most prosperous and active years in the history of the Cape — those from the thirties to the fifties — were not occupied exclusively with building bridges and dikes, erecting factories and salt works, drying codfish, and greeting deep-water shipmasters on their return from the antipodes. Such activities were marred by a less desirable manifestation of energy — schism in the churches. Not that schism was anything new or particularly undesirable. Usually it is an indication that progress is in the offing. Furthermore, this particular rift in the ranks of the church was brought about by a sufficiently righteous motive on the part of those who left the fold. They refused to support any longer a church which preached Christianity on the one hand and on the other received into membership men who tolerated slavery. Those who broke away were called 'Come-Outers' (or 'Comers Out'), a name which was not restricted to these groups of Abolitionists, but had been given pretty generally to all who for any reason had seceded from an established church.

The Come-Outers were not essentially riotous or seditious people. They merely had the courage of their convictions and refused to remain loyal to a church whose tenets they believed were unchristian. The two camps would doubtless have rubbed along with no more friction than is usual between dissenting organizations, if it had not been for agitators from elsewhere. Such agitators there were, of course, all over New England, and occasionally a band of them invaded the Cape. They did not come often, for the Cape was out of their way; but when they did arrive, trouble was sure to follow.

The most sensational instance of such a visit occurred in Harwich in 1848. A report had been spread in anti-slavery circles in Boston that a Harwich coasting captain, whose name is not recorded, had taken one hundred dollars from a Negro in Norfolk to bring him and a friend North on his schooner, and had then seized him and had him advertised as a runaway slave.

Such indignation was aroused by this outrage that a group of distinguished Boston Abolitionists visited Harwich and held an indignation meeting. Among them were Parker Pillsbury, Stephen Foster, and Lucy Stone. No building in Harwich, or for that matter on the Cape, was big enough to hold the crowd that assembled; men and women poured in from the neighboring towns until, according to one estimate, three thousand had gathered in the grove where the convention was held.

The first speaker was Parker Pillsbury — a young enthusiast whose emotions were stronger than his judgment. His share in the programme was to state the case against the captain of the schooner, without mentioning his name. Writing of the event thirty-three years later, when time and age, if not the Civil War itself, should have somewhat calmed his ardor, Pillsbury calls the Captain's deed one 'that no Modoc nor Apache Indian under Heaven would ever have done! In cold, unprovoked blood — never!' Such ringing phrases written in his old age give some notion of what Pillsbury's oratorical style must have been in his youth. It is no wonder that his speech started a tumult which subsided only when the Captain himself took the platform and said that a friend had just told him that he had been accused of stealing. Pillsbury hedged, declaring that he had named no names and had not used the word 'steal.' But the Captain demanded a hearing, and the crowd became silent.

The Captain's speech was a striking example of the perfectly natural moral blindness that afflicted so many otherwise estimable and pious citizens when they looked at slavery or were mixed up in the slave trade. The phenomenon has not disappeared with the abolition of this particular business: most men are still able to close the shutter that blots from the mental vision a view of the suffering that their profitable ruthlessness creates, and if they keep the shutter closed long enough, they may even forget that there is any suffering and so finally become unaware of any wrongdoing. Something of the sort, at all events, had taken place in the soul of the Harwich Captain. He seems to have pigeonholed his religion even more successfully than most people do nowadays. He calmly told the story from his own point of view, contradicting nothing that Pillsbury had accused him of, and on concluding, took a seat on the

platform. One of Pillsbury's accusations, which the Captain
admitted, was that he was a member in good standing of the
Baptist Church. Taking this admission as his text, the next
speaker, Stephen Foster, launched forth on an invective that
evoked from Pillsbury the admiring comment that he seemed to
be 'Father of the seven thunders of Patmos.' There is little
doubt that the tribute is deserved, for his speech provoked such
a riot that Pillsbury says, 'I have seen many mobs and riots in
my more than forty years of humble service in the cause of
Freedom and Humanity. But I never encountered one more
desperate in determination, nor fiendish in spirit, than was that
in Harwich, in the year 1848.'

It started when some of the Captain's friends in the crowd
stormed round the platform, calling on him to pitch Foster
down to them; but the Captain, who had not commanded vessels in vain, kept calm and told the rioters that he had no need
of their interference. Shortly afterwards he left the scene.
Foster went on with his speech, declaring that any church
which admitted such men as members was no less than the
'bulwark of American Slavery.' This was too much for the
Harwich Baptists. One of them, 'a member of the Orthodox
Church, who had just come from his meeting (and it was said
from the Sacrament) leaped like a lion on to the platform. His
eyes flashed fury if not fire; his teeth and fists were clenched,
and he seemed a spirit from the pit, who might have been com-
missioned to lead its myrmidons in a deadly fray for such a
faith and such a church as his.... His first note was a shriek;
"It's a lie; what you say is a lie; a damned lie! and I'll defend
the church!"'

He had plenty of support. A group of fanatics jumped to the
platform, seized Pillsbury and hurled him to the ground with
kicks and blows. Two Harwich Abolitionists, Captain Chase
and Captain Smith, who had been seated near him, sprang to his
defense and were knocked senseless. Another speaker, William
Wells Brown, was thrown over the back of the platform, and
Foster, the blasts of whose eloquence had kicked up this ugly
sea, was rescued from his assailants only after his 'Sunday frock
coat had been rent in twain from bottom to top, and his body
considerably battered and bruised.'

Thus ended a lurid Anti-Slavery Convention. Certain inferences may be drawn from the proceedings.

Seafaring is a broad school where men see customs that are not their own and learn tolerance. Not all Cape shipmasters approved of slavery (Sandwich and Barnstable had anti-slavery societies as early as 1837), but they did approve of minding their own business and letting the slave-owner mind his. There is much to censure in this attitude; it is not one that hastens the millennium; it seems even to suggest that the millennium had arrived and had taken different forms in different places: slaves for the Virginia planter; smart crews for the New England shipmaster. And this view — too tolerant to commend itself in the High Court of Progress — may account not only for the placidity of many Cape Abolitionists, but also for the stubborn standpatters in the church, who, with an inconsistency almost too perfect for human beings to have achieved, regarded the Come Outers as traitors and the Southerners as within their rights.

Some of the seafaring Abolitionists adopted other measures to show their convictions, and used their vessels to bring slaves North to safety. Among these kind-hearted smugglers was George Lovell, of Osterville, who died in 1861. He was a wealthy and very influential South Side shipowner with strong anti-slavery convictions. It was quite natural, therefore, that he should slip a runaway on board one of his vessels in Norfolk or Savannah now and then, and land him some dark night on the free soil of Cape Cod. The slaves made their way across the Cape, via a pretty well-established 'underground railroad,' to Barnstable, where they were always welcome guests at the houses of Ezekiel Thacher and Alvin Howes. Yet the atmosphere of these New England homes seems not always to have proved congenial to the Negroes; for they frequently sought their own level in some hang-out in the woods on Mary Dunn's road, where rum and a less rarefied environment put them more at their ease.

So matters stood when the opening shot at Fort Sumter cleared the air for all Cape-Codders. Faced by a common enemy, Come Outer and stand-patter alike forgot their differences and joined forces for the coming struggle. The war found greater favor on the Cape than any war had found before.

It has been shown with what difficulty men were drafted for Canada to fight the French and Indians. The Revolution revealed Tories in almost every town. The War of 1812 found the Cape hot and rebellious toward the Administration. But when, in 1861, President Lincoln issued his first call for volunteers, the Cape responded with an enthusiasm that, coming from a maritime community, was surprising. War meant that long-voyage trading could be carried on only at great risk; that whalemen stood an excellent chance of being captured on their way home from the Pacific, and that fishermen would find their old markets closed.

Early in the war, R. B. Forbes, that saltiest of Bostonians, found leisure, while patrolling Cape Cod Bay and the North Shore in his four launches, to comment on the effect the war was having on Cape fishermen. He writes:

BARNSTABLE BAY, *July* 8, 1861

I have visited Salem, Beverly, Gloucester, Provincetown, Barnstable....In all these ports and many others there are hundreds of vessels laying idle and thousands of men, second to none in loyalty, second to none in experience of our Southern Coast, and second to none in all the elements which constitute the accomplished seaman — excepting only a want of knowledge of the art of war.... Their fish markets are cut off, and the stock of last season is on hand to a considerable amount, unsold and unsaleable;... At this moment I have in view from my Yacht a hundred sail, more or less, in Provincetown, Wellfleet and Truro laid up for want of work to do.

Confronted with the prospect of such hard times as Captain Forbes describes, the Cape yet went willingly to war. Sandwich led the way, and on May 8, 1861 — about three weeks after Lincoln first called for volunteers — an enthusiastic company that gave itself the name of the Sandwich Guards marched to Boston under the command of Captain Charles Chipman. This organization was the fourth volunteer company in the State to report for service. It was immediately sent to Fortress Monroe and later took part in a number of engagements, including the battles of Antietam and Fredericksburg. The other towns responded valiantly, in almost every case exceeding their quota of men. Provincetown contributed $45,000 and sent two hundred and fifty men, fifty-seven over her quota. Barnstable raised $58,000 and exceeded her quota of men by thirty-five, sending two hundred and seventy-two in all. The prosperity of Harwich is shown by her three hundred and forty-one enlistments and $54,000. The total number of soldiers from the Cape was approximately twenty-five hundred, and her contribution in money amounted to about half a million, $90,000 of which was subsequently refunded.

The Cape's most distinguished army officer was Major Joseph E. Hamblin. He was born in Yarmouth, where he spent his youth; then he moved to Boston, and at the outbreak of the war he was in business in New York. Beginning as Adjutant of the Fifth New York Volunteers, he was within two years promoted to the ranks of Major, Lieutenant-Colonel, and Colonel. He took part in the battles of Antietam, Fredericksburg, Chancellorsville, and Gettysburg, not to mention half a dozen minor engagements. As Colonel at the battle of Cedar Creek, though he had received two wounds early in the fight, he held on and was instrumental in turning apparent defeat into victory. After this engagement, Colonel Hamblin, on Sheridan's recommendation, was promoted to the rank of Brigadier-General, and for brilliant service at Sailor's Creek, he was brevetted Major-General. He died in 1870 and lies in the family tomb in Yarmouthport.

The sea was, of course, the most appropriate theater for Cape activities during the war, and the only reason why more local names are not found in the naval records is that a large part of the country's merchant marine was still dodging the Confederates at sea — with Cape-Codders on the quarterdecks. But, even so, a good many Cape men enlisted in the navy. Some of them, indeed, were steered into it. As early as May, 1862, Charles F. Swift offered a set of resolutions in a Yarmouth town meeting to the effect that, since the enemy had showed signs of sending out 'piratical crafts' to prey upon the commerce of the country, it was especially proper for the citizens of Yarmouth, whose pursuits and training were largely maritime, to 'lend cheerful aid in bringing these pests of the ocean to condign punishment.' These resolutions were not without effect, for fifteen Yarmouth men served their country as officers in the navy, and three acted as pilots in Southern waters.

The effect that the war had on the Cape was to hasten the decline which had already almost imperceptibly begun. No community that depends on the sea for its prosperity can flourish long after it is driven from the sea, and, bit by bit, changing economic conditions were forcing Cape-Codders ashore. Whaling had been virtually abandoned except at Provincetown; fishermen had to begin again with new schooners or else give up entirely; and now the props were being knocked out from under the last and proudest business of Cape men — the merchant marine. No wonder contemporary writers believed the war to be the cause of all their evils. There was probably not a man on the Cape who did not mistakenly curse Jeff Davis as the cause of the hard times — and undeniably the circumstantial evidence against him was strong. Before the war, business had been good; even in the late fifties most shipmasters had had enough to do. Then four years of war, when cargo-carrying was exciting work; and after the war, bad times indeed. The war stood squarely between the good times and the bad; so the war got the blame.

No bright spot appeared, even on the distant horizon; more and more capital kept heading westward; less and less toward the sea and the ships. The inevitable came. Young Cape-Codders, realizing that the sea had failed them, moved inland and became manufacturers or bankers. Writing in 1884, Shebnah Rich says:

Some of the Cape towns have been reduced more than half, Truro among the number. . . . I have counted fourteen houses in a little neighborhood nestled prettily enough for an artist's pencil. For forty years not a house had been added or removed. . . . The next turn of the road opened another picture, where I counted a dozen houses, and in imagination, a dozen more, that had been moved away within as many years. The population of Truro . . . in 1860 was 1883 . . . in 1880 less than 1000. Over one hundred families from Truro now reside in Somerville.

What a falling off was there! The fate of Truro is no solitary instance. In the thirty years that followed the war, the population of the whole Cape shrank from 36,000 to 27,000. It has dropped another thousand since, but the damage was done with the first exodus. The Cape has by this time grown used to commercial insignificance. If there had never been a Civil War, this resignation might not yet have been achieved. But the same end would have been reached ultimately and from exactly the same causes.

CHAPTER XIV

THE CHURCH

THE Pilgrims brought with them to Plymouth a faith that had already removed mountains. It supported the Scrooby band through the troublous days of their persecution in England; it pointed out for them the way to Holland and freedom; it fortified them against the dishonesty of the Merchant Adventurers; walked the waters of the Atlantic by their side, and remained their only comfort through that first terrible winter in the little clearing in the Plymouth woods. Our own age, that vaunts its toleration, can know nothing of such faith as that. Whatever we may say of the Pilgrims' too rigid righteousness, whatever we may think of their theology, we must remember that their righteousness and their theology were real, hammered out at the forge of suffering and sacrifice. If their form was not graceful and the marks of the hammer were still upon them, yet were they as near to Christ as the polished spirals of our own attenuated doctrines. We shall criticize the Pilgrims and some phases of their religion in the following pages, but we shall do so on our knees.

Persecution had united the Pilgrims long before they left England. Certain independent spirits had begun in the first half-dozen years of the seventeenth century to take strong exception to the ritual of the Church of England. They saw, to quote Bradford, 'how not only these base and beggarly ceremonies were unlawful; but also that the lordly and tyranous power of the prelates ought not to be submitted unto.' They consequently withdrew from the Established Church and by degrees, joining with other malcontents whose views were similar to their own, they formed themselves, in 1606, into a new Church at Scrooby and held services in the houses of one or another of their members. Their pastor was Mr. Richard Clifton, and his assistant was Mr. John Robinson. In the course of their wanderings from England to Amsterdam and from Amsterdam to Leyden, Clifton vanished, and Robinson was in charge.

Robinson was one of the sanest progressives in ecclesiastical history. Convinced though he was that his church was an improvement over the Episcopal Church, he did not for a moment believe that it was the last word in organized religion. 'I profess myself,' he writes, 'always one of them who still desire to learn further what the good will of God is.' Though he believed in the infallibility of the Scriptures, he did not believe in the infallibility of man's interpretation of them. 'It is not possible,' says he, 'the Christian world should come so lately out of such thick Antichristian darknesse, and that full perfection of knowledge should break forth at once.' His quarrel was not with the doctrine of the Church of England, but with its government by the Bishops; and for this government he substituted an almost perfect democracy. His church was ruled by Elders, chosen by the congregation and authorized to serve only with the consent of the brethren, 'Who,' he says, 'ought not in contempt to be called the laity, but to be treated as men and brethren in Christ, not as slaves or minors.'

Such was the doctrine which the founders of the Congregational Church in New England brought with them when they came. How far they succeeded in following it will appear anon. 'We must apply ourselves to God's present dealing, not to his wonted dealing,' was a maxim which they knew to be true in theory and which they did their best to put in practice. If Robinson had been able to go with them to Plymouth, their best would have been a good deal better. But he died in Leyden, thwarted in his greatest desire, which was to tend his flock in their new pastures. Their Covenant was couched in general terms, and so sounds broader than it really was:

In the name of our Lord Jesus Christ, and in obedience to his holy will and divine ordinances, we, being by the most wise and good providence of God brought together in this place, and desirous to unite ourselves into one congregation or church under the Lord Jesus our Head, that it may be in such sort as becometh all those whom he hath redeemed and sanctified to himself, we do hereby solemnly and religiously, as in his most holy presence, vouch the Lord Jehovah the only true God to be our God and the God of ours, and do promise and bind ourselves to walk in all our ways according to the rule of the Gospel, and in all sincere conformity to his holy ordinances, and in mutual love to and watchfulness over one another, depending wholly and only upon the Lord our God to enable us by his Grace hereunto.

This Constitution was framed by men who, unlike Robinson, were convinced that they had found the one true faith and so were quick to resent any deviation from it. When settlements began to appear at Sandwich, Yarmouth, and Barnstable, the Court stipulated that each new group should have an *Orthodox* minister, or should be near enough to a town that had one, to go to church on Sunday. If the preaching was in any way irregular — 'weak and unsafe' were the stock adjectives — the minister's record was examined, his doctrines scrutinized, and if he got off with a warning, he was lucky. What Artemus Ward says of the Puritans is, unfortunately, about as true of the Plymouth men: 'I believe we are descended from the Puritans,' he writes, 'who nobly fled from a land of despitism to a land of freedim, where they could not only enjoy their own religion, but prevent everybody else from enjoying *his*.'

One minister who was broader than most in his doctrine and who did as much for religion and civilization on the Cape as any man has ever done, was John Lothrop, who came from Scituate with his flock and settled in Barnstable in 1639. Mr. Lothrop was a marked man even before he came to Scituate. The record of his trial in 1632 for holding a conventicle in the house of a brewer's clerk in Blackfriars, shows clearly enough what the Bishops thought of Congregationalist morals. The custom at such trials was to hurl three or four questions at the defendant before giving him a chance to answer. Lothrop was asked by what authority he preached at the conventicle, and at the same time 'How manie woemen sate crosse legged upon the bedd, whilest you sate on one side and preached and prayed most devoutlie?' (This from the Bishop of London.) Lothrop replied, 'I keepe noe such evill companie, they were not such woemen.' Thereupon the Bishop of London and the Archbishop of Canterbury demanded in chorus, 'Are you a minister?' and the Bishop of Saint David's asked, 'Were you not Dr. King, the Bishop of London's, Sizer in Oxford? I take it you were; and you shew your thankfullness by this.' Lothrop answered that he was a Minister. 'How and by whom qualified?' asked the Bishop of London; 'Where are your orders?' 'I am a Minister of the gospell of Christ,' replied Lothrop; 'and the Lord hath qualified me.' He then refused the oath and was sent back to prison.

Like Robinson, Lothrop was a Congregationalist of the wisest sort. He even admitted to Christian fellowship the persecuted Anabaptists, who not only in England but in the Massachusetts Bay Colony as well, knew the meaning of prison and stocks and banishment. Their method of immersion, to be sure, Lothrop regarded as unnecessarily thorough — 'Whole rivers,' he writes, 'show not forth Christ's suffering, pouring him out like water, besprinkling all his raiment.' But if the Anabaptists preferred extensive immersion, they were welcome to their belief and to fellowship in his Church. Lothrop took no stock in creeds or particularized confessions of faith, for they seemed to him narrow. He substituted the whole Bible for them, and gladly admitted to membership in his church any one who professed faith in God and promised to do his best to keep the Ten Commandments. Though his writings show him to be a student of theology, and though this subject was to him one of great intellectual interest, he wisely realized that to fill sermons with it was to put congregations to sleep; so he chose his texts with a view to the immediate temporal and spiritual needs of his flock, and read theology at his own fireside.

If more men of Lothrop's caliber had been ministers on the Cape, the ugly period of Quaker persecution would have worn a fairer face. Though he died before the Quaker troubles began, yet it was in great measure owing to his tolerant teachings that his own town of Barnstable escaped almost untouched by the tar brush that so thoroughly bespattered the neighboring town of Sandwich. Sandwich, in fact, was the Friends' Headquarters and the scene of most of the trouble. In 1658, eighteen families there belonged to the new sect. Some said, indeed, that almost the whole town had turned Quaker. One reason why the authorities dealt so harshly with Quakers was that this sect was the first to rebel against the standing order of worship. By the middle of the seventeenth century they had established themselves in Sandwich and were enjoying persecution. The following item from the Aspinwall Papers under the date of 1659 is of interest:

I. I. and W. Leddra went ... to a place called Sandwich where there are many friends, who suffer much in the spoiling of their goods; after that they had been there some time, they were taken prisoners at A

Towne called Plymouth. Dearly Beloved C. Holder . . . is passed towards Sandwitch againe, as I have been told, where he had fine service among friends since I. I. and W. L. were Imprisoned.

But the fine service referred to was not without unpleasant interruptions, for on June 23, 1658, Christopher Holder and John Copeland, the first Quaker ministers on the Cape, were arrested on their way to Sandwich, and a little later were sent out of the jurisdiction.

The authorities sometimes tried other tactics before resorting to pains and penalties. In 1659, they made an attempt — apparently sincere but comically ineffectual — to bring the erring brethren back to the Orthodox fold. John Smith, of Barnstable, together with Isaac Robinson of Falmouth, and two Plymouth men, was permitted to attend Quaker meetings with a view to persuading the Friends to abandon their ways. So far from succeeding, the experiment resulted in the conversion of both Robinson and Smith, and three years later Smith was one of a group that broke away from the Barnstable church and formed a Quaker meeting of their own. A joint council of clergy and laymen was called to recommend what measures should be taken in this alarming state of affairs. Their verdict was sufficiently explicit and harsh enough to suit the most vindictive. The gist of it was that other churches might not hold communion with the Quakers, nor the Quakers among themselves.

But neither excommunication nor the disfranchisement that went with it disturbed the Quakers in the least, for they believed that their own consciences were better guides than the decrees of orthodoxy. The authorities, however, did not stop with decrees. They, too, had consciences which drove them to carry on vigorously the war that they had declared. When the Quakers persisted in absenting themselves from church and holding meetings of their own, they were fined. Since they usually had not money enough to pay the fine, their goods were seized, and this, in frontier settlements, where axes and kettles were scarce and horses and cattle indispensable, was hardship, indeed. The marshal whose duty it was thus to plunder the houses of recalcitrant Quakers, had, one would suppose, an unpleasant task. But whether by accident or design, a man had been selected as marshal of the three towns of Sandwich, Barnstable, and Yarmouth, who was as ruthless as the laws he was called upon to enforce. George Barlow, 'the Quaker Terror,' had, so far as can be discovered from contemporary authorities, not a single good trait. A bully, a drunkard, and a hypocrite, he took malicious pleasure in tyrannizing over a sect from whom he was in no danger of suffering physical injury.

There is no need of reciting the long list of Barlow's brutalities. He had no imagination, and his technique never varied. It was his habit to take not what would be most valuable to the authorities, but what would be most poignantly missed by the Quaker families. The story of his visit to the house of William Allen in Sandwich, which has become a local tradition, will serve to illustrate his methods. Allen's thrift and industry had made him prosperous, but his subsequent adherence to the Quaker doctrine made him poor. His house was a rendezvous for Friends; he was therefore a marked man in the eye of the law, and during 1658 and 1659, so much of his property was seized that nothing remained but his house and land, and a single cow. He had himself been driven from town and was, at the time of Barlow's final visit, lying in a Boston jail. His wife Priscilla and the children were alone in the house. The marshal first took the cow, all the corn in the house, and a bag of meal that had been given to Mrs. Allen by the neighbors. Not content with this, he annexed the only copper kettle she had, and said with a leer, 'Now, Priscilla, how will thee cook for thy family and friends? Thee has no kettle.' 'George,' replied Mrs. Allen, 'that God who hears the young ravens when they cry will provide for them. I trust in that God, and I verily believe the time will come when thy necessity will be greater than mine.' Barlow, so the story goes, lived to see Priscilla's prophecy fulfilled.

It is easy enough in this day of toleration, or indifference, in matters of doctrine, to criticize the authorities who harried the Society of Friends. Those dignitaries could see no sense in the reason which the Quakers gave for refusing to contribute to the Orthodox Church, though a sounder reason would be far to seek. They had Biblical precedent, they said, for not giving support to those from whom they had received no benefit. Most of the magistrates, it is true, from Governor Hinckley down to the humblest office-holder, were blind to the inconsistency of an attitude wherein they felt justified in refusing to contribute to the Church of England, but refused to acknowledge that the Quakers were justified in refusing to contribute to the Congregational Church. One should reflect, however, before censuring Hinckley and his assistants too severely, that they were convinced that theirs was the one true church, and that any who refused its doctrine, whether Episcopalians or Quakers, were heretics. The casual citizen had little fault to find with Quakers. He found them, except when expressing their views on the government, agreeable and peace-loving neighbors, temperate, industrious, and helpful. He was never shocked, as citizens in other parts of New England occasionally were, by the spectacle of naked Quakers rushing through village streets, to the glory of God and of the Society of Friends. So he was far from sharing the Court's views that all Quakers should either recant or move away. More than once, in fact, Orthodox citizens, in trying to act as buffers between the Quakers and the authorities, were badly bruised between the rolling side of the Quaker ship and the granite pier of the Government. In 1658, nine citizens of Sandwich were disfranchised for being, or sympathizing with, Quakers. There was danger even for a deputy who lifted up his voice in behalf of the persecuted sect. James Cudworth, for a time a citizen of Barnstable and deputy to the General Court, writes as follows in November, 1658:

Last election Mr. Hatherly, and my Self, left off the Bench, and myself Discharged of my Captainship because I had entertained some of the Quakers at my house (thereby that I might be better acquainted with their Principles). I thought it better so to do, than with the blind World, to Censure, Condem, Rail at, and Revile them, when they neither saw their Persons, nor knew any of their Principles. But the Quakers and my self cannot close in divers things; and so I signified to the Court, I was no Quaker, but must bear my Testimony against sundry things that they held, as I had Occasion and Opportunity: But withal I told them, that as I was no Quaker, so I would be no Persecutor.

Such was the attitude that cost Cudworth his captaincy and his position as deputy.

It would, of course, be an error to suppose that all the punishments the Quakers received were unjust. They were more than exasperating in their 'holier than thou' attitude. Morton says truly that 'they placed their justification upon their patience and suffering for their opinions, and on their righteous life and retired demurity, and affected singularity both in word and gesture.' Furthermore, contempt of court was quite as often the cause of their being punished as their 'corrupt and damnable doctrines.' Governors and magistrates were to them no more than farmers or tanners. Nor did the Quakers always adhere to that 'retired demurity' of life on which they so much prided themselves. Robert Harper undoubtedly got what he deserved when he was whipped for 'intolerably insolent conduct at Barnstable in railing against Mr. Wally and at Sandwich against Mr. Wiswall.' Even to-day there would be a sensation if a high official were called in public 'an impudent man and a pitiful governor.' Yet that is the language that a Sandwich Quaker used toward his chief magistrate; and he went on to taunt the Governor, asking him 'why he did not send him to gaol since his back had long itched to be whipped.' But the limit in abusive language was reached when Humphrey Norton, addressing Governor Prince before the assembled Court, said, 'Thomas, thou liest; Prince, thou art a malicious man.' And again, 'Thy clamorous tongue I regard no more than the dust under my feet.' 'Thou art like a scolding woman.' Imprisonment or whipping for such silly insolence was just enough.

By quick stages the persecution of Quakers began to cease. They first appeared on the Cape about 1656. King Charles's letter of 1661, enjoining all Colonial Governors to cease persecuting them, was followed three years later by a commission which arrived in New England in response to repeated Quaker appeals, to look the situation over, try certain cases, and recommend toleration. The commissioners were respectfully greeted by representatives from Plymouth; the King's men felt no real enthusiasm about the Quaker question; the Plymouth men felt no interest in enlightening them. They talked pleasantly but vaguely; the commissioners began to sigh for the fleshpots of London, and soon sailed back home to the satisfaction of every one but the Quakers. It cannot be asserted, therefore, that either the King's letter or his commission put an end to the persecutions, but they undoubtedly gave the authorities pause.

If the Quakers had the royal ear, it might be as well to walk circumspectly. The death of Governor Prince in 1673 and the succession of Josiah Winslow was another step toward peace, for Winslow was far more tolerant than his predecessor. From this date the policy of leniency grew, in spite of Hinckley's uncompromising attitude, until, in 1717, we find Yarmouth voting in a town meeting that no Quaker need contribute to the support of the Orthodox minister.

Why, it may be asked, was the Court and not the Church the power that punished the Quakers? The answer is twofold. In the first place, Quaker demonstrations were almost always breaches of the peace rather than heresy, and as such they came under the jurisdiction of the Court. In the second place, the worst penalty the Church could inflict was excommunication, which was no punishment at all to the Friends. Furthermore, for a long time there was almost no distinction between the Church and the civil government — certainly nothing like the gulf that separates them to-day. And this was natural, for the Bible in the minds of the Pilgrims was an adequate source of government; they consulted the Mosaic Law, it will be remembered, for the answers to knotty questions in jurisprudence. More often than not new settlements were made by churches, not by scattered individuals. It was Lothrop's church that came with him and settled Barnstable; it was half the Plymouth church that made the town of Eastham. Membership in the church was a requisite for civil distinction and even for the right to vote. The personnel of the parish and of the civil government was identical. It is not surprising, therefore, that for many years parish business was transacted in town meetings. In 1703, when Falmouth decided to dispense with the preaching of Mr. Shiverick, the action was taken in a town meeting because every man at the meeting was necessarily a member of the church. Another Falmouth minister, Mr. Isaiah Mann, died in 1789, and the town voted a supply of wood and rye for his widow. All the early town records are full of ministers' salaries and other church affairs.

The Church, nevertheless, maintained disciplinary powers quite distinct from the Court and held the right to excommunicate brethren who refused to follow what it decreed even in regard to purely civil controversies. Excommunication, though it held no terrors for the Quakers, was a calamity to the Orthodox citizen, for with his loss of membership in the Church came automatically the loss of his vote in town and Colony elections. His only resource lay in his right to appeal to a higher ecclesiastical council.

An interesting case of this sort of Church discipline — and one that is the more striking because it occurred as late as 1868 — was the incident of Joseph Bodfish, of West Barnstable, and the pasture bars. Mr. Bodfish, an elderly and respected member of the Congregational Church, had for years, in getting out his winter's wood, been in the habit of crossing a piece of meadow that belonged to another member of the family. At the owner's death, the meadow went to Joseph's cousin, Sylvanus, also a member of the church. Sylvanus promptly warned Joseph not to cross that way any more, and nailed bars across the gap in the fence. Joseph consulted Judge Marston, who told him that he had a clearly established right of way to the swamp and advised him to pull down the bars himself if Sylvanus wouldn't. Joseph — obviously a lover of peace — asked one of the deacons to try his luck at persuading Sylvanus to remove the bars. The deacon refused and recommended instead that the matter be laid before the church. This Joseph did, but unfortunately intimated that if the church did not decide in his favor, he would take the dispute to Court, and rely on Judge Marston to see him through.

The committee, not unnaturally, were angry at this veiled threat, which reminded them of the unpleasant truth that the Court was a more powerful body than they. So they refused to remonstrate with Sylvanus, but said that they would examine the lot and see whether the wood could not be taken out some other way. This they did and declared that Joseph had no right of way across Sylvanus's pasture and that they 'could not justify a further prosecution of the claim'; they further *required* Joseph to leave the matter for the whole church to decide. He refused, and was promptly suspended from membership for one year, 'to give him opportunity of fully reflecting on the matter.' His wife Asenath and his son Benjamin were likewise suspended. All three appealed in vain for a hearing; their appeal

for a Mutual Council to decide the matter was equally vain, the
parish taking the ground that 'the church is the highest earthly
tribunal to deal with disorderly members.' The year of suspen-
sion ended on May 3, 1868, and Joseph wrote to the committee on July 28, that he was 'willing to right the wrong, but
not to wrong the right.' This smart remark failed to please
the authorities, and three days later he and his wife and son
were excommunicated for 'violation of the church covenant.'

Here was Church discipline with a vengeance. The unhappy
family again appealed in vain for a hearing before a Mutual
Council, and as a last resort proceeded to call a council *ex-parte*
composed of the Reverend Henry Dexter, of Boston, and eight
other clergymen. This Council found that the action of the
West Barnstable church was contrary to the law of Christ and
the fundamental principles and usages of the Congregational
Church; declared that, as such, it ought to be null and void;
and recommended that the three excommunicated members be
readmitted to good standing.

Other and earlier troubles had arisen to disturb the serenity
of the Church. The question of baptism — always an ecclesiastical battle-ground — claimed the attention of the pious in
the intervals between Quaker demonstrations. The subject had
been raised in Plymouth as far back as 1638, and cropped up
again in Yarmouth during the ministry of Mr. Thomas Thornton, about 1670. Thornton was a liberal and fearlessly adopted
the so-called Half-Way Covenant. Up to this time only the
baptized could be church members, and only the children of
church members could be baptized. But the Half-Way Covenant authorized the baptism of the children of any pious persons
professing Orthodoxy, even though they had never been baptized. This reasonable measure raised a few ominous clouds
in the conservative half of the heavens, and resulted in some
rumblings as of an approaching storm. But Thornton forged
ahead without shortening sail, and came through safely. The
Half-Way Covenant flourished in the free air of the New World,
and spread to one town after another up and down the Cape.

The fact is that, as their numbers grew and their prosperity
increased, the settlers began to feel less interest in the minutiæ
of formalized worship, if not in religion itself. The Mayflower

band, with winter knocking at the door of their unwarmed
houses, had found comfort in religion when no other comfort
could be had. So was it with the pioneers on the Cape. But
when the first sharp struggle with the wilderness had been won,
and the settlers began to build adequate houses with wide
hearths, religion came to be less a crying need and more an
extra-curriculum activity. This is doubtless one reason why
there was not a greater storm when Thornton adopted the Half-
Way Covenant. Goodness knows men still read their Bibles and
still went to Church. The Reverend John Simpkins, of Brewster, writing as late as 1809, says, 'It is still, even at the present
day, considered quite unfashionable not to attend the public
worship.' But the motive — the impulse — which is revealed
by the word 'unfashionable' — was very different from the old
motive, and the change had already begun. Of course this state
of affairs did not arrive until long after Thornton had gone to a
well-earned rest, and his children's children, if such there were,
as well. But the ball had begun to roll, and though its momentum was as yet hardly perceptible, it was headed for a steep
slope and a straight track toward the toleration that comes
from indifference.

The old clergy were much concerned at the state of affairs.
Not only was interest in religion waning, but ministers were
becoming scarce. Barnstable went for five years, 1678–83,
without any settled pastor. In 1678, the Reverend John Cotton, writing from Plymouth to Governor Hinckley at Barnstable, says that it is a 'dying time with preachers' — a lament
that is by no means foreign to the ears of our own generation.
Another and important development, which the Old Guard
interpreted as a sign of disintegration, was the tendency of the
Cape towns to split into two parishes, ostensibly because the
outlying houses were too far from the church, but perhaps also,
if the truth were known, because some disliked the teachings
of the settled minister and wanted a new church and a new
minister of their own. The geographical reason was a good one,
however, and no real objection could be raised by any one
against such separations.

Sandwich made two parishes out of one in 1735, though for
several years the members of the new church were compelled

WEST BARNSTABLE CONGREGATIONAL CHURCH, BUILT 1717–18

to contribute to the support of the old parish as well as bear the expenses of their own. Barnstable began to show signs of restlessness as early as 1712, and in spite of considerable opposition, a new parish was formed the same year. The new meetinghouse was not built until four years later; but in 1716 it was well under way on Cobb's Hill in the easterly part of the town. It is interesting to note Cotton Mather's distress when he learned of the proceedings. 'Poor Barnstable,' he writes; 'what shall be done for thee? Give the best Advice that may be, to the afflicted and oppressed young Minister there.' The 'afflicted and oppressed' young minister was the Reverend Jonathan Russell, Jr., who had recently been called to the original Church, in the West Precinct. No doubt it was hard for him to see half his parishioners walk out to serve new gods, it might be, to the eastward. But the path of progress is ever wet with the tears of conservatism or selfishness. In 1721, Yarmouth followed suit by setting off the East Precinct as a new parish, which later became the town of Dennis, and sooner or later Eastham, Harwich, and other Cape towns did likewise, sometimes in the teeth of fierce opposition from the Mother Church; sometimes with her blessing. The fact that almost always the new parishes were in time incorporated as independent towns suggests what may have been another motive for their desire to separate. The fathers of the new church would be the fathers of the new town; and independence was in the air. Thus, with mixed motives and half or quite unconsciously, our ancestors used religion as a means to civil independence.

The new parishes had plenty to think about besides their church. Some were already angling for incorporation; others devoted their energies to acquiring broader acres, neglecting God in the service of mammon. War is never good for morals or religion, and the long French and Indian Wars were playing their part in loosening the bonds that had held men to the Church. The clergy volleyed and thundered as loud as ever, but the spirits of their congregations were not so eager as of yore. The time was ripe for revival, and revival came about 1740 with the dynamic George Whitefield and the Great Awakening, the effects of which were violent and on the whole beneficial.

Whitefield was a young Episcopal clergyman who, like Mark Antony, possessed the 'power of speech to move men's souls.' If he had appeared in New England a hundred years earlier, he would have been jailed as a Papist and a corrupter of the true faith. But the century and a quarter that had passed since the Pilgrims landed had gone far toward obliterating the old hatred of the Church of England. So he was permitted to travel the length and breadth of the Colonies, preaching sometimes in churches but quite as often in the open air. He never visited the Cape, but his disciples did, and the citizens listened at first with interest and then with excitement to the exhortations of the inspired young itinerants. Theirs was the doctrine of hope. Salvation, they said, was waiting for penitent sinners. Such teaching was music to the ears of men who were used to hell-fire sermons like those of Treat. Here were preachers who told them that though their sins were as scarlet, they could be as white as snow. They left the old churches by the score and were again dubbed separatists by the stand-patters, as their grandfathers had been before them. Sometimes they called themselves 'Come-Outers'; sometimes 'New Lights.'

Whitefield's influence was twofold, for the ministers of other denominations copied his custom of traveling from place to place in evangelical fashion. Elisha Paine, for example, a Connecticut Baptist of Cape ancestry, made a flying visit to Harwich in 1744 in the course of a peripatetic career, and held a series of open-air meetings in which he rallied many to the Baptist standard. He writes to his wife in an exultant strain: 'The pine woods of Harwich ring with Hallelujahs and hosannas, even from babes!' and again, 'I felt the spirit of the Lord come upon me. I rose up and exhorted and persuaded them to come to Christ, and immediately there was a screeching and groaning all over the multitude and hath been very powerful ever since.' No doubt reaction followed the screeches and the groans, but the converts were the better for some religious emotion, at least, and a good many of them adhered to the new doctrine.

The Old Guard Congregational ministers, meanwhile, were at their wits' end. No power that they could exercise, no denunciations that they could compose, had any force in checking the stream of separatists that flowed from the churches. The only response that occurred to them was to hold a meeting and draft a document which should explain why itinerant preaching in general, and Whitefield's in particular, was pernicious. Accordingly, in February, 1745, ten of them, representing the seven principal towns, met at Harwich, which had become the center of religious unrest on the Cape. They set about their task with an earnestness born of despair. They composed a pamphlet in which the 'many sad consequents' of itinerant preaching were 'discovered.' If the itinerants wish to wander about preaching, they argued, let them go where the Word of God is not already adequately preached; let them go among the heathen. As for their plea that they have received an 'extraordinary call,' we shall not believe it until we see results commensurate with such a call. All impostors and enthusiasts have pretended to such extraordinary calls. We admit that the itinerants have done some good, but not enough to justify their practice; for 'a sovereign God can and ofttimes doth bring Good out of Evil, but this in no wise excuseth the Evil-Doer.' Furthermore, the chief result of itinerant preaching has been to substitute schism and discord for peace and unity in the established churches, and we do not believe, as the itinerants are reported to declare, that 'Contention is a sign of the Work of God.' Therefore, in conclusion, 'We cannot in Faithfulness to Christ or his People under our several charges, give any Encouragement or Countenance to the Reverend Mr. George Whitefield as an Itinerant Preacher.'

This serious appeal to reason stood no chance against the revivalist's sensational appeals to the emotions. The old Congregational clergy had to content itself with ministering to the staid and cautious, while the nimbler spirits enlisted under the flag of the schismatics. There is no reason to doubt the sincerity of the ministers who drew up the indictment against the itinerants. They believed that unity was the keystone of religion, and that if unity was destroyed, the whole structure would fall in ruins. The fact that their own livelihoods were involved in the crash was naturally present to their minds, for they were human; but it served only to strengthen, not to create, their conviction. The days of ecclesiastical monopoly were at an end. The Quakers were exempt from supporting the Old Church; the

Separatists and New Lights were on the highroad to the same goal. So were the Baptists. No wonder the Reverend Edward Pell, minister of the Congregational Church in the South Parish of Brewster, remarked in 1752 on his deathbed that he would prefer not to be buried in that parish, for fear 'that the Lord would never think to look in such an ungodly place for a right-eous man.'

Religious affairs remained in pretty much this posture until after the Revolution. Then, about 1795, came the Methodists, the last new sect to meet with any appreciable opposition. The scene of Quaker troubles had centered, as we have seen, at Sandwich; the principal activity of the New Lights and Baptists had taken place halfway down the Cape, at Harwich and Chatham. The Methodists began at the tip end of the Cape among the shifting sands and scrubby hills of Provincetown and Truro. Tradition says that a certain Captain William Humbert, a Methodist, whose vessel was becalmed in Province-town Harbor, came ashore and preached to the fishermen. As nearly as can be discovered, this happened in 1793. The Cap-tain's words seem to have found favor with the Province-towners, for within two years plans were under way to build a Methodist meeting-house there, and in 1795, according to Dr. Coggswell, 'the house at last went up; the second Methodist Church in New England.'

Coggswell might well say 'at last,' for the opposition to the new sect was so strong that the town meeting voted that any who would not pay the standing minister's rate should have his interest 'sesed,' and 'that there shall not be a Methodist meet-ing-house built in this town.' Hardly had the vote been recorded when a vessel-load of lumber for the new church arrived at the wharf and was wheeled up to the beach. Provincetown men have always been direct-actionists; a group of determined Orthodox citizens went to the beach by night, cut the lumber into convenient sizes and dragged it to the top of High Pole Hill, where they burned it with an effigy of the Reverend Jesse Lee, the Methodist minister. This gentleman was on hand to watch the performance, which seems not to have been altogether un-expected, for he writes, 'I went to see the timber destroyed by the mob and felt astonished at the conduct of the people, considering that we live in a free country. However, I expect this will be for the good of the little Society.' Nothing daunted, the Methodists got another load of lumber and, with armed men guarding it day and night, built their meeting-house.

This victory gave the opposition its death-blow. Further objections were but whistles against the hurricane. The town fathers were finally forced to yield, for the number of Methodists grew so fast, not only in Provincetown but in Truro and Wellfleet, that in 1830 the Provincetown Congregational Church closed its doors for want of supporters.

It is not hard to see why Methodism made so strong an appeal to the whalemen and cod-fishermen of the lower Cape. A modified form of itineracy which the new denomination practiced provided that no minister should preach in the same town for more than two years and sometimes only for one. There was, therefore, no danger that a congregation should suffer long from the harangues of a dull preacher. But variety of another sort is what made most converts. The Methodist preachers were often men of little education and no religious training. Zeal and 'a call' with them took the place of theological schools. The consequence was a breezy informality in their discourses. They never hesitated to employ startling tricks to keep their hearers awake. On one occasion a Methodist minister in Truro interrupted his sermon by the remark, 'Brethren, your stove pipe is so confoundedly crooked, that I can't preach a straight sermon.' Another whose subject was 'the World, the Flesh, and the Devil,' prefaced his remarks by saying, 'I shall touch lightly upon the World, hasten to the Flesh, and pass on to the Devil, when I will give it to you hot as you can sup it.' It is a consolation, if we are to get the Devil, to be given him in a language that we can understand. There was, in fact, little danger that a Methodist preacher would shoot over the heads of his hearers. This — with a pleasant smattering of rugged wit — went far toward making Methodism popular, for no men appreciate wit more keenly than Cape-Codders. The Reverend Edgar Clark, one of the early Methodist ministers in Provincetown, showed adroitness and much sense when a pharisaic whaleman of his congregation asked him what to do if, after cruising for months without filling a cask, he sighted a hundred-barrel whale on Sunday.

'I think,' said Mr. Clark, 'I should call all hands together and ask the Lord to bless us. Then I would go and get the whale.'

Another pleasant practice of the Methodists was Camp Meeting Week, which began at Wellfleet in 1819 and after a few years moved to Truro. Camp meetings were, and continue to be, not merely religious assemblies, but social outings as well. The women find a few days in camp a pleasant change from the drudgery of their kitchens; the men do not confine their conversation to ecclesiastical topics. The early camp meetings were thronged with enthusiastic citizens of every denomination from all over the Cape:

> 'We saw great gatherings in a grove,
> A grove near Pamet Bay,
> Where thousands heard the preacher's word,
> And dozens knelt to pray.'

Eastham was the next camp meeting town. Here they began in 1828 and were so successful that the Methodists bought a ten-acre lot called Millennium Grove, and put up a big frame building to house the ministers. The congregations lived in tents. Sometimes — especially on Sundays — as many as five thousand persons attended, some of them, it must be confessed, inspired by no loftier motive than curiosity or mischief. Here men and women arose to give testimony as to their religious experiences, and no doubt some who came to scoff remained to pray. Camp meetings are still held every summer in the woods between Yarmouth and Hyannis.

So, before long, for this reason and that, the Methodists outnumbered any other denomination in most of the Cape towns; and as soon as this happened, all question of their being obliged to support the standing order vanished. Town meetings were parish meetings no longer. Religious freedom became a fact, not by any one grand proclamation, but by years of persistent work by Quakers, Itinerants, Baptists, and Methodists. No two towns struck off the shackles at exactly the same time, but in general by 1816, when Wellfleet exempted Methodists from supporting the Orthodox Church, religion on the Cape might take what form it would.

All this was mighty hard on the devout old Congregationalist ministers, whose lot, even in the palmiest days of orthodoxy, had been no easy one. No picture of early ecclesiastical days in the Plymouth Colony would be complete without at least a few words of tribute to these stalwart pillars of a stalwart faith. Taken by and large, no finer or more influential men ever ministered to a nation's welfare. It is no accident that the towns of Bourne, Dennis, and Brewster were named for their pastors. Such men as John Lothrop, Richard Bourne, Timothy Alden, Josiah Dennis, and Samuel Treat are titanic figures in the history of the Cape. Theirs was the task of setting a spiritual and intellectual standard that should permeate every phase of life. Righteous themselves, they demanded righteousness in their followers, and within the limitations of human nature, they got it. Their example gave strength to the weak and courage to the faint-hearted. As often as not they were physicians as well as pastors, ministering to ills of the body with the same rugged energy they employed with the ills of the soul. The Reverend Thomas Thornton was the only doctor in Yarmouth from 1670 until old age forced him to retire. Fifty years later Mr. Greenleaf was both minister and physician for the same town. The Reverend Hugh Adams, who was called to the pulpit in Chatham in 1711, is said to have had an extensive medical practice, even outside his own parish. The tombstone of the Reverend Benjamin Fessenden, who died in Sandwich later in the same century, bears among other eulogistic remarks the following: 'not only as a divine was he useful, but as a discreet and successful physician.'

These early men of God had to be men of fine parts to get their positions in the first place; before they were officially called to a church, they were often required to prove their mettle by a long series of sermons before congregations as critical and as potentially hostile as school boys. Timothy Alden preached sixteen times to the Yarmouth Parish before they were satisfied that he would do; and Mr. Joseph Green, who antedated him by a few years, worked for fifty-two Sundays to earn the same position. Sandwich was still more candid. Unable to decide whether Thomas Tupper or Richard Bourne was the better man, the congregation asked them to preach in competition, and he who had the fuller house was named 'minister for the day.'

The ministers needed ready tact and large sympathies, if they were to cope successfully with such troublesome parishioners as Sunday fishermen, many of whom were for nine months of the year exemplary Christians. What, for example, was the Truro parson to say to a certain noted skipper who used to assert with commendable candor that 'there was no hope for him if he died during the fishing season, but in winter he was all right?' Such questions wanted nice handling. Lack of tact cost the Reverend Charles Boyter his pulpit in Truro. He arrived there about a hundred years ago and decided one day to swell the numbers of his congregation by announcing that his next discourse would be a sermon on Luck. Sunday morning found the church filled with interested fishermen, who knew more about luck than any other class of men in the world. But Mr. Boyter proclaimed that there was no such thing as luck; industry and hard work, not luck, were what brought full fares of fish. 'Bait your hooks with red flannel,' he told them; 'then if you don't catch codfish, it will be because you don't try.' And he compared the rigors of the Grand Banks to 'trouting in the brooks of Vermont with a fly and pole.' Shortly after this sermon, Mr. Boyter left Truro to try his luck in Orange, New Jersey.

Then there was the ticklish question of church music; that, too, craved wary walking. The Old Church fell heir to Calvin's prejudice against instrumental music, though one may properly ask whether their peculiar antipathy to organs was not owing to their cost and the difficulty of getting them, quite as much as to any more pious objection. In 1726, the West Parish of Barnstable was split wide open on the question of music, and had to call in civil authority to decide it. But two years later the progressives won, and the church voted to sing 'the regular or new way,' that is, with the accompaniment of instruments. The Orleans church had no music, other than vocal, until 1810; then a bass viol made its appearance, probably in the face of strong opposition from a conservative minority.

Through quicksands such as these the parson had to pick his way with care, guided by his conscience on the one hand and expediency on the other. But the greatest trials of the ministers arose from the very ardor and attentiveness of the congregations. The Reverend John Robinson's principle that every member should feel responsible for the church's welfare and should have a voice in all its proceedings, was undoubtedly a fine thing; but it made endless trouble for the pastor. Any one felt justified in falling foul of his doctrine. Mr. Marmaduke Matthews, who occupied the pulpit in Yarmouth about 1640, was hauled over the coals for 'weak and unsafe' remarks in his sermons; and this in spite of the fact that he has been characterized as 'able, zealous and devoted.' Mr. Matthews humbly apologized, confessing that 'he might have expressed and delivered himself in terms more free from exception,' and he was allowed to continue his labors.

Yarmouth, in fact, was early a hotbed of trouble for ministers. In 1651, Mr. John Miller, the pastor of the town, was haled before the Plymouth Court for alleged aspersions against the Government. What these aspersions were is not stated. Doubtless they were as chimerical as Mr. Matthews's heresies. The citizens of Falmouth in 1702 voted that they would not employ Samuel Shiverick any more to preach to them, and chose Joseph Parker to tell him of it. What it was in Mr. Shiverick's preaching that offended his hearers one is left to conjecture.

Another celebrated row occurred in Eastham, where the Reverend Samuel Osborn, after preaching from 1718 to 1738, was dismissed by a vote of an ecclesiastical council. The judgment of this august gathering is no surprise, for Osborn had forsaken Calvin for Arminius, and had been indiscreet enough to assert a universal negative, by saying that there were no promises in the Bible but what were conditional. Few Yankees, even today, would let this statement pass without thumbing their Bibles for evidence against it. Yet Osborn, aside from being a powerful preacher, had done much for the temporal welfare of Eastham; he had taught the citizens better ways of growing crops and had showed them how the peat, of which there was a great quantity in the town, might be used for fuel.

While Mr. Osborn was in doctrinal difficulties at Eastham, the Reverend Joseph Metcalfe found himself in sartorial trouble in Falmouth. With no previous warning, he appeared one Sunday in the pulpit sporting a new wig, which, though 'not expressed in fancy, neat, not gaudy,' was yet a sufficient improvement over the old one to set the Falmouth ladies' tongues wagging about vanity and the preacher. The next day he stepped, perhaps by accident, into a house where several prominent ladies were discussing the absorbing topic. Mr. Metcalfe, the soul of urbanity, suggested that they might be better pleased if he gave up wearing a wig altogether? No, that would never do, they declared in scandalized tones. Perhaps they would like the old one reinstated? By no means! 'Then let us alter the new one until it ceases to offend,' said the patient pastor, wherewith he presented it to one of the ladies after another, each of whom clipped from it what she regarded as the sinful lock. The last lady declared that to wear a wig at all was to break the Second Commandment, but Mr. Metcalfe pointed out that the wig in its present condition 'was so unlike anything in the heaven above or on the earth beneath, or in the waters under the earth,' that it was surely exempt from any possible censure.

Quarrels of one sort or another between clergymen and their congregations became so much matters of course that one canny divine, Mr. Hugh Adams, who was called to Chatham in 1711, took precautionary measures. He accepted the call on condition that if any difference arose between him and his parish ('which we should both humbly pray there may never be'), a committee of clergymen should decide on the rights and wrongs of the disagreement; that if the whole blame was found to rest on the people, Adams and his heirs should still be entitled to his salary forever, whether he was dismissed or not. If neither party was found to blame, or if the blame was equally divided, the salary, too, should be equally divided. Mr. Adams's fears were prophetic. After five years, the trouble came, and he was dismissed, stoutly asserting that he did not care, for 'he had a better call elsewhere.' It would be interesting to know whether the town lived up to its agreement regarding his salary. Perhaps, though, he was found *wholly* to blame!

Any treasures which the old clergy laid up for themselves must have been in heaven; certainly they got few enough of them on earth, for ministers in colonial times were paid proportionally no better than they are now; but it does seem hard that for a time they were obliged to collect their own salaries. How they did it, one can only conjecture; perhaps by a door-to-door canvas, hat in hand; perhaps, if they were more discreet, by a fervid reference to the soaring price of beef in the course of a parish call. At any rate, it was a miserable arrangement, which in the words of the Reverend Enoch Pratt 'was attended with much trouble [to the minister] and often impaired his usefulness.' After one generation had suffered under it, the method was changed; but even so, not much actual cash found its way into the parsonage. The fact that parishioners counted on drift whales to pay part of the minister's salary shows that installments must have arrived with some irregularity. In 1659, some of the Yarmouth men refused to contribute anything to the support of Mr. Miller, and were very properly taken to task by the Court.

Sometimes the parishioners tried to dock the ministerial stipend, as the Wellfleeters did with the Reverend Mr. Lewis in 1747. Times were hard, and the rapid depreciation of currency threw all old standards to the winds. His parishioners waited on Mr. Lewis with the suggestion that he accept the sum of sixty pounds, new tenor, as his salary from then on. But Mr. Lewis was a business man and no doubt had a large and hungry family; it is a pleasure to record that he held out for seventy-five pounds, and got it.

A good part of the pastor's pay took the form of wood and salt hay. Just after the Revolution, the Reverend Jude Damon of Truro received a salary of seventy-five pounds in cash besides the use of the parsonage, eighteen cords of wood cut and delivered at his door, and five tons of salt hay. In 1749, Mr. Stephen Emery, the Chatham minister, received a similar allowance of wood. So, taken all in all, and considering the simplicity of the times, the early Cape clergymen lived comfortably enough. If the flock sometimes grew careless and were late with the winter's wood, they were sure to turn up with it sooner or later. Timothy Alden, the beloved pastor of Yarmouth, had this experience on one occasion and chose for his next Sunday's text, 'Where no wood is there the fire goeth out.' Mr. Joseph Green, the Barnstable minister, started the pleasant custom of asking the boys in to a hearty dinner washed down with a glass of flip when the wood was unloaded.

As time went on, freedom of speech, which grew with the progress of civilization, became gall and wormwood to the preacher.

No divinity hedged him; he was fair game for earnest conservative and godless scoffer:

> 'A learned Treat, a pious Webb,
> And Cheever — all no more;
> Mr. Shaw then took the helm
> And run the ship ashore.'

So sang Peter Walker, the unregenerate blacksmith of Eastham, when the Reverend Philander Shaw, after more than forty years of service, retired from the old Congregational Church, which had grown as weak and infirm as its pastor.

During the first half of the nineteenth century, a strange kind of religious fanaticism visited many of the towns, attacking with greater or less violence a small number of estimable persons who, as soon as they became infected with the malady, promptly withdrew from whatever church they had belonged to and styled themselves 'Come-Outers.' They then indulged in antics that rivaled the antics of the Quakers. Frequently, when under the spell of their mania, they walked along the tops of fences instead of on the sidewalks; affected a strange, springing gait, and conversed by singing instead of by ordinary speech, in the distressing manner of characters in light opera. A favorite tune for the purpose was 'Old Dan Tucker.'

If the Come-Outers had confined themselves to these eccentricities, they might have been allowed, quite literally, to go their own gait unmolested, for tolerance was pretty well established all over the Cape. But fanatics are never satisfied while they see the rest of the world sane; they must needs turn reformers and usher all mankind along their special route to paradise. So it was with the Come-Outers, and so their troubles began — troubles that bear a striking analogy to the troubles of the Quakers. Certain of them were in the habit of attending Methodist meetings in Barnstable in order to disturb the proceedings by shouts and songs. After repeated warnings, they were finally brought into Court, and Nymphas Marston was employed in their defense. They lost their case and were ordered to pay the expenses of the trial; they refused, whereupon Marston attached the cattle of one of his recalcitrant clients, and the fun began. The animals were put up at auction before a large crowd that had come on the chance that there might be

some excitement. They were not disappointed. Most of the
Come-Outers in town were there, proclaiming that the sheriff
would never dare to sell the cattle, and that no one would dare
to buy them, for they belonged to God, and that God's curse
would fall upon all who were concerned in the transaction. They
accompanied these announcements with the dances and songs
in which they always indulged when angry, and which they
called 'dancing a person down to hell.' Bidding was slow —
perhaps because the citizens were frightened by the threats,
perhaps because they were being pleasantly entertained by the
performances of the Come-Outers. Finally two of the crowd,
Daniel Scudder and Daniel Smith, walked off, bored at the
leisurely fashion in which the auction progressed. This gave a
fine chance for some improvised lines from the Come-Outers,
one of whom burst into the following couplet to the tune of
'Old Dan Tucker':

> 'I don't wonder Daniel Smith and
> Daniel Scudder flee away!'

But there were hard heads enough in the assemblage to bid on
the cattle at last, and run the risk of incurring God's wrath. So
Mr. Marston got his pay.

Wherever money is at stake, it is usually possible to discover
a thread of reason in men's actions. But to account for the behavior of the persons in the following bits of idiocy is not so
easy. An enthusiastic Barnstable Come-Outer had a pig. A
prophetess of his order told him that he must kill it because the
Devil was in it. He killed it, dressed it nicely, and buried it,
convinced that he was weakening Satan's dominion thereby.
Not only pigs, but money might be the Devil's abode. A good
woman acted as nurse for a sick friend and was paid a small sum
for her services. The friend who gave it to her remarked, with a
Come-Outer's shudder, that the Devil was in it, whereupon the
horrified recipient threw it into Great Pond. The happy sequel
to this anecdote is not that she ever found the money again, but
that she did regain her wits and had many a laugh over the
antics of her Come-Outer days.

The strange sect was flourishing during the years just before
the Civil War, and became curiously involved in the Abolition
Movement which was so active at that time. As has been ex-

plained in another chapter, one reason why certain men and women withdrew from the various regular churches was that the churches tolerated slavery. After they had withdrawn, these persons sometimes called themselves Come-Outers, whether or not they joined with those of the same name whose actions have just been described. But Abolition became linked with Come-Outerism, and slavery was strengthened thereby. In other respects this eccentric spasm of religious possession did little harm. Many of its victims recovered after a time; it vanished altogether after the Civil War.

And what of recent religion on the Cape? There is not much to tell. Quakers, Baptists, and Methodists broke down the bars, and at one time or another during the last seventy-five years, every sect that the ingenuity of man can devise has had its fling. Even those two great churches which our ancestors called the harlots of Babylon — the Roman Catholic and the Episcopal — to-day are given the right hand of fellowship by the old-line Congregational parishes. Charles Jenkins, the lively historian of Falmouth, was among the last of the stand-patters when he wrote, in 1843, 'Already do we hear that motto so offensive to every true son of New England "No Church without a Bishop."' But the Episcopal Church has been represented here since the fifties, and the Cape is the better therefor. The shades of Bradford and Lothrop, if they rise from their graves at the sound of the Te Deum, rise to join in the Amen; for in the light of their abode, where all secrets are revealed, they interpret anew the teachings of their old pastor, John Robinson, who 'still desired to learn further what the good will of God was.' It should be said, however, that the Episcopal churches even to-day are attended almost exclusively by summer visitors.

The Church of Rome came with the Portuguese fishermen to Provincetown, and spread with the prosperity of these hardy seafarers. Within twenty years the Finns, whose numbers have increased amazingly in the neighborhood of West Barnstable, have presented the Cape with various sorts of Lutheran theology. The Universalists are everywhere prospering. Some of the old Congregational churches, like that of the East Parish in Barnstable, went Unitarian, but retained the name and polity of the old organization. Here and there are Christian Scientists;

the Swedenborgians have a number of representatives. The Mormons followed Greenwich Village to Provincetown; a dingy little building in South Yarmouth echoed not long ago to the enthusiastic activities of the Holy Rollers. A group of Dennis men, finding nothing to their taste in existing theology, created for themselves the Free Independent Church of Holiness, and some of their equally dissatisfied neighbors anticipated the Provincetown Mormons by joining the Reorganized Church of Jesus Christ of Latter Day Saints, wherein, let us hope, they found peace at the last.

'Divide and conquer' might well have been the Devil's doctrine in thus splitting into fragments the remains of a once vigorous piety. To-day as one makes his way through the Cape villages, one sees in each two or three great arks of meeting-houses, each of them big enough to accommodate half the regular church-goers in the county, each of them attended, if it is attended at all, by a handful of the devout, who, like the preacher's utterances, are lost among the hollow echoings of empty pews. Some have closed their doors for good and stand as bleak monuments to a transient enthusiasm. Truly as far as church-going is concerned, man has divided, and the Devil has conquered. Perhaps, after all, the despairing stanza of a pessimistic poet is close to the truth:

> 'I dreamed that I went to the City of Gold,
>   To Heaven resplendent and fair,
> And after I entered the beautiful fold
>   By one in authority there I was told
> That not a Cape-Codder was there.'

CHAPTER XV

THE CANAL

As soon as Governor Bradford established an outpost at Manomet in 1627 for trade with the Dutch at New York, the route of the Cape Cod Canal was virtually fixed. Nature had already done a large part of the work; on the north, Scusset Creek wound inland through marshes and low land, until it came within striking distance of Manomet River, which flows south into Buzzards Bay. Then, too, this route cut off the entire Cape — not part of it, as a canal farther east would have done. The Indians used to carry their canoes across the mile or two that separated the headwaters of the two streams; blockade-runners in the War of 1812 did the same with their whaleboats. Every prospect pleased; only man and machinery were needed.

Man was ready to undertake the job and was already talking about it in 1676, as appears from an entry in the diary of Samuel Sewall — that ubiquitous New-Englander whose active mind touched every phase of life and thought. On this occasion he was visiting Mr. Thomas Smith in Sandwich:

26 Octo'r, 1676. Mr. Smith rode with me and showed me the place which some had thought to cut, for to make a passage from the south sea to the north. He said it was about a mile and a half between the utmost flowing of the two seas in Herring River and Scusset — the land very low and level.... Moniment harbor said to be very good.

The project got no farther for the moment than to serve as a subject for speculative conversation, but Smith was still interested twenty years later, when the General Court ordered Mr. John Otis, of Barnstable, and Captain William Bassett and Mr. Thomas Smith, of Sandwich, to look the ground over and report what the cost of a canal would be and whether the scheme was feasible.

Yet the subject was not dropped. Men were fascinated by it who had never been on the Cape, and the chance traveler could hardly get through Sandwich without being taken to inspect the route. Prince, in 1736, refers to 'the place thro' which there has

been a canal talked of this forty years.' The King's ships which
hovered offshore during the Revolution brought the matter up
again with an urgency it had never had before. The General
Court sent a committee, consisting of the Honorable James
Bowdoin and others, to Sandwich to look into the question and
report. The committee very sensibly sought the advice of local
talent before deciding on anything, and invited Colonel Nathaniel Freeman and others to join them in their labors. They were
favorably impressed with the scheme, and engaged a Government engineer, Thomas Machin, to draw up plans and furnish
an estimate of the expenses. But Machin's work was interrupted, as appears from a letter which General Washington
wrote to James Bowdoin at Boston:

NEW YORK, June 10, 1776;

SIR, — Congress having requested my attendance in Philadelphia,
I was in that city when your letter of the 11th ultimo came to this
place, — this day's post therefore, affords me the first opportunity of
acknowledging receipt of it.

I am hopeful that you applied to General Ward, and have received
all the assistance that Mr. Machin could give, in determining upon the
practicability of cutting a canal between Barnstable and Buzzard's
Bay ere this, as the great demand we have for engineers in this department, Canada, &c., has obliged me to order Mr. Machin hither to
assist in that branch of business.

I thank you most heartily for your kind congratulations on the
departure of the troops from Boston, and am, with very great esteem,

Sir, your most obedient, humble servant,

GEO. WASHINGTON

HON. JAMES BOWDOIN, BOSTON.

Before this order came, Machin had gone so far as to propose
a canal fourteen feet deep with two double locks at each end
and two bridges. The expense he estimated at £32,148, 1s., 8d.
— very nice figuring!

The struggling colonies had no money or men to spare for
such work during the next seven years; but almost as soon as
the war was over, they were at it again, this time sending young
James Winthrop from Cambridge to the Cape, first to examine
the old route, and second to survey a possible new course from
Barnstable Harbor to the anchorage at what is now Hyannis-
port, taking in the two Hathaways and Nine Mile Ponds on the

way. Winthrop submitted detailed figures for the Sandwich Canal, but merely rode over the ground from Barnstable to Centerville, took the Reverend Mr. Mellen's word for the height of Kidd's Hill, and relied on local information as to the depth of the various ponds. He rightly regarded the high ridge that runs all along that part of the Cape as a discouraging obstacle, and gave the project of a canal there no further thought. Mr. Mellen, who accompanied Winthrop over the Barnstable–Hyannis course, mentions two others which were contemplated at least as early as 1794. One led from the Bass Hole in Yarmouth to the eastern part of Lewis Bay in Hyannis. This scheme apparently died at birth. The other, which included Bass River, in South Yarmouth, was so alluring that it was not abandoned for more than a century.

It had, indeed, much to commend it, for Bass River is the noblest of all the tidal creeks which wind inland from the Sound, and it terminates in a chain of ponds in Weir Village at no great distance from White's Brook, Yarmouth, which flows into the creeks that thread the beautiful marshes of Hockanom on the Bay shore. Thus the high ridge of the Cape that frightened Winthrop would be avoided, and the route, though by no means straight, presented few obstacles to the engineer. No less eminent a geologist than Professor Shaler thought that this way through the Cape would be better than the Monument River route. He points out that there were only four places where a canal might easily be dug: Monument River, Bass River, Town Cove, Orleans, and Pamet River, Truro. The last two he eliminated because vessels using them would still have dangerous waters to navigate. Of the remaining two he prefers Bass River because it could be used at the last minute in case of bad weather by a vessel whose captain had planned, other things being equal, to sail all the way round and save the toll. If the canal was at Monument River, a captain would have to decide very soon after leaving port whether or not to use it, for it would mean a different course almost from the outset. Shaler's arguments, however, went unheeded, for the old route was still, in the opinion of most people, the best one.

The citizens of Orleans and Eastham, with proper local pride, pinned great faith to the course which Cyprian Southack fol-

lowed in his whaleboat in 1717. He crossed the Cape by water
from the Bay to the Ocean, using Boat Meadow Creek, Jeremiah's Gutter, Town Cove, and Nauset Harbor — all of which
he found connected. This was unusual, but certainly not unprecedented, for geological evidence indicates that at a remote
period the water had a free sweep through this cut, which was
then much wider. While a small canal at this point would have
been easy to dig and a great convenience for local traffic, it
would have eliminated neither the Monomoy Shoals nor Peaked
Hill Bars. This wrote its death warrant. It is said, to be sure,
that the citizens of Orleans and Eastham cut a passage through
at this point during the War of 1812 to enable small boats to
run the blockade, and five years later a more elaborate canal
was contemplated by a corporation known as the Eastham and
Orleans Canal Proprietors; but it was never dug.

Meanwhile, the old Monument River passage was receiving
more attention than all the others put together; and it will be
wise to follow the crowd back to it. On the strength of Winthrop's report in 1791, the Legislature was convinced that a
canal was practicable and agreed to authorize any person to
construct it and charge a reasonable toll. But it was one thing
to ride over the ground with surveying instruments and an-
nounce that the project was an easy one; it was quite another to
construct the canal. Every one, in fact, seemed anxious that a
canal should be dug, but no one seemed at all anxious to dig it.
Wendell Davis, in his description of Sandwich in 1802, urged it
with exuberant eloquence and asserted (on what authority he
does not say) that the owners were ready to *give* the land along
the proposed route to any company that would undertake the
work. At about the same time a certain James Sullivan and
twenty associates appeared at the State House in Boston with
a mysterious scheme which they declared was far better than
any of the old ones, and asked that they be allowed to incorporate and put it through. Nobody paid much attention to
them, and they were heard of no more. Still the ground was
surveyed every few years by one person or another until, in the
language of the late Senator McCall, every grain of sand along
the whole route had been made the victim of an algebraic equa-
tion. In 1812, the strategic advantages of such a waterway in

time of war were repeatedly demonstrated by local blockade-runners. Here was proof enough, said its supporters, that the canal was necessary as a war-time measure, and in 1818 they sent Loammi Baldwin to Sandwich to resurvey the ground that had been trodden hard by the surveyors of a hundred and fifty years. But Baldwin's report, if he ever made one, inspired no more diggers than the reports of his predecessors.

Thanks to the efforts of Senator Lloyd, of Massachusetts, the taverns of Sandwich echoed in 1825 to the pompous tread of Government engineers from Washington with Major Perault at their head. This officer's careful report was just as fruitful as all the others had been, and for a generation after 1830 the legislators in the State House and the Congressmen in Washington had a rest from the monotonous subject of the Cape Cod Canal. The reason for the welcome silence was that the merchants of New England had by this time worked up an impressive foreign trade. Boston capitalists were thinking in terms of big ships and long voyages; coasting was too small game for them, and without their influence and support it was idle for the small fry, who would have used the canal, to keep up the clamor. Short railway lines began to cut into the coasters' business. With the fifties came the clipper ships. During all these activities, the project for a canal took a long and well-earned nap. When in 1861 a few wise shipowners began to realize that the days of sail were numbered, the scheme stirred for a moment as though to awake, half listening to the favorable utterances of Governor Banks in his inaugural message to the Legislature. It came wide awake a little later when a committee arrived with the familiar surveying instruments, but dropped off to sleep again as soon as it saw the same old maneuvers and heard the same old technicalities. But this committee struck one new note when it asked the coöperation of the United States Coast Survey, and incidentally of the United States Treasury. Henry Mitchell, a real authority on tides and their effect on coast lines, was sent down by the Government, together with specialists in other departments, and it began to look as if something might happen at last. But the war drove the subject from everybody's mind for the next four or five years, and by the time Lee had surrendered, the elaborate reports of Mitchell and his colleagues were of academic interest only. It is significant that nobody, from Governor Bradford in 1627 to the group of engineers who went over the ground in 1861, ever reported that a canal was inadvisable or impracticable, but that, almost without exception, they recommended locks rather than a free-water passage.

After the war, in spite of the fact that considerable New England capital began to head westward and that some was still tied up in sailing ships, a group of enthusiasts in 1870 applied for and received incorporation as the Cape Cod Canal Company with authority to raise money and dig the ditch if they could. The Legislature further suggested that the Federal Government might properly pay for the construction of a breakwater at the end of the passage. Washington was still in a friendly mood and sent General Foster to look the situation over. He, like all previous engineers, found nothing to prevent the construction of a canal, but unlike the rest, he recommended a free-water passage rather than one that depended on locks. He also declared that 'its military value in time of war equaled its commercial value in time of peace,' but after seven years in irons, the corporation had apparently done nothing. The Legislature ordered an investigation of their activities or inactivities; the investigators reported that it was doubtful whether that company would ever construct a canal, but they seized the opportunity to add, with more truthfulness than originality, that a canal would be a splendid thing for New England! The State House gave the Cape Cod Canal Company three years more to get started. Clemens Herschel, a distinguished civil engineer, wrote a somewhat rhetorical pamphlet in behalf of the company in 1878, entitled 'The Cape Cod Ship Canal,' but this seems to have been the extent of the organization's accomplishments.

Since nothing was done, a new charter was given in 1880 to Henry M. Whitney and associates under the name of The Cape Cod Ship Canal Company. Whitney's engineer made a number of borings along the route and reported great quantities of quicksand. This so alarmed the corporation that they announced that the work would cost nearer seven million than four million dollars, which was all their charter authorized, and so stepped out of the running. Before they withdrew, however, they made a futile, and as it turned out a disastrous, move toward excavation by importing several hundred Italians from New York and setting them to work with shovels and wheel-barrows. The Cape was not so used to foreigners in the eighties as it has since become. The arrival of even one or two strangers was then an event; the arrival of five hundred was an earth-quake. Before long trouble arose between them and the towns-people. It has been alleged that the Italians were not paid regularly and that they took it out on the town by breaking into shops and terrorizing the inhabitants. Politicians called the disturbance 'the Neapolitan revolt' and declared that 'Sand-wich was for a week under arms;... life and property were ex-posed to the hungry mob, and the entire community terrified at the presence of an army of houseless, starving, unpaid rampant foreigners.... The State came to her protection and assisted in keeping the peace.' Senator McCall refers more mildly to the incident, yet speaks of the 'depredations committed by these Italians.' It was at least a very unfortunate incident and shows clearly enough the incompetence of the Whitney Company's management.

A new company filled the breach and was incorporated in 1883 under the same name as Whitney's — The Cape Cod Ship Canal Company. The chief mover in this company was William Seward, Jr., and another member of it was Samuel Fessenden, of Sandwich. They contracted with Frederick A. Lockwood, head of a construction company in East Boston, to do the work, and from this time on the organization was generally known as the Lockwood Company, for the charter parties remained silently in the background, leaving the whole arena to Lockwood.

They were very soon in trouble. The exact nature of their difficulties does not appear, but the introduction to a reprint of Herschel's pamphlet, which they got out in 1884, states that: 'The same delightful selfishness which has in the past en-deavored to maintain the undue tax and impost it has so far collected from the public, is again opposing the work which has been begun, and is seeking to throttle it, in the selfish fear that its foothold for such undue tax and impost might suffer a slight deterioration.' The railroad had given Whitney trouble in the Legislature, and was perhaps still clogging the wheels of pro-gress for the new company. But whatever the vague language quoted above may refer to, the Lockwood Company met with two very definite obstacles in the first year of its existence. One was a suit by a certain Mr. Fox, of Montreal, alleging that he had had a contract before Lockwood. The other was a suit for land damages brought by one Briggs, who owned some land along the line of the canal and was dissatisfied with the price that Lockwood had condemned it for. All this litigation delayed the work, and the company had to apply for an extension of their charter (the original terms had stipulated that the work should be finished in four years). At the same session of the Legislature, two other persons, Gerard C. Tobey, of Wareham, and Alfred D. Fox, of Montreal, also applied separately for incorporation and authority to dig the canal.

Here was a different state of affairs with a vengeance! Instead of its being impossible to find a company that would tackle the job, as had formerly been the case, the Legislature was now besieged by three rival concerns, all clamoring for the privilege! Beacon Hill became a battle-ground, resounding to the forensic endeavors in behalf of this petitioner or that. Fox, the Montreal applicant, though his claim to a contract antedating Lockwood's had been denied by the Court, was now applying to the Legislature for authority to incorporate separately. The fact that he was a Canadian and relied at least in part on Canadian capital told heavily against him in Boston and is one reason why his application failed. Tobey, the Wareham applicant, was certainly a more logical candidate for the job. He was familiar with the upper Cape and was a man of wide business experience and varied interests. If he and his associates had been given corporate powers on this occasion, they would probably have done at least as well as Lockwood; but because Lockwood was first in the field, already had a charter, and was seeking only an extension of the stipulated time — a courtesy which the Legislature had frequently shown on other occasions — he came off victorious in the triangular bout.

It must be confessed, too, that though he did not accomplish great things, yet he did more than any of his predecessors. At his works in East Boston, he built a dredge specially designed to dig the canal. It arrived off the Sandwich Beach in the early spring of 1884, was floated through a cut in the beach, and began to eat its way through the Scusset marshes while the whole town cheered. This dredge, more than anything else, established Lockwood firmly in favor with the citizens of Sandwich, but it achieved nothing remarkable. By spasmodic activity it dug a deep ditch for a mile into the marsh. Then it stopped for good; there was not money enough to keep its fires stoked, and the dredge was sold where it stood, was quickly dismantled, and finally sank into the grave its own bucket chain had dug, the hull remaining a dilapidated landmark for years.

Fox meantime had formed a corporation which he said could get all the money it wanted from Canada. Some estimable men were on its board. Fox left them in Boston and went to Canada to raise the money; but it was not forthcoming. The board had made pledges which they wished to redeem; by degrees it became evident that they never could redeem them if they relied on Fox. They therefore asked Lockwood to join them and tackle the job again. This Lockwood did — apparently regarding his contract with the Seward-Fessenden Company as dead. Seward instantly bombarded Boston bankers with circulars alleging that his company was the only legal and authorized one, and warning them to beware of Lockwood. Judgment of the rights and wrongs of the question must be sought elsewhere than in the pages of the present volume, for it is quite beyond the author's powers to decide them. If ever a strip of land was a parade-ground for surveyors first and a battle-ground for legislative vituperation afterwards, it was the route of the Cape Cod Canal. One thing, however, is clear; Lockwood's chances of actually completing the job vanished when his dredge was sold. His activities from then on were those of a minor capitalist, a solicitor and a lobbyist, rather than an engineer. If he had lived longer, perhaps he would have succeeded. But his health failed, and he died without digging another cubic yard of sand on the Cape. His backers (among them Colonel Livermore, Quincy A. Shaw, John M. Forbes, and Henry L. Higginson) turned their energies into other channels. So ended the long and complicated struggle among the three applicants, Fox, Tobey, and Lockwood. Though Lockwood was for most of the time on the top of the heap, yet he failed after all to accomplish what had become the dominant desire of his life.

Two other companies were organized between 1892 and 1898 — the Massachusetts Maritime Canal Company and the Old Colony and Interior Canal Company — but neither of them came anywhere near joining the waters of the two Bays.

In 1898, in fact, the citizens of the Cape were commenting with amused cynicism on the amount of activity and oratory expended in their behalf on the floor of the State House. The Barnstable 'Patriot' voiced the sentiment of the majority when its editor wrote, 'No less than seven projects for a Cape Cod Canal are to come before the legislature this year. Meanwhile, despite all threats, the Cape hangs on the mainland with the grim determination characteristic of its people.'

The beginning of the end came on June 1, 1899, when the Legislature granted a charter to the Boston, Cape Cod and New York Canal Company. The incorporators were William Flannagan, De Witt Flannagan, and other New-Yorkers. They bought the land along the proposed route from Colonel Livermore and spent several years in perfecting their arrangements, while their engineer, Charles M. Thompson, of the old Lockwood Company, camped on the ground that he already knew so well. They had moderate success in arousing the interest of capitalists, but never until they applied to Mr. August Belmont did they actually see their way clear to constructing the canal. It was in 1906 that De Witt Flannagan first brought the project to Mr. Belmont's attention. Belmont became so much interested that he consulted a group of the most eminent men in the fields of engineering, transportation, and maritime affairs. Mr. Belmont then spread all their figures before Mr. Barclay Parsons, one of the greatest engineers of his day and a member of the Panama Canal Commission, and requested him to go over the whole problem. Mr. Parsons did so and then went to Sandwich, where he met Mr. Thompson, who exhibited some samples that had been taken from borings along the route under the Livermore régime. The samples contained quicksand, and Parsons was dubious. But Thompson explained that all the borings had been made in the lowest land along the line — the very central axis of the future waterway — and that naturally all the quicksand in the valley had accumulated during the ages along that line. This proved to be the case; no other deposits of quicksand were found; Parsons reported favorably to Belmont, and the work began.

Mr. Belmont's reasons for embarking on the enterprise, in which so many had failed, were numerous. Chief among them was the consideration that if New England was to continue as a manufacturing center, it was imperative for her to import raw material cheaply. Every vessel wrecked involved not only loss of life and property, but in many cases had a far-reaching effect on industry by diminishing the supply of raw material for New England looms. Any means that would help to keep the supply of coal and cotton large and regular deserved the support of all who were interested in New England's prosperity. This state of affairs turned the Canal's old foe, the Railroad, into a friend, for its prosperity depended on the prosperity of New England.

Another element which had great weight with Mr. Belmont was the change which had taken place in the method of coast-wise transportation. Coasting schooners, which had carried nearly all the freight that did not go by rail, were being crowded out by barges in tow. The great advantage of these lay in their regularity (provided the weather was good), and in the enormous amount of material they could transport in a single trip. Their disadvantage was that in rough water they were helpless. The Canal would, therefore, be a blessing to them, and might rely on doing a far bigger business than it would have done if the coasting schooner had remained supreme. Furthermore, the Canal was not an isolated and independent waterway, but was to be the northernmost link in a contemplated 'chain of improved inland waters from Panama to Massachusetts.' Here were reasons enough for Mr. Belmont. Capital presented no difficulties to him. From now on the work was in the hands of contractors and engineers.

The first block of granite for the breakwater was dropped on June 19, 1909; the first trickle of water flowed through a gap that the dredges made in the last dam, on April 21, 1914; and on July 4, Mr. Belmont, with his son and Mr. and Mrs. Parsons, rowed the first craft through the finished breach. The Canal was officially opened on July 29, when eight vessels went through. Its channel is 25 feet deep, 250 feet wide at water level, and 100 feet wide on the bottom; the approaching channels are wider, measuring 250 feet. Exclusive of these approaches, the Canal is 8 miles long. Since its completion, the Canal has been used increasingly. From moderate beginnings, its business by 1920 had reached a gratifying figure: in that year 120,000 passengers and 2,000,000 tons of cargo passed through it on 8140 vessels.

Almost as soon as it was announced that Mr. Belmont was to finance the work, the report went round that the company intended to sell it to the Government. Whether or not this was the case is a question of no importance. The canal was built entirely by private capital, and its financiers got back what money they could on their investment during the fourteen years that it continued under their management. Finally, Western oratory to the contrary notwithstanding, Congress voted to buy it for $11,500,000. The transaction was completed during the winter of 1927–28, and the Government officially took charge of the Canal on April 1. The Cape as a whole favored the change, though it cost the towns of Sandwich and Bourne the taxes on some $1,000,000 worth of real estate.

Such at present is the status of this new waterway — new in reality, old in the dreams of men. What the future has in store for it is a question on which wise men prefer to hold their peace. One reads of plans maturing in the Federal incubator, to spend $10,000,000 of the Nation's money to make the Canal wider and deeper. If events march as slowly in the future as they have in the past, the present generation's grandchildren will see no change in the Canal. But the ways of governments are past finding out. It would hardly be a surprise to the older and shock-proof citizens of Sagamore and Bourne if they awoke some morning to the tune of steam shovels and dredges; if they saw an army of laborers swarming about the Canal, until they had made it big enough for the Leviathan herself to sail through. In the mean time it has its past which nothing can change; Bradford's dream, Sewall's polite interest, George Washington's letter, and Machin and young James Winthrop at the head of a column of surveyors and capitalists that stretches clear to Boston. At the end of the pageant come Belmont and Parsons, each with a crown of laurel and a victor's smile.

EPILOGUE

To-day the tide of old affairs has ebbed from the Cape shores and left them high and dry. Not even sentiment can blow the breath of life into the sails of the vanished fishing fleet nor call back the dead glory of the clippers. No analysis of the sandy soil — however cheering — can lure the young Cape-Codder back to the abandoned farms. Time will not turn backward in its flight, nor can imagination swell the meager gleanings of boat fishermen or the barrels of whiting in the freezers to the bulk of the full fares of cod and mackerel that two hundred schooners piled on the wharves of Wellfleet and Provincetown in the forties. Land and Sea have failed the Cape-Codder; and the best of the rising generation have moved away.

But what of the others — those whose years are ripe enough to recall the salt works and the packets? Has the passing of the old and busy days left them bitter and resentful, or, what is just as bad, are they content to live on the flimsy basis of a prosperous past? They have been saved from both fates by a whimsical sense of humor, half revealed, yet ever present, which guides their sayings and doings through the lean years. Where did they get it? asks the psychologist. Certainly not from the stern brethren of Plymouth nor from the bitter malcontents who left England after the Acts of Conformity. It did not come to them unbidden from their early struggles with a sandy soil. Rather it followed as the result of a true perspective — that great prerequisite for a humorous point of view — and this perspective they learned from seagoing fathers and grandfathers who had picked it up in the far corners of the world: from Shanghai bartenders and San Francisco crimps; from the sultry banks of the Ganges and from matching wits with British captains in the Master Mariners' Club at Calcutta; they pulled perspective along with codfish from the rugged waters of the Grand Banks and pursued it from Hatteras to Nova Scotia with the mackerel. And though their sons and grandsons inherited no ships and sailed on no far voyages, yet they caught the perspective that enables them to-day to distinguish great matters from small, and so to look at life with a humorous slant. The picture of the Ringleader, or the Belle Creole, or the Leading Wind, which hangs over the stove in the sitting-room, is the symbol of this saving and instinctive point of view.

So the Cape-Codder feels no qualms about nailing up roadside apple stands for the automobilists, or about filling his spare rooms with transients for the night. Some have built shore-dinner restaurants or converted the old barn into an antique shop for the summer visitors. Others have set up a garage or a filling station. If whales no longer visit their shores, rich city folk do, and with easy adaptability, Cape men and women take the goods the gods provide them. What, they argue, is the use of a proud history if it does not make them independent? Why claim descent from the Pilgrims if they cannot serve tables without losing their pride? And the twinkle in their eyes, which Grandfather Howes brought from the ends of the world and handed down to them with the teakwood blanket-chest — that twinkle appears for a moment as they put the tourists' money in the till, and they chuckle quietly at the ways of the world.

POST-EPILOGUE, 1930 – 1968
by John Hay

LIVE WITH ME

THIS SECTION must by its very nature serve as an extension of the Epilogue. As written in *Cape Cod*, the history of that sea-lapped land between 1620 and 1930 is all of a piece, a marvelous story of Indians and settlers, revolution and religion, storms and wrecks, fishing and voyages. What has happened since 1930 would probably have more to do with Cape Cod's relation to the world at large and the possible world of the future than to any self-contained character of its own. On page 233 is the statement that "Most wise men on the Cape knew the way to China by sea better than they did the way to Boston by land." That refers to the great merchant marine days of the nineteenth century, but as recently as the end of the Second World War stories were current about Cape-Codders who had not only never been to Boston but had rarely crossed the Cape from one shore to the other. The Cape was not quickly reached from the outside until fairly recently, except by the lost and, to some, lamented Old Colony Railroad. Even in the 1920's the trip by car from Boston might take up most of a day, especially if you had a flat tire or a break-down along the way and stopped for a leisurely picnic lunch in a roadside field.

Thirty years ago, in spite of a great many substantial summer houses and cottages along the shore, the Cape was still a land with the look of a settled rural culture, holding memories of the days when local boys were lost at sea and the great runs of mackerel came in, and Provincetown smelled of fish. Old seamen whittled model boats on the beach to the delight of summer visitors, or stood by their dories as if they were made of the same grain, steeped in the same salt air.

Some of the gray and white cottages still used kerosene lamps, and during winter evenings their inhabitants rocked away and roasted not far from the kitchen stove. Clam chowder, clam cakes, boiled potatoes and fish were part of the staple fare, since the supermarket was still years ahead and the shore abounded with its natural produce. All roads — those narrow ones leading into the woodlots, sandy, flecked with pitch pine needles, or fallen leaves from the much cut-over and abused oaks — even the main roads could still be called local in a country sense. Cape Cod was a land where towns were zealous on behalf of their own identities, and even capable of being furious about them. The term "Cape-Codder" implied a close, cantankerous individualism defended to the last. Town meeting was a time when it did no good for a man to speak up about town affairs merely because he had lived on the Cape for thirty years or owned land there and paid taxes. He had to be born a native son or run the risk of being dismissed as a foreigner.

Anyone living on the Cape during the past momentous twenty-five or thirty years must have noticed that many of the "old-timers" have disappeared. These were the men who had retired from a life at sea, who ran the village store, made the best homemade ice cream on the Cape, sold homemade bread or pie, or cut your hair for twenty-five cents. These were the men who told you stories about rum-running days in the twenties, or timeless tales about house burnings, country dances and chicken stealing. They have not disappeared altogether, but their ranks are much diminished, and with them has gone, or has nearly gone, the native accent, the local phrase, the attachment of colorful, unique verbal images to country objects, neighborly human situations.

Of course, this is a change which is characteristic of many parts of the United States. The local dialect that developed within various fairly definite and circumscribed regions has been not so much altered perhaps, as shunted aside by the invasion of larger populations. And America, although it can still be divided into linguistic regions, now communicates in a modern continental way. Through mass media we span great distances in seconds, and the accents we hear are as likely to be TV-All-American as mountain or seashore style. Although they still exist in strength in many areas, local dialects can no longer be as self-nourished as they were when relatively isolated and protected, and their rootedness in time and place may gradually be overcome. An identifiable, regional accent may have much wider circumferences than it used to. In any case, the twentieth-century storms have not bypassed Cape Cod although it is certainly quieter after Labor Day, and their winds are blowing stronger.

Subsistence farming, and also fishing, both of which have helped nourish the folkways and speech of many a region and kept up a direct relationship between a people and the land they live in, began to wane a long time ago. The Cape's fishing industry developed serious trouble after the Civil War and by the early part of this century it had declined to a fairly low importance. Men, women and children may still have chased their stray cows through the scrub some forty or fifty years ago and had some fairly prosperous truck gardens, but farms, in a country which had limited agriculture anyway, counted for even less than they used to. In order to help both sectors of the economy, there was some agitation, beginning about 1922, for a State Pier with facilities which would enable Cape farmers to market their produce more readily. It was to be built in a strategic place in Buzzards Bay, on hand to meet the Boston boat when it came by every evening at nine. Unfortunately, by the time the Pier was finally completed in 1935, there were not enough farmers and fishermen in the market to make it worthwhile. The location of the State Pier and such of its facilities as were usable are now in the possession of the Maritime Academy.

The cranberry industry still holds its own, but farms have been reduced to a pitiful few and most of the old barns are gone, or converted and unrecognizable as such. The Cape's fishing industry is diversified and still active, but it is not an industry on which the whole economy can depend for money and jobs. Tourism is the mainstay of the region, as well as new developments to attract retired people, commuters, and a growing number of men and women employed in service industries. Also, a Cape Cod which is only an hour and a quarter from Boston by road, or five hours from New York, now listens harder to the wants and values of urban societies whose people were never born there and do not necessarily expect their children to be.

The old historical peninsula, with its woodlots, its sandy roads and semi-isolation, is no more. During the vacation

season, which is now attracting tourists in early spring and fall
as well as summer, the Cape Cod Canal Bridge sometimes
serves as a bottleneck for traffic that comes from eastern
Canada to as far south as New Jersey, and even farther.
Therefore, better access is the cry. The narrow roads get
straightened out and covered with asphalt. There is talk
about a new crossing at the Canal to relieve congestion. The
Mid-Cape Highway, built after World War II and recently
double-barreled to five miles beyond the rotary at Barnstable,
does not seem to be entirely adequate to take the massing
thousands onward. Hyannis, despite facilities at Provincetown, is the principal air terminal. Will the sea itself have to
be looked to for new ways of reaching this seasonally burdened
land?*

The resident population of the Cape doubled between 1940
and 1965, from 37,000 to 74,000. During the decade between
1950 and 1960 the increase, from 47,000, gave the area a
growth rate which was three times that of the state as a whole.
(It might be said, by way of interpretation, that GI's returning
from World War II gave Barnstable County the distinction of
having the highest fertility rate in the Commonwealth.) The
number of summer visitors, many of whom stay for only a day
or two, has gone up to what must be nearly astronomical
heights compared with what it used to be. The total is hard
to calculate, but whether you arrive at 250,000 or 400,000 for
a weekend summer day you have not come on numbers alone
but on a sizable condition and a change.

Some of the people who came to Cape Cod to live during the
postwar years were interested primarily in living in the country; others came simply to escape from pressures of the city,

* One very original landing from the sea in recent years was made by a gaily painted
reproduction of the *Mayflower*, which was brought in tow around Race Point into
Provincetown Harbor on June 13, 1957. This Anglo-American goodwill ship, with
Allan Villiers as the skipper, had set out from England the previous April, and on the
whole may not have met with the kind of roaring reception it could have hoped for on
going back to the place where its predecessor put in in 1620. The town of Truro refused to appropriate $500 for advanced publicity on the apparent grounds that the
voyage itself was just a publicity stunt. On the one hand, many people grumbled at a
long delayed and inexact arrival date which would not even let the local souvenir
salesmen and hot dog vendors get ready in time. But for many others it was a rare
and exciting thing to see the high-pooped ship and the strange Elizabethan masts
come around the sandy point, spanning three hundred years and more.

but most depended on an expanding job market, and in fact their presence and needs helped create it. The increased size of local military establishments, such as Camp Edwards and Otis Air Force Base, made, and has continued to make, demands on local service, and helped to aid and abet the growing population.

This general growth had a marked effect on the character of the towns in which it took place. Yarmouth and Hyannis, for example, within reasonable distance of Otis Air Force Base (which provided a goodly number of shoppers and their relatives, and one fifth of the Cape's annual employment), began to turn into something resembling the outskirts of a city rather than country towns. The growth of these and other built-up areas like Falmouth and Bourne was considerably faster than it was in places which were not so thickly settled originally, and were farther from the mainland. Villages like Barnstable, Yarmouthport, Dennis and Brewster retained some of their old settled security, their shade trees and their ample houses, both because property owners wanted it that way and because they were a little further removed from the pressures of growth. Some towns of the Lower Cape — from Orleans up to the tip at Provincetown — which were in the same category, now face the problems of traffic engendered by the new National Seashore and of commercial growth in the areas along its boundaries.

New jobs were not in manufacturing for the most part. For reasons of distance, an economic base which was primarily seasonal, and a lack of skilled workers to draw on, manufacturers were not attracted to the Cape. But retail trade establishments rose from a business value of $20,479,000 in 1940 to $165,755,000 in 1963. The number of hotels and resorts doubled in number during the same period. The number of what the chamber of commerce calls "dwelling units" almost tripled.

In the off-season, Cape Cod is not quite the shuttered place it used to be. The new people, in real estate, banks, shops, insurance, building, etc., are often as busy as those in other parts of the state. On the other hand, the economy definitely goes into lower gear after the summer visitors have left, and seasonal unemployment becomes relatively severe in some towns. Truro and Provincetown are known to have the worst employment rate in New England. In January of 1964 the unemployment figure for Bourne and Wareham reached the unusually high level of 22 percent, after 7 percent in the month of July. The Cape is still a part-time economy in terms of national standards, which has made it a good place to retire or escape to during the past thirty years, away from urban conflict and noise, but this also makes for instability in jobs and the expectation of jobs.

That the Cape suffers from the problems of temporary employment is partly reflected in the median family income for the region, below that of Massachusetts as a whole. Nineteen percent have an income below $2500 a year, and in spite of the fact that this figure includes some retired people without families to support, it represents continued, basic poverty, not yet lifted up by the new populations and their needs.

Schools, of course, have had to keep pace with the fastest growing county in the Commonwealth of Massachusetts. Between 1950 and 1964, for example, the elementary school enrollment for the town of Barnstable rose from 1,140 to 1,977, and that of Falmouth from 1,128 to 2,963. Even towns less subject to a sudden increase in population showed a general rise in enrollments which has not stopped yet, with very few exceptions.

As a result of an exploding college-age population, and with a growing number of high school students wanting a college education but lacking a local institution within easy commuting distance, the Cape Cod Community College was started in 1961, using renovated buildings in Hyannis. It is part of a state system of two-year colleges, each of which has an Advisory Board composed of local citizens. Under President E. Carleton Nickerson and a strong faculty with an average age of 46, the college offers its students a variety of courses, not only in the liberal arts but also in such fields as teaching and nursing, both of which present professional opportunities in the Cape area, and in the business and secretarial fields. In recent years some 70 percent of the community college graduates have been accepted as junior-year students by major colleges. To meet a great expanse in enrollments and demands the College is constructing new buildings on a 116-acre location in Barnstable, between the Mid-Cape Highway and Route 6A. These facilities are to accommodate 1500 day students.

Growth then, with all its problems, is making a new Cape Cod and threatening the old one; it acts like waves with the incoming tide, receding, then moving on again, stopped here and there by obstacles, but on the whole taking its own course, as water will. Cape Cod is in some degree helpless, without a strong economic base, almost totally dependent on its qualifications as a resort area, subject to many unpredictable forces in this overpopulated and changing world. The new Cape also has to meet its school demands, its commercial and non-commercial development, the summer traffic, and a great many other problems, without many resources from the past it leaves behind. Its people are in a sense part of a world they never made.

In 1920, when the resident population was 27,000, a large proportion of it was native-born. Now, with qualifications as to how you define your terms, the new citizen may have children who were born on the Cape but is himself more likely to have come in since the war than to have been born there. It is up to the new citizens, as much as to the old-timers, to decide how much they value Cape Cod, and for what. Physically, the new Cape may still be allied to the old, but it is no longer the country refuge it used to be. Its visitors are expected to call the economic tune, and they present the question of the future. Who are they, and how many, and how are they to be met?

At one time, college boys used to come up a country road trying to sell you subscriptions; now the stranger who appears outside may want to buy your house and land. There is not a foot of ground on Cape Cod which is not being eyed by someone. Not long ago, a man saw a visitor walking resolutely around his house and grounds as if sizing them up, but showing no signs of coming to the door. He walked out and said, "What can I do for you?"

The visitor replied: "How much do you want for this place?"

Our homeowner, whose family had lived on the Cape for at least a hundred years, said, "It's not for sale."

The incredulous visitor said, "Why not?"

Words followed.

There are many others, of course, who see the Cape not so much in terms of an old identity which they share — in tart and simple human communities, through sandy roads by ponds innumerable, with the blue band of the sea in the background — but just as another place to land on. Cape Cod still has the unconquered Atlantic investing it but it has lost some of its particularity, its secret identities; the human world is, in a sense, trying it on for size, and therefore some barriers are down, an old self-protectiveness gone. Like many others, this is a region now closer to the urban world, more vulnerable to its pressures, less resistant to its denatured values. It is subject to a proliferation of wants which men may justify under the heading of "progress," a term which has had good lodging in American democracy, but may now mean whatever opportunism wants it to mean.

The land itself is subject to a slaughter, a quick removal, that was never before possible. Old fields that seemed indefinitely based, scraggy but deep woodlands that nurtured the box turtle, the hermit thrush and the owl, ponds that held precious, fascinating elements of life, from the perch and the water snake to the shimmering blue damselfly, can go in a day. Unguided and unchecked, the arrogant bulldozers, pushing and snorting, grunting and whining, can strip the earth to a fare-thee-well. An old ground loses not only its age but all the life attendant on it. Not a blade of grass, not a shrub, not a tree remains. An ancient cellar hole, no longer crowded by lilacs and falling inward like a "dent in dough," in Robert Frost's phrase, is not wrecked; it disappears, it is turned into a nothing. A hundred-year-old mulberry tree, perhaps brought in and planted by a sailor returned from a voyage to the Far East, hangs over a pit and then is shoved away across a long dead plain of yellow, denuded earth. So all is made ready for the new subdivision; but when the owners move in to their new, standard, Cape Cod cottages, row on row, how will they know where they are? Even the ghosts have been dispossessed.

But behind the pressure to take the easy and cynical way, the pressure for tourist traps, quick development, and universal asphalt, is another, greater one, that of a universal growth in population. As the world moves toward 4 billion people and the United States toward 300,000,000, those country areas which are closest to the spreading cities, or what may better be called suburbs, are invaded first, and the more remote ones later on. Cape Cod is not escaping, any more than the human race, but in the proportion that this land can be leveled so it needs an understanding and a defense, on home ground. It has become almost impossible for a landscape to defend *itself*.

Except as it strikes back at man for his abuse of it, nature's voice is not as compelling as the human one and may even be fainter than it was when Henry James wrote these words in *The American Scene:*

> The touching appeal of nature, as I have called it therefore, the "Do something kind for me," is not so much a "Live upon me and thrive by me" as a "Live *with* me, somehow, and let us make out together what we may do for each other — something that is not merely estimable in more or less greasy greenbacks. See how "sympathetic I am," the still voice seemed everywhere to proceed, "and how I am therefore better than my fate; see how I lend myself to poetry and sociability — positively to aesthetic use: give me that consolation."

The degree to which a natural region now keeps what is estimable about it depends on a quality of recognition which may have to be brought in from elsewhere; at least it needs outside help. The living *with* now takes a special kind of encouragement, no less because it has joined the context of violent uncertainty and change, a tension of living, which characterizes the whole world.

Perhaps partly because a resident of the Cape was senator from Massachusetts and then President of the United States, a Cape Cod National Seashore was established by Congress in 1961 and dedicated in 1966. A local newspaper, *The Cape Codder*, broke a story in November of 1956 about a preliminary federal report on proposed acquisition of Cape Cod's Great Beach area, with some 12,000 to 16,000 acres, as a major public seashore on the Atlantic coast. Local reaction was immediate and much of it unfavorable, coming from selectmen who feared their towns would lose tax revenues, residents who felt their homes and lands would be taken away from them, and builders and real estate interests for obvious and, in their terms, justified reasons. After several years of this opposition and a number of public hearings during which heated local opinion was allowed its voice — and it should be said that the Park had its strong supporters on the Cape as well — an addition was made to the law which assured its passage. A new concept for such legislation, originating in the offices of Senators Kennedy and Saltonstall, made it possible for owners within the Seashore's boundaries to keep, bequeath to their heirs, or sell property held prior to September of 1958.

Whatever direction park management may take in the future, in favor of strict conservation of natural resources or "recreation," with all the numbers and money and commercial pressure behind that term, some 27,000 acres, twice the number originally envisaged, were saved from the danger of random obliteration. Also, the Lower Cape towns contiguous with the National Seashore, subjected to increasing pressure of population and development, have necessarily become more aware of the need to protect what they have left. Growth, as the Cape has discovered since World War II, is not something which will take care of itself and, in fact, is very much less than desirable if left alone. "Planning" was once fought like the plague at every town meeting in which it was brought up. Even when zoning and planning regulations were finally adopted they were often too timidly devised and enforced to have much effect on indiscriminate growth; but more and more towns are feeling the need to adopt master plans and adequate, up-dated regulations to control those who would be over-predatory on the land. It is true, of course, that planning is still no panacea and that its effectiveness will depend on how forcefully local interests push it and what its contents are. A master plan which has Brockton in mind instead of Brewster or Eastham may be worse than none at all.

It is not easy for a land which is not altogether in control of its present destiny (and that is probably an understatement) to plan for its future. But at least it can be said that more and more people are becoming aware that saturation points can be reached in everything. They are also aware that the relatively small area which comprises Cape Cod is especially vulnerable to unchecked abuse and that its towns and villages, no longer as autonomous as they used to be, can affect each other's future for good or ill. In any case, there are now hideous examples as well as good ones on Cape Cod, which may make the lines of defense somewhat clearer to the mind and eye.

Left to devour what it wants to, the greed for "developable" land can not only burden Cape Cod towns beyond their capacity, but it can also make the good land unrecognizable and certainly less appealing to the all-important visitor. The question also arises as to what the construction industry will do when there is no land left to build on. These thoughts are not entirely lost on the builders. Some of them, at least, have begun to defend the need for natural areas and are against tearing up the waterways, dredging and filling the marshlands, and building overcrowded, low-standard subdivisions. Other defenders have appeared in increasing numbers on town conservation commissions, a conservation association or foundation, women's clubs, a natural history museum, outspoken local newspapers, among summer visitors who love the open, salty, windy feel of the place, among schoolteachers, and the retired, and all those resident Cape-Codders who defend their marshes or their ponds by virtue of long acquaintance. These are some of the people who value living in a natural environment and can encourage others to do so.

"Conservation," as one man put it, "has had a hard sell on the Cape." While salt marshes may be successfully defended, the ponds, swamps and woodlands go. With state aid, some towns have bought large areas of land to be set aside in the public interest; others have lost far more than can be retrieved, but the effort continues, and it is an effort, essentially, to try and reconcile the human world and the natural one, as well as the steady past and the uncertain present. The living *with* has to include all kinds of bedfellows.

The human summer roars on Cape Cod. The highways are crowded. The internal combustion engine bears all comers on and the cars nose through the old, amazingly narrow streets of Provincetown, jammed together like so many cattle in a stockyard pen. It is a funnel for the urban world, if not urbanity, and the shops sell wood and leather, gold and glass, Indian silk, models of the Taj Mahal, as well as London bobby cloaks, prison shirts, and sometimes helmets from old wars, like the small pinched basins the French poilus wore during the First World War, hard and terrible mementos in the midst of unique or hopefully outrageous trappings for the young. Inside a street-level room with a sign outside saying INDECENT MOVIES, there is a boy with a nest of long hair who is leaning over his guitar, and farther down the street there is a severe white wall with some antique glass in the window and a sign that says THIS IS NOT A SHOP. Beyond the town, beyond the psychedelic signs and the cash registers and the cars, the great Atlantic yawns and fishing boats bob in the choppy gray waters along their plain, workmanlike horizon.

Admiral Donald B. MacMillan of Provincetown, the famous Arctic traveler who stands straight at ninety-two and pronounces the word schooner with a short *o*, appears on a television program in his honor and is asked about the disaffected young of today. He says that they lack "experience," and by that you suppose he means the fruits of personal decision, an Arctic or sub-Arctic testing, though the young tribe, in an age less receptive than his own to the self-made, decisive man, might say that the only weapon it has is the experience of being young.

Then fall comes and the summer shops close up, traffic dwindles, and Cape Cod hears its winds, of hurricane force or gentler strength, and undeniable echos of the past seem to sound in the trees. The shore birds gather on the sandy flats, and the terns start to leave for the south. The sandy cliffs on the outer beach prepare for late fall and winter storms to cut them down, the offshore currents roam, the silverside minnows and killifish crowd inshore, flocks of migrating grackles travel through the oaks and chickadees bound through the pitch pines. The salt marsh grasses ripple and sway behind the beaches and the inscrutable sea. Now men have something near them which is more than the development of Cape Cod with a big D, more than a land which is only thought of as negotiable property. They are faced by seasonal change, on their flesh and in the sound of the air. They are faced by an openness at the water's edge, and also by a characteristic outline — the tangible sight of twisted pines, low, cut-over oaks, beach grass and sand, a place which receives the tides of natural, universal change, and the migrants, and those who make their living there, the electrician, or the blue jay. They are faced by an integrity called Cape Cod which is theirs to ignore or in some degree to follow as well as to guide.

NOTES

CHAPTER I

As is explained in the Notes to Chapter II, if such a headland as Webb's Island ever existed, it had vanished before 1606. In fact, however, it must have disappeared centuries earlier. It is a geographical monstrosity for two points to exist close together and at right angles to each other on a coast like Chatham's. The forces that create one would demolish the other. The alleged Webb's Island Point was nearly at right angles to Monomoy Point, and close to it. The two, therefore, could never have been in existence at the same time; Webb's Island Point must have been demolished before Monomoy was made. Monomoy was there in 1606; we can only guess how old it was then; perhaps a thousand years. But its age, whatever it was, must be subtracted from 1606 in order to get back to the date when Webb's Island Point existed.

We are now confronted by the question whether or not, though the rest of this headland vanished at a very remote period, the extreme easterly end of it, Webb's Island, was still above water in colonial times. An article in the 'Massachusetts Magazine' (III, 1791, page 151) says that such an island existed about 1700. This statement is said to be corroborated in Morse's 'Universal Geography,' I, 357, ed. 1793 (Amos Otis, 'Discovery of an Ancient Ship,' page 10, note). To offset this testimony we have only the negative evidence that Champlain failed to mention such an island or to show it in his map. This oversight, however, is not very significant. The chances are, then, that Webb's Island was visible when the first settlers arrived in Chatham, though there had been blue water between it and the mainland for centuries.

CHAPTER II

Few authorities doubt that Gosnold's Tucker's Terror and Point Care were parts of a point of land that formerly projected from the Eastham shore. Captain John Smith, though he never saw this point, had been told of its existence by the Indians, and named it Île Nauset. What Gosnold called Tucker's Terror was the surf on the north side of this point, and Point Care was its eastern extremity.

As to identification of Point Gilbert, authorities differ. It has been argued that this point was the end of another peninsula about nine miles long, something like Île Nauset, that is said to have stretched easterly from Chatham and terminated in Webb's Island. It is possible that such a peninsula existed at a very remote period, but certainly it had vanished before 1604, when Gosnold arrived, for no trace of it appears on the excellent map of the Chatham region that Champlain made in 1606 (Champlain's 'Voyages,' II, opposite page 122), only two years later, and not even the most careless cartographer could have missed such an important feature. The exponents of the Webb's Island theory for Point Gilbert cannot have seen this map, for they go on to say that Monomoy Point had not been formed in Gosnold's time. Champlain, however, shows it on his map substantially as it is to-day. These considerations eliminate Webb's Island and its peninsula as a possible identification for Point Gilbert.

There remains Monomoy, which answers all the requirements save one. Archer, who accompanied Gosnold and wrote an account of the voyage, estimated the distance from Point Care to Point Gilbert as six miles. If he meant from headland to headland, this is too short. But none of the distances recorded by early navigators are to be trusted. Furthermore, it should be remembered that breakers do not confine their attentions to the *end* of Monomoy Beach; they break indiscriminately along its whole length; and breakers were what occupied Gosnold's mind in connection with Point Gilbert. Six miles is near enough for a guess at the distance between Île Nauset and the nearest part of Monomoy Beach — which being white with breakers, like the rest of its length, was from Gosnold's point of view as much a part of Point Gilbert as the southern end of it was. The actual distance is about eight miles.

Some authorities, disturbed by another discrepancy in distance, push the whole scene of Gosnold's activities farther west and make Tucker's Terror and Point Care, Monomoy instead of Île Nauset, and contend that Point Gilbert was the southeastern corner of Great Island, off Hyannis Harbor, now called Point Gammon. One statement supports this theory; Archer says that the distance from Cape Cod to Point Care was twelve leagues; and that is about the right distance from the outer Beach at Provincetown to Monomoy. But, as has been suggested, we must be very cautious in accepting any mileage mentioned by early mariners. It is well known that distances are deceptive when men are navigating unfamiliar waters and are constantly watching for something ahead. Even so accurate a cartographer as Champlain calls the distance from Nauset to Chatham eighteen miles, whereas in fact it is about six. If Archer's guess of twelve leagues was right, it is the only instance of its kind in the history of early Cape Cod navigation.

Point Gammon, too, is high and rocky, and Archer mentions no rocks until the expedition reached the Elizabeth Islands. Furthermore, he writes as follows of Point Gilbert: 'We sent forth the boat to sound over a Breach (that in our course lay) of another Point, by us called Gilbert's Point.... The nineteenth we passed over the breach of Gilbert's Point in foure or five fadome.' The phrase 'the breach of the Point' means the breakers rolling in over shoals that lay off the point. Such shoals, as every seaman knows, lie off Monomoy, and Gosnold sent his ship's boat to try the depth of the water on them. If it had been blowing, this would have been a suicidal maneuver. But Archer tells us that the day was 'faire.' There are no such shoals off Point Gammon.

CHAPTER III

It is impossible to do much more than guess at these figures because our ancestors, with tantalizing piety, regarded Praying Indians as the only ones worth counting, and they did not begin to count even these until late in the seventeenth century. Various estimates follow:

Date	Authority	No. of Praying Indians	Reference
1674........	Richard Bourne, in letter to Major Gookin	About 500 (old and young)	1 M.H.S. Coll., I, 196 ff.
1685........	Governor Hinckley's Report to Stoughton and Dudley	944 (plus three times as many children)	4 M.H.S. Coll., V, 132 f.
1698........	Rawson and Danforth's Report	1100 (approximately — exclusive of children)	1 M.H.S. Coll., X, 129 ff.

In 1763, the census of Indians of all conditions and ages shows a total of 515. The most useful of these figures are Hinckley's for 1685, and Rawson and Danforth's for 1698, because they agree pretty well. It is safe to say that by 1698 (the date of Rawson and Danforth's Report) nearly all the Cape Indians were at least nominally praying Indians, for John Freeman, in a letter to Hinckley, dated Eastham, 1685, says that most Eastham Indians do 'frequent their meetings on the Sabbath, except aged and decrepit persons and infants and some extravagant fellows that run from one place to another.' (4 M.H.S. Coll., V, 131 ff.) So if the number of praying Indians was about 1000 at this time, the total number, including praying and non-praying, could not have been much greater. War, civilization, rum, and most of all pestilence, had been at work reducing them to this number for the past eighty years or so. I hazard the guess that during these eighty years their number had been decreased by half, and therefore give 2000 as the pre-pestilence population. Only adults are included in these figures. If children are included, this number may be multiplied by four.

CHAPTER IV

1. Frequently warning out of town was a purely nominal performance, issued with no expectation or desire that it would be obeyed. Its purpose in such cases was to protect the town against the possibility of having the warned citizen ever become a town charge. 'Admitted' men, if they fell on evil days, were entitled to support by the town; but those who had been warned out had no such rights, though they might continue to live as respected members of the community. The town fathers were sometimes indiscriminate and warned out all newcomers; sometimes they warned only those whom they judged likely to become paupers. (See J. H. Benton, *Warning Out in New England*, Boston, 1911.)

2. Mashpee is an exception. This district was held as a sort of Reservation for the Indians and was not therefore comparable to the other towns. It had five thousand acres of Common Land as late as 1869. (Hearing before Committee on Indians at Mashpee, 1869, House No. 502, page 13.)

CHAPTER IX

This was the opinion of less austere persons than Her Majesty. A certain William Clap, of Provincetown, in a letter to Governor Dudley in 1705, expressed the same conviction. He wrote in part as follows:

CAPE COD, *July* 13*th*, 1705

SQUIRE DUDLEY.

SIR: — After all due sarvis and Respects to your honnor wishing you all hapynes boath hear and hear after I mack bould to inform your honnor that i have liveed at the Cap this 4 year and I have often every year sien that her maiesty has been very much wronged of har dues by these coutry peple and other whall men as coms hear a whallen every year which tacks up drift whales which was never killed by any man which fish i understand belongest to har majesty and had i had power i could have seased several every year....

Your hombled and unworthy sarvant
WM. CLAP

The Governor gave Clap a commission as water bailiff and a warrant to prize drift whales. Thus do tale-bearers prosper when they carry their tidings to the high places.

CHAPTER XI

There was some justice in this rejoinder, for though throughout its entire colonial history, the Cape had not a single lighthouse to bless itself with, and though for fourteen years after we became independent, sailors had to steer by the stars alone in skirting Monomoy and Peaked Hill Bars, yet once they began, our Congressmen kept on voting money for lighthouses until the coast was adequately illuminated.

The first to be built on the Cape was Highland Light. Its foundations were laid in 1797 on what the Reverend Levi Whitman of Wellfleet called 'a mountain which is of solid clay in Truro.' It stood unchanged while two generations of sailors kept a safe offing on even the darkest nights. Then in 1857 it was rebuilt into one of the foremost lighthouses of the world, a position which it has held ever since. Its 182,000 candle-power lantern is unequalled by any other oil burner on this continent.

It was soon evident that the varied maritime activities of New England were a source of great profit to the country. Everything that aided navigation was therefore encouraged in Congress, and another lighthouse was put up in 1816 at Race Point, back of Provincetown. The fact that the next to appear (1822) was on Billingsgate Island, at the entrance to Wellfleet Harbor, shows clearly what the Government thought of the Bay shore fisheries. This light and its nearest neighbor on the Bay, built at Sandy Neck, Barnstable, four years later, guided the destinies of fishermen and packet captains through the busy decades that followed. To-day, though weeks pass without a single sail

to relieve the monotonous blue of the waters of the Bay, these two lights still
blink reminiscently, cheered by the chance of guiding an occasional lobster-
man or yachtsman to port.

In 1823, the Government took a grant to a piece of beach grass and sand
on Monomoy Point and later erected a lighthouse which showed Chatham
fishermen the way home and which, with the Great Point Light on Nantucket,
gave coastwise vessels a cross-bearing through the dangerous water of the
Sound. Georges Bankers were guided in safety around the very tip of the
Cape by the Long Point Light, which made its appearance in 1826. A dozen
years later — thanks largely to the exertions of the same Mr. Collins who
gave Emerson the information about wreckers — three lighthouses were put
up on Nauset Beach about a mile north of the entrance to the Harbor. These,
with the twin lights of Chatham, and a smaller one at Hyannis, handed vessels
on from lighthouse to lighthouse all the way from the Nobsque Point Beacon
at Falmouth (built in 1828) to deep water beyond Peaked Hill Bars and the
Race. The old stone tower on Point Gammon went out of business when
Bishop and Clark's was put up three miles south of it on a ledge in the Sound.
Two others were erected somewhat gratuitously, one at Pamet Harbor, Truro,
in 1849 and the other at Wood End, Provincetown, in 1873. The former was
discontinued after six years, when the harbor silted up to a mere creek; but
Wood End still fills the gap between the Race and Long Point.

BIBLIOGRAPHY

GENERAL:
 Bradford, *History of Plymouth Plantation* (Mass. Hist. Soc. ed. 1912).
 Simeon L. Deyo (editor), *History of Barnstable County, Mass.* (N.Y.,
 1890). Dean Dudley, *Historical Sketches of Towns in Plymouth and Barnstable Counties, Mass.* (Boston, 1873). Frederick Freeman, *History of Cape
 Cod* (Boston, 1858; printed for the author). John Abbot Goodwin, *The
 Pilgrim Republic* (Boston, 1888). Samuel Eliot Morison, *Maritime History
 of Massachusetts* (Boston, 1921). Mourt's *Relation* (H. M. Dexter ed.,
 Boston, 1865). Amos Otis, *Genealogical Notes of Barnstable Families* (Barnstable, 1888). *Population and Resources of Cape Cod* (Mass. Dept. of Labor
 and Industries, Reprinted for the Cape Cod Chamber of Commerce, Bos-
 ton, 1922). Charles F. Swift, *Cape Cod* (Yarmouth, 1897). Alexander
 Young, *Chronicles of the Pilgrim Fathers of the Colony of Plymouth etc.*
 (Boston, 1841). Files of the Barnstable *Patriot* and the Yarmouth *Register*.

TOWN HISTORIES:
 Charles W. Jenkins, *Three Lectures on the Early History of Falmouth* (Fal-
 mouth, 1889). Herman A. Jennings, *Chequocket or Coatuit: The Aboriginal
 Name of Provincetown* (Yarmouthport, 1885). Everett I. Nye, *History
 of Wellfleet* (Hyannis, 1920). Rev. Enoch Pratt, *A Comprehensive History,
 Ecclesiastical and Civil, of Eastham, Wellfleet and Orleans etc.* (Yarmouth,
 1844). Shebnah Rich, *Truro, Cape Cod, or Land Marks and Sea Marks*
 (Boston, 1884). Rev. Nancy W. Paine Smith, *The Provincetown Book*
 (Brockton, 1922). William C. Smith, *A History of Chatham, Mass.*
 (Hyannis, 1909–1913). Charles F. Swift, *Old Yarmouth* (Yarmouthport,
 1884). The Town Records and Proprietors' Records of all towns on the
 Cape.

 For additional information regarding:
GEOLOGY AND CHANGES IN COASTLINE:
 Prof. Albert Perry Brigham, *Cape Cod and the Old Colony* (N.Y., 1920) which
 I have followed very closely. Prof. Nathaniel Shaler, *Geology of the Cape
 District* (from 18th Annual Report of U.S. Geological Survey, 1896–97).
 Henry Mitchell's Article and Charts on Monomoy (U.S. Coast and
 Geodetic Survey, 1886). Amos Otis, *Discovery of an Ancient Ship* (re-
 printed from New Eng. Hist. & Geneal. Register, Albany, 1864). *Mass.
 Magazine*, Vol. III, 1791. Timothy Dwight's *Travels*, Vol. III.

INDIANS:
 Pub. of Col. Soc. of Mass., 1911–13, Vol. 14, Transactions. Winslow's *Good
 Newes.* Smithsonian Report for 1883, *Notes on Wampanoag Indians*, by
 Henry E. Chase. *Purchas His Pilgrimes*, III, XIX (Glasgow, 1906).

M.H.S. Proceedings, XXIV. Mary Farwell Ayer, *Richard Bourne, Missionary to the Mashpee Indians* (Boston, 1908). Timothy Alden, *Collection of American Epitaphs and Inscriptions* (N.Y., 1814). Jedidiah Morse, *Indian Report*, 1820. Hearing before Comm. on Indians at Mashpee, Feb. 9, 1869 (House, No. 502). 1 M.H.S. Coll. V; 2 M.H.S. Coll. III; 1 M.H.S. Coll. I; 1 M.H.S. Coll. VIII; 4 M.H.S. Coll. V; 1 M.H.S. Coll. X; 1 M.H.S. Coll. VI.

EXPLORERS:
Capt. John Smith, *Works*, Part II, 696 ff. (Edward Arber, ed., Westminster, 1895). Sam'l Champlain, *Voyages* (Prince Soc. ed. Boston, 1880). James Rosier's *Narrative*, 3 M.H.S. Coll. VIII. *Purchas His Pilgrimes*, III (Glasgow, 1906). Mourt's *Relation* (H. M. Dexter, ed., Boston, 1865). B. F. DeCosta, *Cavo de Baros, or the Place of Cape Cod in the Old Cartography* (N.Y., 1881). All but the last of these contain also valuable information on the early coastline and the Indians.

THE FIRST SETTLERS AND LIFE IN THE COLONIAL PERIOD:
Official Proceedings of the Quarter Millennial Celebration of Sandwich and Bourne (Falmouth, 1890). J. H. Benton, *Warning Out in New England* (Boston, 1911). Geo. H. Moore, *Notes on Hist. of Slavery in Mass.* (N.Y., 1866). Plym. Col. Rec. V. 173 f; VI, 15; IX, 71. Barnstable Probate Rec. IX, 6; VIII, 473; XIII, 490; IV, 549 f; etc., etc. Daniel Wing, *Old Cape Cod Windmills* (Library of C. Cod Hist. & Geneal., No. 14, C. W. Swift, Yarmouthport). James Brown Scott, *Robert Bacon, Life and Letters* (N.Y. 1923). Timothy Alden, *Memorabilia of Yarmouth* (1 M.H.S. Coll. V). Roy H. Akagi, *The Town Proprietors of the New England Colonies* (U. of Penn. Press, 1924). Edwin Crowell, *A History of Barrington Township and Vicinity, Shelburne Co., Nova Scotia, 1604–1870.* Diary of Sam'l Sewall (5 M.H.S. Coll. VI). William H. Whitmore, *Origin of Names of Towns in Mass.* (M.H.S. Proc., Vol. 12). John W. Dodge, *Hist. of First Cong. Ch., Yarmouth, Mass.* (Yarmouthport, 1873). Yarmouth *Register*, March 9, 1837.

REVOLUTION:
Wm. Tudor, *Life of James Otis* (Boston, 1823). MS. Diary of Benj. Percival, of Sandwich. M.H.S. Proc., Vols. 16 & 23. Augustus C. Buell, *Paul Jones, Founder of the American Navy* (N.Y., 1903). Francis Tiffany Bowles, *The Loyalty of Barnstable in the Revolution* (Pub. of Col. Soc. Mass., Vol. XXV). Gardner Allen, *Mass. Privateers in Revolution* (M.H.S. Coll., Vol. 77. 1927). Diary of Wm. Russell in Old Mill Prison, Jan. 22, 1781 (quoted by Frederick W. Snow in pamph., *Snowden, Orleans, Mass.*, privately printed). Publications of Naval Hist. Soc., Vol. III, 1913. E. A. Grozier, *The Wreck of the Somerset* (Provincetown, 1887).

REVOLUTION TO CIVIL WAR ASHORE:
MS. Papers of Capt. Job Chase. Thomas F. Hall, *Shipbuilding in East Dennis* (Lib. of C. Cod Hist. & Geneal. No. 11, C. F. Swift, Yarmouth-

port, 1925). Constitution and By-Laws of the Barnstable Lyceum (Barnstable, 1824). *Address Delivered before the Brewster Lyceum*, 1836 (Barnstable, 1836). Half-Centennial Celebration of the Yarmouth Institute (Yarmouthport, 1893). Commonwealth of Mass. Report of Commissioners on Cape Cod and East Harbors, Jan. 5, 1853 (Senate No. 6) and Jan. 16, 1854 (Senate No. 5). Report of Committee on C. Cod Harbor, 1857 (Public Doc. No. 36). Report of Commissioners on Provincetown Dike 1872 (Senate No. 5). Senate Report on Condition of Province Lands, Jan. 1838 (Senate No. 6).

WHALING:
Alex. Starbuck, *Hist. of Amer. Whale Fishery etc.* (appended to report of U.S. Commission on Fisheries for 1875–76). John R. Spears, *The Story of the New England Whalers* (N.Y., 1922). Chas. B. Hawes, *Whaling* (N.Y., 1924). Kendall, *Travels.* Pub. of Col. Soc. of Mass. Transactions, 1904–06, Vol. X. M.H.S. Proc., Vol. 43. John A. Cook, *Pursuing the Whale* (Boston, 1926). B. L. Shurtleff, *Songs at Anchor* (privately printed, 1922).

FISHERIES:
M.H.S. Coll., VIII. MS. notes on Wellfleet vessels, found among papers of late Everett I. Nye of Wellfleet. MS. recording bounties paid on porpoise tails. Geo. W. Field, *Report on Shellfisheries of Mass.*, in 41st annual report of the Commission of Fisheries and Game. David L. Belding, *Report upon the Scallop Fisheries of Mass.* for the Commonwealth of Mass., Boston, 1910. Thoreau, *Cape Cod.* Winthrop L. Marvin, *The American Merchant Marine* (N.Y., 1919).

STORMS, WRECKS, ETC.
Alexander Young, *Chronicles of Massachusetts. Autobiography of Zachary G. Lamson* (Boston, 1908). Dow and Edmonds, *Pirates of the New England Coast* (Salem, 1923). Bliss Perry, *The Heart of Emerson's Journals* (Boston, 1926). *Accounts of Shipwreck*, by a Friend of Seamen (Brunswick, Me., 1823). J. W. Dalton, *The Lifesavers of Cape Cod* (Boston, 1902). James Freeman, *A Description of the East Coast of Cape Cod etc.*, etc. (Boston, 1802). *Elegy on the Death of Capt. Isaiah Knowles and his crew etc.*, etc. (contemporary broadside, 1806). I. Morton Small, *Shipwrecks on Cape Cod* (No. Truro, 1925).

THE MERCHANT MARINE:
Francis W. Sprague, *Barnstable and Yarmouth Sea Capts. and Ship-Owners* (privately printed, 1913). J. Henry Sears, *Brewster Shipmasters* (Yarmouthport, 1906). Octavius T. Howe & Fred'k C. Matthews, *Amer. Clipper Ships*, 1833–58 (Salem Marine Research Soc., 1926). *Old Shipping Days in Boston* (State St. Trust Co., Boston). *Some Merchants and Sea Capts. of Old Boston* (ditto). *Other Merchants and Sea Capts. of Old Boston* (ditto). F. W. Howay, *John Kendrick and His Sons* (Oregon Historical Quarterly, Vol. 23, No. 4, Dec., 1922). F. W. Howay, *A Ballad*

of the North West Fur Trade (New England Quarterly, Vol. 1, No. 1, Jan., 1928). Chas. G. Loring, *Memoir of Wm. Sturgis* (M.H.S. Proc., VII). *Elijah Cobb, a Cape Cod Skipper* (Yale Univ. Press, 1925). Basil Lubbock, *The Western Ocean Packets* (Boston, 1925), *Colonial Clippers* (Glasgow, 1921). Arthur H. Clark, *The Clipper Ship Era* (N.Y., 1910). Samuel Eliot Morrison, *The Old Merchant Marine* (*Landmark*, Vol. V, No. 12, Dec., 1923).

CIVIL WAR:

Parker Pillsbury, *In Memoriam*, an address in memory of Capt. Prince S. Crowell, delivered in East Dennis, Dec. 11th, 1881 (Clague & Wegman, Rochester, N.Y.). R. B. Forbes, *To the Naval and Military Committees* (broadside in Harvard College Library).

THE CHURCH:

Reports of Cases in the Courts of Star Chamber and High Commission (Sam'l Rawson Gardiner, ed.; printed for the Camden Society). *Proceedings and Result of an Ecclesiastical Council, ex-parte*, which met at West Barnstable, Mass., 27th Oct., 1868, to advise in the case of Mr. Joseph Bodfish and Family (Boston, 1868). Nath'n'l Morton, *New England's Memorial* (Boston, 1855). *Declaration of Ministers in Barnstable Co. relating to the late Practise of Itinerant Preaching* (Boston, 1745). *Mortuary Record from the Gravestones in Old Burial Ground in Brewster* (Chas. Mayo, ed., Yarmouthport, 1898). *The Old Cemetery, Sandwich, Mass.*, a paper read before the Sandwich Hist. Soc., Oct. 20th, 1908. MS. Notes on the Barnstable Come-Outers. *Cape Cod in Poetry, an Anthology*, Joshua Freeman Crowell and Florence Hathaway Crowell, ed.

THE CANAL:

Numerous Arguments by S. W. McCall, E. C. Carrigan, Richard Olney, and Robt. M. Morse, Jr., delivered before various Legislative Committees relative to one Canal petitioner or another, 1887–91. J. W. Miller, *Cape Cod and its Canal* (1914). J. W. Dalton, *The Cape Cod Canal* (Sandwich, 1911). William Barclay Parsons, *Cape Cod Canal*, an address delivered before the Boston Chamber of Commerce May 25th, 1910. Senate, No. 241, 1883. Senate No. 218, April 9th, 1880. House, No. 459, 1882. *Report of the Joint Committee of 1860* upon Proposed Canal etc., etc. (Pub. Doc. No. 41, printed, Boston, 1864). This volume is also extremely valuable for its statistics on shipwrecks. James Winthrop, *Journal of a Survey in 1791 for a Canal across Cape Cod etc.* (Boston Public Library Hist. MSS., No. 3, 1902). This journal is also interesting for overland travel before stage-coaches.

INDEX

INDEX

(The Post-Epilogue is not included in the Index.)